Brilliant Essays

Study Skills

Academic Success
Academic Writing Skills for International
  Students
Be Well, Learn Well
Brilliant Essays
The Business Student's Phrase Book
Cite Them Right (11th edn)
Critical Thinking and Persuasive Writing for
  Postgraduates
Critical Thinking for Nursing, Health and
  Social Care
Critical Thinking Skills (3rd edn)
Dissertations and Project Reports
Doing Projects and Reports in Engineering
The Employability Journal
Essentials of Essay Writing
The Exam Skills Handbook (2nd edn)
Get Sorted
The Graduate Career Guidebook (2nd edn)
Great Ways to Learn Anatomy and Physiology
  (2nd edn)
How to Use Your Reading in Your Essays (3rd
  edn)
How to Write Better Essays (4th edn)
How to Write Your Undergraduate
  Dissertation (3rd edn)
Improve Your Grammar (2nd edn)
The Macmillan Student Planner
Mindfulness for Students
Presentation Skills for Students (3rd edn)
The Principles of Writing in Psychology
Professional Writing (4th edn)
Reading at University
Reflective Writing for Nursing, Health and
  Social Work
Simplify Your Study
Skills for Business and Management
Skills for Success (3rd edn)
Stand Out from the Crowd
The Student Phrase Book (2nd edn)
The Student's Guide to Writing (3rd edn)
The Study Skills Handbook (5th edn)
Study Skills for International Postgraduates
Studying in English
Studying Law (4th edn)
The Study Success Journal
Success in Academic Writing (2nd edn)
Smart Thinking
Teaching Study Skills and Supporting Learning
The Undergraduate Research Handbook (2nd
  edn)
The Work-Based Learning Student Handbook
  (2nd edn)
Writing for Biomedical Sciences Students
Writing for Engineers (4th edn)
Writing for Nursing and Midwifery Students
  (3rd edn)
Write it Right (2nd edn)
Writing for Science Students
Writing Skills for Education Students
You2Uni: Decide, Prepare, Apply

Pocket Study Skills

14 Days to Exam Success (2nd edn)
Analyzing a Case Study
Brilliant Writing Tips for Students
Completing Your PhD
Doing Research (2nd edn)
Getting Critical (2nd edn)
How to Analyze Data
Managing Stress
Planning Your Dissertation (2nd edn)
Planning Your Essay (3rd edn)
Planning Your PhD
Posters and Presentations
Reading and Making Notes (2nd edn)
Referencing and Understanding Plagiarism
  (2nd edn)
Reflective Writing (2nd edn)
Report Writing (2nd edn)
Science Study Skills
Studying with Dyslexia (2nd edn)
Success in Groupwork
Successful Applications
Time Management
Using Feedback to Boost Your Grades
Where's Your Argument?
Where's Your Evidence?
Writing for University (2nd edn)

50 Ways

50 Ways to Boost Your Grades
50 Ways to Boost Your Employability
50 Ways to Excel at Writing
50 Ways to Manage Stress
50 Ways to Manage Time Effectively
50 Ways to Succeed as an International
  Student

Research Skills

Authoring a PhD
The Foundations of Research (3rd edn)
Getting to Grips with Doctoral Research
Getting Published
The Good Supervisor (2nd edn)
The Lean PhD
Maximizing the Impacts of Academic Research
PhD by Published Work
The PhD Viva
The PhD Writing Handbook
Planning Your Postgraduate Research
The Postgraduate's Guide to Research
  Ethics
The Postgraduate Research Handbook (2nd
  edn)
The Professional Doctorate
Structuring Your Research Thesis

For a complete listing of all our titles in this area
please visit www.macmillanihe.com/study-skills

Brilliant Essays

Ursula Hackett

First published 2021 by
RED GLOBE PRESS

Red Globe Press in the UK is an imprint of Macmillan Education Limited, registered in England, company number 01755588, of 4 Crinan Street, London, N1 9XW.

Red Globe Press® is a registered trademark in the United States, the United Kingdom, Europe and other countries.

ISBN 978-1-352-01137-1 paperback

This book is printed on paper suitable for recycling and made from fully managed and sustained forest sources. Logging, pulping and manufacturing processes are expected to conform to the environmental regulations of the country of origin.

A catalogue record for this book is available from the British Library.

A catalogue record for this book is available from the Library of Congress.

Contents

List of 'have a go' exercises

Acknowledgements

This book is a joint production. I am grateful to Adrienne Baker, Chris Prosser and four anonymous Red Globe Press reviewers, each of whom generously read this manuscript and made suggestions for its improvement. Mark Hackett's brilliant illustrations help illuminate both this text and my video essay-writing guides. Chris Prosser's camera skills brought the *Brilliant Essays* YouTube channel to life. Colleagues at Macmillan Study Skills – Rosemary Maher, Suzie Burywood and Amanda Woolf – facilitated a wonderfully supportive commissioning process. It has been a pleasure to work with them all.

Although they bear no direct responsibility for the content of this book, my undergraduate tutors at the University of Oxford developed and encouraged my own essay-writing abilities. The questions they asked in tutorials, and their kind yet incisive commentary upon my work, crystallized my thinking about essay writing and later shaped my approach as a university tutor in my own right. I would particularly like to acknowledge my debt to Nigel Bowles, Krister Bykvist, Bill Child, Anthony Eagle, Michael Hart, Benjamin Morison and Stephen Whitefield. I carry their advice with me to this day.

During my academic career, I have taught hundreds of undergraduates and postgraduates how to write brilliant essays, and they in turn have taught me how to do my job better. Thank you to all my students, past and present, for your excellent questions and interesting essays. We truly are a community of scholars.

Introduction: The Challenge of Writing Brilliant Essays

This is a practical guide to writing brilliant essays. It is designed to help ambitious students who want to move their essays beyond average grades and to create brilliant, original, high-scoring essays that are enjoyable to write and read. You won't find any ready-made formula or remedial spelling and grammar here! This book will take you beyond the basics. It is designed for those who want to unlock their full potential and write brilliantly.

I am writing primarily for undergraduate and postgraduate students, for those adapting to life at university and those who are moving into their second and third years of study. My message is simple: have confidence. YOU have the ability to write a brilliant essay. Let me show you how.

Many good students find themselves frustrated at university. It seems hard to crack the code. You can turn in a very well-structured essay without gaining an especially good mark, and it may not be obvious just what you did wrong. You may have managed your time well and written something in line with what worked for you in the past. You may have edited and checked your spelling and ensured that there is an introduction, four middle paragraphs and a conclusion, but if the essay simply goes through the motions it is unlikely to gain a distinguished mark.

Tutors do not always emphasize essay-writing skills; they are focused on delivering substantive content. Marking criteria at university are often more ambiguous and less specific than the marking descriptors you encountered at school. The rubrics can seem quite vague. What are 'methodological sophistication', 'exceptional understanding' and 'originality of thought'? How do you achieve 'fluency', 'clarity' and 'authoritative interpretation'? What is a 'convincing response' to a question?

I am not going to give you a firm definition of any of these concepts; there is no single definition. There are many ways to write a brilliant essay and no single 'right' answer. Instead, I will show you, through discussion and plenty of actual examples, what these concepts can mean in practice. We'll walk through these examples together. By the end of this book, you will have absorbed many of the ways in which these qualities manifest themselves in brilliant essays – and you'll have had the chance to polish your own skills and apply them to your own assignments.

Whatever your essay-writing subject – whether you're a classicist, economist, geographer, historian, lawyer, philosopher, political scientist, psychologist or any other essay writer – there is something here for everyone. This book uses accessible examples, taking as its starting point your everyday experience of using language, arguing a case, thinking creatively and communicating with other people. It comes naturally. You can apply many of the skills that you already possess.

Independent thinking is a process that takes place throughout the writing of an essay: during your initial encounters with an essay question, reading, planning, selecting evidence, and writing, reviewing and editing your essay. The key to a brilliant essay is for you to make informed, independent decisions about what to include and what to exclude. That means jettisoning some of the training wheels you might have learned at school – that is, rigid rules about how an essay has to go. If you follow my advice, I'll help you to shake off tired formulas and take greater pleasure in the essay-writing process. If you're enjoying yourself, chances are your readers will too. It won't guarantee you a first-class mark, but it will improve the odds.

It's not about following a prescriptive set of rules. If you give yourself the space to step back and really think, you will have more confidence in your own authoritative interpretation of an essay question. When you convey that confidence to the reader, then you have a brilliant essay on your hands. There are no absolute laws about how things must be done, but I will offer you some guidelines to help avoid certain pitfalls. There are techniques you can learn that will help you craft something interesting and original. In this book, you will encounter practical exercises to help you think around a question. Once you lose the formulaic approach to essays, you'll gain a lot more enjoyment from the writing process.

Who am I? I am an academic with more than a decade of experience at Oxford and Royal Holloway, University of London: writing, reading and marking many hundreds of essays. I remember the experience of writing university essays myself and am passionate about passing on that expertise to fellow students and colleagues. I did *not* start university with the miraculous ability to write brilliant essays, but learned how through a process of trial-and-error, guided by my tutors. We are all part of the same academic community, engaged in a continuous process of learning. Creating brilliant essays is an exciting process, and I hope to convey that excitement throughout the book.

Brilliant Essays is accompanied by my award-winning YouTube Channel, *How to Write Brilliant Essays*, and website, www.brilliant-essays. com, where you will find bespoke video content, downloadable exercise sheets with answers, blogs, top tips, FAQs and a contact form. If you would like to find out more about how to write brilliant essays, I encourage you to subscribe to my video channel and follow my devoted Twitter feed, @Dr_Essays. Fresh and exclusive web content is available for readers of this book at www.macmillanihe.com/hackett-brilliant-essays.

How to read this book

For students:

These chapters can be read in any order. There is no need to work your way through from start to finish, although you can do so if you wish. You may dip in and out as it suits you. One place to start would be to review my top ten pitfalls in essay writing in the next section. Follow the chapter suggestions for those problems that resonate with you.

The chapters are short and punctuated with exercises – interspersed with the text and in a block at the end of each chapter. You can work through these exercises from start to finish or take a pick-and-mix approach. Although there is no special order to the chapters, you may find that Chapters 1, 2 and 3 on examining assumptions, finding comparator classes and interrogating tensions are particularly useful when you first encounter an essay question. You might wish to save Chapter 11 on examination preparation for your revision period.

For tutors and teaching assistants:

There are hundreds of worked examples of actual essay questions throughout the book, across a wide range of subjects – from psychology to anthropology, geography to political science. Every chapter contains 'Have a go' exercises with answers at the back of the book. You can work through the exercises with your students in the classroom or else set them as self-service exercises for students to complete in their own time.

You can also use this book to help set essay and examination questions for students. The first three chapters are designed not only to help students unpack essay questions but also to suggest question wordings that encourage stronger responses. In the final chapter, I answer frequently asked questions. Personal advisors and study skills colleagues may find it helpful to browse these questions when supporting students.

Top Ten Pitfalls in Essay Writing

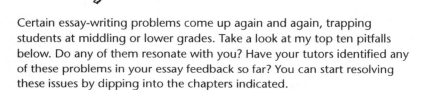

Certain essay-writing problems come up again and again, trapping students at middling or lower grades. Take a look at my top ten pitfalls below. Do any of them resonate with you? Have your tutors identified any of these problems in your essay feedback so far? You can start resolving these issues by dipping into the chapters indicated.

1. Lack of specificity in introductory paragraphs

Most students know roughly what goes into an introduction (definitions of core terms and a summary of the argument), but many introductions set an essay up for a weak grade because they are vague about content. Students might identify the question, say whether they agree or disagree, and leave it at that. How can you make your introductions meatier and informative? Chapter 4 on **the introduction scale** explains.

2. Unnecessary verbiage

You probably know that you need to define your terms, provide evidence and elucidate causal mechanisms, but there's no point spending ages telling your reader that these things need to be done or offering lots of basic background information. Best to just get on with your argument. How can you cut to the chase and write concisely? I show you how in Chapter 6 on **writing elegantly**.

3. The dreaded seesaw

The typical essay does contain some sort of engagement with counter-arguments. A student often identifies both sides of the question ('on the one hand, X; on the other hand, Y') and tries to insert some balance by asserting one side, followed by the word 'however', and then asserting the other side. The effect is a seesaw, and the reader is left with no idea what the author's position actually is. How should you build your case by responding to counter-arguments and adjudicating competing claims? Chapter 5 on **controlling your argument** breaks this process down.

4. A smattering of illustrations, but no evidence

Unless you are answering a very abstract or theoretical question in philosophy or an allied discipline, you will need to produce empirical evidence to help support your argument. Most essays identify some sort of evidence, but it often comes in the form of anecdotes, superficial mentions or examples offered without context. How can you deploy evidence effectively? Chapter 7 on **using empirical evidence** helps you to make clear, defensible decisions about which cases to include or exclude.

5. Excessive deference to the scholarly literature

Many students are understandably wary of seeming arrogant in their essays, particularly when they are new to university life, but this reticence often makes students weaken their arguments with unnecessary hedges ('*arguably*, it *seems* to be *relatively* clear that...'). I show how to avoid these hedges in Chapter 6 on **elegant writing**. Lack of confidence also shows up in excessive deference to the scholarly literature. Students might simply describe a scholar's views rather than telling the reader what the student thinks about that scholarly perspective. How can you engage with the scholarly literature with respectful confidence and authority? Chapter 10 on **reading critically** offers practical tips.

6. Definitions marooned

Every student knows they need to provide definitions, but in middling-grade essays this exercise is just a chore. The student has gone to the Oxford English Dictionary, or some other source, extracted the definition and plonked it into the first paragraph. It is never referred to again. Marooning your definitions at the start of the essay like this is a bad idea because the definitions of your key terms help shape the essay as a whole. Defining the boundaries of a concept can identify relevant comparators, and clashing definitions are a fruitful source of debate. How can you use your definitions more effectively? There are practical techniques to help you do so in Chapters 2 and 9 on **finding comparator classes** and **losing the training wheels**.

7. Laundry lists

A middling-grade essay might be quite structured, with a series of points one after the other, but it often reads like a laundry list: here is one point, here is another point, and another... The reader has no sense of how these points relate to one another. The essay is a workmanlike, solid-but-uninspired listicle[1]. By contrast, a brilliant essay guides the reader through

---

1 A listicle is a piece of writing presented wholly in the form of a list ('14 reasons why X'; '156 sorts of Y'). Readers may be familiar with listicles from sources such as Buzzfeed.

the argument. How can you guide your reader effectively? See Chapter 5 on **controlling your argument**. You can also find ways to avoid the laundry list in Chapter 3 on **interrogating tensions in questions**.

8. Not spelling out one's reasoning

A great deal of planning goes into essay writing, and a student writing a second-class essay will certainly have thought in advance about what they want to assert. The problem is that they may not spell out the reasoning that underpins the argument, so the reader cannot easily see why the student draws certain inferences and comes to a particular conclusion. A brilliant essay makes it crystal clear how the author reached their conclusions. How can you make the links in your argument explicit? For answers, take a look at Chapters 5 and 8 on **controlling your argument** and **syllogisms and summaries**. You may also find the visual mapping tools helpful in Chapter 10 on **reading critically**.

9. Formulaic five-paragraph essays

At school, you might have been told that an essay 'must' consist in five paragraphs, namely an introduction, a list of pros, a list of cons, a 'debate' paragraph and a conclusion. This formulaic approach may save you from drifting away from the question entirely, but it will trap you at the vanilla middle grades by preventing you from responding to the nuances of the question at hand. At university, a more flexible approach is preferable, but how do you respond flexibly to a question without drifting totally off-piste? Chapter 9 on **losing the training wheels** explains how.

10. Leaping without looking

In coursework essays and examinations, students sometimes leap in with an answer to the question without thinking about what it is really asking them to do. A student might score a low to middle grade if they have some sort of answer to the question, but if that answer ignores the wording of the question, neglects to consider its underlying assumptions and contains no nuance, then there is no hope of a better grade. How can you unlock higher grades by reading a question critically? Chapters 1, 2 and 3 on **examining assumptions**, **finding comparator classes** and **interrogating tensions** offer practical techniques for approaching your essay questions. You can find out more about examination essay planning specifically in Chapter 11 on **examination preparation**.

In the first chapter, we'll start at the very beginning: the essay question itself. Before you attempt to plan your essay, you should give your question a long, critical look. We'll discuss how to use the techniques of everyday language – techniques you possess without even knowing it – to interrogate your essay questions. You might be surprised how much you can do with a single line of text.

CHAPTER

1

Examining Assumptions in Questions

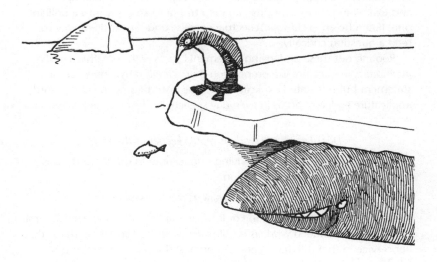

All advice about how to write essays urges you to read the question, but what does *read the question* really mean? Skimming isn't enough. You need to take your time. Define the key concepts, think about how they relate to one another and root out any assumptions the question is making. 'Read the question' means read the question *critically* – that is, actively evaluate the question and come to an informed judgement about it.

Reading the question involves spending enough time working out what the question is really asking you to do, instead of leaping in with a response prematurely. I expect you know this already. I am sure you also know that you must define the main terms of the question. In my experience, university students – including very clever ones – already know what they need to do in general but don't always apply what they know to their own work. It is one thing to know these things in the abstract but quite another to put them into practice. This chapter provides some techniques to help you to read the question critically.

Finding an assumption lurking beneath the surface

One way to read the question critically is to consider whether the question contains any underlying assumptions: propositions that are accepted without proof, hidden in the background, and that may not be immediately obvious to the casual reader. Exposing those assumptions and examining them explicitly can help turn a so-so essay into a brilliant one. It can be an exciting intellectual exercise and an excellent way to read a question critically.

Rooting out these underlying statements starts with something called *implicature*. Implicature is a proposition that is *implied* by a question or statement but not stated explicitly. Don't be disturbed by the fancy word; implicature is all around us in everyday speech. For instance, if I were to ask you:

Does Emma still work as reptile keeper at the zoo?

The word *still* indicates an underlying implication. In other words, this question is based on an assumption.

Assumption: *Emma used to work as reptile keeper at the zoo.*

When we use the word 'still' in English, we imply that *at some point in the past* Emma did indeed work as reptile keeper at the zoo and perhaps that her service in that role has been continuous. The question at hand is whether or not she does so *now*. The answer to the question will be either 'yes' or 'no' but – additionally and entirely separately – that underlying assumption may or may not be true. Since I am using the word 'still', the chances are that we both know that assumption is correct. But if I am wrong, then it might be a good idea to correct that assumption.

Correcting the assumption: *You are confusing Emma with Anna. Emma is a primatologist. She has never worked with reptiles. In fact, she hates them.*

Another way to correct the assumption: *Emma is trainee reptile keeper, but she got the job yesterday so she hasn't been doing it long. She's only just started.*

The assumption arises as a result of a single word. If I had simply asked you (note the missing word):

Does Emma work as reptile keeper at the zoo?

Without the word 'still' in the question, there is no assumption about whether or not Emma has ever been a reptile keeper before. The focus is solely on the present.

Similarly, implicature can arise if I use the word 'too' or 'also'. I could ask you:

Is Ben also a vegetarian?

There is a surface question here – I am asking if Ben is a vegetarian or not – but there is also an assumption (or several) underlying the question.

Assumption: *Somebody else (probably someone we both know) is a vegetarian.*

Or: There is at least one other vegetarian.
Or: You are a vegetarian.

These assumptions may or may not be true, and the precise nature of the assumption is usually clear from the context of utterance. If I come up to you while you're loading your plate with tofu and ask:

Is your brother a vegetarian too?

Then, in addition to asking you a question about your brother, I have probably also implied that *you* are a vegetarian. Perhaps you're not. Perhaps you are a carnivore who happens to enjoy coagulated soy milk.

Although we don't often think about it explicitly, everyday speech is riddled with implicature. For instance, if I say 'the problem with the cat is that it doesn't know how to use the cat flap', then my use of the definite article ('the') implies that there is *just one* problem and *one* cat and *one* cat flap. If we had several cats, I would most likely have identified it by name (*Felix*) or description (*our fattest cat*).

Typically, people converse politely and reasonably, so it is rare to spot an incorrect assumption. It might seem rude to interrupt the flow of the conversation to inform someone they have a faulty assumption; anyway, we can usually be confident that they are correct. In academic essays, however, the best stance is friendly but informed scepticism: start with an open mind and a willingness to question what you are being told, both explicitly and implicitly.

Implicatures such as the ones above often come up in essay questions too, so paying close attention to the wording of the question can help you to assess the question critically. For instance, you might be asked:

Do presidential election debates still matter?

Recall the implicature 'still' in the question: Does Emma still work as reptile keeper at the zoo? This question implies that presidential election debates *used to matter,* and it is asking you whether or not they matter *now.*

Assumption: *Presidential election debates used to matter.*
In other words, the question is: *Do presidential election debates matter now?*

Weaker answers to this question would ignore the assumption and simply list the ways in which presidential election debates do or do not 'matter'. But the assumption underlying the question may be true or false, depending upon what is meant by 'matter' (Matter to whom? Matter in what way?) and the scope conditions of the argument (that is, its empirical boundaries). In this case, the conditions are temporal parameters (What period of time are we talking about? Televised presidential election debates started in 1960: how and when did they change? How far back in time does 'now' stretch?)

A cleverer approach would be to consider whether the assumption is true or not when responding to the question at hand. If the assumption is false, you should correct it.

One way to correct the assumption and answer the question:
Presidential election debates have never mattered.

Another way to correct the assumption and answer the question:
Presidential election debates did not matter in the past, but they do matter now.

Alternatively, it might be that the assumption is indeed true: such debates *did* used to matter.

Affirming the assumption and answering the question in the negative:
Presidential election debates used to matter, but they do not matter now.

Affirming the assumption and answering the question in the affirmative:
Presidential election debates have always mattered.

Even if you ultimately affirm the assumption underlying a question, it is still important that you seriously consider whether or not it is indeed true.

Why is it so vital to drag these assumptions out of their hiding places and address them, even if they turn out to be true? Because it forces you to slow down and really think about what the question is asking. It also allows you to practise your critical thinking skills – the essence of a brilliant essay – because you are not simply taking that assumption as given but actively evaluating it: is it true or false?

EXERCISE 1.1

Have a go at finding hidden assumptions

Find the assumptions underlying the following questions and write them out as full sentences. It doesn't matter if you don't understand the question! The answers are on p. 144.

1 Is catastrophism still a useful theory of geological change?
2 In his theory of *simulacra*, does Lucretius address non-visual senses too?
3 Do modern Chinese people continue to wear white for mourning?
4 'The problem with moral relativism is that it denies societal change.' Discuss.
5 'T.S. Eliot's *Four Quartets* poem can also be seen as a criticism of classicizing conventions.' Discuss.
6 Is the ideal of a democratic transnational public sphere realistic nowadays?
7 From a firm's perspective, what is the advantage of giving workers a fixed annual pay increase instead of paying them based on measures of performance?
8 Few philosophers today are substance dualists. Why?
9 What is the obstacle to adolescent girls' participating in sporting activities?
10 How has increased computational power revolutionized contemporary ecology?

The best place to consider the assumptions underlying an essay question is right at the start, as you unpack the terms of the question and set out the direction your essay will take. If the question does make an interesting or questionable assumption (there might not always be one, of course, and if there is, it might not be particularly interesting), then you can use it as a springboard into your argument.

A middling-grade essay might mention an underlying assumption briefly – for example, by introducing a historical quotation about the importance of presidential election debates, followed by the word 'however' and some points about the importance of such debates in the present day only. In this case, the assumption is merely mentioned in passing, relegated to the background, and dispatched without a second thought. When a question makes an interesting and questionable assumption, it is better to consider the assumption explicitly and integrate that discussion into the essay as a whole.

One note of warning: as you consider the assumptions underlying your essay questions, take care not to stray too far from the question you have been asked. Imagine that you were asked to write an essay on the following question:

Is Malthusian theory still valid today?

You might think the words 'still... today' indicate an assumption:

Assumption: *Malthusian theory was once valid (at some point in the past).*

This is a vulnerable assumption. Even in 1798, when he first laid out his ideas, Malthus's theories of population growth had detractors. It would be a good idea to evaluate this assumption explicitly. Decide before you put pen to paper whether you intend to affirm the assumption (Malthusian ideas did have merit at some point in the past) or reject it (Malthusian ideas were not valid in the past), but remember also to decide whether you will answer *the question* in the affirmative (Malthusian ideas are valid today) or negative (Malthusian ideas are invalid today).

You mustn't write your entire essay about whether Malthus's theories were valid in 1798 and neglect the question of whether they are valid in the twenty-first century. The latter must be the crux of your argument or you won't have answered the question set. A brilliant essay tackles the assumption(s), if there are any, *and* the question. If an assumption is interesting and vulnerable, then examining it can help you answer the question too.

If Malthus's theories weren't valid in 1798, then we might think they wouldn't *ever* be valid. If we can identify time-invariant factors that lead us to reject the assumption, we might apply those same principles to help answer the question at hand: Malthusian theory cannot ever be valid. Similarly, if we affirm the assumption (Malthusian theories did once work), answering the question in the negative (Malthusian theories don't work today) becomes harder though by no means impossible. We would need to show what changed such that the theory is no longer true.

However you choose to answer the question, looking for assumptions is a great way to read a question carefully and approach it sceptically. We *Homo sapiens* are naturally good at communicating; if you are able to identify hidden assumptions in everyday speech, you are perfectly capable of doing exactly the same with an academic essay question. In the next chapter, we'll use the examining assumptions technique for an additional purpose: to highlight possible comparator classes, the set of things you are comparing in your essay. By the end of the next chapter, you'll be all set to ask the crucial questions: Of what is this a case? And compared with what?

Chapter 1 Exercises
Examining assumptions in questions

An implicature is a proposition that is *implied* by a question or statement but not stated explicitly. For example, 'Jane is sad <u>too</u>' implies 'There are at least two sad people' or 'Jane has several emotions'.

PART A: Find the implicatures in each of the following questions and statements. Underline the word or words that indicate implicature and write the implicatures as grammatical sentences.

1 Is John still studying geology?
2 Oh! Do you also like kickboxing?
3 Nowadays Sarah lives a quiet life.
4 Lin hasn't got a dance partner at the moment.
5 When you finally get your car going on a cold morning, the icy seats make your life miserable too.

6 The problem with the youth of today is that they don't respect their elders.

7 I've packed the inflatable dinghy as well, just in case.

8 Charlotte ate the sandwich.

PART B: Find the implicatures in each of the following essay questions. Underline the word or words that indicate implicature and write the implicatures as grammatical sentences. Be careful to distinguish what is *asserted* (the surface statement, such as 'Jane is sad') from what is *assumed* (the statement that is implied but not stated directly, such as 'More than one person is sad').

9 Is 'the Third World' still a useful concept?

10 Are perceptual motor skills a type of intellectual learning as well?

11 In *The City of the Sun*, 'the walls are also the curtains of an extraordinary theatre and the pages of an illustrated encyclopaedia of knowledge'. Discuss.

12 Explain how science-fiction films came to prominence in 1950s Hollywood.

13 Does the Victorian aesthetic sensibility survive today?

14 What is the problem with Meinongianism?

15 Does John Locke also apply the concept of tacit consent to the ongoing evaluation of the performance of a political regime?

16 What explains the current bias towards states in international law?

17 Is it true that any standard of virtue will be contestable in a diverse modern society?

18 'Problem-solving policing doesn't just mean looking at incidents only.' Discuss.

19 'Nowadays, metals are infinitely recyclable.' Discuss.

20 'The problem with geothermal energy is its adverse effect upon land stability.' Discuss

PART C: For each of the implicatures you identified in Part B, say how likely these assumptions are to be true, to the best of your knowledge: Definitely true/Probably true/Probably false/Definitely false/I can't say*.

*If you can't say whether an assumption is true or not, try to explain why. Is it just because *you* don't know enough? Is the assumption true in some senses, false in others? Is it *impossible* to say?

Finding Comparator Classes in Questions

In the previous chapter, we searched for hidden assumptions in essay questions as a way to slow down and read a question critically, but this technique can do far more than just force you to look at questions carefully. By considering underlying assumptions explicitly, you can identify possible comparators and get a clear sense of your domain of reference: that is, the set of things to which the question refers. By clarifying your comparators, you'll produce a more confident, convincing essay (I offer more advice about how to select cases in Chapter 7 on **using evidence effectively**.) Let's have a go, using similar techniques to the previous chapter.

Emphasizing words to find comparators

Many ordinary words can indicate an assumption. For example, if I say:

Even Harry knows it's unethical.

Maybe you sniggered. In effect, I am making two completely separable statements because there is an assumption underlying the surface statement, indicated by the word 'even', which implies that something has occurred which is counter-expectation.

> **Surface statement (that which is asserted):** *Harry knows it's unethical.*
> **Underlying assumption:** *Harry is not a very ethical person.*

If Harry were an upstanding gentleman, then it would be odd to claim that 'even' he knows something is unethical. Harry is clearly a rat or, at the very least, he is not very bright. We expect him to be unethical, but he has (surprisingly) bucked our expectations in this instance.

One way to bring out the assumptions in an essay question or discussion statement is to read it out loud, putting emphasis on different words in turn. Read 'Even *Harry* knows it's unethical' out loud with the emphasis on the second word: does speaking make the assumption jump out at you? Reading out your essay questions and putting emphasis on different words in turn can help you to identify hidden assumptions. This tactic can also help you to think around a question, by which I mean, considering what your core concepts are and what relevant comparators might be. For instance, imagine I said to you:

> *Al didn't even dance with Pete*

The use of the word 'even' implies that it is surprising that Al didn't dance with Pete; we would expect Al to dance with Pete, but the precise meaning of this statement can change depending upon where we place the emphasis. Read the statement 'Al didn't even dance with Pete' aloud three times, emphasizing the first, fourth and sixth words in turn. Can you hear the different implicatures?

> **Emphasis on the first word:** <u>Al</u> *didn't even dance with Pete.*
> **Emphasis on the fourth word:** *Al didn't even* <u>dance</u> *with Pete.*
> **Emphasis on the sixth word:** *Al didn't even dance with* <u>Pete</u>.

When we emphasize different words, the statements differ subtly in meaning, so the implicatures differ too. Some assumptions we might uncover include the following:

> **Assumption (if we emphasize 'Al'):** *Al is a good dancer; we expect him to dance.*
> **Assumption (if we emphasize 'dance'):** *Al likes Pete; we expect him to be friendly to Pete.*
> **Assumption (if we emphasize 'Pete'):** *Pete is a good dancer; we expect people to choose him as a partner.*

Putting the emphasis on each of these words in turn might prompt different responses because we are focusing on different things: Emphasizing 'Al' or 'Pete' points us toward the two actors in this scenario, whereas emphasizing 'dance' nudges us to consider different ways to interact with somebody.

Our relevant comparators differ. We might be invited to consider whether Al or Pete is a better dancer than, say, Joe, Tom or Richard. Or else to consider whether dancing with somebody is more or less friendly than chatting to them, giving them a present or buying them a drink. We can think about the set of things we are comparing as our *comparator class*. For instance, sheep can be compared with other farmyard animals (ducks, pigs, chickens), other fluffy things (knitwear, slippers, cotton candy), other graminivorous quadrupeds (horses, cows, sauropod dinosaurs) and so on. The same concept or object can have any number of different comparator classes.

In the same way, emphasizing different words in essay questions can lead to different comparator classes.

> *'Even hydroelectric power does not reduce methane emissions.' Discuss.*

> *'Even Titus Andronicus is no longer seen as an embarrassingly violent aberration in Shakespeare's early work.' Discuss.*

> *'A punishment so bloodthirsty, even the Romans baulked at deploying it against non-citizen criminals.' Discuss this view of poena cullei.*

Just as 'even Harry thinks it's unethical' indicates that Harry is not very ethical, the word 'even' in these statements suggests that hydroelectric power is likely the best way to reduce emissions, that the violence in *Titus Andronicus* is totally gratuitous and that the Romans were a vicious and insular bunch. These implicit assumptions need careful consideration. A so-so essay leaves them unexamined; a brilliant essay considers them critically. Advances in hydropower research and development, textual criticism or historical criminology might debunk any one of them.

Putting the emphasis on different words in these discussion statements can also invoke different comparator classes. By emphasizing either 'hydroelectric' or 'methane', you can direct readers' attention toward either forms of power (comparator class 1) or forms of emission (comparator class 2) correspondingly.

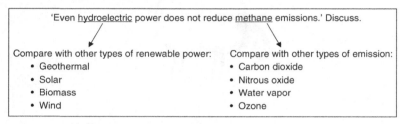

'Even hydroelectric power does not reduce methane emissions.' Discuss.

Compare with other types of renewable power:
- Geothermal
- Solar
- Biomass
- Wind

Compare with other types of emission:
- Carbon dioxide
- Nitrous oxide
- Water vapor
- Ozone

By emphasizing 'Titus Andronicus', 'embarrassingly', 'aberration' or 'early', you can direct readers to all of Shakespeare's plays (comparator class 1), violence that provokes emotions other than embarrassment (comparator class 2), Shakespeare's many other uses of violence (comparator class 3) or Shakespeare's later work (comparator class 4) in turn.

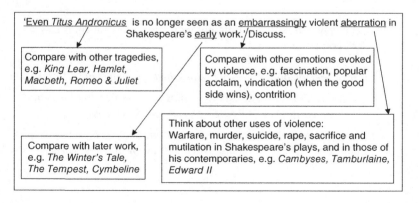

'Even *Titus Andronicus* is no longer seen as an embarrassingly violent aberration in Shakespeare's early work.' Discuss.

Compare with other tragedies, e.g. *King Lear, Hamlet, Macbeth, Romeo & Juliet*

Compare with other emotions evoked by violence, e.g. fascination, popular acclaim, vindication (when the good side wins), contrition

Compare with later work, e.g. *The Winter's Tale, The Tempest, Cymbeline*

Think about other uses of violence: Warfare, murder, suicide, rape, sacrifice and mutilation in Shakespeare's plays, and in those of his contemporaries, e.g. *Cambyses, Tamburlaine, Edward II*

By emphasizing 'Romans', 'non-citizens' or '*poena cullei*', you can direct readers to other civilizations (comparator class 1), other classes of person (comparator class 2) or other types of punishment (comparator class 3), respectively.

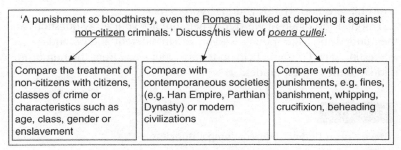

'A punishment so bloodthirsty, even the <u>Romans</u> baulked at deploying it against <u>non-citizen</u> criminals.' Discuss this view of *poena cullei*.

| Compare the treatment of non-citizens with citizens, classes of crime or characteristics such as age, class, gender or enslavement | Compare with contemporaneous societies (e.g. Han Empire, Parthian Dynasty) or modern civilizations | Compare with other punishments, e.g. fines, banishment, whipping, crucifixion, beheading |

These different emphases, assumptions and comparators lead to very different sorts of essay but that is the joy of academia: there are multiple pathways to excellent work. In my experience, students tend to fail quite predictably (incoherent argument, missing data or failure to define terms, for example), but they succeed in a huge variety of different ways, many of which I hadn't even considered when I first set an essay question. Don't be frightened to forge your own path. Often, anxious students ask me if they have the single 'correct' interpretation or if there is a 'wrong way' to interpret a question, but this worry is merely a training wheel left over from school. (For more school habits you should lose, see Chapter 9 on **losing the training wheels**.)

There is no single 'correct' interpretation, and a good question-setter will leave enough ambiguity and meaty concepts in a question to allow the top performers to put their own stamp on their answer. At university, truly brilliant essays are interesting to write and read precisely because their authors have thought around the question and decided independently how to interpret it.

A note of caution: do not attempt to cover every one of these pathways. It can be intoxicating to hunt for different assumptions, meanings and comparator classes by emphasizing different words out loud. Unpacking your questions like this is a chance to open up the possibilities, shake off the obvious, superficial and formulaic responses, and write something truly original, but beware of trying to cover too many different comparator classes in a single essay.

For instance, imagine that you have read the statement about *Titus Andronicus* aloud with different emphases and determined that you could then compare all of Shakespeare's plays, violence that provokes emotions other than embarrassment, Shakespeare's many other uses of violence or Shakespeare's later work. A single essay that attempted to cover all of these angles would be an almighty mess. The process of writing a brilliant essay is making an authoritative decision about which of those pathways is most interesting. That is your decision to make.

Emphasizing different words can help unpack your essay questions and their underlying assumptions, leading you in different and potentially interesting directions and helping to raise your essay from the humdrum middle to the highest grades.

EXERCISE 2.1

Have a go at finding different comparator classes

Read aloud the questions below, emphasizing different words and phrases in turn, and note down possible comparator classes. You can also have a go at uncovering assumptions by looking for indicator words. The answers are on p. 145.

1 'The international refugee regime is ill suited to dealing with contemporary problems in forced migration.' Discuss.
2 'Even eliminating luck cannot solve Gettier's epistemology problems.' Discuss.
3 'The global consequences of al-Qaeda's jihad have outstripped its local causes.' Discuss.
4 Are hard engineering projects still favoured for flood management in the Netherlands?
5 Can class-based accounts of voting behaviour explain Labour's share of the vote in the 2010 general election?
6 How important is public awareness in the management of environmental problems?
7 Why do suicide attacks generate the most newspaper coverage?
8 How stable has the sitcom genre been since the 1950s?
9 What is the difference between imagination and belief?
10 How does screening based on higher education help overcome the adverse selection problem associated with hiring?

By now, I hope you're feeling more confident about uncovering assumptions underlying an essay question. In the next chapter, we'll use the same techniques to deconstruct some of the most common words in essay questions: 'but', 'or', 'why', 'when' and 'how'. By paying close attention to underlying assumptions, you can identify false dichotomies (where you're presented with two choices that aren't really mutually exclusive or collectively exhaustive) and avoid laundry list essays (weak essays that simply rattle off a list of reasons why X without stopping to consider whether X is actually true or not). This third chapter on questioning assumptions will boost your ability to think critically about a whole variety of questions.

Chapter 2 Exercises
Finding comparator classes in questions

An implicature is a proposition that is *implied* by a question or statement but not stated explicitly. For example, 'Tom has a crown-shaped birthmark <u>too</u>' implies 'Someone else has a crown-shaped birthmark' or 'Tom has two birthmarks, of which one is crown-shaped'.

PART A: Find the implicatures in each of the following questions and statements. Underline the word or words that indicate implicature and write the implicatures as grammatical sentences.

1 Even Ali is late for the meeting!
2 Even Sophie thinks this meeting is a waste of time.
3 If you keep on flashing the cash, even the local cops are going to smell a rat.
4 'A racial pattern so obvious, even the Supreme Court might see it.' Discuss this view of peremptory challenges in death penalty cases.
5 Tsongkhapa argues that not only is the intellectual act itself utterly devoid of any essential reality, even the sense-faculties also lack any essential reality. Evaluate Tsongkhapa's claim.
6 Why do scientists appeal to the covering law model, even in cases where nothing resembling a law appears to be available?
7 'At a transcendental level, even causally determined nature is explained in light of the self-positing ego.' Discuss Fichte's theory of the I's absolute self-positing nature.

PART B: By reading your questions aloud and putting emphasis on different words in turn, you can identify different comparator classes: the set of things from which you are drawing cases. For the following questions, underline the word (or words) that might help you find a comparator class. Note down what those comparator classes are.

8 How does eighteenth-century literature manifest gender divisions?
9 Why might employees be less productive following promotion?

10 'Economic valuation and markets can save Nature.' Discuss.

11 Why did the film *Raise the Red Lantern* appeal to audiences in the West?

12 What is the causal effect of education upon individual involvement in crime?

13 How does overloading the atmosphere with contaminants lead to change in that system?

14 How do US economic interests influence American newspapers' coverage of terrorism?

15 Evaluate the role of glacial meltwater in the formation of drumlins and lakes.

16 How might top football players react to increased taxation if they had to play football in their country of citizenship?

PART C: Read aloud some questions in your own discipline, placing emphasis on different words in turn. Consider how this change of emphasis alters the meaning of the question and identify different comparator classes to which the questions direct you.

3

Interrogating Tensions in Questions

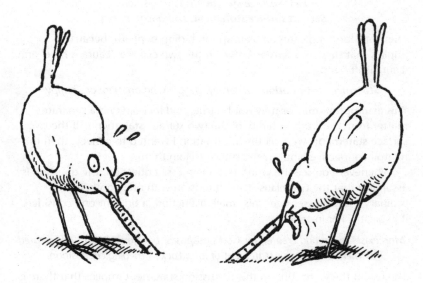

You might be thinking, 'This is all well and good, but I've never seen words like "even" or "still" in *my* essay questions. How relevant is "implicature" to my work?' The words we have considered up to now have been fairly obvious flags for underlying assumptions. There are many other words that indicate hidden assumptions, which are ubiquitous in essay questions and also harder to spot because they are very small and common. These words are 'but' and 'or'. You are bound to encounter these in essay questions at some point. Let us examine them in turn.

BUT: Are your propositions complementary or in tension?

Like 'and', the word 'but' is a connective, yet 'but' always gives rise to an assumption that the word 'and' does not. Any speaker of English knows that these words are not perfectly interchangeable. For instance, if I say:

Laura is here but she isn't happy.

I am making not one but two separate surface statements – that is, explicit propositions about the world:

First surface statement*: Laura is here.*
Second surface statement*: Laura isn't happy.*

The word 'but' indicates an assumption hiding beneath, because it implies that there is a *tension* between the two clauses: 'Laura is here' and 'Laura isn't happy'.

Statement assumption*: Generally, people who are here are happy.*

This assumption may or may not be true, and its validity is a separate matter from the truth or falsity of the two surface statements. If the two surface statements were all the information I wanted to convey, then the neutral connective 'and' would suffice to join them.

Whenever you see the word 'but' in an essay question, the question is assuming that the two clauses are in tension with one another. An ordinary essay glosses over this small distinction; a brilliant one considers it explicitly. For instance:

Man exists in a world created for God's purposes, but governments are created by men. Discuss this statement of John Locke's theological position.

The use of the word 'but' in this discussion statement implies that there is a tension between the idea that God's purposes animate the world and the idea that governments are created by men. That tension must be resolved somehow. A weaker essay simply describes Locke's position; a stronger one might consider how Locke and his interlocutors set up this tension, whether there is indeed a real tension and, if there is, how these two clauses might be reconciled.

OR: Are your options mutually exclusive and collectively exhaustive?

A small word that appears even more frequently than 'but' is the word 'or', and this little fragment has several different meanings. The word 'or' in English is used in both inclusive and exclusive ways. An inclusive 'or' is really 'A or B or both'. An exclusive 'or' is 'A or B but not both'. We would say in the latter case that the two options are *mutually exclusive*: you cannot have both (Hackett 2015; 2016). Context matters a great deal. For instance, imagine that you and your great friend Emma, the famous primatologist, meet for a bite to eat at a local café. The waitress says:

Your tea comes with a biscuit or a slice of cake.

Instinctively you know that this is an exclusive 'or', particularly if the waitress puts the emphasis on the word 'or'. You can't have *both* biscuit *and* cake with your tea, only one of them. If you want both, then you will have to pay extra. Back in Emma's flat, however, the statement 'biscuit or cake' has a more inclusive feel – if Emma's baking is particularly good or[1] you are feeling particularly greedy, then you might feel comfortable responding: 'both, please'. The inclusive 'or' is roomy enough to include 'and'. Whenever you see the word 'or' in an essay question, try adding 'or both', then 'but not both' afterwards, and consider which phrase sounds more plausible.

In addition to the *mutual exclusivity* implicature – that the answer cannot be 'both' – there is a further assumption embedded in many uses of the word 'or': the assumption that the answer has to come from the options laid down on the table and not something else entirely. We call this assumption *collective exhaustiveness*. 'Collective exhaustiveness' is the concept that the available options jointly exhaust all of the possibilities. The numbers one, two, three, four, five and six collectively exhaust the possible outcomes of a single throw of an ordinary die. The waitress who told you about the tea in that café would be surprised if you asked for, say, a hotdog with your tea when she has already laid out what we assume to be collectively exhaustive options: biscuit or cake – and nothing else. Imagine being asked:

Is archaeology fun or tedious?

You might take issue with the assumption that the answer is definitely one or the other and nothing else. The question is nudging you to choose one of these options and go all in on that side and that side only. A weaker essay would simply follow that nudge; a brilliant essay would question it. A clever way to interrogate this question would be to consider whether the question poses a *false dichotomy*. A false dichotomy is a distinction between two alternatives where the choice is not mutually

---

1 This is an inclusive or: either of these conditions may obtain (or indeed *both*!)

exclusive (the answer can be a bit of both) and not collectively exclusive (there are other possibilities that have not been presented).

Many essay questions ask students to choose between two (or more) options, and they tend to carry the assumptions of mutual exclusivity and collective exhaustiveness. For example:

Is David Hume a 'sceptic' or a 'naturalist'?

Was the Obama administration's foreign policy a continuation of, or a break with, his predecessor's?

Were the Aztecs an empire or merely a hegemony?

Which is the most powerful institution in the European Union: the Council, the Commission or the European Parliament?

Sometimes, a full-throated endorsement of one side or another is warranted, in line with these assumptions of mutual exclusivity and collective exhaustiveness, but often nuance is needed. Perhaps Hume is *both* sceptic and naturalist; Obama shared Bush's commitment to regime change in the Middle East yet took a more measured approach than his predecessor; Aztec rule involved political control but little homogenization; and the European Court of Justice or the European Central Bank (which the last question did not even mention) might have legitimate claims upon the title of 'most powerful institution in the European Union'.

Occasionally, an even more radical interpretation of the question is warranted. A really provocative response to these questions might query even the existence of the categories mentioned, debunk the assumption that at least *some* option must be true or consider fundamentally different options in addition to the named categories. For example, one thought-provoking response to the question about the Obama administration's foreign policy might query even the idea that the Obama administration had a foreign 'policy' at all, if 'policy' refers to grand strategy rather than just a set of aspirations about how the world should be. If the categories presented lack internal coherence, this line of thinking goes, then the categories themselves are useless.

A stimulating answer to the question about the European Union might ignore the obvious steer[2] toward policymaking bodies alone and compare them with alternative sources of institutional power: media, pressure groups and private sector companies. Or it might focus on factions *within* the institutions mentioned in the question. In both cases, the radical answer considers and rejects the categorization schema laid out by the question.

---

2 A steer is the path the questioner is indicating that the author should take.

I do not imply that such a radical response is always, or even often, needed. It is certainly not necessary for a top grade and it can be a risky strategy. Everything will depend upon your ability to support and justify such an original position, to argue persuasively against the existing categorization and to ensure that your answer does actually answer the question set. There is a danger of stretching the meaning of the question so far that it becomes a different question, which would be disastrous. After all, the categories set out in your question almost certainly have at least *some* merit; your tutor did not set the question in order to trick you.

Yet it is still helpful to think sceptically about the options contained in the questions you are set, and to at least *consider* a more radical response, because brilliant essays do need deep, confident and original thinking. By considering explicitly whether the choice you are presented with is mutually exclusive and collectively exhaustive, you can start to develop a critical response to a question.

EXERCISE 3.1

Have a go at uncovering false dichotomies (or trichotomies)

Take a look at the 'but' and 'or' questions and statements below. Say whether you think the set of categories presented are mutually exclusive, collectively exhaustive, one but not the other, or neither. If the categories are not collectively exhaustive, suggest alternative options.

1 Are bananas disgusting or delicious?
2 You are either part of the solution or part of the problem.
3 Is Macbeth a criminal sociopath or a victim?
4 Which of these solutions will ultimately reverse climate change: more wind turbines, tropical rainforest reforestation or better family planning?
5 I thought Mia was a good person but she did not attend church on Sunday.
6 Is the news media the friend or foe of prime ministers?
7 Is rape a criminal act or an act of war?
8 Are populist radical right parties successful because they are radical right or because they are populist?
9 Which poses the greater threat: small arms or 'weapons of mass destruction'?
10 Where do food taboos come from: magico-religious beliefs or utilitarian principles?
11 Was Aztec emperor Montezuma a cruel, power-hungry tyrant or an emotional, credulous weakling?
12 Is urbanization a cause or an effect of economic growth?

Why questions

The most common word you will come across in essay questions is 'why', and this word *always* carries an implicature. Asking 'Why X?' *implies that 'X' is indeed the case.* Since your tutor set the question and asked you 'Why X?' in good faith, it is unlikely that 'X' will be outright false, but it may not be true without qualification. For instance:

Why is utilitarianism such an influential moral theory?

Why does resource wealth harm economic growth?

Why did the peace process in Afghanistan fail?

Why are third parties so weak in the United States?

These questions contain the following implicatures:

Assumption: *Utilitarianism is a very influential moral theory.*

Assumption: *Resource wealth harms economic growth.*

Assumption: *The Afghan peace process failed.*

Assumption: *Third parties are very weak in the United States.*

None of these assumptions is obviously false – indeed, they all seem plausible – but they may not be true under every circumstance or time period or for every specification of the most ambiguous part of each question ('influential', 'harm', 'fail' and 'weak'). Other moral theories may be more influential than utilitarianism, particularly in non-Western cultures. The 'resource curse' is a blight, but Norway and Botswana have avoided it. The ongoing Afghan peace process involves both challenges and successes. When historian Richard Hofstadter claimed that third parties are like bees ('once they have stung, they die'), he did at least acknowledge third parties' strength in their 'sting' – since their temporary existence prompts changes to mainstream parties' policy commitments.

Don't fall into the trap of simply rattling off a list of reasons why utilitarianism is influential, resource wealth harms growth, the peace process failed, and third parties are weak. Instead, a wise strategy is to first consider whether these assumptions are indeed true. If they are only partly true, or true under certain circumstances or for some specification of the question, then you should say so. We discuss how to qualify statements like this in Chapter 6 on **elegant writing**.

Of course, sometimes the implicature to which a 'why' question gives rise is just empirically true, so there is no point in questioning that underlying statement. For instance:

Why did civil war occur in England and Normandy between 1135 and 1153?

Why do cabinet ministers resign?

According to Immanuel Kant, why should we 'treat humanity... never merely as a means to an end, but always at the same time as an end'?

The implicatures of these questions are:

Implicature: *Civil war occurred in England and Normandy between 1135 and 1153.*

Implicature: *Cabinet ministers resign.*

Implicature: *Kant states that we should 'treat humanity... never merely as a means to an end, but always at the same time as an end'.*

These implicatures are simply true. Civil war *did* break out in 1135, cabinet ministers *do* resign, and the third question contains a direct quotation from Kant. The questions about utilitarianism, resource wealth, the Afghan peace process and American third parties each contain some ambiguity or require qualification, but the implicatures underpinning these questions about civil war, cabinet ministers and Kant are simple statements of empirical fact. No crack here into which you can insert the crowbar of curiosity, alas.

Sometimes, you will find that the spoilsport question-setter has qualified the statement already, so that questioning the assumption seems like pedantry. For instance:

Why does urbanization tend to exacerbate flooding?

Recall the question: *Why does resource wealth harm economic growth?* The insertion of the word 'tend' in this question about urbanization has moderated the implicature of this question. Compared with the resource wealth question's assumption, which could be read as a blanket statement to the effect that resource wealth *necessarily, always or irrevocably* harms economic growth, the urbanization question's implicature is softer: that urbanization has a *tendency* (which may be reversed or forestalled) to *exacerbate* (not create or determine) flooding. The stronger assumption in the resource wealth question is naturally easier to criticize than the slippery customer in the urbanization question because the former cannot easily accommodate counter-examples. When you identify the implicature of a 'why' question, consider how vulnerable or resilient that underlying assumption is to attack.

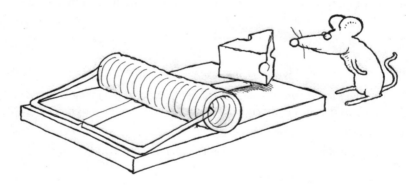

'How', 'what' and 'when' questions

The same hidden implicatures can accompany 'how', 'what' or 'when' questions in precisely the same way as 'why' questions. If you are asked 'How X', 'What X' or 'When 'X', there is an assumption *that X is indeed the case*. The classic example of a loaded question is framed as a 'when' question (although it could also be a 'why' question):

When did you stop beating your wife?

This is a loaded question because it contains an unjustified assumption: that you do not beat your wife now but you used to do so. Simply answering 'never' would imply that you never stopped, so you *are still doing it*. The correct way to approach such a loaded question would be to reject the assumption at the outset: 'I have never beaten my wife'.

Essay questions do not contain such horrible and unjustified assumptions but their assumptions may not always be true. For instance:

When does urban sprawl benefit minority neighbourhoods?

How does form follow function in architecture?

What do improvisational jazz musicians communicate?

These questions contain the following implicatures:

Assumption: *Urban sprawl benefits minority neighbourhoods.*

Assumption: *Form follows function.*

Assumption: *Improvisational jazz musicians communicate.*

Faced with any of these questions, a middling-grade essay simply enumerates the situations in which urban sprawl benefits minority neighbourhoods, the ways form follows function, and the messages jazz musicians communicate. It answers the question set, but it comes across as a workmanlike, solid-but-uninspired listicle. Planning for a brilliant essay requires a more critical approach.

Dare to consider whether urban sprawl does in fact benefit minority neighbourhoods before you plod on with your answer! *Venture to imagine* an architecture which rejects the principle that buildings must be functional! *Risk your professor's ire* by examining whether improvisational jazz does in fact 'communicate' anything! A brilliant essay is one that takes some (calculated) risks in order to convey an original and interesting argument.

EXERCISE 3.2

Have a go at identifying assumptions in 'how', 'when' and 'why' questions

Take a look at the following questions. Find the assumption underlying each question and write it out as a single grammatical sentence. The answers are on p. 147.

1 How do children's rights differ from other human rights?
2 What challenge do Gettier problems pose to internalist accounts of knowledge?
3 Why did John Locke argue for a limited state?
4 What can attention to the phenomenology of everyday life tell us about the mind–world relation?
5 Why is international police cooperation so difficult?
6 How did Queen Elizabeth I unite the English nation?
7 What problems does terrorism present for international law?
8 What does the concept of the sublime offer to our understanding of art?
9 Why do women need female representatives in Parliament?
10 How have humans impacted tropical ecosystems during the Holocene?
11 When should citizens obey the state?
12 Why did the dinosaurs die out?

I do not suggest that there is an assumption underlying every question. Many questions are quite straightforward, but at university it is good to be alive to the possibility that there is something going on underneath the surface, because identifying assumptions helps you pick a question apart and think about its underlying tensions critically – to really *read the question* – and this is a characteristic of a truly brilliant essay.

In the next chapter, we'll move from your essay question to the first part of the essay proper: your introduction. It is crucial that you give your reader the best possible first impression of your work. Using practical worked examples, we'll build up your introductory paragraphs in four key stages.

Chapter 3 Exercises
Interrogating tensions in questions

An implicature is a proposition that is *implied* by a question or statement but not stated explicitly. For example, 'Phil is wrong <u>too</u>' implies 'Someone else is wrong' or 'Phil is right in many respects but wrong in this particular'.

PART A: Find the implicatures in each of the following questions and statements. Underline the word or words that indicate implicature and write the implicatures as grammatical sentences.

1 Was *The Terminator* a brilliant or terrible film?
2 Why has Tina become so miserable?
3 I like Mae as a person but she is a fan of *The Big Bang Theory*.
4 When did you realize you were wrong?
5 Which is your favourite cephalopod?
6 How do bees gather honey from flowers?

PART B: Find the implicature (or implicatures) in each of the following essay questions. Underline the word or words that indicate implicature and write it as a grammatical sentence. Be careful to distinguish what is *asserted* (e.g. 'Phil is wrong') from what is *assumed* (e.g. 'More than one person is wrong').

7 Why has the rollout of autonomous vehicles been so slow?
8 Is the Tea Party an interest group, a faction or a party?
9 How do computers think?
10 Why has the US Congress become so dysfunctional?
11 How should we account for the failure of Descartes's mind–body thesis?

12 What has knowledge got to do with bravery?

13 Was New Labour an ideology or a style of governing?

14 When do our moral intuitions fail us?

15 Is British multiculturalism a symbol of a liberal, cosmopolitan society or a colonial throw-back?

16 How do multinational corporations threaten state authority?

17 What impact did the film *Cathy Come Home* have upon policymakers' willingness to address the social problems it identified?

18 Is social media beneficial or harmful for democracy?

19 'Some landscapes are shaped by human activities.' Discuss.

20 'It may truly be said to have neither FORCE nor WILL, but merely judgment.' Discuss Alexander Hamilton's view of the judiciary in *Federalist 78*.

PART C: For each of the implicatures you identified in Part B, say how likely these assumptions or implied statements are to be true, to the best of your knowledge: Definitely true / Probably true / Probably false / Definitely false / I can't say*.

*If you can't say whether an assumption is true or not, try to explain why. Is it just because *you* don't know enough? Is the assumption true in some senses, false in others? Is it *impossible* to say?

The Introduction Scale

In this chapter, we will focus on the most crucial part of your essay: the introduction. Why is the introduction so important? It's your shop window – the first thing your reader sees. When I'm marking, a student will occasionally surprise me by offering a weak introduction followed by an essay that picks up steam (or, rarer still, a strong introduction leading to a weak essay), but usually the introduction sets the tone for the entire essay that follows. I can often give a ballpark grade from an introduction alone. First impressions count, so it is essential that you nail the opening. If you do it well, the whole argument will flow from your introductory set-up, making the rest of your essay much easier to write.

I'm going to help you build up your introduction on four levels. We can think of these levels as forming four stages of a scale. At the entrance level, the bottom, are the weakest introductions. Those slightly higher up the scale are a bit stronger. Our aim is to reach the pinnacle of the scale: level 4.

The weakest introductions, at level 1, simply identify the question. Level 2 gives the reader a bare 'I agree' or 'I disagree'. At level 3, the writer outlines their own view. At level 4, the writer briefly *explains* their own view. In my experience, many students don't get past level 2. To reach the highest grades, you really need to be on level 4. Throughout this chapter, I'll provide real-world examples of introductions at each level, so you can see what sorts of introduction produce the best impression, and there will be a chance for you to practise polishing up your own introductions. Let's take the following three questions:

'The problem with the US presidency is that expectations always exceed capacity.' Discuss.

How was the island of Britain Romanized and de-Romanized?

Can animals think?

While we work through these examples, keep essay questions from your own area of study in mind.

Level 1 introductions identify a question

The weakest introductions are easy to write, but only because they tell the reader nothing at all. At level 1, an author simply restates the question.

I am going to ask whether presidential capacity exceeds expectations.

I will consider how the island of Britain was Romanized and de-Romanized.

Can animals think? That is the question we need to answer.

These are truly terrible introductions! The reader already knows what the question is, because it's right there at the top of the document. Even if you dress it up a bit, you're still wasting words. In fact, if you try to elaborate on the question in a more long-winded style, you'll irritate your reader even more.

It is absolutely crucial for us to understand whether or not presidential capacity always exceeds expectations, and to discuss the ins-and-outs of this question.

How did the island of Britain become Romanized, and how did that very same island become de-Romanized?

I am going to ask whether animals can indeed think. Answering that question is extremely important, although it is a difficult question to answer properly.

That's 24 wasted words for the presidential capacity question, 17 for the Roman Britain question, and 25 for the animal thought question. All essays will feature the title at the top (or, in the case of exams, it will be easily accessible to the examiner because they will have the paper at hand), so there is no point in restating the question. You have limited space, so avoid wasting words. We discuss how to avoid word wastage in Chapters 6 and 11 on **elegant writing** and **examination preparation**. No amount of variants on 'this is a really, really important question, honestly!' will impress your reader. Better to cut to the chase.

Instead of merely restating the question in the introduction, aim to craft an introduction from which a clever reader could *deduce* the question. The introduction must contain your answer to the question, stated succinctly, and for well-written introductions it should be possible to infer what the questioner was asking. For instance, imagine an introductory paragraph that started with these statements:

Iraqi federalism can succeed only if the institutional capacity of provincial administrations is strengthened and petro-dollar resources shared more equally. The current constitution's deliberate ambiguity on resource-sharing and security responsibilities creates tensions between national, regional and local governments.[1]

It would not be too challenging to identify the question set, judging purely by these introductory sentences:

Can federalism succeed in Iraq?

Have a go at identifying the questions for the introductory paragraphs in the exercise box below.[2] Pay particular attention to the opening sentences for clues.

---

1 With thanks to Natali 2011 for this material.

2 With thanks to Khan and Fazili 2019; Bruce and Young 1986 for some of the material used in this 'Have a go' exercise.

EXERCISE 4.1

Have a go at deducing the question from the introductory paragraphs

Take a look at the following introductory paragraphs. Can you reconstruct an essay question from the answers offered here? Pay particular attention to the first sentence in each introduction, which is likely to offer you the most information about the question. The answers are on p. 149.

1 The surprising thing about the French Fourth Republic was not that it collapsed but that it managed to survive for 12 years. Its chief problems were institutional – a weak legislature riven by ideological disagreement – and its political predicament was exacerbated by economic inflation, agricultural overproduction and war.

2 If Plato's arguments against art and poetry were invalid, then his arguments about the ideal city and the education of its guardians would also fail. It is fortunate, then, that Plato's strictures do have validity, but since they lack clarity, intuitiveness and plausibility, this is a hollow victory for Plato.

3 The combination of price consciousness and the need for social status drives a consumer's intention to buy counterfeit luxury goods. Without diluting the equity of the parent brand, marketers of luxury brands can inhibit consumption of counterfeit luxury items by extending the brand downwards to attract the 'real gainers' group: price-conscious consumers with high need for social status.

4 We derive seven distinct types of information from faces we see: pictorial, structural, visually derived semantic, identity-specific semantic, name, expression and facial speech codes. Recognizing familiar faces involves a match between the encoding of this information and previously stored codes. I show that the cognitive system plays an active role in deciding whether or not the initial match is sufficiently close to indicate true recognition.

5 In opposition to Kripke, I argue that Frege is right to argue that proper names have a 'sense' as well as a reference, that is, a mode of presentation which gives the thought that is expressed by the proper name and accounts for its cognitive significance and its meaning in certain contexts. A cluster-descriptivist construal of 'sense' as a disjunction of descriptions is robust against Kripke's charge that proper names and definite description clusters have different modal profiles.

Level 2 introductions offer a bare 'agree' or 'disagree'

Recall the questions we are considering as we build up our introduction scale:

> 'The problem with the US presidency is that expectations always exceed capacity.' Discuss.

How was the island of Britain Romanized and de-Romanized?

Can animals think?

An introduction at level 1 merely restates the question, whereas a level 2 introduction offers a basic 'I agree' or 'I disagree'. There is still no whiff of an argument in a level 2 introductory paragraph, but the reader at least gets the impression that the author has *some* sort of opinion on the matter, whatever that may be. For our three examples, a level 2 introduction might state:

I am going to argue that presidential capacity does exceed expectations.

The island of Britain was Romanized for many reasons, and de-Romanized when circumstances changed.

I say, no, animals cannot think.

These introductory statements are a *bit* better than level 1 introductions – at least there is a shadow of an answer rather than endless questions – but they are all bare skeletons. There is no sense of what the author understands by 'capacity' and 'expectations', or 'Romanization' and 'de-Romanization', or 'thinking'. A brilliant introduction must introduce its readers to the core conceptual apparatus as soon as possible. That means you should define technical terms as soon as they are first used. University essays often ask you to pick apart juicy concepts like these. The introduction is where that process starts (although it does not end there). A succinct, single-sentence definition is all that is needed. Lengthy paragraphs and extended examples should be placed in the main body of the essay.

These level 2 introductions are also deficient in that they do not offer any reasoning to help the reader see why the author takes a particular view. As with the definitions, you do not want your reasoning to take up too much space at the outset, but you do need to offer your reader a taste of what is to come. One or two sentences – no more – should suffice to express the reasoning behind the answer. Chapter 8 on **syllogisms and summaries** offers more tips to help you summarize succinctly.

The other problem with level 2 introductions is that they give the reader no sign of the independent thinking which characterizes all brilliant essays. In other words, they are quite uncritical of the question. Students often simply accept title quotations without question ('yes, *the* problem with the US presidency is indeed that expectations *always* exceed capacity') or accept the steer given by the question ('can animals think?' sounds a bit negative – 'can they *really*?' – so many answers to this question will accordingly answer in the negative).

Chapter 1 on **examining assumptions** demonstrates how to read an essay question in a critical way. Depending upon your definition of 'Romanization' and 'de-Romanization', your answer might kick back against the twin assumptions embedded in this question: that the island of Britain was fully Romanized and that it was fully de-Romanized later. Either or both might be false, or only partially true, or true in certain senses but not others. The steers in our questions are as follows:

Possible assumption: Expectations of American Presidents always exceed capacity.

Possible assumption: The <u>main</u> (or perhaps even the <u>only</u>) problem with the American Presidency is that expectations always exceed capacity (there are no other problems).

Possible assumption: The island of Britain was fully Romanized.

Possible assumption: The island of Britain was fully de-Romanized (no aspects of Romanization remain).

Possible assumption: The processes of Romanization and de-Romanization mirror one another (they are similar and symmetrical).

Possible assumption: Animals cannot really think.

It is useful to consider what the question is steering you to do, especially when that question consists of a quotation. It isn't that you *must* reject the steer in order to write a brilliant essay – you might find, on reflection, that you accept the underlying premise of the question – but you mustn't simply take it as a given. Level 2 introductions give the reader no reassurance that the writer has thought independently about whether to accept or reject the title proposition. For the discussion questions in the box below, have a go at identifying the proposition or propositions you're being steered to affirm and the ones you're being steered to reject.

EXERCISE 4.2

Have a go at identifying the question steer

Take a look at the following questions. What position is each question steering you to take? The answers are on p. 149.

Some questions steer you to accept a single proposition. For example, the question:

On what basis do some individuals deserve to earn more than others?

steers you to accept the proposition:

Some individuals <u>do</u> deserve to earn more than others.

Other questions steer you to accept several propositions. For example, in the question:

'Elections to the European Parliament are a triumph of democratic participation and provide a mandate for the President of the European Commission.' Really?

the sceptical 'really?' might steer you to <u>reject</u> the twin propositions:

1) Elections to the European Parliament are a triumph of democratic participation.

2) Elections to the European Parliament provide a mandate for the European Commission President.

Summarize the affirmative position (the one which agrees with the quotation or the steer in the question) as a grammatical sentence. Then write out the negative position (the one that rejects the quotation or the steer in the question) as another sentence. As in the examples above, there could be more than one proposition on each side.

---

1. 'To understand the operation of power, there is no need to look beyond access to economic resources.' Discuss.
2. 'We cannot reduce beliefs and desires to neurophysiological states; therefore, we should eliminate them.' Discuss.
3. Why is privacy important?
4. 'The concept of "new social movements" seems increasingly dated and of limited analytical value.' Discuss
5. 'Consciousness is an entirely private, first-person phenomenon' (Damasio). Has philosophy given us reason to doubt this?
6. Do you agree that the European Union is simply an international organization controlled by the governments of its member states?
7. 'Logic is ontologically neutral; therefore, Tarski's account of logical consequence is false.' Discuss.
8. Which theories of political economy can help us understand the governance of climate change?
9. 'Religion is politically significant, but its relationship with "party" is not its main significance.' Discuss with reference to at least two countries.
10. Why is the problem of evil so important and so problematic for Augustine's philosophy?

Level 3 introductions present the author's view

You've seen that level 2 introductions merely gesture toward an 'agree' or 'disagree' with a question or title quotation. They do not unpack the terms of the question or provide an account of the author's reasoning, and they are often uncritically accepting of the steer in the question – that is, the path the questioner is indicating the author should take. At level 3, writers start to remedy some of these deficiencies. Instead of merely hand waving in opposition to or in favour of a particular question, level 3 introductions offer an outline of the core argument.

I argue that it is lack of capacity, not the growth of expectations, which matters most.

The island of Britain was Romanized through Roman expansion, imperialism and economic exploitation, and it was de-Romanized in the fifth century when Rome could no longer defend itself against the incursion of Germanic tribes in Western Europe.

Human animals can think – and so can many non-human ones – because we are neurologically similar.

You can see how much better these level 3 introductions are than their level 2 counterparts. We know more about the writer's own views. There are some interesting thoughts here.

In the presidency question, we are not simply accepting or rejecting a quotation but thinking about how the two elements of the question ('capacity' and 'expectations') interact with each other. For the Romanization question, we are not simply asserting that Romanization and de-Romanization happened, but considering various factors that prompted these processes. Moreover, it looks as if the author rejects the steer in the question – that Romanization and de-Romanization are basically mirror images of one another – by emphasizing economic considerations in explaining Romanization but military ones in explaining de-Romanization. With the animals example, the author advances an intriguing thesis about the neurological similarity of non-human and human animals.

Level 3 is clearly a step up, but we're not quite there yet. Although these introductions present the writer's own views and give the reader an outline of the argument to come, they are still too coy about what the core concepts mean and why the authors take the line that they do. As we discuss in Chapter 5 on **controlling your argument**, you mustn't tease your readers. Readers need to know precisely what the author understands by the question and exactly how they intend to answer it. The introduction provides a roadmap for what follows.

Level 4 introductions explain the author's view

At level 4, the author does not merely outline their own view, but explains it as succinctly as possible. Consider the journal abstracts you have read recently. On the basis of an abstract alone, it is possible to extract not only the question but also the writer's core argument, sources of empirical evidence and theoretical contribution. The abstract contains a succinct summary of the main take-home of the article. In your introductory paragraph, you should aim to achieve both the brevity and the explanatory power of a journal abstract.

For our three example essay questions, a level 4 introductory paragraph might proceed as follows. (Don't take these examples as the definitive response, though. There are as many ways to write a top-notch introduction as there are writers.)

'The problem with the US presidency is that expectations always exceed capacity.' Discuss.

There are three main forms of presidential capacity: rhetorical (the power to persuade), despotic (the power to control other branches of government) and transformative (the power to enact a substantive agenda). Expectations of despotic capacity are always too high because the US is a separated system. Excessive expectations of transformative capacity have become more frequent since the Johnson presidency, but rhetorical capacity is not always exceeded by expectations because it is contingent upon an individual president's skill.

How was the island of Britain Romanized and de-Romanized?

Romanization involves two distinct processes: Roman conquest and acculturation. Compared with continental Europe, Britain was unevenly Romanized on the former dimension and only weakly Romanized on the latter, because of its geographical peripherality and relatively small Latin-speaking population. Its approximation of Roman culture was weaker than that of Gaul. I argue that this uneven acculturation – not pestilence or Anglo-Saxon invasions – was the primary cause of the destruction of Roman Britain. Invasions and plagues are better understood as symptoms rather than the chief causes of Roman decline because the regime was already fatally weakened by societal and economic problems stemming from incomplete acculturation.

Can animals think?

The most rigorous ethological experiments indicate that certain non-human animals do possess phenomenal consciousness, not just wakefulness or basic environmental perception. Those who deny the ability of animals to think are guilty of unsystematic, unscientific methods (Cartesians) or an overly thick and anthropocentric conception of consciousness (Dennett, Carothers). I maintain that consciousness is not a binary state but a spectrum. Deploying progressively 'harder' cases: great apes, corvids, cephalopods, insects and single-celled organisms, I argue that even cephalopods display complex learning, number sense and foresight worthy of the term 'thinking'. But advances in our understanding of the neurobiological substrates of conscious experience are unlikely to shift deeply held folk theories about animals and moral taboos about eating them.

These level 4 examples are brilliant introductions. Why? Several reasons. First, the author has thought carefully about the core concepts in the questions – presidential capacity, Romanization, de-Romanization and thinking – recognizing that these concepts have multiple meanings and dimensions and *briefly* unpacking them. Note that these introductions do not give lengthy definitions, footnotes or long quotations from the scholarly literature. Those elements are better suited to the main body of the essay, not the introductory paragraph. If you find your introductory paragraph extending into two paragraphs or reaching onto a second page (please, no!), then it is too long. A brief summary of the essentials is required, not a lengthy digression. Remember that journal article abstracts are never more than a single paragraph long, often 100 to 150 words.

Second, these introductory paragraphs tell the reader what the answers will be, right at the start. They give away the punchline; no murder mystery novel here! The reader should be able to extract the author's core argument as a single grammatical sentence from the introductory paragraph without difficulty. For the examples above, the reader might identify the essence of each argument as follows:

Expectations of presidents' despotic capacity are inherently excessive, but expectations of transformative or rhetorical capacity are only contingently so.

Britain's low levels of acculturation under Roman rule weakened the Roman regime's ability to withstand Anglo-Saxon invasions.

Even cephalopods display some indications of phenomenal consciousness, including complex learning, number sense and foresight.

Third, these introductory paragraphs are interesting and nuanced. Don't they make you want to read on? Think about your audience, those who mark your work. Your tutors will likely be reading dozens of scripts, many on the exact same question. Take it from me, a tutor who has had to prop up her eyelids to read level 1 or level 2 introductions on many occasions (so many unnecessary words and restatements of the question!), your tutor will be absolutely delighted to read something meatier. The introduction encapsulates the essay as a whole: clear, focused argument delivered without unnecessary hedging or preamble, showing nuanced thinking about the terms of the question.

Fourth, these introductory paragraphs offer a logical structure for the essay. By unpacking the question and defining the core concepts, the authors provide the reader with a clear path forward for the essay as a whole. They help the reader navigate the essay.

For the presidency essay, the three types of capacity the author has uncovered (despotic, transformative and rhetorical) each constitute a natural section. A reader who has read this introductory paragraph will be primed to consider the three forms of capacity in turn. The author can start talking about despotic capacity, and the reader will already know that transformative capacity comes next, to be followed by the rhetorical dimension. No need for any additional language to signpost what will be considered when ('in the first part of this essay I will... in the next part I will...'). That saves space and makes the essay more elegant.

In the Roman Britain example, the author makes an analytical distinction between the conquest and acculturation dimensions of Romanization and signals that they will consider three core explanations for de-Romanization: invasion, pestilence and societal problems stemming from incomplete acculturation. Logically, the essay could be structured in two parts: the first weighs the two dimensions of Romanization, and the second explains how this incomplete acculturation fatally weakened the

Roman regime. This second part would explicitly consider the societal problems explanation for Roman collapse in comparison with external factors focused upon disease or Anglo-Saxon activity.

For the animal consciousness example, the author signals that phenomenal consciousness is a spectrum rather than a dichotomy. So their essay is logically structured around the progressively more challenging cases for theories of animal consciousness: great apes, corvids, cephalopods, insects and single-celled organisms. They could consider each case in turn according to the criteria laid out in the introductory paragraph, showing precisely where other philosophers would draw the line and why we might have principled reasons for rejecting these alternative approaches.

Occasionally, a few signposts in the introduction can be helpful (First I consider X... next I examine Y...), but these introductory paragraphs are so strong that they negate the need for such obvious roadmaps for readers, thereby saving their authors some boring set-up words. In the exercise box below, I provide some example introductory paragraphs. Have a go at drawing out possible structures for the ensuing essays from the introductory statements alone. The introduction should indicate the author's core argument and the main empirical and theoretical

EXERCISE 4.3

Have a go at identifying a logical essay structure

Take a look at the following introductory paragraphs, focusing on the core theoretical and empirical distinctions the author is making and their main argument. How would you structure the ensuing essay?

Sketch out a couple of bullet points indicating a possible structure for the essay. Remember there is not just one way to structure an essay well – this exercise is open to many valid interpretations. The answers are on p. 151.

Q1: What, if anything, is problematic about the involvement of celebrities in democratic politics?

Celebrities' fame gives them the ability to influence what others think and to endorse or discredit other individuals. Those who have found fame for reasons other than their political achievements possess this 'epistemic power' because they have a platform and enjoy concentrated attention. I argue that where celebrities enjoy concentrated attention but do not possess relevant expertise, the use of such unchecked and unwarranted power has a corrosive effect upon the legitimacy of democracies by leaving it open to coercion or manipulation. Their illegitimate ability to set political agendas and their immunity from ordinary checks on power make celebrities damaging to deliberative, epistemic and plebiscitary theories of democracy.

Q2: What explains racial disparities in discipline and punishment rates in schools?
I argue that micro-processes lead to structural inequality within education for black children. The under-diagnosis of disabilities such as attention deficit hyperactive disorder in black children is a result of racism that is structurally and institutionally embedded within school policing policies and the failure to recognize black illness. I show how racism within some schools helps contribute to the under-diagnosis and lack of treatment for disabled black children, their over-punishment and thus their over-representation in today's school-to-prison pipeline.

Q3: How do urban governments respond to immigrants?
In opposition to theories of multilevel urban governance, which emphasize a 'spider web of interactions' consisting in both vertical and horizontal dimensions across localities and sectors, I argue that top-down influence remains most prominent in urban responses to immigrants. Federal policies shape local officials' immediate behaviour, views and actions through constraints upon local policymaking autonomy. They require urban areas to educate immigrants and frame immigrants as clients of local government services, frequently pre-empting local and state policies.

distinctions they will make. These can help structure the essay into different sections.[3]

    In sum, polish up your introductions by giving away the punchline right at the start and thinking very carefully about the terms of the question, including any assumptions that might be lurking beneath.

---

3 With thanks to Archer et al. 2020; Moody 2016; Williamson 2020 for their papers on these subjects.

Don't pad out your introductions with fluff – common knowledge or irrelevant information – and don't simply restate the question, but offer your reader your main argument as succinctly as possible. If your introductory paragraph has set up your essay on a sound footing with a logical structure, you will find it much easier to keep your argument on track in the main body of your essay.

In the next chapter – **controlling your argument** – we will move on from the introductory paragraph to consider how to sustain an argument throughout your essay. Using practical worked examples, we'll examine how to stay on track and avoid meandering. By the end of the chapter, you'll know how to construct a consistent argument to persuade a reader, with each section following logically from the previous one.

Chapter 4 Exercises
The introduction scale

PART A: The weakest introductions (level 1) simply identify the question. Level 2 gives the reader a bare 'I agree' or 'I disagree'. At level 3, the writer outlines his or her own view. At level 4, the writer briefly explains his or her own view. The aim is to reach the top of the scale.

Assess the level (1, 2, 3 or 4) of the following seven introductions for the question: *How does the built environment shape physical activity?*

1 This question asks us to consider the effect of the built environment upon physical activity.

2 Rural, suburban and urban infrastructure differ in their impact upon physical activity because they represent different 'choice architectures'; that is, they present people with choices in different ways. Attractive, leafy streets and widely spaced houses in suburban areas can nudge people to engage in more physical activity by inviting people outside, but densely populated urban areas have the same effect if they are well lit. The effect of the built environment is small in comparison with factors such as age, gender, disability and financial circumstances, but it has a measurable effect if planners design choice architecture carefully.

3 I argue that infrastructure does shape physical activity.

4 Physical activity is very important, and the built environment plays a big role in whether or not people engage in it. I argue that infrastructure profoundly shapes physical activity.

5 What is 'the built environment'? There are many different definitions and many different ways to understand the relationship between the built environment and physical activity.

6 There are many complex factors that affect the relationship between the built environment and physical activity, including house spacing, public transportation and maintained green space. I will consider each of them in turn in order to assess how environmental factors affect physicality. Green space is the most important factor.

7 Does the built environment shape physical activity? This question assumes that the built environment does in fact shape physical activity. I will assess whether or not it does.

PART B: An introduction is your shop window. Avoid padding it out with fluff: basic background, restatements of the question or irrelevant details. Which of the following, if any, would you include?

1 The built environment is created by human beings.

2 In the study of the ancient world, a city is defined as a large populated urban centre.

3 Smart devices have transformed the relationship between built environment and exercise.

4 Physical activity strengths your heart and improves your circulation.

PART C: Take an essay question in your discipline and practise writing an introduction that hits levels 1, 2, 3 and finally 4.

Controlling Your Argument

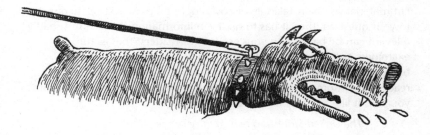

A brilliant essay develops a *controlled argument*. By 'controlling your argument', I mean making a clear, consistent, convincing case through-out the essay, where each section follows logically from the previous one. To write a controlled argument, you need to be ruthless about cutting all information that does not contribute directly to answering the question at hand. You should avoid meandering along without a clear purpose or moving off-piste in the middle of your essay, and you must give your key take-home at the outset rather than leaving the final reveal until your concluding paragraph.

An essay plan anchors your essay by providing a logical structure. I am sure you already know the basics of planning: define the terms of the question; gather ideas and assemble them in sequence; aim for roughly one idea per paragraph; and identify the broader implications of your argument in the concluding section. You already know that you need to spend time preparing and thinking before you write, so I will pass over these simple prescriptions here. You will have encountered essay planning at school, and your university's study skills team will be able to help you if you need a refresher, but how to turn a so-so essay into a brilliant one? In this chapter, we will show how to control your argument in the service of a truly brilliant essay.

Be ruthless

To write a controlled argument, you need to be ruthless about cutting irrelevant and unnecessary material, right from the start. By the time you have finished reading for an essay, you will know a great deal about your topic, but you don't want to simply tell your reader all about it. Instead, you must extract only those pieces of information that are essential for your argument.

Clearly, you must remove irrelevant information. It can be painful to cut material you painstakingly discovered, but if it doesn't relate directly to your question, then it has to go. Even information that seems broadly relevant can be harmful to your essay. Your readers (that is, tutors, examiners and fellow students) are already conversant with basic, background knowledge on the topic. You aren't going to give your readers the impression that you're writing a first-class, A-grade essay if you start it like a school homework assignment:

The United States is a rich country composed of fifty states.

Crocodiles are large reptiles that live in water.

Macroeconomics is a field of study concerned with how the whole economy functions.

Many students start an essay with a bit of fluff like this, which you might think wouldn't hurt, but it wastes words and gives the wrong impression. It makes the reader think that you don't know how to control your argument, as if this elementary information is news to you. Don't insult your reader's intelligence. Instead, get straight on with your argument and assume that your professors already know that basic stuff.

Depending on the actual question at hand, the following statements might be a more informative way to begin an essay.

During economic downturns, the American public looks primarily to the federal government to prevent the situation from worsening, by providing fiscal support to the states.

Crocodilians' navigational skills give them impressive homing ability, but they are easily disturbed by human activity.

I argue that credit market frictions influence the transmission of monetary policy.

Context is everything. In some circumstances, even these meatier statements could come across as trite and uninformative. The distinction between unnecessary background and the real meat-and-potatoes of your essay depends on your question and audience. Think about journal articles in your area: how much background information do they provide, and what do they assume their audience already knows? Ultimately, you need to make your own judgement about what constitutes basic background and what constitutes an informative response to a question.

EXERCISE 5.1

Have a go at ruthlessly cutting basic background information

Take a look at the statements below in response to the question: Does Marx have a consistent theory of the state? For each statement, decide the following: Is this useful, irrelevant or mere background information? Would you cut this sentence or keep it? Are there any borderline cases? Imagine you were writing for Professor Smith, the renowned scholar of Marxism, and fellow students in your political theory class. What can you reasonably expect your audience to know already? Try being ruthless: keep only those statements that actually help answer the question at hand. The answers are on p. 153.

1 Karl Marx was a nineteenth-century German philosopher, economist, historian and socialist revolutionary.
2 The state is an important organization.
3 Marx has been described as one of the most influential figures in human history.
4 By 1857, Marx accumulated over 800 pages of notes and short essays on capital, landed property, wage labour and the state.
5 Marx did not deliberately set out to create a systematic theory of the state.
6 There are many theories of the state.
7 It is important to remain neutral with regard to Marx's writings on the state, which are difficult to understand.
8 Marx's earliest writings identify the state as the guardian of the general interest, but in his later works he reimagines the state as a weapon used by the bourgeoisie to oppress the workers.

Avoid the voyage of discovery

In the main body of your essay, be careful not to send your reader on a voyage of discovery. In other words, don't meander around without a clear purpose at the outset. Growing up, I would regularly embark on voyages of discovery because my younger brother was a confident but unreliable guide. For instance, if I asked him where my coat was, he'd be puppyishly keen to help. He'd say 'Yes, I know where it is!' and we'd set off together. I'd follow him, expecting him to show me the way to my coat, but after a lengthy period of searching, I would eventually realize that he had no idea where it was either. He so wanted to help that he'd managed to convince himself he knew where it was, but we were just searching together! He was no use as a guide at all. It was the blind leading the blind.

In a university essay, the analogous situation is an essay that meanders about and leads the reader into a series of blind alleys – repetition of the question, vague statements, a series of unconnected assertions, rather than a clear argumentative goal combined with a controlled set of steps leading the reader straight to that goal. In the table below, I've laid out some successive sentences in an imaginary essay, showing a meandering voyage of discovery rather than an authoritative guide. The question is: *How did the ordering of space within Neolithic sites contribute to the production and maintenance of religious discourses?*

Essay sentences	What is going on? What's the problem?
This essay is on the topic of Neolithic monuments.	This is a weak opening because it contains only a vague gesture towards a topic. Better to get stuck straight into the question. Take your reader straight to the coat!
The question asks us to find out 'how the ordering of space within Neolithic sites contributed to the production and maintenance of religious discourses'.	Repeats the question – unnecessary! The reader already knows what the question is. It's written at the top of the document. This looks like you're buying time, like my brother trying desperately to think of places where that coat might be – after he'd promised to show me straight there.

Essay sentences	What is going on? What's the problem?
To find out how the ordering of space within Neolithic sites contributed to the production and maintenance of dominant discourses, we first need to consider what is meant by 'ordering', 'space', 'contributed', 'production', 'maintenance' 'religious' and 'discourses'.	Certainly you need to define your terms, but don't waste time repeating the question or telling your reader that you *must define your terms*. Again, this looks like you're buying time. I might start doubting my guide's navigational abilities (and your essay-writing skills) about now.
It might be said that ordering is about creating or maintaining order.	The weasel word is 'might', but the worst thing here is that it's an entirely circular definition. Exasperatingly, we've just looped back to the place we started the coat hunt. We're no closer to achieving any goal.
It might also be said that production is about producing something and that discourses are where you're discoursing with someone.	Another set of circular definitions. You get the picture! Definitions should be informative.
Neolithic monuments were made many, many years ago, around 10,000 years ago.	A random piece of basic background information. Credit your reader with some intelligence – your tutor will appreciate it – by avoiding fluff like this. Say if my brother asked the colour of my missing coat *after* he already promised he knew where it was, he'd reveal that he didn't really know what he was talking about. Adding fluff isn't harmless. It makes your reader think this basic information is news to you – so they adjust downwards their expectations of your work.
Neolithic monuments often include megaliths and dolmens, and some examples are Gobekli Tepe and Nevali Core in Turkey, and they were often built in the Levant.	A clutch of extra pieces of information, added without a clear sense of how they help answer the specific question set. You're like my brother grabbing random clothing items on our coat hunt; your credibility is totally shot now!

The imaginary essay on Neolithic monuments might garner some points here and there for including information that could be (generously) construed as relevant to the question, and it might be given a little credit for recognizing the need to define the key terms, but it will not impress the reader. This essay could never reach the highest grades; it is too meandering. A brilliant essay needs a carefully controlled argument: you tell your reader exactly where you're both going, then you lead them along step-by-step in a logical, coherent fashion.

To write a brilliant essay, you need to be an authoritative guide for your reader. That means knowing exactly where you're going before you set out. You need a take-home, a core argument, not a vague meander in search of an argument that never materializes. Before you put pen to paper – or fingers to keyboard – you must know exactly what your destination will be and how you're planning to get there. In the table below, I've laid out some successive sentences in another imaginary essay – this time showing how to control your argument by acting as an authoritative guide for your reader. No meandering voyage of discovery here! The question is a philosophical one: *Will your death be bad for you?*

Essay sentences	What is going on? Why is this good practice?
The strength of the argument that death is bad for you depends on whether 'your death' refers to the process of dying or the state of having died.	Immediately, the reader's attention is grabbed by an interesting analytical distinction. The scene is set. There's no meandering about on vague topics.
It is easier to return an affirmative answer to this question if 'your death' means the process of dying because it involves weakening and (sometimes undignified, painful and drawn-out) loss of functionality.	This authoritative statement details the easiest way to answer the question in the affirmative. It is informative, displaying the author's reasoning.
It is harder to return an affirmative answer to this question if it means the state of being dead. Epicurus says that death is not bad for us because when we are dead there is no 'us' to experience anything.	A second statement follows logically from the preceding one, according to the distinction laid out in the first sentence. This authoritative statement details the hardest way to answer the question in the affirmative, seamlessly integrating a major thinker.

Essay sentences	What is going on? Why is this good practice?
I argue that Epicurus's arguments are unsound: death is bad for you, even if we mean the state of being dead rather than a drawn-out process of dying.	A critical approach to a major thinker, showing precisely the scale of the task: I'll take on the harder challenge (that of showing how even the state of being dead is bad for you, not just a painful process of dying) and I'll meet that challenge.
The obvious riposte – that my position simply reflects a squeamish reaction to death and thus unclear thinking – is flawed, because fears of loss, upset and incapacitation are psychologically well founded.	A confident response to the most important counter-argument is the next logical part of the essay. Always respond to the strongest of your imagined opponents – don't shy away from counter-arguments, but meet them head-on in the service of your own argument.
The question is not 'is your death bad for you?', but 'just how bad for you is it?' Using McMahon's Life Comparative Account, we can calculate the comparative badness of death for different people by reference to expected lifetime well-being.	An original departure, broadening out the question by showing how we might calibrate the level of badness of death. It provides a satisfying next stage, once the main question has been addressed directly.

A controlled argument starts with a confident, authoritative interpretation of the question (in this case, making the analytical distinction between the process of dying and the state of being dead). It specifies the parameters within which the question will be answered (here: the easier way to affirm the question is to state that the process of dying is bad for you, whereas the hardest case to prove is that the state of being dead is bad for you). It states the case directly. (Epicurus is wrong: death in either sense is bad for you. The degree of badness varies depending on age, suffering, friendships and other factors.) There is a clear structure here and no meandering about.

I think the voyage-of-discovery problem comes about when students use the essay itself to organize their thinking. It's true that writing helps you think, but you need to do the messy work beforehand, in the planning stage, so that the final essay you hand in has a crystal clear take-home. You're not just writing generally about a topic, but answering a specific question.

Don't move off-piste

In the middle sections of your essay, it can be tempting to move off-piste into a set of allied arguments or even into completely new territory. I have read essays on American politics with surreal interludes of German existentialist philosophy and essays on psychological priming which make an unscheduled stop in the history of social reform policies. You might not make such crazy leaps, but you still need to look at every assertion with a sceptical eye: is this point strictly relevant to my argument? Leaving in irrelevant information is a sure-fire way to confuse your reader and decrease your grade.

Certainly, you want to develop your argument over the course of the essay – in the death essay example above, the argument moves on after the initial response to incorporate a more complex calibration of the degree of death's badness – but you must ensure that everything you add really does serve your argument. If you move off-topic, you'll lose precious momentum in the middle. A controlled argument retains the reader's attention throughout. Have a go at spotting where an essay has gone off-piste by reading the essay extracts in the box below.

EXERCISE 5.2

Have a go at staying on-piste

Take a look at the statements below in response to the question: **How does polarization affect Congressional law-making in the United States?** *When does the essay start to go off-piste? Underline the off-piste section or draw a line to show where the rot sets in. Could these essays get back on track in answering the question? The answers are on p. 153.*

1 The greater the party polarization, the greater the gridlock effect on congressional law-making. Polarization is the combination of ideological homogenization within parties and ideological divergence between parties. In Japan, the National Diet was largely controlled by the Liberal Democratic Party for much of its history. In Nicaragua, by contrast, you have a unicameral legislature that is overwhelmingly composed of members representing the Sandinista National Liberation Front. There are many different party types around the world.

2 Polarization comes in several varieties: ideological polarization, where elites and the public express increasingly distinct issue positions around a left–right continuum; and affective polarization, which is about growing tribalism and dislike of the opposing party. Hegel's concept of *geist* (spirit) and *Aufhebung* (sublation of contradictory or opposing factors) expresses a dichotomy of opposites, which is about lifting us

> mentally to a higher unity. Psychologically, these dispositions arise from moral foundations, because it is important for people to cooperate in groups. Even more than ideological polarization, affective polarization contributes to gridlock by making it harder for law-makers to cooperate.
>
> 3 Division in politics has made it extremely hard for most legislation to pass. The term 'bipartisan' is becoming less and less applicable to the real-world US politics. If we look at history, the biggest legislative achievements have usually been done during or in response to a crisis, such as the New Deal, which created the Civilian Conservation Corps, the Agricultural Adjustment Act, the National Industrial Recovery Act and many other programmes. The New Deal sustained the Democratic Party and was attacked by Barry Goldwater, the conservative Republican who ran for president during the 1960s.

In a brilliant essay, you should make your reasoning explicit. Many essays I read are too elliptical, by which I mean, the author simply asserts that something is the case without providing reasoning that would enable the reader to understand why they take the position they do. Your thinking should be absolutely explicit. For example, rather than baldly asserting:

Physical details of a novel's publication are clearly vital for how we read it

you must tell the reader why you take that position:

Physical details of a novel's publication affect the way we navigate text and immerse ourselves in content, because navigational features are part of a work's signifying structure.

Use the word 'because' more often and get rid of words like 'clearly', 'obviously', 'certainly' and 'definitely'. You don't persuade a reader of the validity of your argument just by putting extra emphasis in the text: 'honestly, I really, really believe this is true (obviously it is!), so please, please believe me' – that's what words like 'clearly' or 'definitely' do. It sounds a bit desperate. Instead, you *persuade* the reader by explaining why you take the position you do and providing the reasoning and empirical evidence that support your argument. In short, show don't tell.

Spill the beans

Once you have your core take-home, you need to give it away as soon as possible. SPILL. THE. BEANS. This isn't a murder mystery novel where there's value in puzzling your audience before the final reveal.

…So to conclude, it was all a fiendish plot involving a fake bell-pull, a snake and a safe.

No! Give it away in your very first paragraph. No spoiler alert required.

This is one of the ways that good academic writing differs from journalism. With really good journalism, you're telling a story – often through colourful characters. So you might lead with a little vignette to get people interested, and then the take-home might come part way in. Here are some recent journalist openers in major news outlets:

On 7th August 2016, Zhang Chaolin, a 49-year-old tailor, was savagely beaten by a group of youths in Aubervilliers, a deprived suburb on the northern outskirts of Paris (Aw 2019).

Edinburgh's old Royal Infirmary has been abandoned for more than a decade, its doors boarded up, its gutters overgrown with buddleia and fireweed (Francis 2019).

On a beautiful summer day a few months ago, I walked down to the part of the Connecticut River that separates Vermont from New Hampshire, and rented a kayak (Mounk 2019).

Few chance encounters have had a greater political impact than Gordon Brown's fateful meeting with Gillian Duffy on an April morning in Rochdale in 2010 (Shabi 2019).

Don't these examples make you want to read on? Surely they do! They set a scene, introduce interesting people and places, and intrigue the reader with teasing details. Yet none of them would be at home in an academic essay. They're too elliptical, for one thing. Professors don't like being teased. It isn't clear exactly what the question is: who knows where these sentences will lead? They indicate only a broad topic, perhaps not even that. Magazine readers might appreciate a bit of mystery but professors do not. These openers are scene-setters for a story – they are 'Once Upon a Time' – not a clear, focused response to a question.

In contrast to much long-form journalism, a really good academic essay gives it all up front, and I mean page one: as early as humanly possible.

He's actually a ghost.
It was a snake.
The butler did it.

In an academic essay, this means you need to know exactly what your argument will be before you begin writing.

Q: Why did the Neanderthals die out?
A: The most plausible explanation for Neanderthal extinction is a combination of inbreeding and natural fluctuations in birth and death rates. Competition from Homo sapiens most likely accelerated, but did not by itself cause, the Neanderthals' demise.

Q: Is consequentialism alienating?
A: Consequentialism is alienating in four senses: it alienates people from their intuitions because its prescriptions are counter-intuitive; it is distressing when it alienates people from ordinary desires; it alienates people from their friends since a friendship is based on considerations that impersonal and agent-neutral consequentialism rules out; and it alienates people from society, by treating people impersonally rather than citizens with rights and responsibilities, community ties and family.

Q: What explains cross-national variation in support for redistribution?
A: Contrary to the welfare regimes approach, I argue that attitudes toward redistribution are not determined by stable ideological traditions, but are affected more by economic prosperity and the maturity of a social system.

The above examples reveal the author's argument at the very beginning. All three answers would be a fitting opening sentence in an essay. None of this sort of thing:

I am going to answer a question on the topic of X.

Is it Y or Z? That's a very good question, and I'm going to try to find out the answer.

I bet you wish you knew who dunnit. Well, I'm not going to tell you until page 459!

But instead, something like this:

The answer is Z, not Y.

I argue X.

The key analytical distinction in this question is between V and W.

In the exercise box below, you can practise spilling the beans. Try to summarize your key take-home as succinctly as possible. That means one clear grammatical sentence with the smallest number of words and clauses you can manage.

Have a go at spilling the beans

I'm sure you've heard of Aesop's fables. The Ancient Greek storyteller is associated with a number of parables, each containing some key take-home or moral. Below are some selected fables. For each fable, extract the key take-home and state it in propositional form (as a single grammatical sentence). The answers are on p. 154.

Example: The Hawk, the Kite and the Pigeons. The pigeons, frightened by a Kite, called out to the Hawk: 'Please defend us!' The Hawk agreed, but as soon as the pigeons let him into the dovecote he pounced on them and slaughtered a larger number than the Kite could have managed to kill in an entire year.

Take-home message: Avoid a remedy that is worse than the disease.

1 *The Kid and the Wolf.* A little goat, standing safely on the roof of a little tin shack, laughed at a passing Wolf. 'Can't catch me!' The Wolf looked up at the goat and said: 'I hear you, young goat, yet it is not you who mocks me but the roof on which you stand'.

2 *The Hunter and the Woodman.* A cowardly hunter set off in search of lion tracks. He asked a passing woodcutter if he had seen any paw marks in the area. 'I have', said the woodcutter, 'and I can go one better – I'll show you to the lion!' 'Oh gosh, no', said the hunter, 'I'm looking for the tracks, not the lion himself!'

3 *The Oak and the Reeds.* A huge oak tree fell over in high winds and found himself next to a stream surrounded by reeds. 'How is it that you weak little thin things haven't been uprooted by these winds, as I have?' said the Oak to the Reeds. They replied: 'You try to fight with the wind, and it destroys you in the end, whereas we just bend with every breath of air. That is how we avoid destruction.'

4 *The Seaside Travellers.* From the top of a cliff overlooking the sea, a group of travellers spotted what they thought was a huge ship in the distance. They signalled to the ship and it drew closer to them, but as it came nearer to the shore they saw that it could only be a small boat, not a ship. They rushed down to the beach to climb aboard, but stopped in dismay: when they came up-close, they could see that the boat was nothing but a pile of sticks. 'What a waste of time', they said, 'for there's nothing here but a bit of old driftwood!'

5 *The Sick Kite.* A dying Kite said to his mother: 'Please pray to the gods to grant me a longer life!' She responded: 'Oh dear, my son, do you really

think any of the gods will take pity on you? Is there even one god you haven't infuriated by stealing part of the meat sacrifice offered to them from their very altars?'

6   *The Boy and the Nettles.* A little boy was stung by a nettle. Crying, he said to his mother: 'I only touched it gently, and it hurt me so much!' 'That's just why it stung you so badly', said his mother. 'Next time, grasp the nettle boldly and it will be as soft as silk.'

To control your argument, you need to be ruthless, avoid meandering on a voyage of discovery – that is, be an authoritative guide for your reader – and give away your take-home as soon as possible. When you state your argument up front, you need to be able to write clearly and authoritatively, so that your reader is able to discern exactly what you mean. That is the subject of the next chapter – **writing elegantly** – in which I'll show you how to make your essay writing more lively and confident.

Chapter 5 Exercises
Controlling your argument

PART A: To write a controlled argument, you need to be ruthless about cutting background information if it doesn't contribute *directly* to the case you are making. For the following questions, identify the most promising opening sentence (a, b or c). Explain your answer.

1   What are the consequences of partisan polarization in Congress for presidential power?

   a. Congress is the legislative branch of the United States government.
   b. Barack Obama was the 44th US President.
   c. Polarization takes both affective (dislike) and positional (issue-based) forms, each with distinct effects upon presidential power.

2   Is Wittgenstein's private language argument a defence of or attack on behaviourism?

   a. The private language argument was articulated by Ludwig Wittgenstein in his seminal work *Philosophical Investigations*, which was published posthumously in 1953.

   b. Wittgenstein constructs neither an attack on nor a defence of behaviourism but rather an approach to agreed practices.

   c. Wittgenstein was an Austrian philosopher who worked on philosophy of language, including the private language argument.

3 Is psychoanalytic theory a useful approach in modern psychology?

   a. Psychoanalytic theory is more useful to therapists than to scientists.

   b. Psychoanalytic theory was founded by Sigmund Freud.

   c. Psychoanalytic theory came to prominence in the latter third of the twentieth century and is linked to psychoanalysis.

4 Why are the failures of the US Constitution not remedied by amending the Constitution?

   a. The first ten amendments to the Constitution are collectively known as the Bill of Rights.

   b. Failure implies non-fulfilment of expectations, but the Constitution has not 'failed' because its procedures operate as the Founding Fathers anticipated.

   c. The US Constitution is the supreme law of the United States, a large country in the Western hemisphere with 50 states and more than 320 million inhabitants.

PART B: You must give away your punchline at the beginning. If you are familiar with the following stories, summarize the main argument or take-home as a single grammatical sentence. For example, the take-home of *Little Red Riding Hood* could be 'children should always follow directions', 'the grandmother has already been eaten' or simply 'never trust wolves'.

   5 *The Three Little Pigs*

   6 Biblical account of Adam and Eve

   7 *The Sixth Sense*

   8 *Hansel and Gretel*

   9 The myth of Sisyphus

   10 *Jurassic Park*

PART C: Extract the core take-home from the following introduction (on the question '*What price does the US pay for its exceptionalism?*') Write the take-home as a single grammatical sentence.

   'To answer the question of what price the United States pays for its exceptionalism, it is important to first understand what is meant in this case by "its exceptionalism". Obviously, the asking of this question implies an assumption that the United States is in fact exceptional, and if one accepts that assumption, then one must understand how the United States is exceptional, or rather, what specifically, be it culture or material wealth, makes the United States exceptional. Of course, one does not have to accept this assumption, and can argue that the United States is not in fact exceptional and is just another country. It is also important to focus on the former half of the question. Is the price something that must be paid by all or something that must be paid by some? That this imbalance exists, that this exceptionalism is something that is fuelled by the suffering of particular people, particular groups in the United States, is what I will be arguing in this essay.'

Writing Elegantly

There are plenty of excellent guides for the basics of essay writing: grammar, punctuation, formalizing your prose. If you're writing in your second or third language or you need a refresher, I advise you to read a basic style guide before you take up this chapter. Many universities provide such a guide for students. Ask your university librarian, academic skills department or personal tutor for suggestions.

Most people master the basics of writing at school, but some of the things you learn at school are... less than helpful when it comes to university essays. In particular, some students are taught a very formulaic approach to essay writing, which becomes a straitjacket later on. Taking too risk-averse an approach can make essays stilted and boring to read. A brilliant essay is lively and confident in tone. In this chapter, I will show you how to avoid excessive signposting, hedging and slipping between empirical and emotive arguments. If you can avoid these slips, your writing will become more elegant.

Excessive signposting

Linguist Stephen Pinker writes eloquently about the misery inflicted by what he calls 'excessive signposting' in writing (Pinker 2014). I see myriad examples of this when I mark essays. Essay writers often say what they've been asked to ask, say what they plan to say, say it, and then say what they've said all over again. Often, the signposts overwhelm the actual answer, so the reader's impression is of a student who knows what needs to be done alright, but never actually does it. Take the following example:

Firstly, this essay shall look at the problems with the question and define any ambiguous terms. Secondly, this essay shall move onto the main body of the essay which shall cover the main arguments, which shall lead into a logical conclusion that shall answer the question in a clear and concise manner.

That's 52 totally unnecessary words, right there! Think before you write: does your professor really need to know that you will look at the question (we can take that as read), that there will be some 'main arguments' in the 'main body of the essay' (where else would they be?) and that the essay will end with a conclusion (it would be strange without one)?

When it comes to speaking or writing at greater length – in a dissertation, for example – it *is* helpful to signpost a bit because it's hard to keep all the content in your head at once. The audience might get lost, and the signposts help them to stay on track, but in a short student essay of 1500, 2000 or 3000 words, excessive signposting is wasteful and boring to read. If you've laid out your argument in brief in the introduction, you don't need loads of signposts. Some of the worst offenders are phrases like these:

It is important to define the key terms.

First, I'm going to define the terms of the question, and then I'm going to consider which definition is most appropriate, and then I'm going to assess whether the title quote is true or not.

The last paragraph argued that...

It is good that you know what needs to be done, but there is no point telling your professor that you know what needs to be done. Heavy-handed writing like this is such a drag to read and it wastes space that could be filled with interesting material instead.

Probably the most common comment I have when I mark students' essays is JUST DO IT. Don't spend ages saying you need to define this or that. Just define your terms, right there, and avoid a bunch of boring words. Don't give me a general commentary on what a good essay is supposed to contain. I want your answer to the actual question at hand, not some half-baked essay advice. If you've got a logical structure, there's no need to say what you said in your previous paragraph. I just read it!

EXERCISE 6.1

Have a go at avoiding excessive signposting

Take a look at the statements below and decide whether it's an unnecessary signpost or a useful statement that you'd keep in your essay. The answers are on p. 155.

1 It is important to define the key terms.
2 Our first question is: what is the main concept? I will consider what the main concept in the question is and define it before moving on.
3 Mathematicians view measurement as the mapping of qualitative empirical relations to relations among numbers.
4 First we will consider the core concepts, then we will make some arguments in structured sequence, and finally we will conclude with some reflections on what the question means more broadly.
5 I will criticize the gender binary, arguing that it contributes to the maintenance of oppressive and gendered social orders, and conclude that correcting such oppressions requires attention to multiple aspects of identity, including race, class and disability.
6 Do justice considerations apply to intergenerational relations? That is the question we need to answer in this essay.
7 Inspections by street-level bureaucrats reveal the relationship between power, ethics and status amongst migrant communities.
8 The last paragraph argued that inspections by street-level bureaucrats reveal the relationship between power, ethics and status amongst migrant communities.
9 Why does this question matter? We need to consider what the implications of this argument are for the broader scholarly literature.
10 There are many different ways to interpret the core concepts in the question, including 'renewal' and 'subjunctive politics', and I will consider the various ambiguities within these core concepts.

How can you recognize excessive signposting in practice? It is a matter of judgement, and reasonable people might disagree about what counts as 'excessive'. I don't mean to suggest that you can never signpost in your essay, but that you should try to reduce the number of set-up words wherever possible. Think about what each sentence is doing for your essay: is it helping you to answer the question at hand?

One rule of thumb is to imagine that you had transplanted a sentence from one essay into another essay on a completely different topic. Would you have to change any of the words for that sentence to make sense in a totally new essay? If you wouldn't need to change any words, then that section is a good candidate for the chop. Here is a particularly egregious example of excessive signposting:

When considering the question at hand, it is necessary for us to address the main issues raised, define some of the words and phrases used in the question we are considering, and bring to bear either qualitative or quantitative data upon the subject of this question.

These 46 words could appear in literally any essay because they are so general. They tell the reader absolutely nothing. Even signposting phrases with some words relevant to a particular question can be excessive. For instance:

This essay examines the relationship between the branches of government respective to the courts, and the ways by which they influence each other to determine the power balance (providing insight on whether the courts have any influence at all). I will explore the mechanisms used to achieve this influence, developed by theoretical justifications and empirical support.

Yes, there are a few words in this signpost that point us towards the question at hand ('government', 'courts', 'influence'), but you would need to change only six words (at most) out of 56 in order to transplant this signpost into a totally different essay. This is practically an entire paragraph in which nothing is asserted. Cut it out! Replace it with concrete answers to the following questions: do courts have any influence at all? If so, what sorts of influence? What are the causal mechanisms? Name them. What are the theoretical justifications? State them. What are the sources of empirical support? Identify them precisely.

Compulsive hedging

Excessive signposting can sometimes indicate low confidence in an essay. Another manifestation of a lack of confidence is compulsive hedging: words such as 'arguably', 'comparatively', 'to a certain degree', 'to some extent' and 'relatively'. These phrases are meaningless in themselves and they make the writer seem vague and cowardly. Steven Pinker takes particular issue with the phrase 'I would argue' (Pinker 2014) – a staple of student essay writing! The 'would' is the main issue: do you mean you *would* argue a particular point if things were different? The English subjunctive is typically used to convey a wish, particularly wishes that are counter to fact, but nine times out of ten, the student who uses 'I would argue' simply means 'I DO argue'. Cut out the word 'would' ('I argue that X') or simply dispense with the whole phrase (just assert 'X').

A really brilliant essay is confident in tone. That means, instead of hedging, qualify. Spell out the circumstances in which a statement does or does not hold, rather than leaving yourself an escape hatch (which leaves the reader unsure whether you really mean it). Convey the magnitude of the effect and the degree of certainty explicitly. For instance, rather than:

Republicans are united to some extent, and Democrats are somewhat divided

Say:

Republicans are united and energized by cultural conservatism (as measured by survey items tapping support for building a wall on the Mexican border, respect for the American flag and concerns about discrimination against whites). Democrats are more divided by these cultural questions than Republicans are, but they are united by support for an activist government.

Rather than:

Arguably, Supreme Court justices are relatively constrained

Say:

The Court enjoys greater implementation power in 'vertical' cases (those involving criminal and civil liability) than in 'lateral' cases (all others).

Hedges aren't fatal for your essay, but they waste words and weaken your essay by making you sound unsure of yourself.

Be wary of going too far the other way, though. Confident writing doesn't mean making any old bold, unqualified statement. Writing a university-level essay often involves making complex, nuanced points, but the correct way to write such statements is to be concrete and specific about precisely how far, in what ways, and in what circumstances a statement holds true. Instead of saying 'to some extent', say exactly to *what* extent? Instead of saying something is 'arguably' true, actually argue that case. The words 'predominantly', 'fairly', 'relatively' and 'apparently' are crying out for some specificity.

EXERCISE 6.2

Have a go at avoiding compulsive hedging

Take a look at the statements below. Which words and phrases are unnecessary hedges? Underline them and reread the statement without any hedges. If you can, replace the hedge with an appropriate qualifier: specify under what circumstances, in what ways, or to what degree a statement holds. The answers are on p. 155.

1. Legislation has been effective, but only to a certain degree, to improve racial discrimination.
2. I would argue that Israel/Palestine is a site of bitter struggle over definitions of indigeneity and settlerness.
3. Having a justified true belief is arguably insufficient for knowledge.
4. During the nineteenth century, the Muslim Mediterranean became to some extent a locus of competing imperial projects.
5. The developing culture of mass private automobile ownership in Russia became a relatively prominent platform for post-Soviet citizen-drivers to renegotiate their relationship with the state.
6. In the last few decades, the field of food history has come to fruition, so to speak.
7. It is fairly difficult for Christians to solve the problem of evil.
8. Enslaved property could be relatively easily integrated into aristocratic forms of property-ownership in eighteenth-century Britain.
9. Haitian sea migration and US maritime policing apparently emerged in tandem.
10. Predominantly, an account of consciousness needs an account of mind.

Writing about academia versus writing about the subject matter

As you work your way through university, you spend time reading, going to lectures, writing essays and keeping up with the latest scholarship in your field. In so doing, you engage with the subject you came to university to study: ideas, theories, debates, evidence and models. Here are two different universes: the process of studying and the substantive material. Given that studying, reading and considering evidence are everyday experiences, perhaps it isn't surprising that students sometimes write their essay about *scholarly activities* rather than the ideas that underpin them. The result is pretty dry. Consider the two examples below:

In recent years, an increasing number of political scientists have turned their attention to the American welfare state. In this essay, recent research on these institutions will be reviewed.

By examining the large research literature on the subject, students of social work can consider the relative advantages and disadvantages of adoption and long-term fostering.

In the above examples, the student writes about what they actually *do* on a day-to-day basis – reviewing literature, thinking about scholarly issues, weighing up competing considerations – but not about the actual ideas that underpin these debates. Compare the two examples above with those below:

Americans hate welfare but love social benefits. They seek to shrink the state but expand its reach. Survey research reveals that these tensions are most likely to arise when welfare policy is delivered through private intermediaries.

Adoption confers significant advantages to children who cannot be returned to their birth families, particularly in offering them emotional security, but long-term fostering can still be appropriate for children with continuous birth family involvement.

Aren't these later examples far more interesting? Your essay will be more engaging if you can focus the reader's attention upon the subject matter itself rather than upon the ways scholars spend their time. Be clear about which universe you are inhabiting when you write: the world of studying or the world of ideas. Try to direct your reader toward the ideas themselves rather than the processes by which scholars pursue those ideas.[1]

---

1 With thanks to Frewer et al. 2005; Albarella, Johnstone, and Vickers 2008; Trakakis 2008; Gomes, Vadjunec, and Perz 2012; Smith 2012 for the scholarly papers that underpin the 'Have a go' exercises in this section.

EXERCISE 6.3

Have a go at identifying the world of studying and the world of ideas

Take a look at the statements below and identify which ones relate to the world of studying and which to the world of ideas. The latter are far more interesting, livelier and worthier candidates for inclusion in your essays. The answers are on p. 155.

1 Consumers value a transparent, enforceable and traceable monitoring system for animal welfare-friendly products.

2 In recent years, debates about the relationship between culture contact and change following the Roman invasion have become more febrile, as scholars consider new zooarchaeological evidence which may shed light upon these discussions.

3 Many surveys have been conducted by scholars to consider the significance of rubber tapping in the Amazon.

4 Rubber tapping is a sustainable alternative to forest destruction in the Amazon.

5 In this essay, I argue that sensory interaction with multiple goods helped eighteenth-century consumers to comprehend concepts of design and workmanship.

6 In this essay, I will review the scholarly literature on haptic skills as they were practised by eighteenth-century consumers, focusing upon scholarly disagreements and looking at various literary sources.

7 Apart from certain scholars' efforts, there is very little discussion today within analytical philosophy of religion about meta-theodical questions, so in this paper I shall review the state of such debates, bringing new arguments to bear upon these fundamental questions.

8 Theodicy may set out to reconcile the existence of God with that of evil but this detached perspective disregards the testimony of sufferers and effaces our humanity and God's divinity.

Avoid slipping between empirical and emotional statements

As you write, remember not to get drawn into emotional arguments if you are writing a piece of empirical analysis or reasoning. Leave emotive language (like 'disgusting', 'despicable', 'laudable', 'excellent' or 'groovy') out of your essay. Remember you are making an analytical argument in politics, philosophy, history, geography or whatever discipline you're in, not talking to your friends over a coffee. You are making a convincing empirical or reasoned case.

If you feel strongly about the subject matter, good for you! We all do research because we care about our subject, but an elegant essay does not contain emotional language unless your tutor has explicitly called for a reflective, normative piece. Unlike many journalistic op-eds you read in your favourite news outlets, academic writing requires you to keep the tone formal and a little aloof from your subject matter. Leave the emotive language for your blog or for comments below the line. Work out your feelings elsewhere and focus on making a convincing case instead.

EXERCISE 6.4

Have a go at separating empirical and emotional statements

Take a look at the statements below in response to this question on environmental ethics:

Is it morally wrong for human beings to pollute the natural environment because a sustainable environment is essential to human well-being or because the natural environment has values in its own right?

Which words or phrases are unnecessarily emotional (that is, which ones would you relegate to the comments section, a blog or conversation with friends)? Which statements would you keep in your essay (which statements actually help you to answer the question at hand)? The answers are on p. 155.

1 Polluters are despicable human beings.
2 Possession of intrinsic value generates a *prima facie* direct moral duty on the part of moral agents to protect it or at least refrain from damaging it.
3 Anyone who says it's okay to pollute has blood on their hands.
4 Eco-warrior types are just virtue-signalling.
5 This question assumes that it *is* morally wrong for human beings to pollute the environment, an assumption some anthropocentric ethical perspectives dispute.
6 We should be ashamed. Nobody is willing to do anything about pollution. It's all our fault.
7 Why should I have to feel ashamed about flying? We're all screwed anyway.
8 Thomas Aquinas argued that non-human animals are 'ordered to man's use'.
9 Mainstream environmentalism is hugely arrogant.
10 If trees, forests and mountains could be given standing in law, then they could be represented in their own right in the courts by groups such as the Sierra Club.

Why get rid of hedging and signposting?

My students recently asked me why I am so opposed to phrases such as 'in my opinion' or 'I believe that' or 'from my perspective' in essays. 'After all', said these students, 'it's rude and arrogant to assert your opinion as fact, so you should always signal that it's only an opinion. It's just subjective'. Here's what I said to them in response:

In writing an essay, you are taking part in a scholarly conversation where reasonable disagreement exists. If there were no disagreement, there would be no conversation in the first place! To write a brilliant essay, you need to see yourself as part of a community of scholars. Rather than unthinkingly deferring to the arguments you read in journal articles and books, a top-grade essay marks itself out as such by taking a sceptical approach. You have read what the authors have to say about their reasoning, and you've assessed their empirical evidence. What do you think? Are you persuaded that they're right? How would you adjudicate disputes in the literature? What have these authors missed? Are there alternative sources of reasoning and evidence that could further bolster their case or undermine it? You have to think for yourself. For tips about reading for essays, see Chapter 10 on **reading critically**.

If you disagree with a particular scholar, you do so for good reasons, which you should spell out in your essay. If you believe X and you can back up what you say, it is perfectly reasonable to say 'I argue X' or simply 'X'. It isn't disrespectful to disagree with someone and assert a contrary position – disagreement is what academia is all about! In fact, it's a mark of respect to take someone's argument seriously, think about it, and propose a counter-argument. You signal your respect by providing strong reasoning and powerful empirical evidence in favour of *your* position, not by weakening yourself with mealy-mouthed expressions like 'in my opinion' or 'from my perspective'.

I say this to everyone: male or female, undergraduate, postgraduate and colleague: have confidence! You deserve to consider yourself a part of this community of scholars. A brilliant essay is respectful but not unthinkingly deferential. If you can back up what you say, make sure you assert yourself.

To polish up your writing: don't signpost excessively, JUST DO IT. Get on with it! Get rid of the compulsive hedging; instead, spell out the circumstances in which the statement does and does not hold. Write about the world of ideas, not the world of being a student, and don't get drawn into emotional arguments. Keep your essay formal and analytical in tone. If you can write confidently and elegantly, your reader will enjoy your essay far more than they would if it were a stylistic mess.

Just as your writing needs to be confident in tone, you also need the confidence to select and deploy evidence in support of your argument. A brilliant essay has a clear and defensible case selection. In the next chapter, we will discuss how to use empirical evidence more effectively.

Chapter 6 Exercises
Writing elegantly

Part A: For each of the following statements, underline any words that indicate (a) excessive signposting, (b) compulsive hedging and (c) emotive arguments, which substitute emotional claims for facts and evidence.

1 I would argue that endogenous growth theory is fairly problematic.
2 Donald Trump is the worst president ever, but Hillary Clinton is downright evil.
3 First, I am going to define my key terms and consider which definition of 'development' is most appropriate and then I am going to assess how useful the human development index is.
4 The last paragraph argued that David Hume's scepticism is to some extent warranted.

5 Arguably, King Edward I should never have joined the Ninth Crusade.
6 Hollywood celebrities: what do they know? Do they know things? Let's find out!
7 We have been asked to consider which glacial landforms are depositional and which ones are erosional. We will start by considering what 'depositional' and 'erosional' mean and then move on to discuss which landforms count as 'depositional' and which as 'erosional'.
8 In my opinion, enclosure of arable land in the sixteenth century was wrong.
9 In order to answer the question at hand, we need to define our core concepts and consider any underlying assumptions before moving on to a conclusion that follows from the argument I am going to make.

PART B: In the sentences below, underline the compulsive hedge and use the fact box provided to rewrite the sentence so that it *qualifies* rather than hedges.

Qualifying a sentence means spelling out what a statement means and the circumstances in which the statement does or does not hold.

UK quick facts: Population = 66 million (2017), 59 million (2000), 57 million (1990). A unitary parliamentary democracy and constitutional monarchy. Four constituent countries. Devolved governments in Cardiff, Edinburgh and Belfast. World's fifth largest economy (nominal GDP) or ninth largest (purchasing power parity). Sixth largest military expenditure in the world.

10 The United Kingdom is quite large and powerful.
11 Apparently the UK is monarchical, but mostly it is not.
12 I would argue that the UK seems to be politically split into various components.
13 The UK is relatively developed.
14 To some extent, you could say that the UK has grown a bit recently.

PART C: Which elements do you need in a brilliant (analytical, not normative) essay?

(a) Exact restatement of the question, using the same words
(b) Introductory statement of the argument, in a nutshell
(c) Formal academic prose
(d) Vivid personal statement concerning how you feel, morally, about the subject
(e) Always put 'in my opinion' to indicate which parts are your view.
(f) Always convey the magnitude of any effects explicitly.

Using Empirical Evidence Effectively

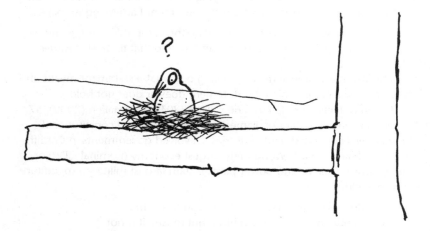

Students often ask how to use empirical evidence effectively. The key is to be absolutely explicit and deliberate about your case selection, and that requires you to develop your knowledge of the universe of cases such that you can make clear, defensible decisions about what to include and exclude. You show mastery of the material by addressing obvious empirical counter-examples and by being crystal clear about which sorts of cases your argument covers and which it does not.

By 'case' I mean a set of empirical observations about a real-world phenomenon. A case is an instance of the sort of thing that you are trying to explain. You might be trying to understand why individuals act as they do or describing the features of political units such as cities, regions or nation states; you might seek to explain differences and similarities

amongst institutions such as businesses, charities or parties; environments; or social phenomena, such as novels, religions and cultures.
Whatever your subject, you need to be clear about what sort of thing you
are trying to understand.

A brilliant argument needs support, which is given by explicit reasoning and high-quality empirical evidence. What makes evidence 'high-
quality' is discipline-specific: it could mean observational data collected
systematically over many years; it could mean experimental evidence
conducted according to scientific protocols; it could mean intensive study
of one or a few instances of a phenomenon, drawing out causal mechanisms and individual subjects' own understanding of the things they are
experiencing. Whatever your discipline's standards and expectations,
writing a brilliant essay requires you to choose your evidence with care,
rather than relying on mere mentions, anecdotes or illustrative examples
that are not organized in a systematic way. This chapter offers some
principles for selecting cases and deploying empirical evidence.

Be systematic in your approach

The first thing to do is to be systematic about surveying the field. In my
marking, I see two major pitfalls in the use of empirical evidence.
Although they manifest very differently, both are symptoms of the same
problem: not making a clear, authoritative and defensible decision about
which empirical cases to cite. The first pitfall is *being led by the nose by the
scholarly literature*. You can be sure that your whole class will have read
the core reading on the list, so it is also likely that the whole class will start
thinking about a topic by looking at the same set of empirical examples:
those cited and discussed in the core reading.

If Professor Jones focuses on Tennyson and Blake in his evaluation of
women's role in heroic myth in Victorian literature, Tennyson and Blake
will be Professor Jones's class's first encounter with the subject. If Professor
Thurston's arguments about racial discrimination in homeownership
formed part of her group's core reading on civil rights and the modern
American state, then her students will naturally be primed to emphasize
housing discrimination, as opposed to discrimination in other spheres,
when writing about civil rights.

There is nothing wrong with drawing from these cases in your
essays – after all, your tutor will have selected particular readings because

they are the most important works in that area – but you mustn't cite those empirical cases *simply because they are the first ones that come to mind*. Your empirical evidence should be carefully chosen to help build your argument.

Think about how your essay will read to your tutor, who is marking dozens of similar papers. If you just pepper your essay with empirical examples plucked from the secondary literature without giving them a clear sense of why you have selected those cases, then your essay will look like an average- to lower-grade effort, identical to many others. It is fine to cite Tennyson and Blake in your discussion of women's role in heroic myth, but you need to explain why you have selected these authors. ('Professor Jones happens to cite them too' is not a good reason!) You can certainly discuss housing discrimination in your analysis of civil rights (make your debt to Professor Thurston clear), but a brilliant essay will situate this arena of conflict within the broader universe of civil rights activity. Resist the lazy option. You need to be systematic in surveying the field.

The second pitfall students often encounter in using empirical evidence is *plucking odd cases from thin air*. Sometimes, in an effort to avoid the first pitfall (being led by the nose), authors will embark on a tour of the further reaches of Google Scholar or Wikipedia. Just like clinging closely to the scholarly literature, taking this approach is not *all* bad but it can lead to problems. It is *good* to be proactive about finding new sources of empirical evidence, but you don't want your essay to consist entirely of wacky examples that aren't substantively important.

For instance, your essay on the history of technological change in cartography would be strangely skewed if you overemphasized Manchurian map inscriptions or experimental uses of modern location-based services but failed to discuss the compass and sextant. An essay on the advocacy of nonviolence in the American Civil Rights Movement that had nothing to say about Martin Luther King would be missing a crucial part of the story. Your tutor can guide you here. They will draw upon key empirical cases and data in lectures and seminars. You should ensure that the empirical evidence in your essays covers the most important cases, facts and figures in your field, even if you also cite a variety of other examples.

EXERCISE 7.1

Have a go at identifying core empirical cases and data

Take a look at the following questions and identify the empirical case or type of empirical data you would definitely want to discuss in response. These cases or data types are the obvious, central examples of a particular phenomenon, so excluding them would make the essay seem incomplete.

Some of the more obscure examples or data sources might also be helpful in your essay, but it would be dangerous to pursue them exclusively at the expense of missing key pieces of empirical evidence. The answers are on p. 161.

1 How do financial crises change understandings of economic globalization?
   a   Case: The 2008 financial crisis
   b   Case: The 1904 dollarization in Panama
   c   Case: Swaziland's weakness to fiscal shocks
   d   Case: Periodic financial crises in Guam between 2001 and 2002

2 Why did the Roman Empire become Christian?
   a   Case: Jovian, a Christian who ruled for eight months in 363–364 CE
   b   Case: Valens, a 'conscientious administrator' and Christian protector who diminished the burden of taxes
   c   Case: Constantine the Great, first Christian Emperor and founder of Constantinople
   d   Case: Honorius, the Christian emperor under whose precarious and chaotic reign Rome was sacked for the first time in 800 years

3 How has the American party system evolved over time?
   a   Data source: Voteview: plots every Members of Congress's ideology and partisan identity using roll call votes, 1789–2020
   b   Data source: California State Archives: historical voter identification statistics in Orange County
   c   Data source: Nineteenth-century presidential campaign posters at the Library of Congress
   d   Data source: The Andrew Jackson papers: documentary evidence on President Jackson's life

4 How does music in a video game help to construct a virtual world?
   a   Case: Dr Jekyll and Mr Hyde, a 1988 side-scrolling action video game that made the top ten worst games of the 1980s
   b   Case: Cho Aniki, a single-player game released on CD-ROM in 1992
   c   Case: Guardian Heroes, a 2D fighting game criticized for its long-winded dialogue
   d   Case: Super Mario Bros, one of the best-selling games of all time

5 When should drugs be decriminalized?
  a   Case: The treatment of methamphetamine under the Czech
       Republic's Regulation No. 467/2009
  b   Case: The American 'War on Drugs'
  c   Case: The 2016 failure of Bill 4533 on psychotropic substances and
       precursors in Ukraine
  d   Case: Article 364 of the Ecuadorian Constitution, which sees drug
       consumption as a health concern

Of what is this a case? Compared with what?

To make your use of empirical evidence as systematic as possible, you
should be clear about where your cases fit within the broader universe of
cases. That means knowing how representative, or otherwise, your cases
are. Rather than plodding through the empirical examples identified in
the core course reading or drawing in an arbitrary selection of data
sources or cases you happen to find online, you need to select your cases
with care and explain to your reader how they compare with other cases
and the broader universe of empirical evidence.

Every time you think about a particular empirical case, you should ask
yourself *of what* is this a case and compared *with what*? One of my
undergraduate tutors used to ask us these questions continually, so we
got into the habit of thinking explicitly about the sort of case we were
discussing (what kind of thing are we considering here?) and the relevant
comparator class (what other things are we comparing it with?). For
instance, imagine you were answering the question:

*To what extent did the Holy Lands Crusades fulfil the intentions of the
Popes?*

The first thing to get clear about is the sort of thing we are discussing: of
what is this a case? There are several different answers to this question
depending on your definition of a 'Crusade'. Crusades were medieval
religious wars, proclaimed by the Latin Church, to remove certain areas
from Islamic rule. Some historians take a narrower definition of 'Crusade'
to mean only certain armed pilgrimages to Jerusalem, whereas others use
the term more broadly to refer to a whole variety of church-sanctioned
campaigns and religious wars.

What sort of case is a Crusade? A campaign explicitly sanctioned by the Church? A political ideology? A nationalistic exercise directed toward the capture of Jerusalem? A stage in the development of Western civilization? *Any* sort of religious campaign against pagans or heretics? How did contemporaneous commentators understand these conflicts, and how did later historians reimagine them? The term 'Crusade' is contested. Your definitions of the key terms of the question should not be marooned at the beginning of the essay with no connection to the rest; your definitions should help you to select your cases.

If you take the Crusades to mean only those conflicts later identified as the First through Eighth Crusades, your universe of cases is narrower than if you had considered all sorts of religious warfare directed against those deemed to lack the true faith. The definition and the selection of cases need to match up. Before you put pen to paper, consider the implications of each definition. Talking about Pope Urban II's First Crusade as one of eight major episodes of church-sanctioned pilgrimage directed toward particular church-sanctioned ends is different from considering it part of a grab bag of medieval religious conflicts playing out across a wider theatre.

Your selection of cases will differ depending upon what you understand the term 'Crusade' to encompass, and your answer to this question about fulfilment of Papal intentions will differ depending upon how you define the terms of the question: of what is this a case? In particular, you are more likely to return an affirmative answer to this question (*'did the Crusades fulfil papal intentions?'*) if you define Crusades as episodes of religious warfare that received explicit Papal sanction, rather than the more general category of medieval violence in the Holy Land directed toward the suppression of heretics.

The second thing you'll need to think about is your comparator class: compared with what? A comparator class is the set of things with which you are comparing your case. We can also call it your domain of reference. In Chapter 2 on **finding comparator classes**, we considered how to emphasize different words in turn in order to reveal different comparators hidden inside a question. In order to be convincing in your use of empirical evidence, you need to be absolutely clear about the boundaries of your comparator class. Many essays I mark bring in illustrative examples but neglect the comparator class. The result is disjointed and unconvincing because there is no principle that explains case selection.

On its own, an example proves nothing. Only by situating a case within the broader set of comparators can its proper significance be understood. For instance, your answer to the Crusades question might focus upon Pope Urban II's First Crusade, it might consider each of the eight major episodes labelled the First through Eighth Crusades, or it might compare 'official' with 'popular' crusades or even examine various other types of religious warfare conducted in Palestine, Egypt and Syria throughout the medieval period.

A brilliant essay shows the reader what sort of cases it is dealing with and how each individual example of Crusader warfare relates to its comparator class, so that the reader knows how the author's example fits within their broader argument about the Holy Land Crusades more generally. Situating each empirical case within its broader domain of reference helps an author to build his or her argument.

Start thinking about comparator classes by considering different definitions of the terms of your question. For example, just as the word 'Crusade' has many different definitions, the word *reason* can mean:

(1) A public justification for action

(2) Intellectual power

(3) Moderate (as in, 'within reason')

Three distinct comparator classes corresponding to these definitions could be:

(1) Motivations (for action) other than reason: impulse, external rewards, loss aversion, curiosity, moods

(2) Other human powers: physical strength, empathy, intuition, creativity, passion

(3) Quantities or qualities (in objects or people) other than moderation: extreme strength or weakness; conservatism, liberalism or independence; intensity, severity or violence

Each of these definitions leads you to a different sort of comparison and a different sort of essay. None of them is 'the right way'; there are many different pathways to a brilliant essay.

EXERCISE 7.2

Have a go at situating an example within different comparator classes

Examine the concepts, names and objects below. For each, identify three possible definitions and their corresponding comparator classes. The answers are on p. 161.

1 Queen Elizabeth II
2 Rats
3 Peru
4 A skipping rope
5 Greed
6 Bark
7 Earth
8 Strength
9 Pattern
10 Race

Note that there may be some comparators that fit in more than one of your definitions. Passion, for instance, could be described as *both* a human power and a motivation. Other comparators fit only one category: liberalism is an ideology, not a power; curiosity is a motivation, but it is not a comparator for moderation. As you work your way through this exercise, consider how the different definitions' comparator classes converge and diverge – and what the implications might be if you were to answer a question containing that word. Where does each of these different definitions and comparators lead you?

There is no right or wrong answer about which cases to select. You shouldn't worry about citing the 'right' number of cases, as if there were some minimum or maximum set in stone. A brilliant essay could involve a working out of a particular case in detail, or it could compare a large number of different cases for a more bird's-eye approach. Often, a mixture of these two approaches can be effective. Zoom in for a more detailed working out of the causal mechanisms; zoom out to give the reader the big picture.

Typical and telling cases

So far, we have considered that to use evidence effectively you need to make deliberate, authoritative choices about which cases and sources to use, and you need to be alive to the connections between your definitions and the various comparator classes they invoke, but what principles can you use to decide which cases to select? Simply knowing that your choices need to be deliberate and not just unthinkingly cribbed from the core reading, or pulled arbitrarily from the further reaches of Google Scholar, doesn't give you that much guidance. There are several principles you can use to help you select cases. One of them is the distinction between typical and telling cases.

Typical or *representative cases* are those that most easily generalize to the broader population of which they are part. They are supposed to stand in for a larger population of cases on a particular dimension or dimensions of interest. *Telling cases,* by contrast, are extreme or unusual: not typical of the broader population. Such cases might yet be of interest to you in your essay because they allow you to probe causal mechanisms or explore relationships in a more open-ended way. For example, your essay on the powers of the Chief Justice of the United States Supreme Court might discuss any of the Chiefs who have held the role since the Founding. Those 17 men represent the universe of cases; there are no more. Inevitably, some of them come to mind more easily than others.

Say you were answering a question on the relative power of the Chief Justice vis-à-vis the eight Associate Justices who sit on the Court:

How much power does the Chief Justice of the Supreme Court wield?

There is a huge scholarly literature on Earl Warren, who held the Chief Justiceship between 1953 and 1969 and pursued a number of important liberal rulings on race, religion, voting and criminal procedure. For students who have studied the Supreme Court, Warren rightly looms large as a particularly important Chief Justice, but his tenure was in many ways an unusual one. Most Chief Justices had less spectacular periods of time in office.

If you focused on Earl Warren in your discussion of the powers of the Chief Justice, you could tell your reader about one of the most crucial periods in the history of the Supreme Court, a period that reshaped the Court's jurisprudence and prompted a furious backlash from the nascent religious right. The case is important because of Warren's masterful use of his Chief Justice powers as leader, agenda-setter and opinion allocator. This is a telling case, not a typical one. If you draw upon the Warren example, you can make many arguments about one of the most important periods in Supreme Court history, but these arguments will not necessarily generalize across the whole period the Court has been in existence.

On one level, each case presents itself as baldly idiosyncratic, but those who study the Court know that there are various ways we can group Chief Justices so that we can consider them in the aggregate. For instance, chronologically (according to the period of time in which the Court was operating); those whose tenures incorporated periods of national crisis (such as war or economic depression); those ideologically aligned with, or diverging from, the forces occupying the White House or Congress; and those who faced external threats to the Court's independence (such as court packing or enforcement challenges).

Any of these grouping principles could be applied to the set of cases you face, to help you construct a defensible selection strategy. A Chief Justice may be representative of those operating in a particular era or typical of a leader during times of crisis. You would need to state at the outset of your essay that *this* is the grouping that you have chosen and why you have chosen the particular cases you will discuss. It doesn't matter if you aren't able to cover the whole ground – what student essay could? Much better to be thorough about those cases you do choose to cover, stating the essay's scope conditions at the beginning. It is your responsibility to choose a grouping that interests you most and that will allow you to be systematic in your choice of cases.

In order to reach the point where you will have a defensible case selection strategy, you need to develop deeper knowledge of particular cases of whatever it is you're writing about. Be proactive! Find data sources and statistics. Ask your tutor for help and search independently online.

Hard and easy cases

Another principle that can help you to select cases for your essays is the distinction between hard and easy cases. In social sciences, these sorts of cases are known as 'least likely' and 'most likely' cases, respectively. An easy case is a case that you expect will conform to a pattern and prove a thesis right. At the outset, the scholar anticipates that his or her theory will easily cover and explain the easy cases. Hard cases are those which are much less likely to conform to a particular pattern, thus presenting a particularly difficult test for a hypothesis.

Why is it helpful to think about hard and easy cases? Each type of case can play a powerful distinctive role in building an argument. If a hypothesis fails to account for an easy case, then that hypothesis is in trouble. We had a strong prior belief that the argument would easily account for such cases, so failure in these circumstances is a strong mark against that argument. On the other hand, if a hypothesis manages to account for a hard case, then that is strong evidence in favour of that hypothesis. An argument that manages to account for a case that we previously thought would be a poor fit is considerably strengthened by discussion of this case.

When selecting empirical evidence, it is important to consider the scale of the task you are setting yourself. The key to writing a brilliant essay is to advance a persuasive argument, supported by powerful empirical evidence. Some arguments are more ambitious (and harder to evidence) than others. If you make the task ahead too easy, by picking and choosing only very easy cases that you know confirm the argument you want to make, then the reader is unlikely to be impressed. On the other hand, if you give yourself an impossible task, then the reader won't be surprised to find the argument fail.

I often read essays where the student has set themselves too easy a task. They might cherry-pick a few easy cases so that, lo and behold, the cases conform to the expected pattern and the argument seems to succeed. Or does it? As marker in such circumstances, I am disappointed by the lack of ambition and concerned about obvious counter-arguments. I find the essay basically unconvincing because it fails to account for more challenging cases.

Conversely, students sometimes set out hard cases that almost guarantee the failure of an argument, particularly when they are critiquing other scholars. They've set an argument up to fail. Does this approach make for a more powerful essay? Often not, because it seems to admit defeat before the essay has even begun. When a student lines up a bunch of hard cases in order to debunk some alternative argument, they are not being fair to their imagined opponent. In those cases, the arguments are dismissed too readily and this sort of essay, too, fails to convince.

A brilliant essay sets itself an achievable task, selecting cases in a defensible way and building an argument – or knocking down an opponent's argument – in a fair fight. For example, imagine you were writing an essay on weapon impact analysis:

Do better weapons win battles?

The easiest possible empirical cases to establish this proposition might draw from the Roman Empire. The Annals of Tacitus, the great Roman historian, describes the defeat of the Druids on the Island of Anglesey off the west coast of Wales in 60 CE. The Druids, armed with nothing but their bare skin, bloodcurdling curses and a few rudimentary weapons, tried to see off the might of the Roman army under the command of the Governor of Britain, Suetonius Paulinus. They were utterly crushed, of course.

That same year, Suetonius Paulinus put down the Boudican revolt at the Battle of Watling Street. Though heavily outnumbered by Boudica's army, Paulinus inflicted a savage defeat upon the Britons because the Romans had superior weaponry, including javelins, shields, armour and swords. Unlike the Britons, they also had cavalry, well drilled.

In modern times, episodes of 'gunboat diplomacy' – shows of superior naval might – are also easy cases for establishing the proposition that better weapons win battles. For instance, the Anglo–Zanzibar War holds the distinction of being the shortest war in history, at just 38 minutes long[1]. The British defeated the Zanzibar Sultanate at a cost of just one injured man compared with 500 dead Zanzibaris, because they fired more than 4000 deadly machine-gun rounds and turned high-explosive shells upon a mostly wooden palace.

An essay seeking to establish the proposition that better weapons win battles might draw upon these cases, but the author would face the charge that they were simply cherry-picking the very easiest cases and ignoring evidence that might undermine the central claim. There are several cases that seem to undermine this thesis, and a brilliant essay should address possible counter-arguments.

Much harder cases might come from episodes such as the Battle of Isandlwana, where Zulu forces inflicted a humiliating defeat upon the

---

1 Perhaps 45 minutes at the outside. There is some disagreement about precisely when the war started.

British in 1879. The British forces enjoyed modern breechloading rifles, mountain guns and a field battery, while their opponents fought mostly with traditional assegai iron spears and cow-hide shields. Despite their clear technological superiority, the British were overwhelmed by the Zulu's greater numbers and tactical nous.

The experience of the Americans fighting the Viet Cong's guerrilla warfare in Vietnam during the 1960s and the modern US army's deployment of drones against insurgent fighters in Afghanistan and elsewhere also seem like hard cases for the proposition that better weapons win battles. A brilliant essay might use these cases to examine the terms of the question. Did the Americans 'win' in Vietnam? What are the criteria of success for conflicts like those in Afghanistan? Can certain types of weaponry win battles but lose wars? Hard cases prompt hard questions.

A brilliant essay positions itself skilfully between easy and hard cases. Selecting only the hard cases makes it too easy to dismiss a central claim, but selecting only the easy cases makes it too easy to *accept* that claim. By thinking carefully about whether a particular case is easy or hard, you can make a judgement about which sorts of empirical evidence will best support your argument and convince the reader. Your essay will be strengthened to the extent that you can show that your argument fits much of the available empirical evidence and deals with possible counter-arguments.

EXERCISE 7.3

Have a go at identifying hard and easy cases

Examine the statements below and imagine you were writing an essay asserting each of these propositions in turn. Of the empirical cases listed afterwards, consider which cases are 'easy' (you expect it to conform to the pattern and prove the thesis right, so if the case doesn't conform to the pattern, then the thesis is in trouble) and which cases are 'hard' (the case is less likely to conform to the pattern, so if the case does conform to the pattern, then it really strengthens the thesis).

Underline the 'easiest' case for establishing the truth of the proposition. Highlight the 'hardest' case for establishing the truth of the proposition. Suggested the answers are on p. 161.

1 'Christmas activities cause family stress.'
   a   Watching the Queen's Speech
   b   Gathering with close family
   c   Eating chocolate in pyjamas
   d   Opening stockings

2 'Role models inspire children to participate in sport.'
   a   Lionel Messi, footballer
   b   Lance Armstrong, cyclist
   c   Paula Radcliffe, runner
   d   Greg Rutherford, javelin thrower
3 'Students in wealthy countries achieve better education results.'
   a   Saudi Arabia
   b   Singapore
   c   Spain
   d   Switzerland
4 'English monarchs are powerful and well respected.'
   a   King Edward IV (1461–1483), who was briefly exiled in 1470 but returned to the throne quickly.
   b   Queen Elizabeth I (1558–1603), who defeated the Spanish Armada
   c   King John (1199–1216), who was forced to sign the Magna Carta
   d   Queen Mary II (1689–1694), who endowed the College of William and Mary
5 'Retailers created the obesity crisis.'
   a   Supermarkets
   b   Newsagents
   c   Takeaway shops
   d   Farmers' markets

A brilliant essay uses empirical evidence deftly, by establishing a clear, deliberate and defensible case selection strategy. You need to have developed your understanding of the topic at hand to the point where you feel able to select the best examples to make your case. Rather than reading, say, Stephen Skowronek's seminal treatment of presidential leadership and simply citing the cases he cites without commentary, the authors of brilliant essays think for themselves about which cases to employ. You don't want to simply pepper your essay with examples plucked from the secondary literature.

To write a brilliant essay, you need to show mastery of the material. In light of your knowledge of the topic at hand, consider which cases might be most likely to help you return an affirmative answer to your question. These are the easy cases – you expect them to conform to the pattern. If they don't, that thesis is in trouble! What about hard cases? Cases which do not obviously conform to the pattern you would expect? If there is an obvious counter-example, you need to address it.

To convince the reader, you need a careful and considered case selection. If you make things too easy for yourself, your reader will think you've missed out too much. If you make things too hard, it'll look like a straw man argument: you'll have defeated the argument, but nobody would reasonably hold that opinion. It is perfectly fine to confine your attention to a particular policy area or time period or region if you say so explicitly at the start. You won't be able to cover life, the universe and everything in 2000-odd words. Just make sure you've chosen your case studies in an informed way rather than relying on a sprinkling of examples that other people used for some other purpose.

By adopting a clear selection strategy for empirical evidence, your essay will become more persuasive to your reader. In the next chapter – **syllogisms and summaries** – we will consider how you can boil your essay down to its essentials. My practical summarizing exercises will help you assess how best to persuade your reader that your argument is correct and to pick holes in possible counter-arguments.

Chapter 7 Exercises
Using empirical evidence effectively

PART A: Of what is this a case? And compared with what? The most important thing to remember when using empirical evidence is that it should be a deliberate and authoritative process.

For each of the questions below, underline the phenomenon or phenomena it is asking you about. Then, identify two comparator classes for each phenomenon. For instance, if you were asked: *What are the challenges of measuring urban poverty in Brazil?* You would consider: of what is Brazil a case? It is a developing country, part of the Global South. It is a Latin American country. It was the last country in the Western Hemisphere to abolish slavery (in 1888). Each of these characteristics points us toward different comparator classes.

1 Do we have ethical responsibilities toward the great apes?
2 How did Victorian authors understand the sublime in mountain landscapes?
3 Did the US have an obligation to intervene in the 1994 Rwandan Genocide?
4 Why are the seeds of birch trees so easily dispersed?
5 Is the United Nations a powerful organization?

6 'Human greenhouse gas emissions explain almost all of the climate change we see in the Quaternary period.' Discuss.

7 Can we ever prevent human trafficking?

PART B: For each of the following theses, consider which cases are easy (you expect it to conform to the pattern and prove the thesis right, so if it doesn't then the thesis is in trouble) and which cases are hard (the case is less likely to conform to the pattern, so conforming really strengthens the thesis).

8 'Food makes people happy.' (lettuce, milk, bread, chocolate)

9 'Children's stories empower girls.' (*Cinderella, Frozen, Rapunzel, Little Red Riding Hood*)

10 'Taking public transport reduces stress.' (train, subway, bus, gondola)

11 'Superheroes are excellent role models.' (Superman, Batman, Silver Surfer, Wolverine)

12 'Sport is dangerous.' (table tennis, American football, tenpin bowling, skiing)

PART C: Another principle of case selection for essays is to consider whether your cases are typical (those that most easily generalize to the broader population of which they are part) or telling (atypical cases selected specifically to showcase certain unusual features). For the questions below, identify the population and distinguish typical from telling cases.

13 How did Google Earth break from previous mapping genres? (European maps that use the Mercator projection, Polynesian stick charts, military maps, 25,000-year-old mammoth tusk carvings)

14 How did the transition from live to recording affect the sitcom genre? (*Friends, The Big Bang Theory, Slattery's People, The Office, The Tammy Grimes Show*)

15 What challenges do policymakers face in regulating mergers and acquisitions in the carbonated soft drink industry? (Leninade (a 'simple Soviet-style soda'), Brain Wash Blue, Dr Pepper, Fanta)

16 How do children acquire perceptual motor skills? (plate spinning, kicking a ball, playing with blocks, slackwire balancing)

17 What do historians know about the everyday experiences of the medieval peasantry? (reaping, sowing, haymaking, eating pottage, leading peasants' revolts, being executed for participating in peasants' revolts)

8

Syllogisms and Summaries

When you write an essay, you are not just talking about a topic or theme in general. You are making an *argument* in response to a particular question. In other words, you are trying to persuade the reader of a set of propositions. A really brilliant essay is one in which the reader can easily discern those propositions. The argument you make has to be crystal clear.

To make your argument obvious to the reader, your writing should be elegant yet succinct – so you should use academic English, define all technical terms the moment they are introduced in the text, and avoid excessive hedging or signposting (phrases we encounter in Chapters 6 and 9 on **elegant writing** and **losing the training wheels**, such as 'in my opinion', 'relatively', 'to some extent' or lengthy re-statements of the question). But making your argument crystal clear doesn't hinge on just the quality of your prose.

You want the reader to be able to identify the take-home argument at the beginning, be convinced by your evidence and your response to counter-arguments, and then remember what your argument was afterwards. Not just that the essay was 'something about the Aztecs', but that the essay asserted the following proposition:

Rigid class stratification bolstered the power of ruling Aztecs by integrating traditional leaders into a centralized system.

Not just that the essay was 'on the theme of civic engagement' generally, but specifically that the author's argument was:

Resource-rich organizations are more able to engage in civic life, and among these resource-rich organizations, a close connection with the state is associated with high levels of activity.

Not just that the essay was 'about presidential TV debates', but specifically:

Television images prime people to rely more on personality perceptions in their evaluations of presidential candidates.

You need to make your argument concrete and specific by putting the core assertion right at the start of the essay.

Many students start an essay with a bit of hand-waving about the themes and issues the essay will address. It isn't a bad thing to give the reader a sense of the big picture in an essay, but that means situating your argument within the broader scholarly literature and giving a reader a clear, specific answer to the 'Why should we care?' question. It doesn't mean merely gesturing towards a set of topics.

For example, in your essay on the development of the medieval English longbow, you might argue that your essay 'challenges technologically deterministic accounts of English military success in the Hundred Years War', even though longbows were decisive in battles at Poitiers and Agincourt. You don't want to start with a few generic statements about broad issues. Don't say your essay is 'about the military' or 'on the theme of warfare' or that it 'will deal with issues surrounding weapons' or 'look at the medieval period'. Better to state your core argument up front.

Similarly, your essay on the decline of linguistic heterogeneity might argue that migration is even more important than economic development in explaining language death. That's your take-home and it should be made totally explicit to your reader. You shouldn't simply gesture towards 'the diverse nature of the world's many languages' or 'the variety of social and cultural factors affecting various parts of the world'. In short, give your reader a concrete and specific statement of your argument, not just a casual mention of general themes and issues.

One way to practise this skill (and it is certainly something that can be practised – you'll get better as you become more experienced) is to summarize the core argument of books and articles you read. Practise writing the core argument out as one, two or at most three grammatical sentences. You should be able to sum up the main point of each paper succinctly. That is a skill that lawyers use a lot and it is vital in clarifying the point of the whole piece of writing.

EXERCISE 8.1

Have a go at moving from general theme to proposition

Examine the following topics. Using your background knowledge, assert three propositions about each topic. Each proposition should be written out as a single grammatical sentence. Don't just hand-wave towards a general 'theme'. You should aim to be as concrete, specific and informative as you can. Suggested answers are on p. 164.

1 Making a cup of tea
2 Ghosts and the supernatural
3 Chocolate
4 Learning to drive
5 Weddings
6 Gaining self-confidence
7 Trees
8 Young people's use of social media

Some students find it helpful to create a mind map when they first encounter an essay. At the first stage in writing an essay, the purpose is to open up the discussion and think as widely and creatively about a subject as possible, but you can't leave things there because it will come across to the reader as a bit of a jumble. After you have opened up the conversation and explored the various dimensions and assumptions within the question, you need to make an authoritative choice about which avenues are most promising. That choice will dictate the propositions you advance.

Summarizing effectively by paraphrasing an argument

Sometimes essays get bogged down in irrelevant detail, so the reader loses the thread of the argument. There are so many elements that go into a brilliant essay – definitions and discussion, theory, empirical evidence and scholarly literature – it can be hard to convey your meaning clearly. If you learn how to summarize effectively, you'll know how to extract the core argument and avoid drifting off-piste.

To take notes effectively, you have to engage in summarizing. There's no point simply copying out an entire text, or highlighting long sections, except for shortish direct quotations. I discuss note-taking at greater length in Chapter 10 on **reading critically**. What do you do when you summarize? You read a whole section for meaning and then you make a decision about which sections are most important. Of these important parts, you show that you understand what it means by writing it out in your own words: that is, paraphrasing.

EXERCISE 8.2

Have a go at paraphrasing

Consider the following classic stories. Each one has some sort of moral or key conclusion. We can think of this conclusion as a proposition the story advances. For each, try to identify the core proposition of each story. Write it out as a single grammatical sentence. Suggested answers are on p. 164.

1 *The Wizard of Oz*
2 *Cinderella*
3 Mowgli's experiences in Rudyard Kipling's *The Jungle Book*
4 Bram Stoker's *Dracula*
5 The Biblical parable of the Good Samaritan
6 *Catch-22*

You should take this approach to your own draft essays. Read it one paragraph at a time. Can you extract the key point you're making? Next, summarize that key point as a single grammatical sentence. Why a grammatical sentence? Writing something out in your own words as a proposition forces you to think rather than just replicate an entire paragraph. It should be an assertion rather than a question. You want to avoid simply asking questions; your job is to *answer* them.

Some students pose excellent questions in their essays, but they don't always answer them. Imagine you were writing an essay in response to the following question:

'The presidency is the illusion of choice.' Discuss.

As you tear this question apart you could ask many questions about its terms and underlying assumptions. You might ask: what is choice? What is the relationship between choice and power? What does choice look like in practice? What counts as an illusion? Who holds the illusion? Is this proposition falsifiable? How can the choices be measured and described? What sorts of empirical evidence can we bring to bear upon this question? What constraints are there upon the presidency? What determines the extent of presidential power? These are all excellent questions to pose. Consider them carefully as you draft your essay but don't leave them in the essay itself. The reader wants answers, not just questions. It is your job to adjudicate these questions.

Similarly, imagine you were writing an essay on *Vita Basilii*, the biography of the first Byzantine emperor of the Macedonian dynasty, written by the emperor's grandson, Constantine VII.

'An effective rebranding of a ruthless and ineffective emperor.' Consider this view of Constantine VII's Life of Basil I.

As you chew over this question, you need to consider its moving parts. 'Rebranding' implies that the subject was formerly branded otherwise: when was this? What changed? What counts as an 'effective' rebranding? How does an effective rebranding differ from an effective emperor? Can someone be both ruthless and ineffective? Is the idea of 'ruthlessness' an anachronism, transplanted from the modern day to the ninth century, and how can we place the concept of ruthlessness in historical context? Again, you want to answer such questions, not just pose them.

If you learn to summarize effectively in your own words, you will be able to put your essential points across more easily, and your argument will become clear to the reader. Certain types of summarizing are particularly good at helping you lay bare the core of the argument.

Using syllogisms to boost the power of your arguments

It can help to write out an argument as a syllogism. A syllogism is a form of reasoning that derives a conclusion from some premises, usually two (although there could be more). For example:

Premise 1: All dogs walk on their toes.

Premise 2: Spaniels are dogs.

Therefore,

Conclusion: Spaniels walk on their toes.

A more interesting example, still in this 'Premise 1, Premise 2, therefore Conclusion' form, could be:

Presidential power is the power to persuade.

Polarization makes persuasion more difficult.

Therefore,

Polarization makes it harder for presidents to exert power.

Here is a syllogism that paraphrases musicologist Elizabeth Eva Leach's arguments about nature and music (Leach 2007):

'Humans are qualitatively different from other animals because they have reason...

Music is fundamentally rational.

Therefore,

Music can only be a human activity'. Discuss.

To make a convincing argument in this syllogistic form, you need to do two things: establish the truth of your propositions – make sure that the premises of your argument are well evidenced and convincing – and show that the conclusion follows from these premises.

There are two main ways that an argument can fail. Maybe one or both of the premises are false. Or maybe the premises are sound but the conclusion doesn't follow.

For example, in the presidential power syllogism above, the argument could fail at any of these points. Richard Neustadt famously defined presidential power as the power to persuade, but there are rival characterizations. Polarization may make inter-party persuasion more difficult, but it might increase the likelihood of intra-party persuasion.

And even if we accept the truth of these two premises, it is possible to argue that the conclusion does not flow from them – in other words, that this is not a valid argument – because, maybe, the separated nature of the American political system is so impervious to the exercise of presidential power in domestic matters that polarization per se doesn't make much difference. In this case, the critique might be that we have missed out a whole additional factor that should be addressed: the institutional configuration established by the Constitution. You need to be able to pick out the key premises in the argument and assess whether they are true or false. You also need to think about the relationship between the premises and the conclusion.

In the music example, you might question either of the premises or the connection between the conclusion and its premises. Many philosophers have taken it as axiomatic that human beings are the only creatures who possess reason, but the truth of this statement depends crucially upon our definition of 'reasoning'. Language is a key differentiator between humans and other animals, but a wide variety of animals, including elephants, chimpanzees, ravens and lions, exhibit executive control when it comes to making decisions: consciously choosing their goals and ways to reach those goals before acting.

Alternatively, we might question the second premise. Even if we grant the rationality of the tonal structure of music, it is still possible to argue that it rests upon fundamentally irrational premises, as Max Weber believed. Perhaps the problem lies with the connection between the premises and the conclusion. Something that is fundamentally rational might still be accessible in some form to beings that do not possess rationality. If you seek to question this statement, you need to decide precisely which angle you want to attack, and if you seek to defend it – that is, you believe that Elizabeth Leach has reasoned soundly – then you will need to respond to the strongest counter-arguments. You had better have a powerful response up your sleeve to respond to those who seek to annihilate the weakest premise or the connection between premises and conclusion.

Occasionally, you get an essay question that is explicitly formulated as a syllogism:

> 'If the Constitution is the source of governmental power, and the judiciary interprets the Constitution, then the judiciary is the most powerful branch of government.' Discuss.

Let's break this statement down into its premises and conclusion:

> Premise 1: The Constitution is the source of governmental power.
> Premise 2: The judiciary interprets the Constitution.
> Therefore,
> Conclusion: The judiciary is the most powerful branch of government.

You might think that this is a good argument, but if so you would need to defend it from the charge that it is false or invalid. There's one concept here that is highly contested, which appears in both Premise 1 and the Conclusion and which you would need to interrogate in order to come to a judgement about this syllogism: 'power'. Whether the first premise is true, and whether the conclusion follows from the two premises, will depend crucially upon how you define this concept.

You might also want to look into the 'interprets' part of the second premise. After zooming in on the core concepts, take a step back and consider the argument as a whole in light of your definitions. Does it make sense? Are the premises true? Is the argument valid?

Using syllogisms to problematize a question

Sometimes, writing the argument out as a syllogism can help to problematize a question. For example, if you were answering the question:

> Since the foetal period is a time of enormous growth and development, and childhood cancer is fundamentally a disease of dysregulated development, why are babies so rarely born with cancer?

The argument might run:

> Premise 1: The foetal period is a time of enormous growth and development.
> Premise 2: Childhood cancer is fundamentally a disease of dysregulated development.
> Therefore,
> Conclusion: Babies are often born with cancer.

But the fact is that, contrary to this argument's conclusion, babies *aren't* often born with cancer. Writing the argument out as a syllogism can raise the stakes here. Something has got to give. Premise 1 seems pretty secure, but perhaps Premise 2 needs additional scrutiny, and if Premises 1 and 2 are correct, then the argument must be invalid: some factor we haven't taken account of yet is needed to explain why the conclusion does not follow from these premises.

Your task is to explain why the conclusion does not follow from these premises. That's the problem – the puzzle – which will animate your writing. It should be made clear from the start why this problem is so puzzling, so that the reader knows exactly what you have achieved when you help to unravel it. Writing the argument out in terms of premises and conclusion can help you to spell out the problem for the reader.

EXERCISE 8.3

Have a go at writing an argument as a syllogism

Consider the following questions. For each, flesh out what the question is asking you to do by writing it out as a syllogism: in the form 'Premise 1, Premise 2, therefore Conclusion'. Some of these questions are arguments that purport to be valid; others can be written out syllogistically in order to problematize them, as in the cancer example. Answers are on p. 164.

1 'If I have an idea of a supremely perfect being, and one of those perfections is necessary existence, then a supremely perfect being exists.' Does the ontological argument for the existence of God succeed?
2 Doing statistical social science is pointless! In the social sciences, knowing all of the confounding variables and measuring them properly are basically impossible. But without accounting for omitted confounding variables, our estimates of causal effects will be wrong.
3 'If being a woman is one cultural interpretation of being female, and if that interpretation is in no way necessitated by being female, then it appears that the female body is the arbitrary locus of the gender "woman".' Discuss Judith Butler's comment on Simone de Beauvoir's *The Second Sex*.
4 Descartes asserts that if the mind is not made of parts, it cannot be made of matter because anything material has parts. What do you think of his arguments for dualism?
5 Why, despite the opposition of the City authorities, did playhouses flourish in fifteenth-century London?
6 'If the first ruler is excellent and his rulership truly excellent, then in what he prescribes he seeks only to obtain, for himself and for everyone under his rulership, the ultimate happiness that is truly happiness; and that religion will be the excellent religion.' (Al-Farabi, *Book of Religion* 1: 93). Discuss.
7. Why did the Visigoths succeed in establishing a lasting kingdom from the fifth to the eighth centuries, whereas the Huns did not – in spite of the Huns' military prowess?
8 Given that the New Economic Policy had stabilized its economy, why did the Soviet Union abandon the Policy in 1928–29?

You won't always, or even often, have an essay question that is explicitly formulated as a syllogism, but it's still a very good exercise to try to draw out the key assertions and conclusion of each paper you read. Why does it help? Instead of talking about vague 'themes', you'll be considering actual propositions: assertions that might be true or false.

By extracting the core premises and conclusion, you can cut through extraneous material, and make it clear to your reader precisely what the paper is arguing. It also helps you to check how persuasive your argument is and protect it from counter-arguments. The ability to synthesize large amounts of material in a succinct and coherent fashion is a hallmark of a truly brilliant essay.

Now that you have read this far, you are ready to start discarding some of the rules and procedures for essay writing you learned at school. Not all of the things you were taught about essay writing will turn out to be wrong, of course, yet there are many tired formulas and rules of thumb that might have worked for more basic high-school assignments but that hamper your ability to reach for the highest grades at university. In the next chapter – **losing the training wheels** – we will discuss which prescriptive rules you can safely jettison to liberate your essay writing.

Chapter 8 Exercises
Syllogisms and summaries

How strong are the arguments below? For each argument, decide whether you find the argument basically plausible or basically implausible overall.

Identify the weakest parts of the arguments below: the Premise(s), the Conclusion or the argument's overall validity (the connection between the premises and the conclusion).

1 Premise 1: International treaties mean no one has ever laid claim to Antarctica.
Premise 2: International treaties never last for long when real land claims are at stake.
Conclusion: Antarctica is not a continent but a 360° ice mass, and the earth is flat.
2 Premise 1: The Crusades were sanctioned by the Church.
Premise 2: Crusaders pillaged and massacred as they travelled.
Conclusion: The Church condoned massacres in the name of God.

3 Premise 1: There are similar-sounding words in languages around the globe.
Premise 2: Word similarities are too extensive to be a coincidence.
Conclusion: All natural languages must have a single origin (a 'Proto-World' language).

4 Premise 1: Languages vary by how much they make speakers attend to gender.
Premise 2: Emphasizing gender makes people less likely to support gender equality.
Conclusion: Genderless languages liberalize attitudes toward gender equality.

5 Premise 1: Justice is nothing but the advantage of the stronger.
Premise 2: Justice is obedience to laws.
Conclusion: Injustice, if it is on a large enough scale, is stronger than justice.

6 Premise 1: It is hard for states generally to maintain the rule of law at times of crisis.
Premise 2: Colonial Burma faced rebellion in the 1930s but retained the rule of law.
Conclusion: *Colonial* states are particularly in need of the rule of law at times of crisis.

7 Premise 1: Americans no longer report racist attitudes or support segregation.
Premise 2: When people stop reporting racist attitudes or supporting segregation, they also support programmes to redress racial discrimination, such as affirmative action.
Conclusion: Affirmative action programmes are popular.

8 Premise 1: The will of God is identical with the laws of nature.
Premise 2: A miracle is a violation of the laws of nature.
Premise 3: Necessarily, God's will is inviolable.
Conclusion: Miracles cannot happen.

Losing the Training Wheels

There are things you were told to do at school: strict rules about precisely how an essay has to go. For example, 'never, ever use the word "I" in your essays' or 'you must write five paragraphs, of which the second is the pros, the third the cons, and the fourth the "debate"'. These are training wheels, like side bars in bowling alleys, which can prevent you from languishing in the very lowest grades. But they come at a cost: preventing you from reaching for the highest grades that demand original thinking, critical analysis and beautiful writing.

Why might these training wheels stop you from writing, thinking and analyzing at the highest levels? Because they make essays formulaic and boring to write. They impede your ability to think creatively and critically about a question by forcing you to follow a preordained structure. They are a straitjacket. You might get a low-ish, solid but not stellar mark for such an essay (and you're unlikely to crash and burn) but it's not going to be much fun to write.

In this chapter, I will run through some common training wheels and show you how to shake them off in order to write truly original, brilliant essays. The key point is that although following very strict rules about writing, structure, argument, evidence, literature and citations can help you avoid total wipe-out if you're struggling, they also prevent you from stepping back and truly thinking about what you need to do. A brilliant essay is controlled by its author: you are in the driving seat, not some rigid rule half-remembered from school.

There's a reason this chapter comes so late in the book. Now that you know more about examining assumptions, controlling your argument, writing elegantly, and deploying evidence, you should feel confident enough to jettison certain practices that are trapping you in the vanilla middling grades. Like training wheels, such practices probably helped you when you were starting out. Now it's time to discard them and fly free!

Training wheel #1: The pro–con procedure

One of the training wheels you might have encountered at school is the *pro–con procedure*. This procedure involves drawing a line down the middle of the page, with 'pros' on one side and 'cons' on the other. You list the pros, list the cons, and then write an essay consisting of five paragraphs:

1. The introduction
2. The pros
3. The cons
4. A 'debate' between pros and cons
5. The conclusion

For example, imagine you were answering one of the following questions:

Are Marxist theories still valid?

To what extent can Mozart's operas be considered 'religious' works?

Do our personality traits influence our political behaviour?

According to the pro–con procedure, you would line up reasons on either side of each question, ready to plug them into paragraphs 2 and 3.

Are Marxist theories still valid?

PROS: Reasons that Marxist theories are valid

- Marx's theories generate empirically verifiable predictions, which have been applied successfully in fields as varied as criminology, economics and political science.
- Marx presents a clear vision of the problems of class-based capitalism.
- Marx's methodologies are hugely influential and are still in use in some segments of the academy today.

CONS: Reasons that Marxist theories are invalid

- Historical materialism proposes a circular relationship between base and superstructure.
- Marxist theories are overly deterministic.
- According to John Maynard Keynes, *Capital* is 'an obsolete textbook which I know to be not only scientifically erroneous but without interest or application for the modern world' (Keynes 2010).

To what extent can Mozart's operas be considered 'religious' works?

PROS: Reasons that Mozart's operas are religious works

- The music itself is divine, Mozart himself was a devout Roman Catholic throughout his life, and he composed more than 60 pieces of sacred music.
- Karl Barth, the Reformed theologian, sees Mozart as a composer who sounds the glory of the Creator.
- Hans Kung, the Roman Catholic theologian, argues that Mozart's music signals 'traces of transcendence' (Kung 1992).

CONS: Reasons that Mozart's operas are not religious works

- Comic and low-brow art forms are irreverent and irreligious. Mozart produced comic operas in the form of *opera buffa* and *singspiel*.
- Mozart's music was influenced by the Enlightenment and by non-religious considerations.
- Soren Kierkegaard's non-religious aesthete celebrates a 'daemonic Mozart' in operas such as *Don Giovanni* (Kierkegaard 1992).

Do our personality traits influence our political behaviour?

PROS: Ways personality traits influence political behaviour

- Conscientiousness is associated with greater political conservatism.
- People who score highly in 'openness' tend to be politically liberal.
- Conservatives like well-done steak and tend to prioritize group hierarchies. Liberals like their meat rare and prioritize individuals.

CONS: *Ways personality traits do not influence political behaviour*

- Political behaviour is influenced by lots of things besides personality, including friendship networks, family and socioeconomic background.
- Extroversion and introversion are not clearly associated with liberalism or conservatism.
- There is no evidence that turnout is particularly affected by personality traits, one way or the other.

Writing down the arguments on each side of the question might help you to think about both sides but, reading these disparate points through, don't they seem a bit of a jumble? The points are not all of the same type, so they do not add up to a coherent argument. For example, to argue that Mozart's operas are *non*-religious is not the same as describing them as *anti*-religious, and to argue that we *lack evidence* that personality traits influence political behaviour is not the same as stating that personality traits definitely do *not* influence political behaviour.

The pros and cons do not speak to each other directly. For instance, some of the 'reasons to think that Marxist theories are valid' pertain to empirical verification, and others to influence in the academy, but the counterpart 'reasons to think Marxist theories are invalid' are mostly about theoretical consistency instead, not verification or influence. The author of the political behaviour essay has also assembled a disparate collection of reasons on each side of an argument: a selection of personality traits that do seem to be associated with political behaviour, a selection that do not, and a global assessment that personality is not as important as, say, socioeconomic background in explaining behaviour. Weaker essays often present a list of reasons on each side of an argument (just like a shopping list: dishwasher tablets, cat food, milk, noodles…) without clarifying how each point relates to the others and to the argument as a whole.

These pro–con lists present another problem for a student trying to reach the highest grades: by focusing entirely on the five-paragraph formula – one paragraph of 'pros', another paragraph of 'cons' and so on – the writer ignores certain intriguing aspects of the questions at hand. Let's come back to our three example questions:

Are Marxist theories still valid?

The word 'still' in this question suggests that a temporal perspective is needed. The question is not 'Are Marxist theories valid full stop?' but 'Are they valid *today*? (implying that they were once valid, an assumption you may wish to question). The clodhopping pro–con listicle ploughs straight on with reasons on each side of the validity question without stopping to consider what the question is really asking.

To what extent can Mozart's operas be considered 'religious' works?

The question asks 'to what extent', implying that there is at least some sense in which Mozart's operas were 'religious' – but it is up to the author to make it crystal clear what they understand by 'religious'. There are many potential definitions. The pro–con approach results in a set of arguments that seem to talk past one another because the author has not clarified what 'religious' (or 'non-religious') actually means.

Do our personality traits influence our political behaviour?

One consideration the pro–con approach ignores is that the question rests upon the assumption that 'personality traits' are analytically and empirically separable from 'political behaviours' – but that is a questionable assumption. Behaviours, including political ones, may not be rigidly distinguished from personality, because a person's personality is constituted by their behavioural responses to the world. By sticking to the five-paragraph, list-the-pros-and-cons procedure, the author has missed the chance to think through the question more deeply and challenge its underlying assumptions.

An essay that adheres rigidly to the pro–con procedure presents its readers with a seesaw effect: 'on the one hand this... on the other hand that'. The reader is pushed one way, and then another, without a clear sense of what the author's own position is.

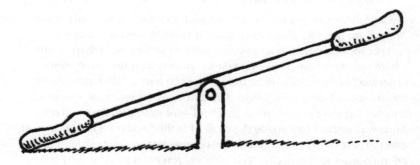

Each paragraph seems completely divorced from the others, so the writer doesn't actually engage with the arguments presented except near the end: that awful 'debate' paragraph 4, according to the pro–con procedure. Many students are keen to write a balanced essay, but 'balance' does not mean providing three (or however many) points on each side and zigzagging between them. Seesaws are dizzying.

One way to practise eliminating the seesaw effect is to try removing the word 'however' from your essays. My first undergraduate tutor suggested I eliminate that word, and it was surprisingly effective – provided that I also stopped using weasel substitutes such as 'conversely', 'nevertheless' and 'on the other hand'. I had been in the habit of presenting arguments on one side followed by a huge 'However...' and a set of counter-arguments. My tutor was left to adjudicate between the two sides himself, but that should be the author's job, not a burden the reader has to carry. A brilliant essay makes a case by sustaining an argument over the whole essay. That doesn't mean you ignore the counter-arguments. On the contrary, you engage with them.

How does this work? Imagine you're arguing with your friend Sheena in the Student Union about who was the most effective president of the Argentinian Tango Society. You think Anna was the most effective. Sheena thinks Ben was the most effective. You want to convince Sheena that Anna, not Ben, was the most effective. How do you do this? Not just by listing Anna's excellent qualities:

Anna is the best president of the Tango Society because she is so organised, such a good communicator, completely inspirational to the new dancers, so fantastic at...

And not just by putting a line down the page with Anna's case on one side and Ben's on the other.

Anna is organised, but Ben has great integrity.
Anna is a good communicator; however, Ben is very confident.
Anna inspires the new dancers, but Ben is an innovative choreographer.

If you do this, Sheena might be confused about what your argument is. Are you on her side after all? How do you weigh up these arguments?

Instead, you establish what your metric of success is. Perhaps that's where you differ. Anna has more dance awards than Ben. Sure, Ben's organized more social events, but being president of the Tango Society is mostly about being an excellent dancer. You assess which of Sheena's counter-arguments is the most powerful – for example, Sheena thinks Anna was *efficient* (she made the most of limited resources) but not most *effective* (she didn't put on many big competitions) – and respond to that counter-argument explicitly. Throughout, you need to show why your arguments trump hers. For instance:

I can see why you care about competitions, Sheena, but you're not taking financial context into account. If we consider the level of resources available, Anna put on a comparable number of big competitions to previous presidents of the Tango Society AND she won more dance awards to boot.

In an essay, you build your argument by responding to counter-arguments explicitly, not by simply laying out a selection of reasons on either side.

EXERCISE 9.1

Have a go at responding to counter-arguments

Take a look at the questions and possible arguments for and against, below. Make up your mind where you stand with respect to each question. Then write down the most persuasive response you can think of to deal with the counter-arguments.

You want to build your case by responding to the strongest of your opponents rather than seesawing between each side.

If you can think of an even stronger counter-argument than those proposed here, have a go at responding to that counter-argument. Suggested answers are on p. 169.

1 How safe are winter sports?
   NOT SAFE: Travel insurance costs more if it includes winter sports, and every year many people are injured by skiing, snowboarding, ice skating and tobogganing.
   SAFE: Cycling, football and swimming cause thousands more injuries each year than winter sports do. If you are fit, winter sports are quite safe.
2 Is it more important for children to be considerate or well behaved?
   CONSIDERATE: Children need to learn how to develop their own moral code and act independently. An obedient teenager or adult is a doormat.
   WELL BEHAVED: Children need to be taught to obey rules, so that they can fit in with society. Spare the rod and spoil the child.
3 How disgusting are koalas?
   NOT DISGUSTING: Koalas are adorable symbols of Australia, voted #1 cutest animal in a poll conducted by the tourism site Experience Oz.
   VERY DISGUSTING: Chlamydia, a sexually transmitted disease, is so rife amongst koalas that some wild populations have a 100% infection rate. Young koalas also contract it in the pouch by eating their mothers' pap: a nutrient-rich faecal matter.
4 Do holidaymakers have a nicer time at the seaside or in the countryside?
   SEASIDE: The seaside offers fresh sea air and a free natural place to swim, helping people to relax and destress. Living by the sea is extremely calming.
   COUNTRYSIDE: A rural idyll provides tranquillity and relaxation. Countryside destinations are regarded as safe, welcoming and comfortable.
5 Are things getting better?
   YES THEY ARE: Extreme poverty, hunger and child labour have all fallen. Life expectancy is rising. We have drastically reduced the number of nuclear weapons.
   NO THEY AREN'T: According to Freedom House, democracy is under assault around the globe. Climate-warming gases such as carbon dioxide, methane and nitrous oxide have risen to record highs.

Training wheel #2: Eliminating all uses of the word 'I'

One of the rules you might have learned at school, or when starting out at university, is the rule that one should *never* use the words 'I', 'me' or 'my' in an essay. Eliminating 'I' might stop you from using horrible constructions such as 'In my opinion' or 'I believe that'. These are excessive hedges, which I discuss in Chapter 6 on **elegant writing**. They bespeak a lack of confidence in whatever you're asserting. You don't turn to your friend over lunch and say 'I believe that there is a fork in front of me' when it's right in front of you.

But eliminating all uses of 'I' is throwing the baby out with the bathwater. It can force you into nasty passive constructions like: 'On the basis of the analysis which was made of the data which were collected, it is suggested that the null hypothesis can be rejected'. Such statements would be much more easily expressed as 'I argue' or 'I did X'. You need to own up: 'I collected data. I reject the null hypothesis. It's me, me, me!' 'As I made clear in paragraph 3' is better than 'paragraph 3 argues that' because a paragraph is not a person. People, organizations and institutions act in the world. They do things. Paragraphs don't.

Avoiding the passive voice at all costs is not the way to go either; sometimes you do not need to mention the agent who did something. This is one of those rules that shouldn't be replaced by a blanket ban. Suffice to say, eliminating 'I' is a training wheel that ought to be replaced by a good read-through by you, a tutor or a friend. Sometimes 'I' is useful. Sometimes it isn't. The key is to write confidently by taking responsibility for your argument. That means eliminating both weak-kneed hedges such as 'I believe that' *and* passive constructions such as 'on the basis of the evidence presented, it is suggested that'.

EXERCISE 9.2

Have a go at identifying appropriate uses of 'I', 'me', 'my' and the passive voice

Take a look at the following sentences and decide whether you would include it in your essay or not. If you would not include the sentence, re-write it so as to eliminate the use of 'I', 'me' or 'my' or add 'I', 'me' or 'my' or otherwise turn the passive into the active.[1]

The aims of the game are to write confidently and take responsibility for your argument without hedging your bets, being too timid or engaging in long-winded, unnecessarily cagey constructions. Answers are on p. 169.

1 With thanks to Hanß 2019; Barnett 2020; Greenfield 2020 for some of the examples used in this 'Have a go' exercise.

1 In my opinion, African elephants are the most impressive of all African mammals.

2 My research on featherwork in colonial Peru demonstrates that artisanship linked indigenous Andean and European societies.

3 On the basis of the survey that was conducted, it is asserted that the effect of greater representation among the police is largely negative, for whites at least.

4 From my perspective, anxiety is a normal part of the human condition.

5 'A system hostile or antagonistic to women' has been held by many to have been facilitated by globalization.

6 I believe that social status and gender are intertwined with the Victorian processes of grieving and remembering the dead.

7 It is argued, using archival and published sources, that three of the consequences of the failure of the French expedition to Mexico from 1862 to 1867 were the undermining of the French Second Empire, the convulsing of the fiscal–military system and the hindering of the Second Empire's ability to confront the Prussian threat.

8 Conservatism is a philosophy of common sense and everyday experience, in my view.

9 I argue that eating was a spiritually rewarding exercise for English Protestants in the sixteenth and seventeenth centuries.

10 I am convinced that compassion acts as a mechanism for coping with stressful public service conditions.

11 A rigid designator, which designates the same object with respect to all possible worlds, was suggested by Kripke.

12 Tests for capacity need to be assessed for their reliability, and major concepts and theories need to be empirically validated.

Training wheel #3: Defining your terms and moving on

All students know that they need to define their terms at the outset of an essay. The training wheels approach makes defining terms into a formulaic, perfunctory exercise that bears no relation to the remainder of the essay. One idea you may have picked up at school is that there is a single, agreed-upon definition that you have to get 'right', after which you can ignore it and move onto the next thing.

In some A-Level examinations, you received five marks for a 'correct' definition, but university essays often ask you to consider essentially contested concepts, such as 'power', 'consciousness', 'beauty', 'freedom', 'strength', 'rigidity', 'rationality', 'globalization' and 'democracy'. A brilliant essay acknowledges that there may be several different dimensions to these concepts and different metrics to measure them. As we discuss in Chapters 2 and 7 on **finding comparator classes** and **using evidence effectively**, your definitions of a term will help to define the universe of cases and your comparator class. Definitions are crucially important.

One way to write a brilliant essay is to tear apart these meaty concepts into their component dimensions and consider the question in relation to each of them. *You* make a decision about which definition you find most persuasive. *You* make a decision about the implications of each definition. For example, imagine you were considering the question:

'Arguments that America is exceptional can be neither proved nor disproved.'
Discuss.

Some definitions of 'exceptionalism' are not the sorts of propositions that can be proved or disproved: 'America is the greatest.' 'Yay, America!' These are expressions of a feeling or emotional response, not a truth claim, necessarily. Other definitions of exceptionalism *do* make truth claims. For example: 'The United States has a tendency to act unilaterally in foreign engagements' – is that true or false? There are religious claims to exceptionalism, political–institutional claims, economic claims, values or cultural claims, and many others. The point is don't simply define and move on. Think about the different definitions that might be proposed and explicitly consider what the implications of each might be.

EXERCISE 9.3

Have a go at identifying different definitions

Examine the following words. All of them are in use in everyday language, although some of them have more technical definitions as well. Using your background knowledge and understanding of language, offer at least two definitions of each term. This exercise assumes no particular scholarly reading. Suggested answers are on p. 169.

1 Freedom
2 Rational
3 Beauty
4 Thinking
5 Power
6 Representation
7 Soul
8 Conservative
9 Living
10 Organization

In this 'Have a go' exercise, you are asked to provide different definitions. In your university courses, you will encounter many terms of art, and you will be exposed to scholarly definitions and perspectives that will expand your ability to think around the core terms of the question. If you have studied any allied subjects and encountered these concepts before, you may have more fleshed-out definitions. If you haven't encountered these terms in a technical or specialist context, your definitions will likely be based on your ordinary understanding of language – but that's okay. The key here is to think carefully about the core terms of a question. An ordinary understanding of language is a good place to start!

Getting rid of tired old formulas for essay writing

So to recap: loosen up! Get rid of those training wheels! Think carefully about your definitions (plural) and consider their various dimensions. Don't stick rigidly to the 'no "I"' rule at the expense of bad writing. Jettison the pro–con procedure you may have learned at school. Don't simply lay out your arguments, followed by a list of counter-arguments, and leave it to your reader to decide. 'X might be true, but here are reasons to think it isn't true.' Or: 'Here are some arguments on one side, and here are some arguments on the other side.' That's bad writing because the reader doesn't know where you stand.

Instead, always respond to the strongest of your imagined opponents – don't shy away from counter-arguments, but meet them head-on in the service of your own argument. For example, an essay on the philosophical question *'Do we have free will?'* might argue:

> *We lack free will because assigning ultimate moral responsibility for action requires an infinite regress of past decisions, decisions that influence how we make subsequent choices.*

It should respond to counter-arguments directly:

> *Mele's argument that freedom is a feature of actions, not characters, fails to save free will by shifting the locus of moral responsibility away from the agent and his or her past actions, because a complete source of any action can always be found that is external to an agent.*[2]

Your job is to adjudicate between competing claims rather than making the reader do the thinking for you. Tell your reader where you stand at the outset, and build your argument by responding to opponents. Some

---

2 With thanks to Stanford Encyclopedia of Philosophy 2018a for source material.

students say they're worried about being disrespectful to their opponents, so they don't want to come on too strong in their arguments. Yet by responding to counter-arguments firmly and reasonably, you *are* respecting your opponents. This is a scholarly conversation. Stop thinking rigidly about pros and cons and start thinking about how you can best persuade your reader.

When you are planning and writing your essay, you are taking part in a scholarly conversation with a range of thinkers. How can you read for an essay most effectively? The next chapter – **reading critically** – offers guidance about reading with confidence and authority.

Chapter 9 Exercises
Losing the training wheels

PART A: You sustain an argument partly by responding to counter-arguments. Imagine that you were defending the following propositions. Write down the strongest *counter-argument* you can think of, then say how you would *respond* to it in support of each proposition.

1 For something to be classified as a 'sport', it must involve physical exertion.
2 Donald Trump is the most effective President in US history.
3 Human beings cannot truly know anything about the world.
4 Successful people tend to have extrovert traits.
5 Friendship is the most important determinant of human happiness.

PART B: One training wheel you may have been exposed to – *never use 'I' in your essays* – is too rigid for top-flight essays. 'I' can lead you to hedge excessively, but it also helps avoid nasty passive constructions. Which of the following uses of 'I', 'me' or 'my' would you lose in your essays, and which would you keep?

6 In my opinion
7 I argue
8 I would argue
9 I believe that
10 I collected and analyzed the data
11 My data show that
12 I reject the null hypothesis
13 For me personally, this is problematic

PART C: A third training wheel is the idea that there is a single, agreed-upon definition, but academics often confront meaty and contested concepts. Underline the contested concept(s) in each question below and give *at least two* definitions, empirical manifestations or dimensions for each.

14 Does the European Union retain its legitimacy?
15 As rational agents, are we free?
16 How does environmentalism balance relations between humans and natural systems?
17 How do education systems resolve frictions between diversity and standardization?
18 Does conservatism depoliticize inequality?
19 Why do empires collapse?

10

Reading Critically

Effective reading at university is thoughtful and goal-directed rather than aimless and indiscriminate. Before you start, you should be clear about your purpose. Are you reading for an essay, presentation, examination, your own background information, class discussion or some combination of these? As you read, aim to forge connections between what you have read and other authors have written and to apply what you have read to real-world examples. Reading is thinking.

I have an acronym I use when marking: LFZ, which stands for literature-free zone. There is no way you can get a good mark without engaging the literature. Some tutors give you training wheels: 'You must cite at least five bits of literature'. We encounter some of these writing formulas in Chapter 9 on **losing the training wheels**. To write a brilliant essay, you need to lose such a formulaic approach. How long is a piece of string? There is no hard and fast rule about how much literature to cite. The caveat: obviously, if your tutor has a strict rule, conform to it! Otherwise, think about the practice of reading more carefully.

Fundamentally, you're trying to convince the reader, which means you need to enter into a conversation with the literature. Don't argue by citation – that is, simply re-explaining the literature. Instead, tell the reader what you think of the literature. What are the controversies in the literature? What does the literature miss? Where does your argument fit with respect to the claims in the literature? In order to engage with the literature properly, you need to know what it says. Read as widely as possible and practise summarizing the key arguments in your own words. Active reading will help you enter into a conversation with the authors you encounter.

Active reading

By active reading, I mean reading thoughtfully, critically and purposefully. How do you do that? First, you need to set yourself a clear goal for your reading. This analytical approach is not the same as reading for pure pleasure. When you snuggle down in bed to read a pot-boiler thriller or a piece of low-brow romantic fiction, you're seeking to relax and lose yourself in the book. You certainly aren't expecting to be quizzed on its contents. If you forget what you've read, who cares? Reading for scholarly purposes may also be very enjoyable, but it has a totally different character.

Before you begin, know why you are being asked to read. If you are reading for classroom discussions, write down any questions your tutor has set ahead of time and have them in front of you as you read. If there are no guiding questions available, take a moment to consider what sorts of queries might come up in class. What has your tutor asked in previous seminars? What issues did they draw your attention to in lectures on this subject? If you can give your reading purpose and structure, it will be a quicker and more interesting process. You will be able to recall more of it afterwards.

If you are reading in order to write an essay or presentation, note down your question and have a think about it first, before you even open a book. You should consider the core terms of the question: what parts need defining? What do you know – or think you know – about this subject already? Are there any assumptions buried in the question? We encounter many words that indicate underlying assumptions in Chapters 1, 2 and 3 on **examining assumptions, finding comparator classes** and **interrogating tensions in questions**. It is astonishing how much you can dig into a question before you even start reading, based on your understanding of everyday language. If you have thought about the question a bit first, you will know what to look out for in your reading. An aimless meander is transformed into a purposeful expedition.

Note-taking

Reasonable people disagree about approaches to note-taking. The key is to do what works for you, but there are some broad-brush guidelines you would be wise to adhere to. Imagine my crestfallen face when I started revising for my University Finals and discovered that half my first-year notes – written more than two years before – had faded to a pale orange colour. Alas, who knew that non-permanent black fountain-pen ink can fade almost to unreadability like that? Since that unfortunate experience, I have always written in permanent ink and stored the notes properly.

Handwritten note-taking forces you to read at a slower pace, helping you to think at the same time as you read, but there may be times and purposes for which notes typed directly into your computer are a better option. Obviously, it's easier to save typed notes, decipher them, and rework them later. Take note of basic bibliographic information at the time, especially page numbers for direct quotations, and consider downloading bibliographic management software to save yourself the trouble of laboriously constructing a references list from scratch afterwards. To avoid accidental plagiarism, use a clear labelling system to distinguish your own ideas from those of your lecturer or another author.

Whatever your personal system, spacing it out and keeping it logical, with headers and sub-headers, will always be a good approach. There is no point in duplicating your lecture slides if they will be made available afterwards. Some people find highlighters and coloured pens helpful but these should be used very sparingly and deliberately. Don't bother to colour in large segments of text. Far better to rephrase the author's statements in your own words, as we discuss in Chapter 8 on **syllogisms and summaries**. That way you are forced to think actively about what the author is asserting.

You need to find a happy medium between writing at such length that you might as well have photocopied the original text and writing so sparingly that you cannot later decode your own notes. Copying things out verbatim is a bad idea, but so are notes that consist of single-word themes or cryptic squiggles. Somewhere between these two poles are helpful notes which draw out the most important parts of an author's argument, summarize them succinctly, but are sufficiently future-proof that you can return in a few months or years and still understand what you were trying to convey. Coming back to our old friend – the proposition written out as a grammatical sentence – can help you here. The very act of constructing a single clear, grammatical sentence helps you to synthesize complex arguments without losing too much meaning.

Questions to ask yourself as you read

You can greatly improve the quality and focus of your reading by considering three sorts of questions in relation to the literature you encounter: definitions, connections and critical response.

Definitions: If you have a specific essay question in mind when you start reading, you should already have considered how you would define the key terms. As you read, you will encounter an author's own definition of that core terminology. Make a note of how each author defines the terms in the question. Consider how they differ from your own definitions and from the definitions proposed elsewhere in the literature. For instance, your naïve understanding of the word 'power' might consist in something like 'the ability to affect something strongly'. When you read Michel Foucault, you could consider how his concept of 'power-knowledge' – the idea that power is intrinsically bound up with knowl-edge – compares with your own definition and that of other authors. What do you think of Foucault's definition? Does it capture the essence of the concept of 'power'? Does it leave anything out?

Similarly, your everyday understanding of the term 'biodiversity' might simply be 'the variety of animal and plant life', but when you dig into the literature you will note that biodiversity is a contested concept. The intuitive definition leaves something to be desired because it is very loose. If preserving biodiversity is our aim but 'biodiversity' is simply the sum total of all life on earth in its myriad forms, then biodiversity is simply biology in general and the idea of preserving biodiversity seems either meaningless or impossibly ambitious. Your reading of conservation biology might prompt you to reconsider the boundaries of the concept, the relative value of rare and common habitats, the distinction between wild and farmed populations and the consequences of each definition for actual conservation practices.

If a piece of terminology is very discipline-specific or unusual, it is a good idea to copy down a particular author's definition precisely as they describe it. For instance, you may have no prior understanding of technical terms such as Leibniz's distinction between esoteric and exoteric presentations of his philosophy; the biological concept of allopatric speciation; the descriptivist theory of names known as 'Millianism'; or archotontology, the study of historical offices of state. Once you have read, identified and digested the technical definitions you read, you may also wish to summarize that definition in your own words to ensure that you have retained the information and understood what is at stake. The exercises below will help you practise these skills.[1]

EXERCISE 10.1

Have a go at rewriting definitions in your own words

Take a look at the technical terms below, along with their definitions. Have a go at re-writing the definition in your own words. The answers are on p. 169.

1 *Secession*: 'Used to render Latin *secession (plebis)*, the temporary migration of the plebeians to a place outside the city, in order to compel the patricians to grant redress of their grievances.' (Oxford English Dictionary)

2 *Medieval semiotics*: 'To speak of medieval semiotics is not to speak of a precisely defined discipline besides, and distinct from, other medieval arts and sciences; it is rather to speak of a complex field of... elaborate reflections on the concept of sign, its nature, function, and classification.' (Stanford Encyclopedia of Philosophy, 2011a)

3 *Agent autonomy*: '... a relationship between an agent and her motivational states which can be roughly characterized as the agent's ability to decide which of them to follow: it is a type of *self-control* or self-government that persons (usually) have and that nonhuman animals do not have.' (Arpaly, 2004: 173–174)

4 *Phylogeny*: 'A diagram or theoretical model of the sequence of evolutionary divergence of species or other groups of organisms from their common ancestors.' (Oxford English Dictionary)

5 *Tax expenditures*: 'Tax expenditures are a diverse group, and can be large (such as tax relief on pension contributions), complex (such as some corporation tax reliefs) or small tax reliefs intended to recognise certain taxpayers (such as relief on war disablement benefits)... they can have more than one objective, some incentive behaviour, while others simply reflect a government policy choice to reduce the tax burden on particular groups or sectors.' (Davies, 2020: 14)

6 *'Games of truth'*: '... it is their mutual development [of the subject of knowledge and what it knows] and their reciprocal relation which gives birth to what we call the "games of truth"; that is to say not the discovery of true things, but of rules according to which, in relation to certain things, what a subject can say about specific things becomes accessible as true or false.' (Foucault, 1994: 632)

1 With thanks to Arpaly 2004; Stanford Encylopedia of Philosophy 2011a; Foucault 1994, IV:632; Davies 2020, 14 for the examples used in this 'Have a go' exercise.

Connections: Active reading involves constantly forging connections between what you read and what you are trying to do with that reading. Ask yourself how the assertions of the authors you are reading stack up against your own background assumptions about the field. Do you need to re-evaluate anything you previously thought to be true, in light of your reading? What new questions does the literature prompt? Scholarly reading should take you on a journey, moving from limited understanding to a fuller and richer picture of the issues. You use the literature to join up the dots between your own background knowledge and the wider scholarly vista.

One way to think about this process is in Bayesian terms. Before you read a piece of literature and examine the evidence that other scholars present, you have some *priors*: a set of beliefs about how the world is, based on your background information, which you possess before the moment you take new information into account. Once you start reading, you begin the process of *updating your priors*: tweaking (and sometimes even overturning) what you previously thought, based on the information and ideas you have encountered. At the end, you arrive at a set of *posterior* beliefs, taking into account what you have discovered. The beauty of the Bayesian approach is its acknowledgement that you don't come to a piece of scholarly literature with a blank slate. Reading involves updating your priors by connecting what you already know, or think you know, to the scholarly insights of others.

You will also use your readings to connect each author to others in the field. How does your reading compare with other pieces of writing you have studied? Imagine bringing the authors you read into a conversation with one another, even if they were writing at entirely different times and in different contexts. Would they understand one another, or are they talking past one another? Where do these authors agree and disagree? Acting as referee, how would you adjudicate any disputes between them? The more you are able to read, the fuller your understanding of the webs of connections between different scholars.

In addition to connecting your readings to your own background knowledge and to other authors, you need to connect your readings to the empirical world. Ask yourself: what are the real-world applications of this reading? What are the implications of these scholarly insights? How might these readings be applied to other contexts, thought experiments or cases? Think! How does this reading help me to answer the question at hand?

As we discuss in Chapters 6 and 8 on **elegant writing** and **syllogisms and summaries**, being concrete and specific is vital in essay writing. Your understanding of what you have read will be greatly enhanced by the act of applying an abstract theory to an empirical case, considering how an idea might translate into a different context, or using a set of scholarly readings to help answer a new question. This is truly *active* reading.

Forging connections between the scholarly reading and your own priors, other authors, empirical cases and essay questions is a task specific to your discipline, but that doesn't mean you cannot practise the skill of connecting up the dots. The exercises below will help you get used to making such connections, using your own background knowledge of familiar topics and issues.[2]

EXERCISE 10.2

Have a go at joining up the dots

Take a look at the technical terms listed below, alongside their definitions. You may not have encountered them all before. Consider how you might apply these new concepts to a topic that you do know something about: the three suggestions under each question. The answers are on p. 169.

1　Cultural anthropologist Clifford Geertz's concept of *thick descriptions*: in which 'behavioural practices are described in sufficient detail to trace inferential associations between observed events... Ideally, the anthropologist can present a culture from the point of view of its members'. (Stanford Encyclopedia of Philosophy, 2011b)

Consider how you might apply this concept to (a) marriage, (b) children's play and (c) University Freshers' Week.

---

2 With thanks to Stanford Encylopaedia of Philosophy 2003, 2011b, 2018b; Churchill 2020 for the examples used in this 'Have a go' exercise.

2   *The Free Rider Problem*: in which 'all of the individual members of a group can benefit from the efforts of each member, and all can benefit substantially from collective action' but there is no way to prevent individuals from not contributing their share, and so free-riding on the beneficial actions of others. (Stanford Encyclopedia of Philosophy, 2003)

Consider how you might apply this concept to (a) cleaning the communal kitchen, (b) Wikipedia and (c) producing a class presentation.

3   Feminist Betty Friedan's concept of *feminine mystique* to 'describe the societal assumption that women could find fulfilment through housework, marriage, sexual passivity, and child rearing alone'. (Churchill, 2020)

Consider how you might apply this concept to (a) women's magazines, (b) the school curriculum and (c) advertising.

4   The religious concept of *dispensation*: 'A religious order or system, conceived as divinely instituted, or as a stage in a progressive revelation, expressly adapted to the needs of a particular period of time.' (Oxford English Dictionary)

Consider how you might apply this concept to (a) the Garden of Eden, (b) US foreign policy and (c) climate science.

5   *The Doctrine of Double Effect*: 'It is permissible to cause a harm as a side effect (or "double effect") of bringing about a good result even though it would not be permissible to cause such a harm as a means to bringing about the same good end.' (Stanford Encyclopedia of Philosophy, 2018b)

Consider how you might apply this concept to (a) a teenager holding a messy house party, (b) a vaccination programme and (c) driving an SUV.

Critical approach: You should approach readings with cautious scepticism. That doesn't mean dismissing things out of hand or deferring to other authors but, rather, being prepared to question what you are being told. Ask yourself whether you agree with author X. How persuasive are his or her arguments? Keep these questions in mind as you read; jot down your thoughts about an author's reasoning and evidence along the way. One way to get clear about precisely what is being asserted is to map out the causal mechanisms and arguments as diagrams.

Mapping out causal mechanisms and arguments as diagrams

Diagrams can help you to identify and critique arguments you encounter in the literature because they lay everything out in the open. Instead of burying an idea or argument in a dense thicket of text, a diagram can extract the most important points and show how they connect with each other. The act of drawing a diagram can also be a useful exercise in helping you to understand what you have read. Just like the syllogisms we encounter in Chapter 8 on **syllogisms and summaries**, diagrams are summaries of essential nodes (points where lines intersect) and vectors (lines connecting different ideas).

For instance, imagine you were reading a scholarly article about lowering the voting age to 16. In order to fully understand the argument, you might find it helpful to draw the connections that the authors make.

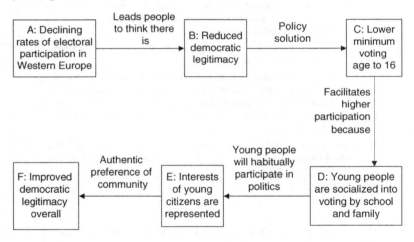

Showing the argument as a diagram can help you to pick it apart and respond critically. By labelling the vectors as well as the nodes, we can clarify the nature of the connections between different points. For example, A is a description of empirically verifiable facts about electoral participation, but B is a value judgement about the effect of this state of affairs upon democratic legitimacy. Whenever you see a connection that moves from empirical fact to normative assertion, it is worth considering whether that connection is warranted. On what basis might someone draw a normative conclusion? What is the nature of 'democratic legitimacy'? What is the connection between participation and legitimacy? Are there other characterizations of 'legitimacy' that do not draw so strongly upon participation rates? Overall, do you think the author's move from point A to point B is warranted?

This diagram also highlights several empirical steps in the author's argument. To move from C to D to E, the policy solution (lowering the voting age) needs to reliably induce young people to vote in greater numbers and to do so in a way that truly represents their interests and calls policymakers to account for their promises rather than just providing a vehicle for a select few to express themselves. The posited moderators (listed under D) are the fact that young people typically live at home with their parents and go to school, so those whose parents and schools encourage them to vote are even more likely to develop a habit of voting – one that proponents of the lower voting age hope will last long into the future. These assertions may seem reasonable to you, or not. You should ask yourself what other factors might affect this relationship and how strong you think the relationship will be. All of these critical questions will help you to understand what you have read and come to conclusions about it.

In order to read effectively, you need to lose the formulaic approach (the idea you *have* to cite a certain number of pieces of literature) and instead think how you can best convince your reader. Avoid the literature-free zone and enter into a conversation with other scholars. It is good to be proactive about finding new readings, and your tutor will appreciate your efforts to move beyond the standard list, but you don't want to miss the contributions from the heart of the field. Your tutor is there to guide you to the canonical works.

As you read, consider how the authors define the core terms in your field – and the terms of the essay questions you have been set. Update your priors by connecting the things you read to your own background knowledge and assumptions and consider the connections between different authors. How would they speak to one another? Can you adjudicate a real or imagined debate between them? Think also about the connections between the ideas you are presented with and their real-world applications. Throughout, you should maintain a position of cautious scepticism. To read is to think.

Passive meandering is even more dangerous in the ultimate essay-writing test: examination essays. The next chapter – **examination preparation** – takes you through the stages of preparing to write examination essays.

Chapter 10 Exercises
Reading critically

PART A: No amount of practice will help you if you don't know your stuff. As there's no substitute for simply *knowing what the literature says*, this exercise requires you to take a subject you know well and extract its core propositions.

1 For each journal article, chapter or book that you have read on a topic, write down up to three grammatical sentences, in your own words, which summarize its main arguments.
2 Write down the three main *controversies* in that literature.
3 Consider what the literature *doesn't say*. Write down what scholars fail to consider or explain.

For example, three works on prison policy could be summarized as follows:

- Alexander: Mass incarceration is a system of social control that resembles Jim Crow.
- Miller: Institutional fragmentation facilitates a punitive response by policymakers.
- Weaver: Conservatives rhetorically sharpened the connection between civil rights and crime.

There is disagreement about the extent to which state punitivity is related to actual crime, the level of support for punishment in violent areas and the appropriateness of the Jim Crow metaphor.

PART B: One way to summarize an author's argument in scholarly articles and books is to draw it as a diagram, labelling nodes and vectors. Draw the following arguments as a diagram and think about how sound the connections are.

1 *On how to suppress political factions*: 'There are two methods of curing the mischiefs of faction: the one, by removing its causes; the other, by controlling its effects. There are again two methods of removing the causes of faction: the one, by destroying the liberty which is essential to its existence; the other, by giving to every citizen the same opinions, the same passions, and the same interests. It could never be more truly said than of the first remedy, that it was worse than the disease... The second expedient is as impracticable as the first would be unwise... The inference to which we are brought is, that the CAUSES of faction cannot be removed, and that relief is only to be sought in the means of controlling its EFFECTS. If a faction consists of less than a majority, relief

is supplied by the republican principle, which enables the majority to defeat its sinister views by regular vote.' (Hamilton, Madison and Jay 2008, bk. Federalist 10)

2 *On achieving successful crop rotation*: 'The success of rotation systems for weed suppression appears to be based on the use of crop sequences that create varying patterns of resource competition, allelopathic interference, soil disturbance, and mechanical damage to provide an unstable and frequently inhospitable environment that prevents the proliferation of a particular weed species... Many aspects of crop rotation and intercropping are compatible with current farming practices and could become more accessible to farmers if government policies are restructured to reflect the true environmental costs of agricultural production.' (Liebman and Dyck 1993, [abstract])

3 *On recruitment to the British House of Lords*: 'New entrants to the British peerage between 1700 and 1850 included both traditional landed magnates and men from humbler backgrounds. The rate of recruitment accelerated rapidly after 1782... While the inclusion of large numbers of Irish and Scottish grandees sustained the longitudinal sinews of the peerage, war and empire produced an increasing number of titles awarded on merit. Men of modest backgrounds had always been admitted to the elite, but 'Old Corruption' and the marriage market allowed most of their descendants to blend in with the old peerage after a few generations. The wave of new recruits, especially after 1782, included numerous relatively poor or landless men, and governments increasingly intervened with grants of multi-generational annuities in order to protect the status of the peerage while continuing to use titles to reward new men. Ministers boldly and astutely acted both to preserve the pre-eminence of the old order and encourage the prowess of state servants as Britain bestrode the globe...' (McCahill and Wasson 2003, [abstract])

4 *On autonomous vehicles*: 'Autonomous vehicles (AVs) should reduce traffic accidents, but they will sometimes have to choose between two evils, such as running over pedestrians or sacrificing themselves and their passenger to save the pedestrians. Defining the algorithms that will help AVs make these moral decisions is a formidable challenge. We found that participants in six Amazon Mechanical Turk studies approved of utilitarian AVs (that is, AVs that sacrifice their passengers for the greater good) and would like others to buy them, but they would themselves prefer to ride in AVs that protect their passengers at all costs. The study participants disapprove of enforcing utilitarian regulations for AVs and would be less willing to buy such an

AV. Accordingly, regulating for utilitarian algorithms may paradoxically increase casualties by postponing the adoption of a safer technology.' (Bonnefon, Shariff and Rahwan 2016, [abstract])

5 *On conspiracy theories*: 'Focusing on a contemporary conspiracy theory popularized in the novel *The Da Vinci Code* (Brown, 2002), we examined the underlying psychological factors and individual differences that may predict belief in conspiracy theories, and assessed such beliefs' resistance to counterevidence. Our results suggest that belief in the *Da Vinci Code* conspiracy may be associated with coping with existential threat and death-related anxiety. In addition, the extent to which participants believed in the conspiracy was associated with the endorsement of congruent (New Age spiritual) and competing (Christian religious) beliefs, in opposite directions. Finally, exposure to counterevidence resulted in belief reduction, specifically among more religious participants (i.e. among those endorsing a competing belief system). We suggest that belief in modern conspiracy theories may help individuals attain or maintain a sense of meaning, control, and security.' (Newheiser, Farias and Tausch 2011, [abstract])

Examination Preparation

Essay technique in examinations is fundamentally the same as regular essay writing in that you are answering a specific question by making a clear, consistent, convincing argument. You deploy evidence and enter into a conversation with the scholarly literature. Above all, examinations are about *thinking*, not just remembering (although remembering is also important, as I discuss later in this chapter). You should plan to do fresh thinking in an examination rather than merely regurgitating what you have learned during the year. You will need to construct an original response to a question you have not seen before. Don't fall into the trap of spotting a familiar concept and writing a rehearsed answer on that topic. It is unlikely to address the question set – and will rule you out of the top grades.

You are in the business of persuading readers: your professors and external examiners. Think about that audience. These are not your parents, friends, fellow blog commentators or a newspaper audience. Academics reading your work already know plenty about your area of study, so they don't want to read a load of basic facts or everything you happen to be able to remember about a topic. Instead, what they want is an answer that *you* have come up with in response to a *particular* question. Think about what that question is really asking you to do, using the techniques we identified in Chapters 1, 2 and 3 on **examining assumptions, finding comparator classes** and **interrogating tensions in questions**.

These points about clear, consistent, convincing arguments – and avoiding the splurge of random information – are the same regardless of whether you are writing a regular essay or an examination one, but there are some key differences between examinations and regular essays. In this chapter, I'll go through each one and offer some tips to improve your examination performance.

First, you have a very short time frame. For a standard university examination, you have only an hour per question. Make sure you check precisely how long your examinations will be so you can prepare accordingly. The short time frame means two things: that you need to prioritize thinking time and that you must be extra careful to avoid any word wastage. Let's look at these in turn.

Prioritizing thinking time and avoiding word wastage

Prioritizing thinking time means that you should never just start scribbling as soon as you open the paper. One of my wonderful undergraduate tutors gave us a great examination tip, which I hereby bequeath to you, my readers: No matter how hard your pulse is racing when you're sitting in that dreaded examination hall and the invigilator says 'You may turn over your papers now', you should sit back in your chair for a minute, fold your arms, spot the people in the hall who are already writing, and mentally say to yourself: 'fail', 'she's failed', 'he's failed over there'.

The point is that writing straight away is a terrible idea because you are pretty much guaranteed to write third-rate material. Anticipate devoting a good 20% or so of your entire essay-writing time to preparation and essay planning. Don't take the 20% figure as set in stone, however. There is no strict formula about precisely how many minutes you should spend on this question or that; you should aim to respond flexibly to the material you are given. Some essay questions require more planning time than others, and how you break down that time will depend upon your own essay-writing style, your subject and the question.

Your planning stage will involve some combination of reading and re-reading the essay questions, defining your key terms and considering whether there are any hidden assumptions embedded in your chosen questions, identifying the key argument you will make in the essay – your main take-home – and writing it out as a single grammatical sentence, considering which empirical cases you might deploy in the service of your argument and thinking about how representative those cases are of the broader phenomenon you are considering. This way, once you start writing you will have a crystal clear sense of precisely where you answers are going. This approach will actually save you time because you won't have to pause much during the essay writing itself to consider your next step. You will have prepared thoroughly enough that writing is simply a matter of executing your plan.

If you have done enough preparation, you should be able to avoid word wastage, which is a big pitfall in timed examinations. By 'word wastage', I mean unnecessary verbiage:

> *For many years, scholars have argued that one of the things that it is important for people to know about the topic of Guattari's notion of rhizomatic assemblages...*

Or simple restatements of the question:

> *This question asks whether television has influenced interest groups' strategies and behaviour, so I will consider whether television has influenced interest groups' strategies and behaviour.*

Or phrases that state the obvious:

> *In order to answer this question, we need to define our key terms.*

Instead of writing these long, boring, tangled sentences, you should substitute clean, lean prose. I, your professor, know what the question is, because I set it. I don't need a restatement of the question. I just need your answer! Also, I don't need to be told that it's important to define your key terms. If I had a penny for every time an earnest student wrote that phrase in my exams, I'd be a rich person rather than just a frustrated one. JUST DO IT. Just define your terms right there and save yourself time. Give your answer as clearly and as early as humanly possible.

In short, you need lean meat with absolutely no fat on it at all. Before the examination, I recommend practising writing timed essay introductions (ten minutes a pop), swapping with a friend, and ruthlessly cutting out each other's unnecessary verbiage. I guarantee *that* will be time well spent.

Have a go at avoiding word wastage

Imagine you were answering the examination question: **Is democracy a universal concept?** *For each of the statements below, consider whether you would cut, modify or keep it in your examination essay. The answers are on p. 172.*

1 It is important to define the term 'democracy'.
2 This question asks us whether democracy is a universal concept or not.
3 Democracy is a mode of group decision-making characterized by participant equality.
4 Is democracy a universal concept?
5 There are many possible definitions of 'democracy'.
6 Does democracy really apply to everyone, everywhere? Should it?
7 I will start by considering the term 'democracy' and then I will go on to discuss the concept of universality.
8 A form of democracy acceptable to all peoples in the world must respect unique cultural identities but retain sufficient internal homogeneity that it can still be termed 'democracy': namely mechanisms of accountability, the rule of law and free exchange of information.
9 This examination essay will discuss the issue of whether democracy in fact applies to every person, everywhere in the world, and if so, what the implications of this fact might be.
10 In order to be able to answer the title question, it is necessary to examine and define some of the words and phrases used in order to establish what this essay will consider and answer.
11 Several case studies shall be presented to suggest how democracy might or might not be understood as a universal concept.
12 Even if we say that democracy is a superior type of government, the question still remains about which conception of democracy (if there is one) would actually be acceptable to every person in the world.

Revising well

The second thing that distinguishes examinations is that you can't look things up. It all needs to be in your head, so be canny about what you put there. It is important to select your cases with care. You don't want to simply litter your examination paper with random examples. That is where rote learning can help. If you take a bit of time to learn some lists of figures, dates and quantitative data, not only will you be able to deploy that evidence in the exam but you should be able to contextualize your case studies better. I don't mean just splurge out that data in a big descriptive wodge. I mean select the pieces of evidence that help you make your case, and use the wider lists of data you've rote-learned to contextualize that evidence.

For example, let's say that in addition to your excellent class work on the US Supreme Court, you have learned off-by-heart the names of all 17 of the Chief Justices going back to the American founding. You followed up by developing your knowledge of particular cases. If there is a question about the power of the Chief Justice vis-à-vis Associate Justices, then you can not only talk knowledgeably about particular Chiefs but also show your reader how similar he was to Chiefs who preceded or succeeded him in office. That is much more compelling for the reader than just focusing on the Chief Justice most mentioned in your textbook. Rote learning helps you choose and contextualize cases.

EXERCISE 11.2

Have a go at rote learning for examinations

For an examination, some rote learning can give you confidence and context. Take a set of names, dates or places from your own subject and time yourself: ten minutes to memorize them, ten minutes to check and correct and another five minutes to write them out in order without notes.

To see how much you can remember, try the following:

- Post-war presidents of the United States up to the 2020 presidential election (13)
- English monarchs (Houses of Plantagenet, Lancaster and York) from 1216 to 1485 (13)
- Member countries of NATO (30)
- Transition metals in the periodic table (36)

The answers are on p. 173.

Students often ask me how many topics they should revise. The answer is 'How long is a piece of string?' But I generally warn students against sailing too close to the wind by revising too little of the course; you never know when you'll find a stinker of a question on your preferred topic. For more on the question of revision strategies, see the **frequently asked questions** in the next chapter. It's up to your individual willingness to take risks and your knowledge of the past papers. One way to revise smart is to think about which bits of information could be connected with others, repurposed under different sorts of questions, and play different roles under various rubrics. That should help you to cover enough ground to avoid wipe-out, without forcing you to spread your revision too thinly.

On its own, of course, rote learning can take you only so far. There is no substitute for the deep learning you will have engaged in during your courses throughout your time at university. You certainly cannot write a brilliant examination answer without deep knowledge and understanding of the material the exam covers, but *some* rote learning, alongside the work you have done throughout the year, can help you increase the speed and efficiency of your examination technique.

Handwritten essays

The third thing that distinguishes examinations from regular essay writing is that your examinations are generally handwritten from start to finish, without the opportunity to go back and insert sections. Some students write the introduction last, inserting it after leaving a space, but this often looks clunky. I would advise against it. If you've spent enough time thinking before you put pen to paper, then you should know before you even start writing precisely what your main take-homes are going to be. You write them in your introduction, and then the remainder of your essay will flow logically from those premises.

An examination essay should be like a beautiful wedding cake: clear, smooth layers without any indication of the mess and hard work that went into making it.

Your examiners, like your wedding guests, shouldn't have to see you actually working things out in your examination essay. That part comes beforehand, and you present only the smooth finished product – the core argument, answering the specific question asked, using carefully selected literature and evidence. I recommend practising moving all the way from start to finish in a smooth and logical fashion, using hand-written test papers.

EXERCISE 11.3

Have a go at examination planning

Take another timed challenge! For each of the questions below, take no more than ten minutes to rough out a plan for how you would approach the essay in an examination.

Make sure your plan is as concrete and specific as possible. That means, don't just identify the thing you need to do, but actually do it. Don't just say: 'I need to define my terms at the start', but actually define them, according to your knowledge of each topic. At the start of each plan, write out your core take-home (your main argument) as a single grammatical sentence. Suggested essay plans are the answers are on p. 173.

1 Why are trees vital for humanity?
2 Should assisted dying be legalized?
3 Which are the most important human rights?
4 Are we all feminists now?
5 What explains national variations in crime rates?

A brilliant examination essay contains, in condensed form, all of the elements that we have discussed throughout this book. You need to consider the terms of the question: what is it really asking? Are there any assumptions hidden under the surface that need to be brought to light? Are those assumptions (if there are any) justified? How can we define the key concepts in the question? Your core take-home should be identified in propositional form at the outset, so the reader is left in no doubt about your position on the question at hand. You may not need an elaborate bibliography or lengthy references, but you will need to situate your argument with respect to relevant scholarly literature, and you will need to advance empirical evidence and sound reasoning to build your case.

Cut out all unnecessary verbiage. Rote learn so that you can select your cases with care on the day, and make your essays as smooth as a wedding cake by spending plenty of time thinking before you write.

Chapter 11 Exercises
Examination preparation

PART A: Try cutting the unnecessary verbiage in the following sentences, leaving only lean meat behind.

1 Can computers think? In terms of clarifying what is meant by 'think', in this essay I will consider what various scholars have said about what 'thinking' comprises and will consider four possible ways of describing something as 'thinking', to wit, thinking in terms of emotions, images, abstract concepts and raw intelligence.

2 The American state is a relatively young and intricate formulation of institutions, agencies and establishments among its different branches (legislative, executive and judicial) which are crucial and that have progressively evolved and sufficed the operation of the US since the Declaration of Independence in 1776.

3 To answer the question of why the Mongol empire disintegrated during the late thirteenth century, it is important to first understand what is meant in this case by disintegration (such as changing loyalties, factionalism and civil war) because there are many different ways for us to try to understand this question, as several scholars have noted.

PART B: For each of the sentences below, say whether you would (a) include it in your examination script in its *current* form, (b) include it in your examination script in *modified* form or (c) *cut* the sentence entirely. If you choose (b), say how you would improve it. If you choose (a) or (c), explain why.

4 In order to answer this question, we need to define our key terminology and consider any assumptions underlying the question.

5 For decades, neo-colonialism has been the subject of much study by scholars.

6 By asking what price the US pays for its exceptionalism, this question assumes that the US is indeed exceptional.

7 Is the presidency the illusion of choice? The question, though concise, leads to a series of ongoing questions highlighting its ambiguity. This in turn intensifies the difficulty of answering the question, where do I begin?

8 I argue that a misplaced focus on comparing the American state to European states has led to inaccurate claims of apparent weakness. Not only was the American state *not* weak from its birth, but it has only grown in strength.

9 Throughout history, there has been strong and continual debate about how the landscape is shaped by human activity.

PART C: Take on the timed examination challenge! Spend 15 minutes planning and 15 minutes writing a handwritten exam-style introduction on a question of your choice. Alternatively, practise your technique with this question: 'Why is [insert your university's name here] the best place to study?'

Frequently Asked Questions

General questions

What counts as originality of thought?

You've looked at the marking guidelines for your course, and under the top-grade banding is listed 'originality of thought' – but what on earth is that? It can be many things: drawing new theoretical distinctions, introducing a novel argument, collecting fresh empirical evidence or making connections by applying a theory in one discipline to another. Nobody is expecting you to redraw the boundaries of your discipline in a single university essay, but you can stick out from the crowd by actively evaluating a question and coming to a judgement about it. Use the 'Have a go' exercises throughout this book to practise critically evaluating each question.

My advice is not to stress unduly about 'demonstrating originality' –
that can seem a mountain to climb – but simply focus on developing an
interesting and persuasive answer to the question at hand. Chapters 1, 2
and 3 on **examining assumptions, finding comparator classes**
and **interrogating tensions** are a good starting point. You may also
wish to take a look through the suggestions in the Conclusion to this
volume.

How do I choose my own essay title?

It can be bewildering to have to create an essay title from scratch. Take
advice from people in your discipline. Many tutors will allow you to
modify existing course questions, or you could take a provocative
quotation from the scholarly literature as your starting point (add
'Discuss' afterwards). Make sure your question allows you to use higher-
order skills of evaluation and analysis, so don't create purely descriptive
questions. For inspiration, read a clutch of journal articles in your field,
drawing out the research question each one tackles. What sorts of
questions do scholars consider?

What should I do if my essay is under the word count?

Universities typically have penalties for over-length work, but many don't
have specific rules about under-length essays. An over-length essay is
often a bit flabby: padded out with the sort of unnecessary verbiage we
encountered in Chapter 6 on **writing elegantly**. Fewer essays come up
significantly under-length. If you find yourself with a yawning chasm in
your work, don't be tempted to extend the length of your sentences or
fluff it up with basic background information. That approach is all but
guaranteed to reduce your grade.

Under-length essays may have an argument that is too brief or does
not spell out its reasoning for the reader. Take another look at your
argument and try mapping out your reasoning using a diagram, as we
did in Chapter 10 on **reading critically**. As you identify the propositions
that build up your arguments, check that you have evidenced them
properly. What would a sceptical reader say? What possible counter-
arguments might they advance? If you have some shaky propositions in
there, beef up your reasoning and empirical evidence to support them.
Check also that the links in your argument are explicit to the reader. You
might wish to swap essays with a classmate and ask them whether they
can follow your reasoning, point by point.

Questions about reading

How do I find good readings?

Start with the reading list, obviously, and follow up by looking through the references section of each journal article or book. Snowballing – that is, using these references to find recommendations for other materials – will help you identify additional readings fast. Next, check in with your course tutor and ask them for reading recommendations. I also suggest using the search function for the top-rated scholarly journals in your field (if you are in doubt about which journals these are, ask your tutor) to look for key words in your question.

Feel free to use Google Scholar too, but always use your common sense to detect whether a particular reading is important and relevant to your question. You don't want your essay to spin off in a weird direction. Identify the core proposition advanced by each new piece of literature you encounter; consider how that proposition fits with the canonical texts you have read for your course.

As long as you keep your question and the core reading firmly in mind, you should feel free to search beyond the lists. The fun of writing an essay is that this is your party: the more creative and purposeful you can be in searching out books and articles that truly interest you, the more enjoyable the task of putting together an essay – and the more impressive it will be to your audience.

How do I pick out essential information when reading for an essay?

Personally, I hate highlighters. They encourage you to underline sections of text mindlessly without truly taking anything in. A better way to pick out essential information is to take five minutes at the end to jot down the core take-home of each article you read in propositional form – that is, as one, two or at most three grammatical sentences. You'll find that you get more efficient at this as you practise. Like a lawyer, you'll be constantly scanning the document for the main arguments – even as you zone in on particular details. See Chapters 8 and 10 on **syllogisms and summaries** and **reading critically** for more advice.

How should I structure a literature review?

If you are writing a dissertation or a much longer piece of coursework, you may be required to write a literature review: a survey and discussion of the main findings in the scholarly literature. For regular coursework with shorter word limits or for examination essays, you still need to show knowledge of relevant scholarly literature but you should not write a separate 'literature review' section unless your tutor has specifically asked for one. A separate literature review takes up too large a proportion of the word count of regular essays. Better to situate your own argument with respect to the literature throughout, integrating discussion of other scholars as you answer the question at hand rather than writing a separate section. Your writing will flow better that way too, and it will be easier to stay focused on the question and avoid getting side-tracked from your argument.

For longer pieces of writing where you *have* been asked for a separate literature review, there are many compelling ways to structure it. Avoid a descriptive laundry list of claims ('Professor X says this, Professor Y says that, Professor Z argues this other thing'). Instead, think about how you might organize the material in a way that suits your question. As we discussed in Chapter 10 on **reading critically**, you should read *actively*: summarize authors' key claims in your own words as grammatical sentences, jot down their definitions of core terminology, and forge connections between different authors by considering how you would adjudicate disputes between them. A good literature review is the product of active reading.

When reading, you notice where the disputes lie in the literature and consider any gaps: what do we (collectively, as scholars) know about this issue, and what *don't* we know? One way to structure a literature review is to identify the main problems or puzzles in your discipline and show how different scholars seek to resolve each of them in turn. Another way to structure the review section would be to take a chronological approach, showing how each subsequent generation of scholarship built upon (or sought to demolish) the ones that went before. Alternatively, you could start with the meatiest and most complex concept in your question ('power', 'consciousness', 'history') and unpack its various dimensions, showing the reader how other scholars have sought to define this core concept and the implications of each definition.

However you choose to structure your literature review, remember that you are in charge. A literature review exists to help you craft a larger argument. You are not simply describing scholarly debates for the sake of it, but to set the stage for your own argument. That means you should take a sceptical approach. If you think a certain scholar has missed a crucial piece of evidence or that a particular scholar's definition of the core terminology is unreasonable or that a proposed resolution to a puzzle fails, then *say so* right there in your literature review and explain why. You are guiding your reader through the literature review, so your voice needs to come to the fore.

How many authors should I cite?

There is no hard and fast rule about how many authors to cite. One of the characteristics of a brilliant essay is that it is deeply informed by – and in conversation with – a range of scholarly literature, but since you have limited space you'll need to make an intelligent choice about what to cite. It's not just about name-checking. Think what each citation does for your argument: are you agreeing or disagreeing with these scholars? Do they introduce a theoretical distinction or empirical finding that will help you build your argument? Do they propose a counter-argument that you need to address? See Chapters 7 and 10 on **using empirical evidence** and **reading critically** for more advice.

Are examples better if they're provided in the literature?

In short, no. There are no special marks to be gained from using examples the literature cites. Of course, there may be good reasons why a particular example is frequently deployed in the literature – and those reasons may persuade you to cite that example too – but beware of mindlessly sprinkling your essay with examples plucked from the secondary literature *simply because they feature* in that literature. Better to make your own judgement about which examples are most appropriate for your purposes.

Questions about evidence

Should I pick a single case or compare a variety of different cases?

A brilliant essay could do either. If your tutor has asked explicitly for a comparative account or a single case study, obviously follow their steer. If not, then the choice is up to you. There is no strict formula! Both approaches have advantages and disadvantages, as we discussed in Chapter 7 on **using empirical evidence**. The answer to this question depends upon the question asked. Even if you are writing a single case study, you should always be able to answer the questions we considered in Chapter 2 on **finding comparator classes**: of what is this a case? And compared with what? You need to know your domain of reference so that you can be clear about precisely what your essay is asserting about a particular case. Zooming out and offering a broad-brush comparative account can be a successful strategy, but even if you are comparing many different cases you will always need to be aware of what is happening in particular cases, so that you can make the logic of your argument explicit to your reader.

What is the relative weight of evidence and theory in a brilliant essay?

This question is 'How long is a piece of string?' because there is no single best way to balance theory and evidence. A top-grade essay could be highly theoretical or a deeply informed empirical piece. If your tutor has specific guidelines, then obviously you should follow them. If not, step back from the question and consider what it is asking you to do. Have confidence in your own judgement.

Questions about examinations

When it comes to examinations, how many topics should I revise?

The question of how many topics to revise comes down to your individual appetite for risk. Some students take a riskier approach by concentrating their revision on only part of the course, whereas others take a more risk-averse (but potentially less efficient) approach by revising absolutely everything. I recommend revising enough so you can be confident of answering the required number of questions well, with enough back-up in case you don't like the questions on your preferred material.

Beware of thinking about 'topics' as insulated silos. 'Topics' on a university course are not usually separated very precisely. The course tutor will have divided up the material in whichever way facilitated the delivery of the appropriate number of lectures and seminars, but you will have encountered synoptic material straddling multiple weeks of teaching. Rather than taking the formulaic topic-by-topic approach to revision that you may have adopted (with some success!) in school, step back and consider how the material you learned in one part of the course informs the material you encountered later. How did your ideas change over the course? Were your expectations of the course at the outset confirmed or disconfirmed by the course material? Can you bring the scholars you encountered at different ends of the course into dialogue with each other?

Thinking about how different parts of the course fit together will stop you from trying to recall specific 'topics' (a boring task) and help you start thinking about the material from new angles (an interesting task). Thinking afresh will boost your recall into the bargain. Revise as much of the course as will make you confident you can answer the correct number of questions, leaving space for choice, and keep in mind how each part fits into the whole.

How should I reference scholarly literature in an examination? Is it like a coursework essay?

Your university or course tutor may have specific guidelines on referencing in examinations, so check those first and follow them. If you don't have any institutional rules on referencing, allow yourself to be guided by the examination format. Most likely, you will be handwriting answers to unseen questions under a time limit, or you might have an online take-home paper to be completed in a few hours. Obviously, this is no time for fancy bibliographies or perfectly formatted endnotes. Think about the purpose of a citation: it is to help the reader to identify the scholarly literature to which you are speaking.

As with a regular coursework essay, you will need to bring your argument into a dialogue with relevant scholarly literature, so your citations need to make it possible for the reader to identify the correct authors. A surname and date should suffice for most journal papers and books. If there is a crucial difference between (Campbell 1993a) and (Campbell 1993b) – and it is essential that your reader know which of the prolific Campbell's outputs you are referring to – then you should certainly mark it out as such, but it's unlikely you will need to refer to two papers with that degree of specificity.

If the reader knows who and what you're talking about, job done. Don't waste any time memorizing extraneous bibliographic elements (except spelling: get the trickier names of professors right – especially the ones that formed part of your core readings – and avoid irritating your examiner unnecessarily!) Your examiner is most interested in your *thinking* on the question, rather than your ability to format a pristine bibliography.

Questions about anxiety and confidence

I feel completely stuck. What should I do?

Writing brilliant essays – like all scholarly activities – is fundamentally a creative process. You need to *think afresh* about a scholarly puzzle and craft your own answer to a question. Such creativity cannot be forced. It might seem frightening to embark on a new essay when you are unsure at the outset where your thinking will take you. It may be tempting to fall back on the tried and tested approaches from school, but resist the temptation: it will lead you to vanilla middling grades at best. Jettisoning the training wheels and shaking off the tired old school formulas is a risk, but with risk comes reward! To write a brilliant essay, you need to have confidence in yourself.

How to induce such confidence? By being as practical about the task as possible: break down the process into manageable steps, use your natural understanding of everyday language to guide your initial thinking, and read as much of the scholarly literature as you can. Start with the question itself and use the techniques we identified in Chapters 1, 2 and 3 on **examining assumptions, finding comparator classes** and **interrogating tensions in questions** to consider what your question is really asking. You may be surprised how much you can glean from the question alone.

Ask yourself which are the core concepts in the question and jot down various possible definitions. Do those concepts have different dimensions or manifestations? What are the comparator classes? What relationship does the question assert between two variables? Asking these sorts of questions and bringing your natural understanding of language, everyday knowledge, classroom discussions and literature to bear upon the question at hand often provoke new insights. If inspiration fails to strike, reading what other scholars have had to say will help you map out the field and start to identify connections and gaps that may be relevant to your question.

Resist the temptation to email your course tutor as soon as you feel a twinge of unease. Say to yourself: I will email them in, say, a day's time if I haven't yet made progress. Of course, I don't mean to suggest that you should *never* email your tutor – you should certainly speak to them if you are completely at sea or the demands of the assignment are affecting your mental health – but under normal circumstances, you will feel more confident if you can start to think about these questions by yourself. Give yourself credit and have a go first. If you do need to speak to your tutor, your communications will be far more effective if you can come prepared with some targeted questions arising from your own thinking rather than a vague plea for help.

I am anxious and feeling out of my depth at university. How will I cope with writing essays?

It's perfectly normal to feel a bit anxious. You're not alone. I promise you – we've all been there! I didn't arrive at university already able to write brilliant essays (in fact, I think I only really cracked it towards the end of my undergraduate degree), and nobody is expecting you to write perfectly at the outset either. It takes plenty of trial and error to get better and that's okay. Everybody is learning.

One of the things that can happen when you're anxious is that you fall back on formulaic approaches from school (see Chapter 9 on **losing the training wheels** for examples). If you can loosen up a bit and actively evaluate each question, you'll have a much more rewarding essay-writing experience – and you may start to feel more convinced that you can pull it off.

Conclusion: Techniques for Writing Brilliant Essays

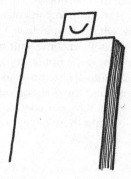

Now that you have read this book, you should feel more confident about your essay-writing abilities. To write a brilliant essay, you need to loosen up and think around your question. Pick the question apart, identifying different possible definitions of the core conceptual apparatus and considering whether the question makes any dubious assumptions. Read actively, give away your take-home at the outset, situate your argument with respect to claims made in the literature, and make defensible decisions about which empirical cases you cite. There is no strict formula for a top grade because there are multiple pathways to brilliant work, but you can use the practical techniques in this book to get better at recognizing and taking advantage of opportunities that come your way.

Remember, it is okay to try new things and make mistakes while you are at university. We are all – academics, postgraduates and undergraduates alike – engaged in a continuous process of learning. We are a scholarly community. Don't allow fear to prevent you from taking some calculated risks. It is only when we open ourselves up to the possibility of failure – and the excitement and enjoyment of writing something truly original – that we can move from the humdrum middle to the highest grades. We need to lose the tedious training wheels.

In this book, you have encountered many techniques for thinking around your essay questions. If you are not sure where to start, you can explore the following avenues:

Approach your essay question critically Define the key concepts, think about how they relate to one another, and root out any assumptions the question is making. In particular, look out for questions phrased as 'why, what, when or how X?' (such questions assume *that X is indeed the case*). Any time your question uses the words 'but' or 'or', consider how the options presented relate to one another: are the categories mutually exclusive and collectively exhaustive? Have a go at reading the question out loud. By putting emphasis on different words in turn, consider various different comparator classes. Where might these different comparators lead your essay?

Read actively Enter into a conversation with the scholarly literature rather than arguing by citation: that is, don't simply re-explain the literature. What are the controversies in the literature? What does the literature miss? Where does your argument fit with respect to the claims in the literature? In order to engage with the literature properly, you need to know what it says. Read as widely as possible and practise summarizing the key arguments in your own words. As you read, look out for the authors' definitions of the concepts in your essay questions and imagine how you would adjudicate a (real or imagined) debate between different scholars.

Control your argument Make a clear, consistent, convincing case throughout the essay, so each section follows logically from the previous one. Be ruthless about cutting all information that does not contribute directly to the question at hand. You could use a syllogism to summarize the premises and conclusion of your own argument and those you read. Are the premises true and does the conclusion follow from them? Give away your key take-home at the outset rather than leaving the final reveal until your concluding paragraph. That means you should briefly explain your own view in your introduction instead of merely identifying the question. Could your reader discern the question on the basis of your opening paragraph alone?

Make your writing more elegant Don't spend ages saying you need to define this or that. Just define your terms, right there in the text, and save yourself many boring words. Don't give your tutor a general commentary on what a good essay is supposed to contain. Write about ideas themselves rather than the scholarly activities needed to produce those ideas. Write with confidence by qualifying rather than hedging: give your readers a concrete and specific account of the conditions in which a particular statement holds true, enlivened by real empirical cases.

Use empirical evidence deliberately Be absolutely explicit and deliberate about your case selection. Develop your knowledge of the universe of cases such that you can make clear, defensible decisions about what to include and exclude. You show mastery of the material by addressing obvious empirical counter-examples and by being crystal clear about which sorts of cases your argument covers and which it does not. Think about hard, easy, telling and typical cases. What is the universe of cases, and which ones could you select to best persuade your reader that what you have said is true?

All of these suggestions really boil down to the same thing: *think*. Instead of executing a formulaic five-paragraph essay as you might have done at school, make time to consider the terms of the question so that you can make deliberate choices about what your essay will contain and what it will exclude. If you have trouble with essay writing, step back and try out some of the practical techniques in this book. If you give yourself a chance to use your natural language skills, common sense, and ability to read, spot connections or argue a case, you may be surprised how pleasurable essay writing can be. Above all, have confidence in yourself. Enjoy the journey!

Answers to Chapter 1 Exercises

Have a go at finding hidden assumptions

1. Is catastrophism <u>still</u> a useful theory of geological change? (Catastrophism used to be a useful theory of geological change.)
2. In his theory of *simulacra*, does Lucretius address non-visual senses <u>too</u>? (Lucretius addresses visual senses in his theory of *simulacra*.)
3. Do <u>modern</u> Chinese people <u>continue to</u> wear white for mourning? (Historically, Chinese people wore white for mourning.)
4. 'The problem with moral relativism is that it denies societal change.' Discuss. (There is only one problem with moral relativism.)
5. 'T.S. Eliot's *Four Quartets* poem can <u>also</u> be seen as a criticism of classicizing conventions.' Discuss. (The *Four Quartets* poem has more than one function [i.e., functions other than criticism of classicizing conventions].)
6. Is the ideal of a democratic transnational public sphere realistic <u>nowadays</u>? (The ideal of a democratic transnational public sphere was, at some point in the past, realistic.)
7. From a firm's perspective, what is <u>the</u> advantage of giving workers a fixed annual pay increase instead of paying them based on measures of performance? (From a firm's perspective, there *is* one – and only one – advantage of fixed pay rates rather than merit pay.)
8. Few philosophers <u>today</u> are substance-dualists. Why? (More philosophers were substance dualists in the past.)
9. What is <u>the</u> obstacle to adolescent girls, participating in sporting activities? (There is only one obstacle to adolescent girls, participating in sports.)
10. How has increased computational power revolutionized <u>contemporary</u> ecology? (Computational power has increased; modern ecology has been affected by this computational power; formerly, ecology was not so affected by computational power.)

Answers to Chapter 2 Exercises

Have a go at finding different comparator classes

1. 'The <u>international refugee</u> regime is ill suited to deal with <u>contemporary</u> problems in <u>forced</u> migration.' Discuss. (Possible comparators: other types of political regime; historical problems in forced migration; migration that is not forced)

2. 'Even eliminating <u>luck</u> cannot solve Gettier's <u>epistemology</u> problems.' Discuss. (Possible comparators: other things philosophers seek to eliminate in order to solve the epistemology problem Gettier poses; other problems posed by Gettier)

3. 'The <u>global</u> consequences of al-Qaeda's jihad have outstripped its <u>local</u> causes.' Discuss. (Possible comparators: other consequences; other causes)

4. Are <u>hard</u> engineering projects still favoured for <u>flood</u> management in the <u>Netherlands</u>? (Possible comparators: soft engineering; other problems to manage; other countries)

5. Can <u>class-based</u> accounts of voting behaviour help explain <u>Labour's</u> share of the vote in <u>the 2010 general election</u>? (Possible comparators: other accounts of voting behaviour; other political parties; other elections)

6. How important is <u>public awareness</u> in the management of <u>environmental</u> problems? (Possible comparators: factors other than public awareness that affect how environmental problems are managed, such as characteristics of the environment itself, public attitudes, industrial activity; other sorts of problem that we need to manage, such as economic growth or the need to ensure that all people are fed)

7. Why do <u>suicide attacks</u> generate the most <u>newspaper</u> coverage? (Possible comparators: other sorts of attack, such as hijackings, non-suicide bombings, or assassinations; other sorts of media coverage, such as radio or TV)

8. How stable has the <u>sitcom genre</u> been since the 1950s? (Possible comparators: other sorts of TV programme, such as police procedurals, drama, chat show and satire)

9. What is the difference between <u>imagination</u> and <u>belief</u>? (Possible comparators: other ways of representing the world, such as perceiving, desiring or anticipating)

10. How does screening <u>based on higher education</u> help overcome the <u>adverse selection problem</u> associated with hiring? (Possible comparators: other ways to screen applicants for jobs, such as entrance tests or interviews; other problems associated with hiring, such as transaction costs and sunk costs associated with hiring bonuses)

Answers to Chapter 3 Exercises

Have a go at uncovering false dichotomies (or trichotomies)

1. 'Are bananas disgusting or delicious?' (Not collectively exhaustive: bananas could be bland.)
2. 'You are either part of the solution or part of the problem.' (Not collectively exhaustive: you could be an innocent bystander.)
3. 'Is Macbeth a criminal sociopath or a victim?' (Neither mutually exclusive nor collectively exhaustive: Sociopaths can be victims too, and Macbeth could be neither.)
4. 'Which of these solutions will ultimately reverse climate change: more wind turbines, tropical rainforest reforestation or better family planning?' (Neither mutually exclusive nor collectively exhaustive: there are many other ways to combat climate change, and a good strategy will incorporate many different solutions. The hubris of the underlying assumption [that one of these solutions will indeed 'reverse' climate change] is eye-popping!)
5. 'I thought Mia was a good person but she did not attend church on Sunday.' (Assumption: either you attend church or you are a bad person. Not mutually exclusive: people are neither clearly 'good' nor 'bad', church-goer or not.)
6. Is the news media the friend or foe of Prime Ministers? (Not collectively exhaustive: the media could be indifferent to Prime Ministers, or a friend at one time and a foe at others.)
7. Is rape a criminal act or an act of war? (Not mutually exclusive: it could be both, and there may be other ways to characterize rape, in addition to ones listed – not collectively exhaustive.)
8. Are populist radical right parties successful because they are radical right or because they are populist? (Assumes that populist radical right parties ARE successful, and needs a definition of 'successful'. Not mutually exclusive: the combination of populism and radical right beliefs might be what makes such parties successful. Not collectively exhaustive: there might be other characteristics of such parties that help account for their electoral success.)

9. Which poses the greater threat: small arms or 'weapons of mass destruction'? (Depends upon what we understand by 'threat'; answer could vary depending upon the time period or arena of conflict.)
10. Where do food taboos come from: magico-religious beliefs or utilitarian principles? (Neither mutually exclusive nor collectively exhaustive: food taboos could originate both for practical reasons and for spiritual ones. Taboos could also originate for other reasons, such as the ability to bind a community together.)
11. Was Aztec Emperor Montezuma a cruel, power-hungry tyrant or an emotional, credulous weakling? (Neither collectively exhaustive nor mutually exclusive: revisionist scholarship might portray Montezuma as an effective politician, a kind and just king, and a strong leader. Also, nothing about being a cruel tyrant means you can't also be emotional and credulous.)
12. Is urbanization a cause or effect of economic growth? (Not mutually exclusive: it is possible, indeed likely, to be both.)

Have a go at identifying assumptions in 'how', 'when' and 'why' questions

1. Children's rights do differ from other human rights.
2. Gettier problems pose a challenge to internalist accounts of knowledge.
3. John Locke argued for a limited state.
4. Attention to the phenomenology of everyday life can tell us something about the mind–world relation.
5. International police cooperation is very difficult.
6. Queen Elizabeth I did manage to unite the English nation.
7. Terrorism presents problems for international law.
8. The concept of the sublime adds something to our understanding of art.
9. Women need female representatives in Parliament.
10. Humans have impacted tropical ecosystems during the Holocene.
11. There are at least some circumstances in which citizens should obey the state.
12. All of the dinosaurs died out.

Answers to Chapter 4 Exercises

Have a go at deducing the question from the introductory paragraphs

There are several possible 'correct' answers to these questions and readers might reasonably disagree. Some suggestions are below.

1. Why was the French Fourth Republic (1946–1958) unable to maintain itself?
2. Do Plato's strictures against art and poetry have any validity?
3. What drives a consumer's intention to buy counterfeit luxury goods?
4. How do we recognize faces?
5. Do proper names have a sense as well as a reference?

Have a go at identifying the question steer

1. To understand the operation of power, there is no need to look beyond access to economic resources. (Accepting the steer)
   To understand the operation of power, we must look beyond access to economic resources. (Rejecting the steer)
2. There are three propositions on each side of this question.
   Accepting the steer:
   i. We cannot reduce beliefs and desires to neurophysiological states.
   ii. We should eliminate beliefs and desires.
   iii. If something cannot be reduced to a set of neurophysiological states, it cannot exist.
   Rejecting the steer:
   i. We <u>can</u> reduce beliefs and desires to neurophysiological states.
   ii. We <u>shouldn't</u> eliminate beliefs and desires.
   iii. Even if something cannot be reduced to a set of neurophysiological states, it may yet exist.
3. Privacy is important. (Accepting the steer)
   Privacy is not important. (Rejecting the steer)

4. There are two propositions on each side of this question.
   Accepting the steer:
   i. The concept of 'new social movements' is increasingly dated.
   ii. The concept of 'new social movements' is of limited analytical value.
   Rejecting the steer:

   i. The concept of 'new social movements' is not dated.
   ii. The concept of 'new social movements' has analytical value.
5. The phrase 'give us reason to doubt this' makes the questioner sound sceptical, so the question steers the reader to doubt the truth of the quotation accordingly: Consciousness is <u>not</u> an entirely private, first-person phenomenon. (Accepting the steer)
   Consciousness is an entirely private, first-person phenomenon. (Rejecting the steer)
6. By using the term 'simply', the questioner prompts the reader to doubt the proposition.
   The European Union is <u>not only</u> an international organization controlled by the governments of its member states <u>but something else too</u>. (Accepting the steer)
   The European Union is <u>simply</u> an international organization controlled by the governments of its member states. (Rejecting the steer)
7. There are three propositions on each side of this question.
   Accepting the steer:
   i. Logic is ontologically neutral.
   ii. Tarski's account of logical consequence is false.
   iii. Tarski's account must be false *because* logic is ontologically neutral.

   Rejecting the steer:
   i. Logic is <u>not</u> ontologically neutral.
   ii. Tarski's account of logical consequence is true.
   iii. Even if logic is ontologically neutral, Tarski's account is not necessarily false.
8. There is at least one theory of political economy which <u>can</u> help us understand the governance of climate change. (Accepting the steer)
   Theories of political economy are useless at helping us understand the governance of climate change. (Rejecting the steer)
9. There are two different ways to reject the steer.
   Religion is politically significant but its relationship with 'party' is not its main significance. (Accepting the steer)
   Religion is <u>not</u> politically significant. (One way to reject the steer)
   Religion <u>is</u> politically significant and its relationship with 'party' <u>is</u> its main significance. (Another way to reject the steer)

10. There are two propositions on each side of this question.
    Accepting the steer:
    i. The problem of evil is important for Augustine's philosophy.
    ii. The problem of evil is problematic for Augustine's philosophy.
    Rejecting the steer:

    i. The problem of evil is <u>not</u> important for Augustine's philosophy.
    ii. The problem of evil is <u>not</u> problematic for Augustine's philosophy.

Have a go at identifying a logical essay structure

There are many possible ways to structure an answer to these essay
questions and readers might reasonably disagree. Some suggestions are
below.

Q1: *What, if anything, is problematic about the involvement of celebrities in
    democratic politics?*

- Elucidate various forms of power; explain why 'epistemic' power is
  important.
- Consider how epistemic power threatens three understandings of
  democracy in turn:
  1. Deliberative democracy
  2. Epistemic democracy
  3. Plebiscitary democracy

Q2: *What explains racial disparities in discipline and punishment rates in
    schools?*

- Situate the under-diagnosis of disabilities in the context of other
  factors explaining racial disparities in disciplinary rates (such as
  poverty, segregation and school governance).
- Examine each stage of the school-to-prison pipeline in chronological order:
  1. Embedded racism in schools leads to...
  2. Schools under-diagnosing and under-treating disabled black
     children, which leads to...
  3. Over-punishment of black children, which leads to...
  4. Greater likelihood of black children becoming enmeshed in the
     justice system.

Q3: How do urban governments respond to immigrants?

- Show how multi-level theories of urban governance differ from top–down and bottom–up models.
- Show how federal constraints upon local policymaking autonomy affect local officials'...
  1. Immediate behaviour
  2. Longer-term views and actions

Answers to Chapter 5 Exercises

Have a go at cutting basic background information

1. Karl Marx was a nineteenth-century German philosopher, economist, historian and socialist revolutionary. – CUT
2. The state is an important organization. – CUT
3. Marx has been described as one of the most influential figures in human history. – CUT
4. By 1857, Marx accumulated over 800 pages of notes and short essays on capital, landed property, wage labour and the state. – CUT
5. Marx did not deliberately set out to create a systematic theory of the state. – KEEP
6. There are many theories of the state. – CUT
7. It is important to remain neutral with regard to Marx's writings on the state, which are difficult to understand. – CUT
8. Marx's earliest writings identify the state as the guardian of the general interest, but in his later works the state is re-imagined as a weapon used by the bourgeoisie to oppress the workers. – KEEP

Have a go at staying on-piste

The underlined sections indicate where the author has gone off-piste, including irrelevant information that does not help answer the question posed.

1. The greater the party polarization, the greater the gridlock effect on congressional law-making. Polarization is the combination of ideological homogenization within parties and ideological divergence between parties. In Japan, the National Diet was largely controlled by the Liberal Democratic Party for much of its history. In Nicaragua, by contrast, you have a unicameral legislature which is overwhelmingly composed of members representing the Sandinista National Liberation Front. There are many different party types around the world.
2. Polarization comes in several varieties: ideological polarization, where elites and the public express increasingly distinct issue positions around

a left–right continuum; and affective polarization, which is about growing tribalism and dislike of the opposing party. Hegel's concept of _geist_ (spirit) and _Aufhebung_ (sublation of contradictory or opposing factors) expresses a dichotomy of opposites, which is about lifting us mentally to a higher unity. Psychologically, these dispositions arise from moral foundations, because it is important for people to cooperate in groups. Even more than ideological polarization, affective polarization contributes to gridlock by making it harder for lawmakers to cooperate.

3. Division in politics has made it extremely hard for most legislation to pass. The term 'bipartisan' is becoming less and less applicable to real-world US politics. If we look at history, the biggest legislative achievements have usually been done during or in response to a crisis, such as the New Deal, which created the Civilian Conservation Core, the Agricultural Adjustment Act, the National Industrial Act, and many other programmes. The New Deal sustained the Democratic Party and was attacked by Barry Goldwater, the conservative Republican who ran for president during the 1960s.

Have a go at spilling the beans

There are several possible interpretations of Aesop's fables, so don't worry if your answer is different from the ones below. These are simply examples. You may also have expressed your take-home differently. This could be a group exercise: show the stories to some friends and discuss your answers.

1. [The Kid and the Wolf] Time and place can advantage the weak over the strong.
2. [The Hunter and the Woodman] The hero is brave in deeds as well as words.
3. [The Oak and the Reeds] Stoop to conquer.
4. [The Seaside Travellers] Our mere anticipations of life outrun its realities.
5. [The Sick Kite] We must make friends in prosperity if we want their help in adversity.
6. [The Boy and the Nettle] Whatever you do, do with all your might.

Answers to Chapter 6 Exercises

Have a go at avoiding excessive signposting

1. It is important to define the key terms. – UNNECESSARY SIGNPOST
2. Our first question is: what is the main concept? I will consider what the main concept in the question is and define it before moving on. – UNNECESSARY SIGNPOST
3. Mathematicians view measurement as the mapping of qualitative empirical relations to relations among numbers. – USEFUL
4. First we will consider the core concepts, then we will make some arguments in structured sequence, and finally we will conclude with some reflections on what the question means more broadly. – UNNECESSARY SIGNPOST
5. I will criticize the gender binary, arguing that it contributes to the maintenance of oppressive and gendered social orders, and conclude that correcting such oppressions requires attention to multiple aspects of identity, including race, class and disability. – USEFUL
6. Do justice considerations apply to intergenerational relations? That is the question we need to answer in this essay. – UNNECESSARY SIGNPOST
7. Inspections by street-level bureaucrats reveal the relationship between power, ethics and status amongst migrant communities. – USEFUL
8. The last paragraph argued that inspections by street-level bureaucrats reveals the relationship between power, ethics and status amongst migrant communities. – UNNECESSARY SIGNPOST AT THE START
9. Why does this question matter? We need to consider what the implications of this argument are for the broader scholarly literature. – UNNECESSARY SIGNPOST
10. There are many different ways to interpret the core concepts in the question, including 'renewal' and 'subjunctive politics', and I will consider the various ambiguities within these core concepts. – UNNECESSARY SIGNPOST

Have a go at avoiding compulsive hedging

1. Legislation has been effective, <u>but only to a certain degree</u>, to improve racial discrimination.
2. <u>I would argue that</u> Israel/Palestine is a site of bitter struggle over definitions of indigeneity and settlerness.
3. Having a justified true belief is <u>arguably</u> insufficient for knowledge.
4. During the nineteenth century, the Muslim Mediterranean became <u>to some extent</u> a locus of competing imperial projects.
5. The developing culture of mass private automobile ownership in Russia became a <u>relatively</u> prominent platform for post-Soviet citizen-drivers to renegotiate their relationship with the state.
6. In the last few decades, the field of food history has come to fruition, <u>so to speak</u>.
7. It is <u>fairly</u> difficult for Christians to solve the problem of evil.
8. Enslaved property could be <u>relatively</u> easily integrated into aristocratic forms of property-ownership in eighteenth-century Britain.
9. Haitian sea migration and US maritime policing <u>apparently</u> emerged in tandem.
10. <u>Predominantly</u>, an account of consciousness needs an account of mind.

Have a go at identifying the world of studying and the world of ideas

1. Consumers value a transparent, enforceable and traceable monitoring system for animal welfare–friendly products. – IDEAS (KEEP)
2. In recent years, debates about the relationship between culture contact and change following the Roman invasion have become more febrile, as scholars consider new zooarchaeological evidence which may shed light upon these discussions. – STUDYING (CUT)
3. Many surveys have been conducted by scholars to consider the significance of rubber tapping in the Amazon. – STUDYING (CUT)
4. Rubber tapping is a sustainable alternative to forest destruction in the Amazon. – IDEAS (KEEP)
5. In this essay, I argue that sensory interaction with multiple goods helped eighteenth-century consumers to comprehend concepts of design and workmanship. – IDEAS (KEEP)
6. In this essay, I will review the scholarly literature on haptic skills as they were practised by eighteenth-century consumers, focusing upon

scholarly disagreements and looking at various literary sources. – STUDYING (CUT)

7. Apart from certain scholars' efforts, there is very little discussion today within analytical philosophy of religion about meta-theodical questions, so in this paper I shall review the state of such debates, bringing new arguments to bear upon these fundamental questions. – STUDYING (CUT)

8. Theodicy may set out to reconcile the existence of God with that of evil but this detached perspective disregards the testimony of sufferers and effaces our humanity and God's divinity. – IDEAS (KEEP)

Have a go at separating empirical and emotional statements

1. Polluters are despicable human beings. – EMOTIONAL
2. Possession of intrinsic value generates a *prima facie* direct moral duty on the part of moral agents to protect it or at least refrain from damaging it. – USEFUL
3. Anyone who says it's okay to pollute has blood on their hands. – EMOTIONAL
4. Eco-warrior types are just virtue-signalling. – EMOTIONAL
5. This question assumes that it *is* morally wrong for human beings to pollute the environment, an assumption anthropocentric ethical perspectives dispute. – USEFUL
6. We should be ashamed. Nobody is willing to do anything about pollution. It's all our fault. – EMOTIONAL
7. Why should I have to feel ashamed about flying? We're all screwed anyway. –EMOTIONAL
8. Thomas Aquinas argued that non-human animals are 'ordered to man's use'. – USEFUL
9. Mainstream environmentalism is hugely arrogant. – EMOTIONAL
10. If trees, forests and mountains could be given standing in law, then they could be represented in their own right in the courts by groups such as the Sierra Club. – USEFUL

Answers to Chapter 7 Exercises

Have a go at identifying core empirical cases and data

1. A – The 2008 financial crisis
2. C – Constantine the Great, first Christian Emperor and founder of Constantinople
3. A – Voteview: plots every Members of Congress's ideology and partisan identity using roll call votes, 1789–2020
4. D – Super Mario Bros, one of the best-selling games of all time
5. B – The US 'War on Drugs'

Have a go at situating an example within different comparator classes

There are many potential definitions and comparator classes, so there is no right or wrong answer here. Some possibilities are below.

*Note that a case might fit into more than one comparator class (e.g. mice are laboratory animals as well as rodents; Uruguay is a Spanish-speaking, South American presidential republic). You can see where the comparator classes for different definitions converge and diverge, with potentially important consequences for your answer to a question.

1. Queen Elizabeth II: (1) British monarch (comparison class includes: George III, William IV, Edward VII); (2) longest-reigning head of state (comparison class includes: Louis XIV of France, Franz Joseph I of Austria-Hungary, Constantine VIII of the Byzantine Empire); (3) queen (comparison class includes: Elizabeth I, Anne, Victoria)
2. Rats: (1) rodent (comparators include: beaver, capybara, squirrel, mouse); (2) subject of scientific research in laboratories (comparators include: monkeys, rabbits, fruit flies); (3) a sneak, someone who trades secrets (comparators include: moles, spies, diplomats, inside traders)
3. Peru: (1) country in South America (comparators: Ecuador, Colombia, Chile, Brazil); (2) predominantly Spanish-speaking territory

(comparators: Spain, Mexico, Puerto Rico, Uruguay); (3) presidential
republic (comparators: United States, Kenya, Zimbabwe,
Turkmenistan)

4. A skipping rope: (1) children's toy (comparators: pogo stick, trampo-
line, scooter, swing); (2) piece of adult gym equipment (comparators:
dumbbells, rowing machine, yoga mat); (3) means to achieve a
cardiovascular workout (comparators: running kit, mountain bike,
swimming costume)

5. Greed: (1) one of the seven deadly sins (comparators: pride, lust,
envy, gluttony, sloth, wrath); (2) a healthy appetite for success
(comparators: ruthlessness, strategic nous, intellectual capability); (3)
a cause of misery (comparators: cruelty, depression, fear, resentment)

6. Bark: (1) vocalization of some animals (comparators: squawk, chatter,
grunt, squeak); (2) the outermost layers of stems and roots of woody
plants (comparators: pith, wood, vascular cambium); (3) garden
material used for landscaping when chipped (comparators: compost,
mulch, playground surfacing)

7. Earth: (1) terrestrial planet of the solar system (comparators: Mercury,
Venus, Mars); (2) planet with important moons (comparators: Pluto,
Jupiter, Saturn); (3) a vital life-support system for humanity (compara-
tors: the sun, the moon, gravity)

8. Strength: (1) individual power or resilience (comparators: individual
failure, incompetence; muscular weakness, moral weakness); (2)
military capability (comparators: infrastructure, economic power,
trade); (3) quality of an argument, convincing (comparators: logical,
structured, well evidenced)

9. Pattern: (1) something used in dressmaking (comparators: sewing
machine, thread, fabric); (2) something used in angling (comparators: fishing rod, floats, feeders); (3) discernible order or arrangement
(comparators: chaos, asynchrony, true randomness)

10. Race: (1) a social construct (comparators: money, language, narratives, the concept of human rights); (2) a way to group people in
survey research (comparators: height, age, gender, education level);
(3) a way to taxonomize animals and plants (comparators: Aristotle's
groups, Linnaeus's kingdoms classification, Darwin's phyletic systems)

Have a go at identifying hard and easy cases

Disagreement is possible about which are the 'hardest' and 'easiest' cases, but some suggested answers are below.

1. 'Christmas activities cause family stress'.
   a. Watching the Queen's Speech
   b. Gathering with close family – EASY CASE
   c. Eating chocolate in pyjamas – HARD CASE
   d. Opening stockings
2. 'Role models inspire children to participate in sport'.
   a. Lionel Messi, footballer – EASY CASE
   b. Lance Armstrong, cyclist – HARD CASE
   c. Paula Radcliffe, runner
   d. Greg Rutherford, javelin thrower
3. 'Students in wealthy countries achieve better education results'.
   a. Saudi Arabia – HARD CASE
   b. Singapore – EASY CASE
   c. Spain
   d. Switzerland – EASY CASE
4. 'English monarchs are powerful and well respected'.
   a. King Edward IV (1461–1483), who was briefly exiled in 1470 but returned to the throne quickly.
   b. Queen Elizabeth I (1558–1603), who defeated the Spanish Armada – EASY CASE
   c. King John (1199–1216), who was forced to sign the Magna Carta – HARD CASE
   d. Queen Mary II (1689–1694), who endowed the College of William and Mary
5. 'Retailers created the obesity crisis'.
   a. Supermarkets
   b. Newsagents
   c. Takeaway shops – EASY CASE
   d. Farmers' markets – HARD CASE

Answers to Chapter 8 Exercises

Have a go at moving from general theme to proposition

This exercise is entirely your own, so there are no right or wrong answers. Some suggested propositions are below:

1. Making a cup of tea
   a. Tea became fashionable to drink among English aristocrats in the seventeenth century, but Methodist John Wesley thought it caused nervous disorders.
   b. Before individual tea bags arrived, around the time of the First World War, making a cup of tea required brewing an entire pot.
   c. Tea is the most popular beverage in the world after plain water.
2. Ghosts and the supernatural
   a. Roman tragedian Seneca's *fabula crepidata* play *Agamemnon* opens with the Ghost of Thyestes urging his son Aegisthus to carry out revenge on his behalf.
   b. In 1597, King James VI of Scotland published *Demonologie*, a book of necromancy, divination and theology.
   c. Mary Todd, Abraham Lincoln's wife, organized séances at the White House after their son died in 1862.
3. Chocolate
   a. Cacao beans used to make chocolate come from the cacao tree, which is native to Central and South America.
   b. Owing to their high procyanidin content, chocolate products display high levels of antioxidant activity.
   c. Roderich Lindt of Switzerland invented 'melting chocolate' in 1879, after which consumption of eating chocolate soared.
4. Learning to drive
   a. Around half of 17- to 20-year-olds could drive in 1992–1994, but the rate had dropped to 29% by 2014.
   b. The British driving test theory pass rate is just 47%, a quarter lower than it was a decade ago.
   c. Japanese driving tests are amongst the toughest in the world.

5. Weddings
   a. White wedding dresses are uncommon in Eastern cultures where white is the colour of mourning.
   b. Pope Innocent III declared that a waiting period should occur between betrothal and marriage, leading to separate engagement and wedding rings.
   c. August is the most popular month for weddings in the UK.
6. Gaining self-confidence
   a. Self-confidence has a greater effect upon sporting performance than cognitive anxiety does.
   b. Females are on average less self-confident than males.
   c. Supervisors who lack confidence in their leadership abilities are significantly less willing to hold face-to-face discussions with subordinates.
7. Trees
   a. Earth now has 46% fewer trees than it did 12,000 years ago.
   b. More than half of all tree species exist in only a single country.
   c. Some trees protect themselves by emitting chemicals to attract the enemies of their enemies.
8. Young people's use of social media
   a. Social media use affects political participation both directly and indirectly.
   b. As platforms for self-expression, social media requires young people to consciously perform their identity (Gabriel 2014).
   c. There is a negative association between social media use and self-esteem.

Have a go at paraphrasing

There are many different, good answers to this question. Some suggested propositions, in grammatical sentences, are below:

1. *The Wonderful Wizard of Oz*: There's no place like home.
2. *Cinderella*: Physical beauty is of paramount importance.
3. Mowgli's experiences in Rudyard Kipling's *The Jungle Book*: Danger is always present in every human society, just as it is in the jungle.
4. Bram Stoker's *Dracula*: Vampires are willing to kill to become immortal.
5. The Biblical parable of the Good Samaritan: Everyone is your neighbour.
6. *Catch 22*: Individuals are subject to absurd bureaucratic constraints according to which, paradoxically, to fight the rule is to accept it.

Have a go at writing an argument as a syllogism

1. Premise 1: I have an idea of a supremely perfect being.
   Premise 2: Necessary existence is a sort of perfection.
   Conclusion: A supremely perfect being exists.

2. Premise 1: If we don't account for omitted confounding variables, our estimates of causal effects will be wrong.
   Premise 2: In the social sciences, knowing all of the confounding variables and measuring them properly is basically impossible.
   Conclusion: Doing statistical social science is pointless!

3. Premise 1: Being a woman is one cultural interpretation of being female.
   Premise 2: That interpretation is in no way necessitated by being female.
   Conclusion: The female body is the arbitrary locus of the gender 'woman'.

4. Premise 1: The mind is not made of parts.
   Premise 2: Anything material has parts.
   Conclusion: The mind cannot be made of matter.

5. Premise 1: City authorities in fifteenth-century London opposed playhouses.
   Premise 2: Whatever institutions the City authorities opposed failed to flourish.
   Conclusion: Playhouses failed to flourish in fifteenth-century London.

6. Premise 1: The first ruler is excellent and his rulership truly excellent.
   Premise 2: Excellent rulers seek only to obtain, for themselves and for everyone under their rulership, the ultimate happiness that is truly happiness.
   Conclusion: That religion will be the excellent religion.

7. Premise 1: Military prowess always creates lasting kingdoms.
   Premise 2: The Huns had military prowess.
   Conclusion: The Huns succeeded in establishing a lasting kingdom.

8. Premise 1: Governments never abandon policies that stabilize their economies.
   Premise 2: The New Economic Policy stabilized the Soviet economy.
   Conclusion: The Soviets never abandoned the New Economic Policy.

Answers to Chapter 9 Exercises

Have a go at responding to counter-arguments

Your answers to this exercise depend on which side you take – and there are any number of possible responses to counter-arguments. Some suggestions are below. Although I list responses to counter-arguments on both sides, you mustn't take this as an opportunity to reinforce the pro–con seesaw effect. A brilliant essay takes a single, clear position and bolsters its argument by responding to counter-arguments. It does not simply list arguments and counter-arguments on each side *ad nauseam*.

1. How safe are winter sports?

NOT SAFE: The key part of the claim for the safety of winter sports is that IF you are fit, winter sports are quite safe, but that is a conditional claim. When I ask 'how safe' something is, I mean for the typical person, not an athlete. Most people are not athletes, and the insurance statistics don't lie. Just because cyclists experience more injuries each year than skiers doesn't prove that skiing is safer than cycling: many more people cycle than ski, so the absolute number of injuries are bound to be higher.

SAFE: It all depends on where you anchor your expectations about safety. No aspect of life is risk-free. If we expand our time frame to include the sorts of risks our grandparents and great-grandparents experienced before modern medical treatments, government responses and scientific risk-prevention, we are living in extraordinarily low-risk times. A modern skiing holiday is nowhere near as unsafe as everyday life was a century or more ago.

2. Is it more important for children to be considerate or well behaved?

CONSIDERATE: 'Spare the rod' is an antiquated expression. Modern studies show that authoritarian parenting styles double the risk of a child developing a drinking problem and other issues in adolescence.

WELL-BEHAVED: Focusing on good behaviour doesn't mean that you have to adopt an authoritarian parenting style. Your answer betrays Western bias, because concern for good behaviour is prominent in many successful parenting cultures around the world – even if it has become less popular in some developed societies.

ALTERNATIVE WAY TO COUNTER AN ARGUMENT ON EITHER SIDE: This question poses a false dichotomy, because being considerate of others *is* the foundation of good behaviour. There is simply no way to separate the two.

3. How disgusting are koalas?

NOT DISGUSTING: The STD response is disingenuously trying to provoke a visceral reaction, by using words such as 'faecal' or 'chlamydia'. Most people don't know about those figures – they love cuddling koalas! If people don't feel disgust, then it isn't disgust*ing*.

VERY DISGUSTING: Once people do know that koalas harbour sexual diseases, they feel differently about them. But how disgusting something is isn't dependent on what any person happens to know about a thing. You may not *think* your aeroplane tray table contains more germs than a toilet seat; nevertheless... it does.

ALTERNATIVE WAY TO COUNTER AN ARGUMENT ON EITHER SIDE: Going all in on one side or the other misses the point, because 'disgusting' has a completely elastic definition. Anything could be 'disgusting' or perhaps nothing is. The concept is too slippery.

4. Do holidaymakers have a nicer time at the seaside or in the countryside?

SEASIDE: In many rural areas, there's poor Wi-Fi and limited shopping opportunities. There are insects and cows. I rest my case.

COUNTRYSIDE: Sea air is all well and good, but what about dive-bombing gulls, dirty amusement arcades and huge crowds of whinging toddlers? The claims made for seaside relaxation are overblown.

ALTERNATIVE WAYS TO COUNTER AN ARGUMENT ON EITHER SIDE: This question rests upon some dodgy premises: (1) 'the seaside' and 'the countryside' are very varied categories (Copacabana and Brighton? The Lake District and the Transylvanian wilderness?) We shouldn't talk about them as if they're a single thing. (2) The sorts of people who seek out seaside or rural holidays are different and have different expectations, so it is problematical to talk in general about 'having a nicer time' in one or the other. People select in to one or the other holiday location.

5. Are things getting better?

YES THEY ARE: Science shows that humans have inbuilt negativity bias (we pay more attention to threats than to positive stimuli), and when problems are rare, we count more things as problems (Burkeman 2018).

NO THEY AREN'T: Climate change is the defining crisis of our time because it concerns the very habitability of our planet. No amount of progress on nuclear weapons or reductions in guinea worm incidence (small fry, comparatively) should distract us from this overarching threat – and the news there is almost all bad.

Have a go at identifying appropriate uses of 'I', 'me', 'my' and the passive voice

1. In my opinion, African elephants are the most impressive of all African mammals. REWRITE AS: 'African elephants are the most impressive of all African mammals.'
2. My research on feather-work in colonial Peru demonstrates that artisanship linked indigenous Andean and European societies. KEEP
3. On the basis of the survey that was conducted, it is asserted that the effect of greater representation among the police is largely negative, for whites at least. (PASSIVE). REWRITE AS: 'My survey shows that the effect of greater representation among the police is largely negative, for whites at least.'
4. From my perspective, anxiety is a normal part of the human condition. REWRITE AS: 'Anxiety is a normal part of the human condition.'
5. 'A system hostile or antagonistic to women' has been held by many to have been facilitated by globalization. (PASSIVE). REWRITE AS: 'Many believe that globalization facilitates "a system hostile or antagonistic to women".' – even better if you can attribute this claim, rather than leaving it general ('many believe')
6. I believe that social status and gender are intertwined with the Victorian processes of grieving and remembering the dead. REWRITE AS: 'Social status and gender are intertwined with the Victorian processes of grieving and remembering the dead.'
7. It is argued, using archival and published sources, that three of the consequences of the failure of the French expedition to Mexico from 1862 to 1867 were the undermining of the French Second Empire, the convulsing of the fiscal-military system, and the hindering of the Second Empire's ability to confront the Prussian threat. (PASSIVE). REWRITE AS: 'Archival and published sources show that the failure of the French expedition to Mexico from 1862 to 1867 undermined the French Second Empire, convulsed the fiscal-military system, and hindered the Second Empire's ability to confront the Prussian threat.'
8. Conservatism is a philosophy of common sense and everyday experience, in my view. REWRITE AS: 'Conservatism is a philosophy of common sense and everyday experience.'

9. I argue that eating was a spiritually rewarding exercise for English Protestants in the sixteenth and seventeenth centuries. KEEP
10. <u>I am convinced that</u> compassion acts as a mechanism for coping with stressful public service conditions. REWRITE AS: 'Compassion acts as a mechanism for coping with stressful public service conditions.'
11. A rigid designator, which designates the same object with respect to all possible worlds, <u>was suggested by</u> Kripke. (PASSIVE). REWRITE AS: 'Kripke suggests that a rigid designator designates the same object with respect to all possible worlds.'
12. Tests for capacity need to be assessed for their reliability, and major concepts and theories need to be empirically validated. KEEP

Have a go at identifying different definitions

There are many possible definitions for each of these concepts. With thanks to the Oxford English Dictionary for some of the suggested definitions below. There are many more – how do yours differ from these selected definitions? Which definitions do you find more compelling and why?

1. Freedom: (1) Absence of obstacles, barriers or constraints. (2) Ability to take control of one's own life and achieve one's own goals. (3) Ability to associate voluntarily with others. (4) Boldness. (5) Civil rights and liberties. (6) Self-determination. (7) Frankness, familiarity and openness in conversation. (8) Different ways in which an object can undergo displacement, translation or deformation.
2. Rational: (1) Decision-making based on choices that result in the optimal level of utility for an individual. (2) Reasonable rather than foolish, absurd or extreme. (3) Being human. (4) Good judgement. (5) Not being too emotional. (6) A quantity that can be expressed as a ratio of two whole numbers.
3. Beauty: (1) One of the ultimate values, like goodness, truth and justice. (2) Subjective – just a question of taste. (3) Something that gives people pleasure. (4) A celebration of a relationship between human and object. (5) Something useful. (6) Something useless.
4. Thinking: (1) Internal mental activity. (2) Meditating or pondering. (3) Purpose or intention. (4) Experiencing wonder. (5) Imagining. (6) Remembering. (7) Making a plan.
5. Power: (1) Ability to affect something strongly. (2) Rule, authority or command. (3) Influence. (4) Mental capacity. (5) The sound expressed by a character or symbol. (6) An angel or other spiritual

being. (7) A quantity obtained by multiplying a given quantity by itself.

6. Representation: (1) Standing in for a person or thing. (2) Symbolism. (3) The workings of a democracy. (4) Portraying an image in art. (5) Pretence.

7. Soul: (1) The essence of life. (2) Intelligence or thought. (3) The spiritual part of a person. (4) Emotional music. (5) Powerful.

8. Conservative: (1) A preserving agent. (2) Paternalism, authority and tradition. (3) Right-wing philosophy. (4) Fear of sudden social change. (5) Scepticism about reason.

9. Living: (1) To be alive and capable of vital functions. (2) To support oneself by means of a source of income. (3) To pass one's life in a specified fashion. (4) To be happy and comfortable.

10. Organization: (1) The study of efficiency of working practices. (2) Systematic ordering or arrangement. (3) The development or coordination of parts in order to carry out vital functions. (4) An organism.

Answers to Chapter 10 Exercises

Have a go at rewriting definitions in your own words

There are many possible answers to these exercises. Some suggestions of plain-language definitions are below.

1. *Secession*: A situation in which a group withdraws from a larger entity, particularly to make a political point.
2. *Medieval semiotics*: How people during the medieval period studied and interpreted signs and symbols.
3. *Agent autonomy:* A person has a choice about which of her own motivations to follow. She is not constrained or interfered with by anyone else.
4. *Phylogeny*: A tree of life, showing how a particular species evolved from its distant ancestors.
5. *Tax expenditures*: Targeted tax reliefs for particular purposes, whereby the government deducts the tax it would otherwise collect on certain income, goods and services.
6. *'Games of truth'*: A set of rules by which truth is produced.

Have a go at joining up the dots

There are many possible answers to these exercises. Some suggestions are below.

1. *Thick description*
   There is not enough space here to attempt an actual thick description, but an application of the concept might explore some or all of the following angles: how wedding ceremonies, university inductions and children's play activities differ around the world and in different cultural traditions; what the participants in these rituals consider themselves to be doing, in their own words; how we weave narratives and stories into our remembrance of these life events.

2. *The Free Rider Problem*
   a. *Cleaning the communal kitchen*: Nobody wants to do the dirty work, but everyone would benefit if the housemates could find a way to unite and get the job done. Passive–aggressive notes left on the fridge in ALL CAPS are an effort to shame recalcitrant housemates into doing their share.
   b. *Wikipedia*: This online platform provides a valuable, free service for the world's internet users but struggles to fund itself because there is an individual incentive to free-ride on the donations of others.
   c. *Producing a class presentation*: Every individual in the group has an incentive to slack off and allow his or her classmates to do most of the work. The problem is that the presentation won't get done unless the students overcome this collective action problem.

3. *The feminine mystique*
   a. *Women's magazines:* Friedan herself wrote for many women's magazines. She was fiercely critical of their portrayal of women as either happy housewives or unhappy careerists.
   b. *The school curriculum*: Sex-segregated curricula, particularly home economics for girls and woodwork for boys; the role of Title IX in promoting anti-discrimination norms in American education.
   c. *Advertising*: Advertisers encouraging housewives to consider themselves professionals in need of special household products, but discouraging women from seeking careers outside the home.

4. *Dispensation*
   a. *The Garden of Eden:* Adam and Eve exist in a state of innocence prior to the fateful fall. A divinely instituted paradise.
   b. *US foreign policy*: For dispensationalists, the state of Israel exists as a revelation of God's will for the Last Days. Israel counts upon the support of many American Evangelical Christians because of their dispensational beliefs.
   c. *Climate science*: If someone believes that the Revelation is imminent, then they may also believe that evidence the planet is heating up catastrophically is a sign for Christians to prepare for the Apocalypse.

5. *The Doctrine of Double Effect*
   a. *A teenager holding a messy house party*: A teen might try to defend the holding of a messy house party in defiance of their parents' orders on the grounds that they foresaw but did not intend to damage the property and that the party was otherwise a good act. Whether their parents would agree is a moot point.

b. *A vaccination programme*: Even if there are some regrettable, fatal side effects of administering a large-scale vaccination programme for a dangerous disease, the intended good and the lack of deliberately intended harm might serve to justify it morally.

c. *Driving an SUV*: You intended to drive to the shops, and you foresaw – but did not intend – that in so doing you would wear down the treads of your car. If you accidentally knocked down a neighbour crossing the road, it would be interesting to consider whether the tread wear, the swerve and its consequences are also covered by the Doctrine of Double Effect.

Answers to Chapter 11 Exercises

Have a go at avoiding word wastage

1. It is important to define the term 'democracy'. – CUT
2. This question asks us whether democracy is a universal concept or not. – CUT
3. Democracy is a mode of group decision-making characterized by participant equality. – KEEP, but will need to flesh this definition out and explain further.
4. Is democracy a universal concept? – CUT
5. There are many possible definitions of 'democracy' – CUT
6. Does democracy really apply to everyone, everywhere? Should it? – CUT
7. I will start by considering the term 'democracy' and then I will go on to discuss the concept of universality. – CUT
8. A form of democracy acceptable to all peoples in the world must respect unique cultural identities but retain sufficient internal homogeneity that it can still be termed 'democracy': namely mechanisms of accountability, the rule of law and free exchange of information. – KEEP
9. This examination essay will discuss the issue of whether democracy in fact applies to every person, everywhere in the world, and if so, what the implications of this fact might be. – CUT
10. In order to be able to answer the title question, it is necessary to examine and define some of the words and phrases used in order to establish what this essay will consider and answer. – CUT
11. Several case studies shall be presented to suggest how democracy might or might not be understood as a universal concept – CUT
12. Even if we say that democracy is a superior type of government, the question still remains about which conception of democracy (if there is one) would actually be acceptable to every person in the world. – CUT OR MODIFY

Have a go at rote learning for examinations

Give yourself marks for each name, date or place you can remember.

- Post-war Presidents of the United States up to the 2020 presidential election (13): Truman, Eisenhower, Kennedy, Johnson, Nixon, Ford, Carter, Reagan, Bush, Clinton, Bush, Obama, Trump.
- English monarchs (Houses of Plantagenet, Lancaster and York) from 1216 to 1485 (13): Henry III, Edward I, Edward II, Edward III, Richard II (Plantagenet), Henry IV, Henry V, Henry VI, Edward IV, Henry VI (again), Edward IV (again), Edward V, Richard III.
- Member countries of NATO (30): Albania, Belgium, Bulgaria, Canada, Croatia, Czech Republic, Denmark, Estonia, France, Germany, Greece, Hungary, Iceland, Italy, Latvia, Lithuania, Luxembourg, Montenegro, The Netherlands, North Macedonia, Norway, Poland, Portugal, Romania, Slovakia, Slovenia, Spain, Turkey, the United Kingdom, the United States.
- Transition metals in the periodic table (36): Ti, V, Cr, Mn, Fe, Co, Ni, Cu, Zn, Zr, Nb, Mo, Tc, Ru, Rh, Pd, Ag, Cd, Hf, Ta, W, Re, Os, Ir, Pt, Au, Hg, Rf, Db, Sg, Bh, Hs, Mt, Ds, Rg, Cn.

Have a go at examination planning

This exercise is entirely a matter of interpretation, so you should not take the following exemplars as the only ways to plan these essays. There are as many possible good plans as there are students! The following exemplars are suggestions only, not a gold standard. The key is to think around the question and consider what it is truly asking you to do, rather than leaping in with a rehearsed examination answer on the topic.

1. Why are trees vital for humanity?

TAKE-HOME: Trees have extrinsic value because they satisfy basic human needs for life, food and shelter, but they do not have intrinsic value.

- Question assumes that trees are vital for humanity and asks about extrinsic value of trees only, not intrinsic value.
- Intrinsic value of trees is non-relational and non-instrumental, a thing's capacity as an objective holder of value.
- Trees do not have subjective mental states, so there are no tree qualities that are good *for trees*. Trees have value only in relation to humans.

- Scale of extrinsic value this essay will use: Maslow's hierarchy of human needs.
- Extrinsic values of trees for humanity in order of importance according to Maslow's hierarchy:
  - make air suitable for breathing,
  - filter soil and prevent erosion,
  - bring rain and preserve freshwater,
  - provide lumber, paper, fibre, dyes, waxes and many other products.
- Two major counter-arguments:
  - (1) aesthetic value of trees does not fit on this scale. Answer: human aesthetic needs are either below utilitarian needs on the hierarchy or incommensurable. Better to take the first approach, as humans can and do adjudicate these apparently incommensurable values in real life: see evidence from court cases.
  - (2) value of trees to life itself cannot be compared with the value of a sheet of A4 paper. It has lexical priority. Answer: just because it is difficult to put something onto a scale doesn't mean that the task is impossible.
- The most dangerous counter-arguments stem from the same source: intuition that trees have intrinsic, rather than only extrinsic, value.
- We find this idea of intrinsic value appealing because it chimes with our intuitions, but intuitions are not always reliable.
- If we grant trees intrinsic value, we will have to grant that value to inorganic substances and deep space → our concept of value dissolves into meaninglessness.

2. Should assisted dying be legalized?

TAKE-HOME: Euthanasia should be legalized under controlled medical conditions for the terminally ill or those experiencing unbearable suffering as a result of an incurable condition, who have the competence to express their desire to die (or in consultation between relatives and medical professionals).

- The question of whether assisted dying should be legalized is not the same as the question of whether assisted dying is morally okay.
- Legalizing euthanasia is a public policy decision with costs and benefits. We could simultaneously hold that something is morally okay without saying that it should be legalized (if there is a compelling public interest in criminalizing, say, certain drugs) or that something is legal yet immoral (if a policy would be impossible to

enforce or have unacceptable consequences, such as for 'mere' failure to rescue a person in mortal danger).

- Our starting point for determining whether euthanasia should be legalized is the need to respect a person's autonomy, in the fullest sense of the term (that is, including their dignity, natural regard for well-being and self-determination about how to live their own life).
  - ○ Better than rival methods for assigning value in these cases (utilitarian calculus, categorical imperatives etc.) because it focuses our attention upon an individual's interest in making decisions about their own lives, and euthanasia concerns the manner and timing of a person's death (and end-of-life care).
- Even if we conclude that euthanasia is morally okay for a wide range of people, including those rendered quadriplegic as a result of accidents or those affected by Alzheimer's, a public policy needs sufficient support within a jurisdiction in order to be legalized, so the class of people for whom euthanasia should be legally available is smaller than the class of people for whom euthanasia is morally okay.
- Euthanasia should be legalized under controlled medical conditions for the terminally ill or those experiencing unbearable suffering as a result of an incurable condition, who have the competence to express their desire to die, or in consultation with the families of those who lack that competence but who would most likely, in the medical professionals' and family members' judgement, have expressed that desire.
- The strongest counter-arguments against the legalization of euthanasia:
  - ○ It is unnecessary given palliative care regimes. Answer: such regimes cannot remove all pain or obviate the need to respect an individual's autonomous choices.
  - ○ It would be a slippery slope. Answer: euthanasia policies can be designed with safeguards against abuse, as in the Netherlands and certain other jurisdictions (comparison of safeguards, policy forms and consequences).
- If the case for the legalization of euthanasia is powerful, why has it *not* been legalized in most jurisdictions? Answer: there is public support for legalizing some forms of euthanasia. Difficulty of surmounting legislative hurdles, competing priorities and interest group activity.

3. Which are the most important human rights?

TAKE-HOME: The most important human rights, judged by their practical political purposes, are freedom from slavery, liberty of conscience and security of ethnic groups from mass murder and genocide.

- Question assumes there are such things as human rights. We cannot identify 'the most important' human rights unless we know the pool of contenders. A relational question: 'most important' means 'more important than something else'.
- There is no agreed basis for the existence of human rights: law (but laws differ), God (but different religionists and atheists disagree, plus Euthyphro's dilemma is a problem for divinely inspired rights regimes), human moralities (but moralities also differ; ontological and anthropological rights universality is philosophically indefensible – see Donnelly 2007), justified ethical perspectives (still contentious, but the best available option since it is the basis for the Universal Declaration of Human Rights, or UDHR).
- The UDHR contains 30 rights, grounded in (1) recognition of inherent human dignity and (2) prudential need to promote freedom, justice and peace in the world.
- Adjudicating the 'most important' human rights – possible criteria:
  - Ordering of rights within the UDHR: life, liberty and security of person rank highest by this metric (Article 3); rights to a cultural life, education and a 'social and international order' rank lower by this metric (Articles 26, 27 and 28). This is a crude calculus: adopted by 58 (then) members of the United Nations in 1948. Ordering reflects needs and desires of particular participants *then*. Not the best way to adjudicate the 'most important' human rights.
  - Human agency and autonomy: if the most important human rights are those that best promote human autonomy, then these are a right to be free from servitude and to freedom of thought, opinion and assembly. Problem is that the 'enhances autonomy' metric expands the pool of 'human rights' beyond the UDHR to incorporate many other norms (back to problem identified at outset: what are human rights?). Approach is too profligate; 'human rights' proliferate; no clear distinction between human rights and other moral norms.
  - Practical and prudential reasons: most important rights are those which play the most prominent political roles and would be recognized as such by competent participants. Advantages:

concrete and helpful in guiding actual practice, not just abstract normative justifications. Special class of urgent rights (Rawls) in peaceful, cooperative international order: freedom from slavery, liberty of conscience and security of ethnic groups from mass murder and genocide.

- Practical, thinner, Rawlsian approach to human rights does not incorporate everything anyone might wish to include in a full list of 'human rights', but it does at least give us a defensible metric for determining importance *within that pool.*

4. Are we all feminists now?

TAKE-HOME: More people *do* accept both the normative and the empirical claims of feminism than they did 50 years ago.

- Assumes that we haven't always been feminists. If by 'feminist' we just mean 'concerned with and theorizing about justice for women', then that assumption is false: ancient philosophers such as Plato can be 'feminists' in this sense. Human societies have always had *some* conception of women's roles, and there has always been *some* resistance to male domination. A thin conception of feminism. Too thin, because every society qualifies.
- Thicker conception of feminism: advocacy of equal rights for women on the basis of the idea of equality between the sexes.
- We need thicker conceptions of feminism because unless there are ways *not* to be a feminist, the title question dissolves into meaning-lessness (do we all [exist, breathe, have views about women and men] now?)
- Feminism consists in *both* an empirical *and* a normative claim: women are currently treated unjustly, and we should do something about it. Some people might reasonably reject the normative or the empirical claim or both. Accepting both claims does not mean belonging to a formal political movement, nor does accepting those claims mean accepting the label of 'feminist'.
- Feminism fights sexist oppression: enclosing structures that systematically disadvantage women *because they are women.* A family resemblance approach is required to develop a sufficiently unified conception of 'sexist oppression' that is also capacious enough to incorporate varied female experiences.
- Sexist oppression is not necessarily deliberately aimed at women, but it is particularly harmful to women. Exploitation, marginaliza-tion, powerlessness, cultural imperialism and systematic violence form the core.

- According to opinion polls, more people *do* accept both the normative and the empirical claims of feminism than they did 50 years ago. Just because they are reluctant to adopt the label 'feminist' does not mean that they are not actually feminists.
  - ○ Counter-argument: social acceptability of publicly voicing opposition to feminism has decreased over that time period. People might not truly believe what they tell pollsters. Answer: techniques such as list experiments can help social scientists to uncover even unpopular views. Reinforces our confidence in this empirical result.
  - ○ Counter-argument: by their nature, polls can ask only relatively superficial questions about equal rights and societal structures. They cannot truly get at the underlying concepts. Answer: people will always differ in their understanding of feminism's precepts. As long as there is sufficient overlap between conceptions, we can understand one another.
- The question makes sense only if we take a mid-range conception of 'feminist': not so capacious that everyone, everywhere, automatically qualifies; not so restrictive that the answer is obviously 'no'. According to my thicker definition of 'feminist', many more people – though not all – are feminists now.

5. What explains national variations in crime rates?

TAKE-HOME: Economic inequality is the best explanation for cross-national variations in homicide rates.

- Differences in the ways crimes are reported by citizens, handled by police and recorded in official statistics make cross-national analysis of crime rates challenging.
- Homicide data are less affected by the inefficiency, corruption and biases that challenge comparative criminologists. Hence, I focus on homicides.
- Modernization theory states that economic development, and associated industrialization and urbanization, is positively associated with property crime and negatively associated with violent crime. By increasing social equality and thus solidarity, development reduces violent crime, but by increasing wealth, materialism and portable goods, it has the opposite effect upon property crime (Neapolitan 2003).
- Problem with modernization theory: GDP is poorly correlated with violent victimization rates.

- Better theory: Dissatisfaction with economic and status inequality. Inequality raises the stakes of fights for status amongst men. Confrontations become more fraught because there is more at stake for winners and losers. Inequality is the best explanation for several reasons:
  - o Most perpetrators and victims of violence are men, but the proportions of male perpetrators and victims are lower in countries with higher levels of social equality, such as the Nordic countries.
  - o Allows us to incorporate cultural variables as moderators. No need for a reductively cultural explanation for variations in homicide rates, but cultural variations in how status differences are expressed and channelled influence the effect of inequality upon violent victimization (empirical case studies of selected Asian countries, Nordic countries and African countries).
  - o Strong, robust empirical relationship between inequality rates and homicide rates cross-nationally and across time.
- Relationship between inequality and homicide rates generates a moral and political imperative to reduce economic inequality. Finding is not easily translated to other sorts of crime, not only for the methodological problems identified at the outset but also because alternative causal mechanisms and expectations are required.

Answers to Chapter Exercises

End of Chapter 1 Exercises: Examining assumptions in questions

PART A:

1. Is John <u>still</u> studying geology? (John used to study geology.)
2. Oh! Do you <u>also</u> like kickboxing? (Someone else likes kickboxing – the questioner.)
3. <u>Nowadays</u> Sarah lives a quiet life. (Sarah used to live a wild life.)
4. Lin hasn't got a dance partner <u>at the moment</u>. (Lin used to have a dance partner.)
5. When you finally get your car going on a cold morning, the icy seats make your life miserable <u>too</u>. (Getting your car going on a cold morning makes your life miserable.)
6. <u>The</u> problem with <u>the</u> youth of today is that they don't respect their elders. (There is only one major problem with the youth of today. We can actually identify a single category of 'youth', and they are sufficiently homogenous that we can describe them as a group.)
7. I've packed the inflatable dinghy <u>as well,</u> just in case. (I've packed other things, besides the dinghy.)
8. Charlotte ate <u>the</u> sandwich. (There is only one sandwich.)

PART B:

9. Is 'the Third World' <u>still</u> a useful concept? (The Third World was once a useful concept.)
10. Are perceptual motor skills a type of intellectual learning <u>as well</u>? (There are other types of intellectual learning.)
11. In *The City of the Sun*, 'the walls are <u>also</u> the curtains of an extraordinary theatre and the pages of an illustrated encyclopaedia of knowledge.' Discuss. (The walls in *The City of the Sun* have functions other than being curtains of extraordinary theatre.)
12. Explain how science-fiction films <u>came to prominence</u> in 1950s Hollywood. (Science-fiction films weren't prominent in Hollywood before the 1950s.)
13. Does <u>the</u> Victorian aesthetic sensibility survive <u>today</u>? (There once existed such a thing as a 'Victorian aesthetic sensibility'.)

14. What is <u>the</u> problem with Meinongianism? (There is only one problem with Meinongianism.)
15. Does John Locke <u>also</u> apply the concept of tacit consent to the ongoing evaluation of the performance of a political regime? (John Locke applies his concept of tacit consent to other points, besides the evaluation of the performance of a regime. Someone other than John Locke applies the concept of tacit consent to the ongoing evaluation of the performance of a political regime.)
16. What explains the <u>current</u> bias towards states in international law? (International law wasn't always biased towards states.)
17. Is it true that any standard of virtue will be contestable in a diverse <u>modern</u> society? (In pre-modern societies, standards of virtue are less likely to be contestable.)
18. 'Problem-solving policing doesn't just mean looking at incidents <u>only</u>.' Discuss. (Problem-solving policing looks at things other than incidents.)
19. '<u>Nowadays</u>, metals are infinitely recyclable.' Discuss. (Metals have not always been infinitely recyclable.)
20. '<u>The</u> problem with geothermal energy is its adverse effect upon land stability.' Discuss. (There is only one problem with geothermal energy.)

PART C: There are no set answers here. Use your knowledge and judgement to argue your case! I think the <u>least</u> plausible assumptions are 9, 12, 14 and 17. What do you think?

End of Chapter 2 Exercises: Finding comparator classes in questions

PART A:

1. Ali is usually on time for meetings.
2. Sophie is a jobsworth.
3. The local cops are not very clever.
4. We do not expect the Supreme Court to spot racial patterns.
5. Sense faculties are the faculties most likely to possess essential reality.
6. Cases where nothing resembling a law appears to be available are least suitable for the application of the covering law model.
7. Causally determined nature is the hardest test for Fichte's theory of a self-positing ego.

PART B:

8. How does eighteenth-century literature manifest gender divisions? (Possible comparators: other time periods; other types of societal division, such political or religious divisions)
9. Why might employees be less productive following promotion? (Possible comparators: other factors that have an impact on productivity, such as having a child or working from home)
10. 'Economic valuation and markets can save Nature.' Discuss. (Possible comparators: other ways to save nature; other purposes served by economic valuation and markets)
11. Why did the film *Raise the Red Lantern* appeal to audiences in the West? (Possible comparators: other films; other international successes in the arts; audiences in other parts of the world)
12. What is the causal effect of education upon individual involvement in crime? (Possible comparators: other factors that influence individual involvement in crime; group involvement in crime; other effects of increasing education upon individual behaviours)
13. How does overloading the atmosphere with contaminants lead to change in that system? (Possible comparators: other natural systems that humans are overloading with contaminants, such as seas, earth and space)
14. How do US economic interests influence American newspapers' coverage of terrorism? (Possible comparators: countries other than the US; other American interests (strategic, political); other newspapers around the world; other American media (TV, websites); other sorts of news coverage)
15. Evaluate the role of glacial meltwater in the formation of drumlins and lakes. (Possible comparators: other features of glaciers, such as ice, weight, rock and debris; other landscape features shaped by glaciers, such as roche moutonnees, moraines and U-shaped valleys)
16. How might top football players react to increased taxation if they had to play football in their country of citizenship? (Possible comparators: weaker football players; other sportspeople, such as cricketers, athletes or basketball players; other policy interventions that might bring down footballer pay)

PART C: Swap your answers with a friend in your class, or your tutor, and talk your suggestions through. What do you think of each other's ideas?

End of Chapter 3 Exercises: Interrogating tensions in questions

PART A:

1. Was *The Terminator* a brilliant <u>or</u> terrible film? (*The Terminator* must be either brilliant or terrible, and nothing else.)
2. <u>Why</u> has Tina <u>become</u> so miserable? (Tina is miserable; Tina used to be less miserable.)
3. I like Mae as a person <u>but</u> she is a fan of *The Big Bang Theory*. (Generally I don't like people who are fans of *The Big Bang Theory*. I think it is an awful show.)
4. <u>When</u> did you realize you were wrong? (You were wrong, and you realized it.)
5. <u>Which</u> is your favourite cephalopod? (You actually have a favourite cephalopod.*)
6. <u>How</u> do bees gather honey from flowers? (Bees gather honey from flowers.**)

---

* It's hard to get beyond octopus. They really are amazing creatures.

** This is actually a false assumption. Bees gather *nectar* from flowers in order to make honey.

PART B:

7. <u>Why</u> has the rollout of autonomous vehicles been so slow? (The rollout of autonomous vehicles has been very slow)
8. Is the Tea Party an interest group, a faction <u>or</u> a party? (The Tea Party must be only one of an interest group, a faction or a party, and nothing else.)
9. <u>How</u> do computers think? (Computers do think.)
10. <u>Why</u> has the US Congress <u>become</u> so dysfunctional? (Congress is dysfunctional; Congress used to be less dysfunctional.)
11. <u>How</u> should we account for the failure of Descartes's mind–body thesis? (Descartes's mind–body thesis does fail.)
12. <u>What</u> has knowledge got to do with bravery? (Knowledge has something to do with bravery.)
13. Was New Labour an ideology <u>or</u> a style of governing? (New Labour was either an ideology or a style of governing but not both.)
14. <u>When</u> do our moral intuitions fail us? (Our moral intuitions do sometimes fail us.)

15. Is British multiculturalism a symbol of a liberal, cosmopolitan society or a colonial throw-back? (Multiculturalism is one or the other and not both.)
16. How do multinational corporations threaten state authority? (Multinational corporations do threaten state authority.)
17. What impact did the film *Cathy Come Home* have upon policymakers' willingness to address the social problems it identified? (*Cathy Come Home* did have an impact on policymakers' willingness to address social problems.)
18. Is social media beneficial or harmful for democracy? (Social media is either wholly beneficial or wholly harmful for democracy.)
19. 'Some landscapes are shaped by human activities.' Discuss. (Not all landscapes are shaped by human activities.)
20. 'It may truly be said to have neither FORCE nor WILL, but merely judgment.' Discuss Alexander Hamilton's view of the judiciary in *Federalist 78*. (Hamilton thinks that judgement is a distinctly third-rate quality, compared with force and will.)

PART C: There are no set answers here. Use your knowledge and judgement to argue your case! I think the least plausible assumptions are 8, 15, 17 and 18. What do you think?

End of Chapter 4 Exercises: The introduction scale

PART A:
1. Level 1 (identifies question)
2. Level 4 (explains own view)
3. Level 2 (bare 'agree'/'disagree')
4. Level 2 (bare 'agree'/'disagree')
5. Level 1 (identifies question)
6. Level 3 (gives own view)
7. Level 1 (identifies question)

PART B:
This is a matter of interpretation – you might reject them all! – but 3 ('Smart devices have transformed the relationship between built environment and exercise') is the worthiest candidate for inclusion.

PART C:
Swap your efforts with a friend and see if you can pinpoint what level each introduction is at. As you read your friend's work, and review your own, consider the following:

- Can you easily spot what the essay take-home is?

- Can you cut any more fluff – background information that doesn't contribute directly to the argument?
- Does the introduction seem interesting? Does it make you want to read on?

End of Chapter 5 Exercises: Controlling your argument

PART A:

1. C – Polarization takes both affective (dislike) and positional (issue-based) forms, each with distinct effects upon presidential power.
2. B – Wittgenstein constructs neither an attack of nor a defence of behaviourism but rather an approach to agreed practices.
3. A – Psychoanalytic theory is more useful to therapists than to scientists.
4. B – Failure implies non-fulfilment of expectations, but the Constitution has not 'failed' because its procedures operate as the Founding Fathers anticipated.

PART B: This is up your interpretation – no single correct answers here! But some suggestions are below.

5. Bricks build stable houses and keep out predators.
6. Humanity is in essence a single family.
7. *Spoiler alert* He is a ghost.
8. Be wary of strangers.
9. Sisyphus has such hubris that Zeus condemns him to unending frustration.*
10. Life finds a way.

---

* This question referred to the original Ancient Greek stories about Sisyphus. Bonus points if you can summarize Albert Camus's 1942 absurdist work, *Le Mythe de Sisyphe*. Now that is a real challenge!

PART C: Again, this is a matter of interpretation because the introduction is quite wordy. A suggestion below:
American exceptionalism is fuelled by the suffering of some groups.

End of Chapter 6 Exercises: Writing elegantly

PART A:

1. <u>I would argue that</u> endogenous growth theory is <u>fairly problematic</u>. ('I would argue' is (b) – you mean you *would* argue it if things were different, or what? 'Fairly' is (b). 'Problematic' is (c))

2. Donald Trump is the <u>worst</u> president ever, but Hillary Clinton is downright <u>evil</u>. (c)
3. <u>First, I am going to define my key terms and consider which defini-</u><u>tion of 'development' is most appropriate, and then I am going to</u> <u>assess how useful the human development index is</u>. (a)
4. <u>The last paragraph argued that</u> David Hume's scepticism is <u>to some</u> <u>extent</u> warranted. ('The last paragraph argued that' is (a). 'To some extent' is (b).)
5. <u>Arguably,</u> King Edward I <u>should</u> never have joined the Ninth Crusade. ('Arguably' is (b). 'Should' *could* be (c) – but feel free to push back on that interpretation.)
6. Hollywood celebrities: <u>what do they know? Do they know things?</u> <u>Let's find out!</u> (a)
7. <u>We have been asked to consider which glacial landforms are deposi-</u><u>tional and which ones are erosional. We will start by considering what</u> <u>'depositional' and 'erosional' mean and then move on to discuss</u> <u>which landforms count as 'depositional' and which as 'erosional'.</u> (a)
8. <u>In my opinion,</u> enclosure of arable land in the sixteenth century was <u>wrong</u>. ('In my opinion' is (b). 'Wrong' is (c)).
9. <u>In order to answer the question at hand, we need to define our core</u> <u>concepts and consider any underlying assumptions, before moving</u> <u>on to a conclusion that follows from the argument I am going to</u> <u>make</u>. (a)

PART B:

10. The United Kingdom is <u>quite</u> large and powerful.
11. <u>Apparently</u> the UK is monarchical, but <u>mostly</u> it is not.
12. <u>I would argue that</u> the UK <u>seems to be</u> politically split into various components.
13. The UK is <u>relatively</u> developed.
14. <u>To some extent, you could say</u> that the UK has grown <u>a bit</u> recently.

Suggested rewrites:

10. The United Kingdom has a population of 66 million and the sixth largest military expenditure in the world.
11. The monarch is the head of the British state, and Acts of State are done in the name of the Crown, but sovereign powers are delegated by statute or convention to ministers or officers of the Crown or to other public bodies.
12. The UK is composed of four countries: England, Scotland, Wales and Northern Ireland.
13. The UK has the world's fifth-largest economy in nominal GDP or ninth-largest at purchasing power parity.

14. The UK population grew by two million in the decade 1990–2000, from 57 to 59 million, but it grew another 7 million in the 7 years from 2000 to 2017, to 66 million inhabitants.

PART C:
The correct answers are (b), (c) and (f).

End of Chapter 7 Exercises: Using empirical evidence effectively

PART A: Of what is this a case? And compared with what?

1. Do we have ethical responsibilities towards <u>great apes</u>?
   Great apes: a non-human animal. Comparators: molluscs, fish, amphibians, birds.
   Great apes: an intelligent species with elaborate social structures. Comparators: elephants, dolphins, whales, pigs, parrots.

2. How did Victorian authors understand the sublime in <u>mountain</u> landscapes?
   Mountains: a type of landscape. Comparators: moors, gardens, rivers, woods.
   Mountains: a place where humans become aware of their vulnerability. Comparators: nighttime, forest wilderness, clifftops, deep space.

3. Did the US have an obligation to intervene in <u>the 1994 Rwandan Genocide</u>?
   The 1994 Rwandan Genocide: a modern genocide. Comparators: Darfur, Bosnia and Herzegovina, Cambodia.
   The 1994 Rwandan Genocide: an international event that poses ethical questions. Comparators: terrorism, civil war, the Coronavirus pandemic, the development of nuclear weapons by unstable regimes.

4. Why are the seeds of <u>birch trees</u> so easily dispersed?
   Birch trees: forms of tree. Comparators: alder trees, rowan, wild cherry, oaks.
   Birch trees: a pioneer species that favours wind dispersal. Comparators: orchids, puffball fungi, willows, Scots pines.

5. Is the <u>United Nations</u> a powerful organization?
   United Nations: an international organization. Comparators: World Health Organization (WHO), International Labour Organization (ILO), International Criminal Police Organization (INTERPOL).
   United Nations: an organization designed to promote peace and security. Comparators: the Organization for Security and Co-operation in Europe (OSCE), the North Atlantic Treaty Organization (NATO), national governments.

6. '<u>Human greenhouse gas emissions</u> explain almost all of the climate change we see in <u>the Quaternary period.</u>' Discuss.
   Quaternary period: a geological epoch. Comparators: Cretaceous, Paleogene, Neogene.
   Greenhouse gas emissions: a source of long-term climate change. Comparators: orbital forcing, solar forcing, volcanic eruptions.

7. Can we ever prevent <u>human trafficking</u>?
   Human trafficking: a sort of crime. Comparators: fraud, robbery, terrorism, cyberwarfare.
   Human trafficking: a lucrative business. Comparators: tax evasion, counterfeiting, accountancy, real estate, banking.

PART B: This exercise is a matter of interpretation, so there is no single correct answer. Here are some suggested answers, but feel free to push back if you can justify alternatives.

8. 'Food makes people happy' (HARD case: lettuce. EASY case: chocolate)
9. 'Children's stories empower girls' (HARD case: *Rapunzel*. EASY case: *Frozen*)
10. 'Taking public transport reduces stress' (HARD case: bus. EASY case: gondola)
11. 'Superheroes are excellent role models' (HARD case: Wolverine. EASY case: Superman)
12. 'Sport is dangerous' (HARD case: tenpin bowling. EASY case: American football)

PART C: This exercise is also a matter of interpretation, but broadly speaking you are looking for cases that are representative of a broader population of cases on some dimension (typical), and those that are atypical of their class, with unusual properties that might be helpful in investigating causal links or developing a theory (telling).

13. How did Google Earth break from previous mapping genres?
    Comparator class: mapping genres. (European maps that use the Mercator projection (TYPICAL), Polynesian stick charts (TELLING), military maps (TYPICAL), 25,000-year-old mammoth tusk carvings (TELLING))
14. How did the transition from live to recording affect the sitcom genre?
    Comparator class: sitcoms. (*Friends* (TYPICAL), *The Big Bang Theory* (TYPICAL), *Slattery's People* (TELLING), *The Office* (TYPICAL), *The Tammy Grimes Show* (TELLING))

15. What challenges do policymakers face in regulating mergers and acquisitions in the carbonated soft drink industry? Comparator class: carbonated soft drinks. (Leninade (a 'simple Soviet-style soda') (TELLING), Brain Wash Blue (TELLING), Dr Pepper (TYPICAL), Fanta (TYPICAL))

16. How do children acquire perceptual motor skills? Comparator class: children's activities. (Plate spinning (TELLING), kicking a ball (TYPICAL), playing with blocks (TYPICAL), slackwire balancing (TELLING))

17. What do historians know about the everyday experiences of the medieval peasantry? Comparator class: peasant activities. (Reaping (TYPICAL), sowing (TYPICAL), haymaking (TYPICAL), eating pottage (TYPICAL), leading peasants' revolts (TELLING), being executed for participating in peasants' revolts (TELLING))

End of Chapter 8 Exercises: Syllogisms and summaries

The plausibility of the arguments is a matter of interpretation. There is no single 'correct' answer here. Some suggestions are below – but you may well feel differently.

Arguments from most plausible to least:

(most plausible) 4, 2, 6, 8, 5, 7, 3, 1 (least plausible)

Do you agree? How would you array the arguments on a plausibility scale?

1. Premise 2 and Conclusion are factually wrong – outrageously so. Conclusion does not follow from the premises.

2. The Premises are supported by historical evidence, but the Conclusion does not necessarily follow, at least in its strongest form. Crusaders joined for a variety of reasons, including the satisfaction of feudal obligations and economic as well as spiritual gain. The Church did not necessarily 'condone' all of their activities.

3. Premise 2 lacks evidence, and Premise 1 is true only for some words and some languages. The Conclusion seems a bit of a leap.

4. The argument seems basically sound, although one might reasonably question the power of the effect asserted by Premise 2. In comparison with all the other things that affect attitudes towards gender equality, language might not be a very important factor. Or the effect might be spurious.

5. There are some obvious tensions between these claims (made by Thrasymachus in Plato's *Republic*). Obedience to law does not necessarily mean the advantage of the stronger, and vice versa. The tension between Premises 1 and 2 and the Conclusion might be resolved if Thrasymachus were read as a nihilist or relativist.

6. Both Premises are strong. The biggest issue is with the inductive leap from the single case (Premise 2) to the global conclusion about colonial states in general (Conclusion).

7. Premise 1 is not uncomplicatedly true, unfortunately. Opinion polls show that Premise 2 corresponds only to a very limited extent with the true state of public opinion, with the rise of 'color-blindness' as a principle of governance and the backlash against affirmative action programs instigated during the Civil Rights era (Hackett and King 2019). The Conclusion is false. Strictly speaking, the argument as a whole is valid, but its components are not true.

8. This is Baruch Spinoza's argument that miracles are 'sheer absurdity'. If it is vulnerable at any point, it is Premise 1. A theist seeking to defend the existence of miracles can reject this Premise and see the argument fall apart. Premises 2 and 3 are true by definition, and the argument as a whole is valid, but if God is distinct from nature then Premise 1 is false.

End of Chapter 9 Exercises: Losing the training wheels

PART A: This exercise is up to you – there are any number of great possible answers. Some possibilities are sketched out below.[†]

1. Counter-argument: Essentialist definitions like 'sport must involve physical exertion' are at odds with the way we actually use language, which is dynamic, elastic and fuzzy. E-sports and motor-sports are both sports – it's in the name!
   Response: we have to draw the line somewhere when we make binary decisions about activities' inclusion in, or exclusion from, sporting competitions such as the Olympics. Our language reasonably reflects existing institutions and norms.

[†] These answers are written in a colloquial style – as you might sketch out notes as you plan. Obviously, they are not written in the formal academic English required for your university essays.

2. Counter-argument: President Trump could not build his wall, even under unified government, and his administration had a 70% loss rate in court during his first two years in office – compared with an average *win* rate for presidential administrations of 70%.

    Response: President Trump twice secured his first-choice nominee to the Supreme Court, and his base expressed satisfaction with his progress on building the wall.

3. Counter-argument: When we talk, we make appropriate causal connections between terms and objects in the world. We reasonably claim to have true justified beliefs.

    Response: Just because we think we can make truthful claims about the world doesn't mean that we are not really in the matrix, or brains in a vat, and thus cannot truly know anything at all about the world.

4. Counter-argument: Introvert traits such as contemplation, empathy and deep and complex thinking are far more important to success than extrovert ones. Gandhi, Rosa Parks and JK Rowling's successes stemmed from introvert traits.

    Response: Some introverts are wildly successful, but extroverts are more likely to seek and win power. The fact that books are written in defence of introversion is a *prima facie* case that extroversion is valued more, at least in the West.

5. Counter-argument: Relationships, meaning and accomplishment are the joint pillars of happiness. Boiling it down to friendship misses romantic and family relationships, which cross-national surveys show are central to happiness.

    Response: Many factors affect human happiness, but for beings who have evolved to be social, friendships are the most important. The romantic and family relationships you describe are fundamentally friendships or *philia* too.

PART B:

6. In my opinion (LOSE)
7. I argue (KEEP)
8. I would argue (LOSE)
9. I believe that (LOSE)
10. I collected and analyzed the data (KEEP)
11. My data show that (KEEP)
12. I reject the null hypothesis (KEEP)
13. For me personally, this is problematic (LOSE)

PART C: Again, this exercise has any number of good answers. Some examples are below:

14. Does the European Union retain its <u>legitimacy</u>? (the implicit consent of the governed; a reservoir of good will; legal controls upon governing majorities that effectively secure equal treatment and individual liberty)
15. As <u>rational</u> agents, are we <u>free</u>? (*Rational*: logical and reasonable; responses that cohere; optimal satisfaction of preferences. *Free*: self-determination; having control over one's actions; striving for inner justice; escaping determinism)
16. How does <u>environmentalism</u> balance relations between humans and natural systems? (deep ecology; conservation; restoration; improvement of natural world)
17. How do education systems resolve frictions between <u>diversity</u> and <u>standardization</u>? (*Diversity*: normative embrace of difference; empowerment. *Standardization*: commoditization; coordination; implementing technical standards)
18. Does <u>conservatism depoliticize inequality</u>? (*Conservatism*: inseparability of ideal and practical; appeal to tradition; right-wing ideology. *Depoliticize*: remove from the sphere of political influence; normative fetishization of 'apolitical' markets. *Inequality*: absolute or relative; social, political and economic disparities)
19. Why do <u>empires</u> collapse? (extensive territories under rule of single sovereign state; transnational corporations; control by force; control by tribute and indirect rule)

End of Chapter 10 Exercises: Reading critically

PART A: The answers to this section are entirely dependent upon which articles and books you have read. Try swapping answers with a friend and consider how useful your summaries are. As you read your friend's efforts, and look back over your own, consider the following:

- Is each summary written as an informative and grammatical sentence rather than just another question?
- Do the summaries make sense?
- Does each summary truly encapsulate the key argument in the article or book it is summarizing?
- Could the summaries be more informative? What could they usefully add?

- Are the summaries a bit wordy? If so, how could they convey the same information in fewer words?

PART B: Some suggested diagrams are below:

1. *On how to suppress political factions*

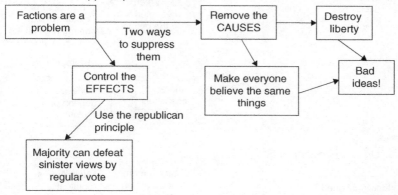

2. *On achieving successful crop rotation*

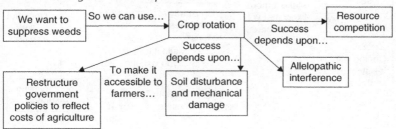

3. *On recruitment to the British House of Lords*

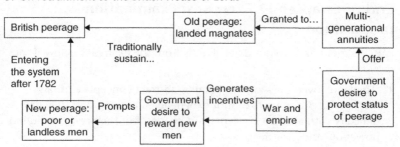

4. *On autonomous vehicles*

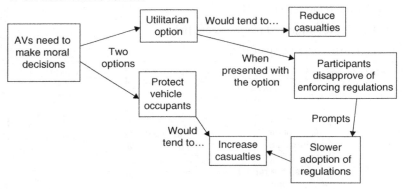

5. *On conspiracy theories*

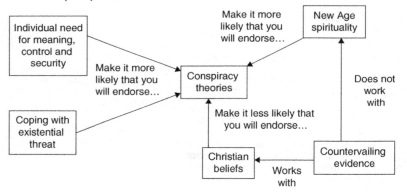

End of Chapter 11 Exercises: Examination preparation

PART A: Your efforts might differ slightly from the examples below. That's okay.

1. 'Thinking' involves emotions, images, abstract concepts and raw intelligence. Computers cannot experience emotions, and they have difficulty with abstract concepts and images, but their raw computing power outstrips our own.
2. The American state is formed by institutions, agencies and establishments distributed among legislative, executive and judicial branches.

3. The Mongol Empire's disintegration was a function of changing loyalties, factionalism and civil war.

PART B:

4. In order to answer this question we need to define our key terminology and consider any assumptions underlying the question. (CUT)
5. For decades, neo-colonialism has been the subject of much study by scholars. (MODIFY, e.g. 'Neo-colonialism was a term originally deployed by Marxists, but post–Cold War, the scope of its condemnation has expanded to include left-wing regimes and conservationism.')
6. By asking what price the US pays for its exceptionalism, this question assumes that the US is indeed exceptional. (KEEP)
7. Is the presidency the illusion of choice? The question, though concise, leads to a series of ongoing questions highlighting its ambiguity. This in turn intensifies the difficulty of answering the question, where do I begin? (CUT)
8. I argue that a misplaced focus on comparing the American state to European states has led to inaccurate claims of apparent weakness. Not only was the American state *not* weak from its birth, but it has only grown in strength. (KEEP)
9. Throughout history, there has been strong and continuous debate about how the landscape is shaped by human activity. (MODIFY, e.g. 'The term 'Anthropocene' is popular but problematic because it blames the entire human race for the crisis caused by relatively few corporations.')

PART C: Swap your efforts with a friend and consider each other's work. Is the argument clear? Could you guess the essay question from that paragraph alone? Can you decipher the handwriting?

References

Albarella, Umberto, Cluny Johnstone, and Kim Vickers. 2008. "The Development of Animal Husbandry from the Late Iron Age to the End of the Roman Period: A Case Study from South-East Britain." Journal of Archaeological Science 35 (7): 1828–48. https://doi.org/10.1016/j.jas.2007.11.016.

Archer, Alfred, Amanda Cawston, Benjamin Matheson, and Machteld Geuskens. 2020. "Celebrity, Democracy, and Epistemic Power." Perspectives on Politics 18 (1): 27–42. https://doi.org/10.1017/S1537592719002615.

Arpaly, Nomy. 2004. "Which Autonomy?" In Freedom and Determinism, edited by Joseph Keim Campbell, Michael O'Rourke, and David Shier, 173–88. MIT Press.

Aw, Tash. 2019. "Coming out of the Shadows: What It Means to Be French and Chinese." The Guardian, November 26, 2019, sec. The Long Read. https://www.theguardian.com/world/2019/nov/26/what-you-hear-about-chinese-people-in-france-feeling-scared-its-true.

Barnett, Eleanor. 2020. "Reforming Food and Eating in Protestant England, C. 1560–C. 1640." The Historical Journal 63 (3): 507–27. https://doi.org/10.1017/S0018246X19000426.

Bonnefon, Jean-François, Azim Shariff, and Iyad Rahwan. 2016. "The Social Dilemma of Autonomous Vehicles." Science 352 (6293): 1573–76. https://doi.org/10.1126/science.aaf2654.

Bruce, Vicki, and Andy Young. 1986. "Understanding Face Recognition." British Journal of Psychology 77 (3): 305–27. https://doi.org/10.1111/j.2044-8295.1986.tb02199.x.

Burkeman, Oliver. 2018. "Are Things Getting Worse – or Does It Just Feel That Way? | Oliver Burkeman." The Guardian, July 20, 2018, sec. Life and style. https://www.theguardian.com/lifeandstyle/2018/jul/20/things-getting-worse-or-feel-that-way.

Churchill, Lindsey Blake. 2020. "The Feminine Mystique." In Encyclopaedia Britannica. https://www.britannica.com/topic/The-Feminine-Mystique.

Davies, Gareth. 2020. "The Management of Tax Expenditures." HM Revenue & Customs, HM Treasury. https://www.nao.org.uk/wp-content/uploads/2020/02/The-management-of-tax-expenditure.pdf.

Foucault, Michel. 1994. Dits et Ecrits. Vol. IV. Paris: Gallimard.

Francis, Gavin. 2019. "What I Have Learned from My Suicidal Patients." The Guardian, November 22, 2019, sec. The Long Read. https://www.theguardian.com/lifeandstyle/2019/nov/22/doctor-gp-what-i-have-learned-from-my-suicidal-patients.

Frewer, L. J., A. Kole, S. M. A. Van de Kroon, and C. de Lauwere. 2005. "Consumer Attitudes Towards the Development of Animal-Friendly Husbandry Systems." Journal of Agricultural and Environmental Ethics 18 (4): 345–67. https://doi.org/10.1007/s10806-005-1489-2.

Gabriel, Fleur. 2014. "Sexting, Selfies and Self-Harm: Young People, Social Media and the Performance of Self-Development." Media International Australia 151 (1): 104–12. https://doi.org/10.1177/1329878X1415100114.

Gomes, Carlos Valério Aguiar, Jacqueline M. Vadjunec, and Stephen G. Perz. 2012. "Rubber Tapper Identities: Political-Economic Dynamics, Livelihood Shifts, and Environmental Implications in a Changing Amazon." Geoforum, SI – Party Politics, the Poor and the City: Reflections from South Africa 43 (2): 260–71. https://doi.org/10.1016/j.geoforum.2011.09.005.

Greenfield, Jerome. 2020. "The Mexican Expedition of 1862–1867 and the End of the French Second Empire." The Historical Journal 63 (3): 660–85. https://doi.org/10.1017/S0018246X19000657.

Hackett, Ursula. 2015. "But Not Both: The Exclusive Disjunction in Qualitative Comparative Analysis (QCA)". Quality and Quantity 49 (1): 75–92. https://doi.org/10.1007/s11135-013-9975-5.

———. 2016. "The Goldilocks Principle: Applying the Exclusive Disjunction to Fuzzy Sets". International Journal of Social Research Methodology 19 (5): 551–74. https://doi.org/10.1080/13645579.2015.1053708.

Hackett, Ursula, and Desmond King. 2019. "The Reinvention of Vouchers for a Color-Blind Era: A Racial Orders Account." Studies in American Political Development 33 (2): 234–57. https://doi.org/10.1017/S0898588X19000075.

Hamilton, Alexander, James Madison, and John Jay. 2008. The Federalist Papers. Oxford: Oxford University Press.

Hanß, Stefan. 2019. "Material Encounters: Knotting Cultures in Early Modern Peru and Spain." The Historical Journal 62 (3): 583–615. https://doi.org/10.1017/S0018246X18000468.

Keynes, John Maynard. 2010. Essays in Persuasion. London: Palgrave Macmillan.

Khan, Sameeullah, and Asif Iqbal Fazili. 2019. "Does the Need for Social Status among Price Conscious Consumers Induce Consumption of Counterfeit Luxury Brands?" Journal of Business and Management 25 (2): 43–70.

Kierkegaard, Soren. 1992. Either/Or: A Fragment of Life. London: Penguin Classics.

Kung, Hans. 1992. Mozart: Traces of Transcendence. SCM Press.

Leach, Elizabeth Eva. 2007. Sung Birds: Music, Nature, and Poetry in the Later Middle Ages. Ithaca, NY: Cornell University Press.

Liebman, Matt, and Elizabeth Dyck. 1993. "Crop Rotation and Intercropping Strategies for Weed Management." Ecological Applications 3 (1): 92–122. https://doi.org/10.2307/1941795.

McCahill, Michael, and Ellis Archer Wasson. 2003. "The New Peerage: Recruitment to the House of Lords, 1704–1847." The Historical Journal 46 (1): 1–38. https://doi.org/10.1017/S0018246X02002820.

Moody, Myles. 2016. "From Under-Diagnoses to Over-Representation: Black Children, ADHD, and the School-To-Prison Pipeline." Journal of African American Studies 20 (2): 152–63. https://doi.org/10.1007/s12111-016-9325-5.

Mounk, Yascha. 2019. "The Great American Eye-Exam Scam." The Atlantic, November 27, 2019. https://www.theatlantic.com/ideas/archive/2019/11/great-american-eye-exam-scam/602482/?utm_source=share&utm_campaign=share.

Natali, Denise. 2011. "Can Federalism Work in Iraq?" Institute for National Strategic Studies. https://www.files.ethz.ch/isn/134644/ER-Iraq%20Federalism.pdf.

Newheiser, Anna-Kaisa, Miguel Farias, and Nicole Tausch. 2011. "The Functional Nature of Conspiracy Beliefs: Examining the Underpinnings of Belief in the Da Vinci Code Conspiracy." Personality and Individual Differences 51 (8): 1007–11. https://doi.org/10.1016/j.paid.2011.08.011.

Pinker, Steven. 2014. The Sense of Style: The Thinking Person's Guide to Writing in the 21st Century. New York: Penguin Books.

Shabi, Rachel. 2019. "How Immigration Became Britain's Most Toxic Political Issue." The Guardian, November 15, 2019, sec. The Long Read. https://www.theguardian.com/politics/2019/nov/15/how-immigration-became-britains-most-toxic-political-issue.

Smith, Kate. 2012. "Sensing Design and Workmanship: The Haptic Skills of Shoppers in Eighteenth-Century London." Journal of Design History 25 (1): 1–10. https://doi.org/10.1093/jdh/epr053.

Stanford Encyclopedia of Philosophy. 2003. "The Free Rider Problem." May 21, 2003. https://plato.stanford.edu/entries/free-rider/.

———. 2011a. "Medieval Semiotics." May 11, 2011. https://plato.stanford.edu/entries/semiotics-medieval/.

———. 2011b. "Culture and Cognitive Science." November 2, 2011. https://plato.stanford.edu/entries/culture-cogsci/.

———. 2018a. "Free Will." August 21, 2018. https://plato.stanford.edu/entries/freewill/#DoWeHaveFreeWill.

———. 2018b. "Doctrine of Double Effect." December 24, 2018. https://plato.stanford.edu/entries/double-effect/.

Trakakis, Nick. 2008. "Theodicy: The Solution to the Problem of Evil, or Part of the Problem?" Sophia 47 (2): 161. https://doi.org/10.1007/s11841-008-0063-6.

Williamson, Abigail Fisher. 2020. "Intergovernmental Policy Feedback and Urban Responses to Immigrants." PS: Political Science & Politics 53 (1): 20–4. https://doi.org/10.1017/S1049096519001355.

Index

Made in the USA
Las Vegas, NV
12 January 2024

84241305R00125

Among the constituents of knowledge are belief and truth: Because the earth is not flat, no one can know that the earth is flat, and no one can know that the earth is round without believing that it is. There are purported counterexamples to these claims, but they are not persuasive. David Lewis, for example, considers a student who, he reports, knows when Columbus discovered America (because he answers correctly on a test), but doesn't believe anything here in virtue of being too uncertain of the date.[1] I reject this account of the case. First, answering correctly on a test is not a litmus test for knowledge. Either the answer is a sheer guess (the student perhaps knows that the discovery had to be in the last thousand years, and randomly picks three numbers to put after the number 1), or the student is answering based in part on information possessed. If the latter, the lack of confidence is not a sign of lack of belief; it is rather an indication of (second-order) uncertainty about the truth of what is believed. In that case, the case looks more like either a case in which the student knows the date but holds no opinion (is uncertain) about whether he or she knows the date, or a case of belief without knowledge. In the former case, in which the answer is a sheer guess, it is wholly implausible to think that a correct answer is an indicator of knowledge, for guesses are not knowledge.

Regarding the connection between knowledge and truth, it is becoming more common for students, infused with relativistic ideas, to maintain that it was once known that the earth is flat, but it is now known that the earth is round. Such students confuse knowledge with justified belief, however. What is true is that to the best of the knowledge at the time, the best viewpoint to adopt was that the earth was flat; in short, the viewpoint that was justified by the evidence was the flat earth viewpoint. Now we know better. That is, the viewpoint best justified by the evidence we possess is that the earth is not flat.

If such misstatement occurs often enough and becomes widespread enough, the term 'knows' will acquire a different meaning than it currently possesses. It may become a synonym for 'justified belief'. But it is not yet one, as is shown by the plausibility of the preceding explanation of the error made in saying that it was once known that the earth is flat. So knowledge requires truth (and always will, even if the meaning of the term 'knows' changes so that the sentence "Knowledge requires truth" comes to express a falsehood). Hence, another way to account for the

---

1. David Lewis, "Elusive Knowledge," *Australasian Journal of Philosophy*, 74,4 (1996): 549–67.

value of knowledge is to derive it in part from the value of truth, or perhaps from the value of truth in combination with belief.

The other constituents of knowledge are more controversial. Some say that justification is a constituent of knowledge, and adherents of this viewpoint may attempt to account for the value of knowledge at least in part by the value of justified belief. Even if justification is required for knowledge, it is not sufficient for knowledge, even when combined with true belief. So at least a fourth condition is required, and the need for a fourth condition can lead one to suspect that justification is not required at all. It may be that whatever fourth condition one accepts makes justification otiose. In any case, the nature of the fourth condition for knowledge may also be appealed to in an account of the value of knowledge.

If we proceed straightforwardly to account for the value of knowledge, we will look at each of its components to see if they have value and explain the value of knowledge in terms of the increase in value contributed by each of these components. But some may not be happy with this manner of proceeding. As we shall see, it is very hard to account for the value of knowledge in terms of the value of its constituents, leading to an interest in a different approach to the question of the value of knowledge. Second, there is the rare breed who thinks knowledge is not composite. In either case, there is motivation for thinking of the value of knowledge in terms of knowledge itself rather than in terms of the value of its constituents, motivation for thinking that knowledge is valuable in itself, independently of its relationship to anything else, including its purported constituents.

As I have pointed out, the historical roots of this inquiry are found in the *Meno*, with the discussion between Meno and Socrates concerning the relationship between the value of knowledge and the value of right opinion. In order not to mislead, however, it is important from the outset to distance the problems and issues of this inquiry from the Platonic issue (or set of issues). I have already intimated that one way in which I diverge from the Platonic setting is that I will approach the problem of the value of knowledge assuming that true belief is a constituent of knowledge. Rather than propose to investigate the Platonic issue of the value of knowledge, I instead use Plato's discussion as a point of origin for an investigation that is a natural extension of it. Besides the point already noted, it would be objectionably anachronistic to introduce issues surrounding the Gettier problem into Plato's discussion of a few millennia earlier. It is also the case that there are a number of lines of inquiry that could claim to be legitimate heirs of Plato's discussion, and I make no pretext against such by labeling the problem I will address the *Meno problem*. The problem of how, and whether, knowledge has a value that exceeds that of its parts, the *Meno* problem, has its roots in the discussion between Socrates and Meno in Plato's dialogue, but I do not claim that it is precisely the problem that interests Plato or that there are no other issues surrounding the value of knowledge that can lay claim to being the natural offspring of Plato's discussion. The previously discussed possibilities of addressing the problem of the value of knowledge arise because of the specific nature of the problem of the value of knowledge that prompts this inquiry, rather than through exegetical inspection of the Platonic text.

These possibilities create a map of exploration of the question of how and whether knowledge has a value exceeding that of its parts. In Chapter 1, I examine attempts to find the value of knowledge in things external to it, including its practical benefits. I argue that such accounts fail to generate an adequate account of the value of knowledge. I consider and reject the practical benefits approach on the same grounds that Socrates rejects it, but I also consider two other proposals about how the value of knowledge involves things external to it. Both proposals originate in the work of Timothy Williamson, the first being that knowledge is more immune to being undermined by future evidence than is true belief, and the second depending on the claim that knowledge is the norm of assertion. I argue that neither of these approaches provides an adequate defense of the value of knowledge.

In Chapters 2 through 5, I explore the value of the purported constituents of knowledge, including truth, belief, justification, reliability, and a variety of approaches to the Gettier problem. These chapters evaluate the attempt to find the value of knowledge in terms of the amalgamation of the value of its parts, and in order to investigate this idea, I want to be liberal in granting theorists as much as I can as to what the constituents of knowledge are. So, for example, even though I have defended the idea that true belief is a constituent of knowledge, my investigation of the value of true belief does not require the endorsement of that idea. Instead, I grant the assumption to see how far the idea of accounting for the value of knowledge in terms of the value of its parts can be taken. A similar point applies to the ideas that justification is required for knowledge or that reliability of belief-forming processes is necessary for knowledge. Regarding each such proposal, I will grant the claim in order to focus on the question of the value of knowledge, rather than following what would be, given my purposes, the red herring path of debating the nature of knowledge.

Granting these assumptions about the nature of knowledge is important for the relevance of these chapters to my project, for a satisfactory answer to the question of the value of knowledge will need to explain why knowledge is, by its very nature, more valuable than its parts. It will not be enough, for example, to show that sometimes or in some places knowledge is more valuable than its parts. Instead, we will need to show that no matter what the world happens to be like, knowledge is more valuable.

An example may help here. Suppose some (and only some) of our knowledge is infallible. If so, then knowledge of this kind is immensely valuable to have, for it involves beliefs about which we cannot be mistaken. Even so, the existence of such infallible knowledge will not assuage my concerns about the value of knowledge, for the existence of such could only show that *some* knowledge is more valuable than its parts. What we are in search of is something stronger: We want to find out whether knowledge is, by its very nature, more valuable than its parts, and no answer to this question can be satisfactory if it appeals to contingent features of knowledge.

So in investigating the relationship between knowledge and purported constituents of it, I grant for the sake of the inquiry the claims of constituency in order to focus on the question of the value of knowledge. In line with this approach, Chapter 2 argues that true belief is valuable, a task I approach by arguing for the value of belief and for the value of truth. I defend the value of belief against views that suggest that some weaker mental state is better or that merely acting as if certain claims are true would be better. Such arguments against the value of belief are commonly associated with Pyrrhonian skepticism and with the constructive empiricism of Bas van Fraassen[2] and related instrumentalist views in the philosophy of science. I argue against the view that some weaker concept than truth, such as empirical adequacy, suffices for our cognitive interests and needs. Chapters 3 and 4 explore the third condition for knowledge, normally expressed in terms of the concept of justification. Chapter 3 argues for the importance of a strongly internalist, subjective kind of justification, and Chapter 4 develops the special promise that virtue epistemology offers in the attempt to account for the value of knowledge. These chapters take us quite a ways toward explaining the value of knowledge in terms of the value of its constituents (assuming, again, that these purported constituents of knowledge are genuine constituents of it). The

2. Bas van Fraassen, *The Scientific Image* (Oxford: Clarenden Press, 1980).

attempt to account for the value of knowledge in terms of the value of its constituents comes to an end in Chapter 5, however, where I argue for a hitherto unnoticed difficulty introduced by the Gettier problem. I explain how the Gettier problem, a difficult problem concerning the nature of knowledge, raises an insoluble problem concerning the value of knowledge. The Gettier problem creates a tension between the two requirements of a theory of knowledge, between the need to account for both the nature and the value of knowledge, for the better one's approach to that problem is in terms of accounting for the nature of knowledge, the less useful it becomes for the task of explaining the value of knowledge. I argue, that is, that the potential of an approach to the Gettier problem for adequately addressing the problem of the nature of knowledge is inversely proportional to the potential for being able to account for the value of knowledge.

Chapters 6 and 7 are motivated by the failure to develop an explanation of the value of knowledge on the basis of the value of its purported constituents, exploring more-direct ways of accounting for the value of knowledge. Chapter 6 argues against the claim that knowledge is valuable independently of any relationship to things external to it or to its purported constituents. Chapter 7 explores how nondescriptive approaches to the nature of knowledge might be used to account for its value and argues that such approaches to knowledge are not especially promising. Such an attitudinalist view of knowledge has been suggested by Hartry Field,[3] and I argue that versions of attitudinalism are also found in Mark Heller's version of contextualism and in John Greco's latest account of knowledge.[4] These chapters thus approach the question of the value of knowledge directly, one with descriptivist assumptions about the nature of knowledge and the other with nondescriptivist assumptions, and I argue that neither approach is successful.

Thus, I will be arguing that knowledge is valuable, but that it fails to have a value exceeding that of its parts, thereby leaving us with no adequate answer to the problem of the value of knowledge first posed by

3. Hartry Field, "The A Priacity of Logic," *Proceedings of the Aristotelian Society*, 96 (1996): 359–79; "Epistemological Nonfactualism and the A Priority of Logic," *Philosophical Studies*, 92 (1998): 1–24.
4. Mark Heller, "The Proper Role for Contextualism in an Anti-Luck Epistemology," *Philosophical Perspectives, 13, Epistemology*, James Tomberlin, ed. (Cambridge, MA: Blackwell, 1999), pp. 115–29; John Greco, "Knowledge as Credit for True Belief," in *Intellectual Virtue: Perspectives from Ethics and Epistemology*, Michael DePaul and Linda Zagzebski, eds. (Oxford: Oxford University Press, forthcoming).

Plato in the *Meno*. I will also be arguing that this conclusion should cause us to rethink our assumptions of the central concepts for epistemological theorizing. For, I will argue, there are other concepts with equal claim to theoretical importance for which we can provide an answer to Socrates' question. That is, we can cite some theoretical achievements that have more value than true belief and are more valuable than their parts, a topic that will occupy us in Chapter 8. In particular, I will argue in that chapter that understanding is just such an achievement, and the pursuit of understanding is no insignificant relative in the cognitive realm to the search for knowledge. The conclusion toward which I drive, then, is that epistemological inquiry deserves at least some enlargement in the direction of concepts other than knowledge.

I have had much help in this endeavor from valued colleagues, friends, and students, among whom are Colin Allen, Richard Feldman, John Greco, Michael Hand, Robert Johnson, Peter Markie, Matt McGrath, Paul McNamara, Cristian Mihut, Michael Pace, Chris Robichaud, Robin Smith, Scott Sturgeon, Paul Weirich, and Timothy Williamson. Ward Jones and Wayne Riggs deserve special mention for their detailed and helpful comments on the entire penultimate draft. My work has benefited immensely from their help, and I am grateful for it.

1

The Value of Knowledge Is External to It

With the scientific sophistication of the local news, I polled some folk (my son and daughter) about the value of knowledge. They apparently think of knowledge as Quine thinks of induction: Those eschewing it tend to fall off cliffs. Knowledge is good, the survey says, because you can make more money with it, get into a better college, get a better job, live a better life.

These answers are examples of finding the value of knowledge in its connection to practical affairs of life. Instead of tracing the value of knowledge to the value of its constituents or some intrinsic value that it has, these accounts claim that knowledge is valuable because it is useful.

The most obvious alternative to this account of the value of knowledge is the view that knowledge has value intrinsically. Academics often lament the pragmatism of undergraduates who prize knowledge only indirectly, in terms of what it can get for them in terms of money, prestige, power, and the like. Academics like to insist, instead, that knowledge is valuable for its own sake and not (just) because it helps you get a good job or get rich.

These two theories provide paradigm examples of the kinds of theories of the value of knowledge I want to explore, but they are only paradigms and not exhaustive of available approaches. The pragmatic theory is paradigmatic of theories that locate the value of knowledge in things logically distinct from knowledge itself, and the intrinsic value theory is paradigmatic of theories that locate the value of knowledge in things logically tied to knowledge itself. In this chapter, I will explore views that explain the value of knowledge in terms of things external to it, starting with the most obvious such theory, the theory that locates the value of knowledge in its usefulness.

1

There is much to be said on behalf of this account. First, we often explain things not going well in terms of a lack of knowledge. Parents often lament not doing a better job raising their children with the phrase "if we'd only known better." And sometimes, at least, the lack of knowledge provides insulation from moral responsibility. Many of our military were told, on assignment in Nagasaki after World War II, that the dangers of radiation exposure could be eliminated by taking a good shower every day. Perhaps the advisors knew better, but if they didn't, they have an excuse for the damage they caused. We often unwittingly hurt the feelings of those we care about and offer as an excuse that we didn't know what effect our actions would have. Medical personnel are exonerated in courtroom proceedings for damaging treatment because they simply didn't know and couldn't be held responsible for not knowing.

On the positive side, we often seek knowledge in order to obtain certain benefits. Those who invest in the stock market often spend enormous amounts of time in knowledge acquisition before making investment decisions, convinced that the additional knowledge will improve their likelihood of success. Good parents reward the search for knowledge in their children, viewing it as an indicator of success in life, and the most common defense given for spending time pursuing a college degree is that one's earning power will be greatly enhanced by the acquisition of knowledge that is required for the degree.

In a similar vein, it is often also said that knowledge is power. This slogan should not be taken literally, but it signals a perceived connection between what we know and the capacity for getting what we want.

It would be one-sided to ignore at this point the negative effects of knowledge as well, however. Knowing what causes pain helps torturers ply their trade; knowing that smallpox was deadly to native populations aided North American immigrants in destroying those populations.

So it is false to say that knowledge produces only good effects. The pragmatic theory of the value of knowledge need make no such claim, however. Instead of claiming that knowledge can only produce good effects, the pragmatic theory bids us to hold certain factors fixed in assessing the value of knowledge. Knowledge is valuable, on this account, because, in the hands of good and honest people, it opens up possibilities of good effects that wouldn't be available without knowledge.

It is in this special way that knowledge is associated with good things and the lack of knowledge with bad things in our ordinary patterns of

2

activity and in our conception of such. It is somewhat of a shock to this way of thinking, then, to find that the earliest philosophical investigations of the value of knowledge begin by challenging this association. In Plato's *Meno*, Socrates challenges Meno on this very question.[1] In particular, Socrates wants to know what makes knowledge more valuable than true opinion, and he points out that true opinions have all the practical benefits of knowledge. His example concerns traveling "to Larissa, or anywhere else you like" (97a). The man who merely judges correctly how to get to Larissa will nonetheless be every bit as successful in his journey as the man who knows the way. So Socrates rejects the idea that knowledge is more valuable than true opinion because of its practical benefits. As he puts it, "Therefore true opinion is as good a guide as knowledge for the purpose of acting rightly" (97b), and "right opinion is something no less useful than knowledge" (97c).

Notice, however, that the question shifts here from the one with which we began. We began wanting to know whether knowledge is valuable, and if so, why. If we infer a negative answer to the first question on the basis of Socrates' discussion, we may be accused of the following mistake. Suppose we want to know whether gold is valuable, and we try to answer that question by asking whether it is more valuable than platinum. Upon learning that it is not more valuable than platinum, we infer that gold is not valuable.

Of course, this analogy is not perfect if we assume that true opinion is among the constituents of knowledge. For once we acknowledge the relationship of constitution, other analogies become more appropriate. If we claim that a diamond ring is valuable, we might be corrected by someone who knows that the diamond taken from its setting would be just as valuable. Or, again, if a hero-worshipping Little Leaguer claims that his Ken Griffey, Jr., autographed baseball bat hits better because of the autograph, he would be wrong. The bat without the signature would be just as good (once we control for the placebo effect of the signature, of course).

We could escape Socrates' counterexample, however, if we were willing to claim that knowledge is valuable but no more valuable than true opinion. Yet, part of the challenge of explaining the value of knowledge is in explaining how it has more value than other things, one of these other things being true opinion – as Meno claims after acquiescing to

---

1. Plato, *Meno*; all quotes are from the W. K. C. Guthrie translation in *The Collected Dialogues of Plato*, Edith Hamilton and Huntington Cairns, eds. (Princeton, NJ: Princeton University Press, 1963), pp. 353–84.

Socrates' point that true belief is every bit as useful as knowledge. "In that case, I wonder why knowledge should be so much more prized than right opinion" (97c–d). Meno expresses here a common presupposition about knowledge, one that is widely, if not universally, shared. Given this presupposition, an account of the value of knowledge must explain more than how knowledge is valuable. It must also explain why the value of knowledge is superior to the value of true opinion.

Socrates' claims are therefore telling against the pragmatic account of the value of knowledge. Knowledge is valuable because it is useful, but an account of the value of knowledge cannot be complete without something further. For true opinion, one of the constituents of knowledge, is equally useful, and yet knowledge is more valuable than true opinion. Hence the value of knowledge must be explained in terms beyond its pragmatic usefulness.

This conclusion holds so long as we refuse to identify knowledge with true opinion, an identification with which Meno toys ("I wonder ... indeed how there is any difference between them" (97c–d)). Socrates uses an "analogy" (98b) to illustrate both the difference between them and the superiority of the value of knowledge over that of true belief, an analogy we shall look at carefully a bit later, and concludes

But it is not, I am sure, a mere guess to say that right opinion and knowledge are different. There are few things that I should claim to know, but that at least is among them, whatever else is. (98b)

Socrates does not tell us how knowledge is different from right opinion, but he is convinced that there is a difference. So Socrates is convinced that he knows that the account of knowledge that Meno suggests is false. That fact is interesting in its own right, coming from a philosopher who conceived of his own wisdom in terms of an understanding of the limitations on what he knows, but equally interesting in the present context is the way in which Meno's theory is prompted. Meno's toying with the identification of knowledge and correct opinion is a result of having his proposed theory of the value of knowledge undermined, indicating an interplay in his mind between accounts of the nature of knowledge and accounts of the value of knowledge. For Meno, counterexamples to his suggestion about the value of knowledge tempt him to endorse an account of the nature of knowledge that blocks the counterexamples. Socrates' response is that even to one who knows (nearly) nothing, Meno's suggestion regarding the nature of knowledge is known to be false. This interplay between accounts of the nature and value of knowledge is no mistake on Meno's

4

part. It would be a strange dialectic to find a theoretician completely satisfied with an account of the nature of knowledge known to be incompatible with any value for knowledge. Coherence might be restored by some further explanation, and the point to note is the need for such further explanation to address the cognitive dissonance present in such a strange conjunction of epistemological views. The interplay between the nature and value of knowledge present in Meno's thinking exists because there is a presumption in favor of holding an epistemological theory responsible to two criteria. A correct account of the nature of knowledge must resist counterexample, but it also ought to be amenable to an account of the value of knowledge. Meno's inclination to abandon an account of the nature of knowledge should still arise, even if that account is able to resist counterexample, provided that account fails to allow an explanation of the value of knowledge.

Note what I am not claiming here: I am not claiming that an adequate account of the nature of knowledge must contain an explanation of the value of knowledge. Nor am I claiming that an adequate account of the nature of knowledge must appeal to elements of knowledge that are themselves valuable. I am not even claiming that knowledge is valuable. I am, instead, claiming a presumption in favor of the view that knowledge is valuable, and more valuable than subsets of its constituents, and that failed attempts to account for the value of knowledge legitimately prompt questioning of one's assumed theory of the nature of knowledge. The presumption in favor of the value of knowledge is strong enough that it gives reason to abandon even a counterexample-free account of the nature of knowledge if that account leaves no way open for defending the value of knowledge.

It is important to note here a further thing that I am not saying. When I say that there is a presumption in favor of the value of knowledge, I am not saying that the only way an account of the nature of knowledge can be adequate is to be capable of being supplemented by some adequate account of the value of knowledge. I leave open the conclusion at which I aim in this work, namely, that we are mistaken to attach such significance to knowledge, that the valuable accomplishments of cognition are to be found in the general area inhabited by knowledge but do not require knowledge itself. That is, when knowledge is valuable, its value is to be explained in ways that do not require the presence of knowledge for that value to obtain. Coming to such a conclusion should change our conception of the tasks for epistemology, and I will indicate some of the differences such a conclusion will make.

But where I will end up is not where I begin, for there is a strong presumption in favor of the view that knowledge is valuable. So we ought to begin by seeking an explanation of the value of knowledge, and my discussion of Plato's *Meno* is meant to highlight dual presumptive conditions of adequacy for a theory of knowledge. First, an adequate theory of knowledge must contain an account of the nature of knowledge that is, at a minimum, counterexample-free. (I ignore for present purposes other theoretical virtues that the account will need to possess to be preferable to other counterexample-free accounts.) Second, the theory must be amenable to an account of the value of knowledge. What do I mean by "amenable to"? At the very least, the theory must be logically consistent with an account of the value of knowledge, but perhaps something stronger is required. Perhaps the two accounts should fit well together or cohere in some way beyond being merely consistent with each other; but we shall start with the minimal requirement of logical consistency.

Given these twin desiderata, Socrates' counterexample to Meno's account of the value of knowledge shows that Meno's account cannot be adequate so long as knowledge is anything more than true belief. Meno's reaction is to consider the possibility that knowledge is nothing more than true belief, but Socrates immediately rejects this idea, and this reaction is nearly universally shared among epistemologists. But only nearly universally shared; recently, Crispin Sartwell has tried to resurrect Meno's theory,[2] seriously defending Meno's first shot from the hip when confronted with the problem of the value of knowledge. It is very hard, however, not to side with Socrates against Sartwell. Socrates provides an interesting analogy to display the difference between knowledge and true belief, as well as the more straightforward route in terms of a counterexample.

Such counterexamples can be multiplied. For example, one need only look at the voluminous body of literature on the Gettier problem to find counterexample after counterexample to the claim that knowledge is true belief. One can even find an unanswered counterexample in Sartwell's own work. He says:

On the other hand, and this is where the present account runs into difficulties, we may be pressing the question of the source of belief. For example, if we find out that the claimant in this case has recently emerged from a mental hospital,

2. Crispin Sartwell, "Knowledge Is True Belief," *American Philosophical Quarterly*, 28, 2 (1991): 157–65.

and regards the voices in her head as reliable sources of information, we may well ask how she knows that $2 + 2 = 4$. If she now replies that one of these voices told her, we may say (though with some strain to common sense) that she didn't know it after all.[3]

Sartwell notes immediately that his account "obliges me to deny this claim,"[4] but all we get by way of argument for such a denial is a remark that "it *is* natural in a case such as this one to say that we *all* know that $2 + 2 = 4$; it is 'common knowledge'; in a typical case it would be perverse to ask of any one person *how* she knows it."[5] None of these claims is a sufficient reply to the counterexample, however. It may be natural to say that everyone knows simple arithmetical truths, but it is false. It is natural to say it because the counterexamples are so rare, not because they do not exist. Second, simple arithmetical truths are among the items of common knowledge, as Sartwell points out, but not everyone knows all of these items. Finally, though it is clearly not perverse to ask someone how he or she knows such simple truths, it is certainly unusual. But many of the questions therapists need to ask mental patients in order to ascertain their degree of sanity are similarly unusual.

Hence, Sartwell has no good response to his own counterexample. In light of this and the multitude of other counterexamples, how could Sartwell maintain the view that knowledge is only true belief? The answer lies in the argument that persuades him to maintain this uncommon and implausible thesis.

Sartwell's argument[6] focuses on the question of the goal, or *telos*, of inquiry with regard to particular propositions, which he maintains is knowledge.[7] He argues that an adequate theory of justification will be teleological, a means to the goal of truth. The argument is, he thinks, simple – that justification is not necessary for knowledge:

If we describe justification as of merely instrumental value with regard to arriving at truth, as BonJour does explicitly, we can no longer maintain both that knowledge is the *telos* of inquiry and that justification is a necessary condition of knowledge. It is incoherent to build a specification of something regarded *merely* as a means of achieving some goal into the description of the goal itself; in such

3. Ibid., p. 162.
4. Ibid.
5. Ibid., p. 163.
6. Crispin Sartwell, "Why Knowledge Is Merely True Belief," *Journal of Philosophy*, 89, 4 (1992): 167–80.
7. Ibid., p. 173.

circumstances, the goal can be described independently of the means. So, if justification is demanded because it is instrumental to true belief, it cannot also be maintained that knowledge is justified true belief.[8]

Before commenting on the argument directly, I want to forestall one misunderstanding of Sartwell's conclusion. Because those familiar with the Gettier literature will balk at the claim that knowledge is justified true belief, it might seem that Sartwell's conclusion can be avoided just by holding that knowledge is more than justified true belief. But, as Sartwell makes clear, that would miss the point of the argument. Better put, Sartwell's conclusion is that if justification is of merely instrumental value, then knowledge is not even *at least* justified true belief. The instrumental value of justification is supposed to force us to take justification as only a criterion for knowledge, a mark we look for when we are trying to answer the question of whether someone knows, rather than a necessary condition for knowledge.[9]

The central stated premise of the argument for this claim is that "it is incoherent to build a specification of something regarded *merely* as a means of achieving some goal into the description of the goal itself." It is not obvious how to get from this claim to Sartwell's conclusion, but I think he is reasoning as follows:

1. Knowledge is the goal of inquiry.
2. Nothing that is merely a means to a goal is a necessary component of that goal.
3. Justification is merely a means to the goal of inquiry.
4. Therefore, justification is not a necessary component of the goal of inquiry.
5. Therefore, justification is not a necessary component of knowledge.

Premise 1, Sartwell admits, is undefended.[10] But that is not the primary defect of the argument. The primary defect is that this assumption simply will not be granted in the presence of premise 3, the claim that justification is a means to the goal of inquiry. Sartwell cites a long list of epistemologists who conceive of justification in instrumental terms, but they do not conceive of it as a means to the goal of inquiry except insofar as that goal is clarified in terms of getting to the truth and avoiding error. They do not conceive of justification as of instrumental value for knowledge,

---

8. Ibid., p. 174.
9. Ibid.
10. Ibid. In fairness to Sartwell, he does claim in footnote 11 that "I hope to establish this claim on completely independent grounds." I am unaware of any place where he tries to so establish the claim.

8

but rather for truth over error. So Sartwell cannot appeal to the views of epistemologists to establish the third premise of this argument unless he first abandons the first premise and clarifies the goal of inquiry in terms of truth.

Of course, if one already holds the view that knowledge is true belief, then one can easily accept both of these premises and even see the claims of epistemologists who endorse the view that justification is instrumentally valuable in the search for truth as supporting one's affirmations. But that is because one has already rejected the necessity of justification for knowledge. It appears, then, that the argument would only be accepted by those who already accept its conclusion.

What of the first premise, though? Is knowledge the goal of inquiry? I do not think that is the correct way to think of inquiry. When we engage in inquiry, we are trying to get to the truth about the subject matter in question. Inquiry ceases when we take ourselves to have found the truth. That is, human beings do not typically conceive of inquiry in terms of knowledge, but rather, to use a common phrase, as "the search for truth." Inquirers describe the task in these terms, and the object of their intentions, when inquiry is accompanied by such, involves the concept of truth. Of course, it can also involve knowledge, but it needn't. So no argument will be forthcoming from reflective descriptions of human beings or from the contents of their intentions that knowledge must be the goal of inquiry. Inquiry is not "directed at" knowledge in either of these senses by its very nature, but instead can be, and often is (perhaps usually is), "directed at" finding the truth and avoiding error.

The best that might be true is that successful inquiry yields knowledge, and so that knowledge is a product of inquiry successfully conducted and hence the, or a, *telos* of inquiry in that sense. This is a claim that, if true, will not rescue Sartwell's argument. If knowledge is the result of successful inquiry in this sense, it is possible for justification to be both a means to it and a constituent of it as well. If becoming elected a senator is the result of a successful campaign, then running a successful campaign can be both a means to this goal and a constituent as well. The tension Sartwell cites between constituents of and means to some item arises at most in the intentional realm, but need not arise once we leave that realm. Indeed, if we consider the general concept of a means to a goal, some compelling examples are where the means are sufficient to produce the effect. So Sartwell's premise implies that no means sufficient to produce X can itself be necessary for X. This claim, however, is obviously false; some means toward a goal are both necessary and sufficient for achieving that goal.

9

Most means to a goal are not sufficient for the achievement of the goal to which they are directed, so Sartwell might restrict the premise to talk only of such insufficient means. This alteration is still false, however. A means toward the goal of getting a million dollars is getting half a million, or getting nine hundred thousand, or getting the first dollar (a journey of a thousand miles begins with the first step). Yet, each of these means is also a necessary constituent of the goal in question, so the alteration won't work either.

So Sartwell's argument is defective on several fronts, leaving his position that knowledge is true belief without adequate argumentative support. The proper conclusion to draw is that there is no reason to satisfy Meno's temptation by adopting the view that knowledge is true belief and many reasons against it in the form of counterexamples.

If knowledge is not true belief, then Socrates' counterexample shows that knowledge is no more practically useful than is true belief. So abandoning the claim that knowledge is true belief forces us to abandon the idea that the value of knowledge is to be accounted for by its practical significance in the lives of those who have it.

This conclusion is compatible with the claim that knowledge gives practical advantage to those who have it. It is just that the advantage they gain would have been achieved even if they had only gained true belief and not knowledge. So it is not their knowledge that explains their advantage but rather the fact that when one knows something, one has a true belief about it. Consider cases from the theory of explanation to make this point clear. A white, crystalline substance is immersed in water, and we want to know why it dissolves. Joe says it is because it is salt, but Billy disagrees. He says it is because it is *hexed* salt that it dissolves. If it is somehow useful to have a substance dissolved in our sample of water, we cannot claim that it is hexed salt that is valuable for that purpose. It does accomplish the goal we have in mind, but not because it is hexed salt; instead, it accomplishes the goal because all hexed salt is salt and salt dissolves in water. So hexed salt will be useful to us, but not because it is hexed salt. Instead, it will be useful to us because it is salt. Just so, knowledge is useful to us, but not because it is knowledge. Instead, it is useful because it involves true belief. Hence, pragmatic usefulness does not explain why knowledge is valuable; in particular, it does not explain why knowledge is more valuable than true belief.

A natural response at this point might be skepticism concerning the value we seek to explain. We began by noting the value of knowledge and have found a sense in which it is valuable and a sense in which it may not be as valuable as we initially thought. Knowledge is valuable because of the practical benefits it provides. The only shadow of a problem is that it is not superior to true belief on this score. But, the skeptic might query, isn't that enough? We now have an account on which knowledge is valuable, and that is what we were looking for. What more do we seek?

The answer is that when we seek the value of knowledge, the description of the search is intended to be completely accurate. That is, it is *knowledge*'s value that we aim to understand, not the value of some of its constituents or the value of something in the logical neighborhood. It may be, in the end, that we will have to claim that what we seek cannot be found, but for the present, finding that true belief is valuable is not sufficient to end the search. What we have found is that when we have knowledge, we have something that is (often) practically useful to have, but it is not in virtue of being knowledge that it is practically useful. Instead, it is in virtue of being true belief. So if we are to succeed in giving an account of the value of knowledge, we will have to go further. In particular, we will have to address Socrates' concern in the *Meno* about what makes knowledge more valuable than true belief.

This skeptical inclination is useful, however, even if it should be resisted at this point. It is easy to mistake questions about the value of knowledge for comparative questions about its value relative to the value of its constituents or other cognitive states in the general conceptual neighborhood of knowledge. Thus, when we claim that knowledge is not more useful from a practical point of view than is true belief, we seem to threaten the view that knowledge is valuable. No such threat exists from this quarter, however. Instead, what is threatened is a further view about the nature and extent of the value of knowledge, a view that requires not only that knowledge is valuable, but that its value exceed that of its conceptual constituents and neighbors. I agree with those who hold that this view is an initially attractive one and that epistemological theorizing should take this attractiveness into account; that was my point in defending the twin desiderata on a theory of knowledge. Still, the twin desiderata are not *indefeasible*, for we might discover that we were mistaken in our assumptions about the value of knowledge. The previous skeptical response helps us to hold this possibility in our minds, for it might be that knowledge is valuable, but not as valuable or not possessing the kind of value that we initially thought. So even though we should reject the skeptical response that maintains that knowledge has no more value than true belief, keeping this response in mind will help us avoid confusing the question we will

11

pursue with the quite different question of whether or not knowledge has any value at all.

So far, I have assumed that true belief is valuable, but this assumption will not go unquestioned. In the following chapters, we will examine accounts of the value of knowledge that explain it in terms of its internal characteristics, one of which is true belief. There we will investigate whether true belief is, in fact, valuable. For present purposes, however, we shall merely assume that it is. For if it is not valuable, we have no explanation of the value of knowledge, and if it is valuable, we do not yet have such an explanation either. So the assumption causes no problems for our investigation at this point.

The conclusion we must draw at this point is that we will not be able to account for the value of knowledge in terms of its practical significance. At first glance, this conclusion would seem to be sufficient to end our search for a value for knowledge that is external to it. For the obvious candidate for knowledge to help us achieve is well-being or happiness – more generally, whatever has practical utility. With the failure of that account, it might seem that we must look to the internal structure of knowledge to find its value, but moving to that position would be premature at this point, for there are two other approaches deserving attention before we abandon the idea that the value of knowledge is found in things external to it. The first tries to find a defensible proposal in Socrates' analogy about the statues of Daedelus, and the second looks for an account in terms of the connection between knowledge and appropriate action. I turn first to Socrates' analogy.

PLATO AND THE TETHERING OF TRUE BELIEF

Return for a moment to the passage in the *Meno* with which we began. In that passage, Socrates first shows that knowledge is no more useful than true belief, leading Meno to wonder whether the two differ at all. Socrates answers by suggesting that the reason for Meno's wonderment is that Meno must not be familiar with the statues of Daedelus:

> **Socrates**: It is because you have not observed the statues of Daedalus. Perhaps you don't have them in your country.
> **Meno**: What makes you say that?
> **Socrates**: They too, if no one ties them down, run away and escape. If tied, they stay where they are put.
> **Meno**: What of it?

Socrates: If you have one of his works untethered, it is not worth much; it gives you the slip like a runaway slave. But a tethered specimen is very valuable, for they are magnificent creations. And that, I may say, has a bearing on the matter of true opinions. True opinions are a fine thing and do all sorts of good so long as they stay in their place, but they will not stay long. They run away from a man's mind; so they are not worth much until you tether them by working out the reason. That process, my dear Meno, is recollection, as we agreed earlier. Once they are tied down, they become knowledge, and are stable. That is why knowledge is something more valuable than right opinion. What distinguishes one from the other is the tether.[11]

Immediately following this passage, Socrates points out that his discussion is at the level of mere analogy, denying that it provides a theoretical basis for explaining the difference between knowledge and true belief. At first glance, Socrates is right to denigrate the theoretical sophistication of the analogy, for the analogy seems to suggest that knowledge is more valuable than true belief because knowledge does not get up and wander off, as do the statues of Daedelus when untethered. Yet, it is clear that knowledge does get up and wander off. Nothing beyond the most casual acquaintance with human forgetfulness and the graceful, and sometimes not so graceful, degradation of our cognitive equipment over time shows that knowledge has no such permanence to it. In short, knowledge, no less than true belief, can be lost. So no simple account of the implications of present knowledge in terms of what the future will hold can be adequate.

Still, there may be more to Socrates' suggestion than this initial glance reveals. At least Timothy Williamson thinks so. He says:

Present knowledge is less vulnerable than mere present true belief to *rational* undermining by future evidence. . . . If your cognitive faculties are in good order, the probability of your believing p tomorrow is greater conditional on your knowing p today than on your merely believing p truly today. . . . Consequently, the probability of your believing p tomorrow is greater conditional on your knowing p today than on your believing p truly today.[12]

Williamson here takes the cross-temporal feature of Plato's analogy seriously, interpreting the value of knowledge in terms of the persistence of known beliefs as opposed to true beliefs. He holds that the likelihood that a belief will be held tomorrow is greater, given that it is known as

---

11. Plato, *Meno*, pp. 97d–98a.
12. Timothy Williamson, *Knowledge and Its Limits* (Oxford: Oxford University Press, 2000), p. 79.

opposed to merely believed truly, and he also holds that knowledge is less susceptible to rational undermining by future evidence than is true belief.

So there are some who find more of substance in Socrates' analogy than Socrates himself thought he could find. Immediately upon giving the analogy, Socrates says, "Well of course, I have only been using an analogy myself, not knowledge. But it is not, I am sure, a mere guess to say that right opinion and knowledge are different."[13] Socrates used the analogy only to make the point that knowledge and true opinion are distinct, but he doubted that his analogy arose from any secure knowledge concerning the proper explanation of the difference between true belief and knowledge. Williamson thinks Socrates is on to something more. He thinks not only that the analogy points to a crucial difference between knowledge and true belief, but also that this difference is an important one for any attempt to explain the value of knowledge. In commenting on the argument previously cited, Williamson says, "[T]he present argument concerns only delayed impact, not action at the 'next' instant. We do not value knowledge more than true belief for instant gratification."[14] Williamson thus holds that cross-temporal differences are at the heart of the difference between the value of true belief and that of knowledge.

Williamson makes two points in the earlier quotation cited. The first claim is that knowledge is more immune from rational undermining by further evidence than is true belief. The second appears to be an attempt to make precise this first idea by employing the language of probability. According to it, "If your cognitive faculties are in good order, the probability of your believing p tomorrow is greater conditional on your knowing p today than on your merely believing p truly today."[15] Williamson notes that this probabilistic inequality is undermined if the true beliefs are thoroughly dogmatic ones, but claims that in such a case the cognitive faculties are not in good order.[16]

One flaw in Williamson's proposal is that it does not attend sufficiently to the pragmatic dimension of the fixation of belief. It is true that discovery of evidence is a primary way in which fixation of belief occurs, but it is also well known that the importance of belief for survival and well-being depends on other factors for belief formation as well. For example, hasty generalizations are often important beliefs for survival, and false positives,

---

13. Plato, *Meno*, p. 98b.
14. Williamson, *Knowledge*.
15. Ibid., p. 79.
16. Ibid.

14

even a high percentage of them, can be produced by cognitive systems for predators that are in good working order and have survival value. In general, our cognitive systems serve a variety of purposes besides truth and are in good working order because of their contribution to these other important goals.

So, in order to assess Williamson's claim, we should divide the class of true beliefs into those whose fixation depends on evidence and those whose fixation depends on nonevidential factors. Among the latter are not only beliefs that result from a cognitive system that is not in good working order, but also beliefs produced by cognitive systems in good working order aimed at some goal other than truth.

If we consider beliefs fixed by mechanisms having survival value, it would not be surprising to find such beliefs very difficult to unseat, perhaps even more difficult to unseat than knowledge would be. Knowledge can cease to exist in a number of ways, from simple forgetting to injury-induced trauma through the deterioration of cognitive abilities, but one would expect beliefs fixed by survival mechanisms to be among the most resistant beliefs one has.

Of equal importance for assessing Williamson's probabilistic inequality is that not all, and perhaps not even a majority of, beliefs fixed by evidence count as knowledge. It is essential that one exist in a cooperative environment for such beliefs to be known to be true, and it is implausible to discount true beliefs fixed by evidence in hostile environments as the product of cognitive equipment not in good working order.

When we compare knowledge with true beliefs fixed by evidence that do not count as knowledge, we find no obvious pattern favoring the retention of the former over the latter. Williamson is correct that the latter beliefs can be undermined by finding information of which one was unaware at the time of belief formation, whereas knowledge is incompatible with the presence of such undermining yet unknown information. This feature does not tell the whole story, however, for there are other ways in which knowledge can be undermined but true belief remains unaffected. In particular, knowledge can be undermined at a later time by future changes of which one is unaware, where true belief is retained. For example, my mathematical knowledge might be undermined tomorrow by the sincere testimony of a renowned mathematician to the effect that what I believe is false. Until such testimony is rendered, I have such knowledge, but I lose it when the defeating testimony is given, even though I am unaware that such testimony has occurred. I thereby lose my knowledge but not my true belief (I am assuming that the renowned mathematician has made an honest mistake, one that will take considerable effort and time to uncover, for even other important mathematicians will be taken in by his remarks). Or, again, consider the similar effect radical changes in nature can have on knowledge. Much of our common knowledge about the patterns in nature can be undercut by events of which we are unaware. The eruption of Mt. St. Helens, for example, caused noticeable shifts in weather patterns, and even more radical changes are imaginable. In such cases, the evidentiary basis for our knowledge of weather patterns can be undercut, even if some particular aspects of our views of such patterns are nonetheless true. In such cases, even before we become aware of the volcanic eruption, its occurrence introduces a defeater regarding our knowledge of weather patterns, but it does not undermine our beliefs (because we are not yet aware of the catastrophic event). So even though there is one respect in which true belief is capable of being undermined in a way in which knowledge is not, there are other respects in which knowledge is capable of being undermined in which true belief is not.

Perhaps a specific example would help in understanding my point. Suppose Joe is building a sand castle on a Japanese beach and wishes to show it to his children, who will arrive tomorrow. Joe thus uses his knowledge of high and low tides to find a location that will not be overrun before his children arrive. In fact, over a month ago he picked an especially safe location, planning the event carefully to ensure success. His knowledge of low and high tides serves as a basis for his knowledge that if he builds a castle at a certain location, the ocean won't ruin it before his children arrive.

His knowledge disappears before he builds the castle in the following way. Two weeks after he decides where to build the castle, an earthquake occurs that causes a *tsunami* headed for the Japanese coast that will arrive the night before his children arrive. He is unaware of these events, however, and so blissfully goes about constructing the castle. He has lost his knowledge but not his true belief (the *tsunami* improbably fails to damage his particular beach).

A defender of Williamson might turn skeptical about claims to knowledge in such cases, holding that we never have knowledge of the future, as this example maintains. Such skepticism would be overdone, however, for its basis would have to be that we can never have knowledge based on patterns of nature if those patterns are not completely exceptionless. I will not press this point here, however, for we already have presented other examples of cases where knowledge is undermined but true belief remains.

It is time to bring these strands of discussion to bear on Williamson's probabilistic inequality, which requires that the likelihood of a belief persisting until tomorrow is greater, given that it is known today as opposed to merely believed truly. The previous information shows, I submit, that whether this claim is true is highly contingent. In some worlds, environments may be very cooperative and pragmatic matters less significant in the process of belief fixation. In such worlds, Williamson's inequality may well be true. The vast majority of beliefs will be fixed by evidence, and the vast majority of beliefs fixed by evidence will be both true and known. Moreover, pragmatic features may be relatively insignificant, implying that beliefs fixed by such factors need not be especially resistant to abandonment. In such worlds, one may be more likely to continue to know tomorrow what one knows today than to believe truly tomorrow what one believes truly today. In other worlds, the pragmatic dimensions may be more dominant, implying the falsity of Williamson's inequality. In such worlds, most of the true beliefs may be fixed by quite strong pragmatic mechanisms, with any other true beliefs having considerable fragility. In such cases, beliefs known today to be true will be much more susceptible to abandonment than will true beliefs fixed by nonevidentiary factors. And even if we restrict our attention to evidentially induced beliefs, there will be worlds in which known beliefs are more susceptible to cessation than are mere true beliefs. Such susceptibility would occur when (i) the unpossessed information that undermines knowledge for some true beliefs is resistant to discovery, while (ii) the universe conspires to generate future defeaters for a large percentage of what is known. So whether Williamson's inequality is true or not depends on what kind of world we live in and is thus a contingent truth at best.

Furthermore, even if we agree with Williamson about which kind of world we inhabit, the contingent truth of his inequality will be of little use in the present context, for the value of knowledge does not covary with the truth value of Williamson's inequality. It is simply false that knowledge loses its value in worlds where the environment is less cooperative and where pragmatics play a more significant role in belief fixation. So this inequality yields no adequate explanation of the value of knowledge.

It might appear that my objections to Williamson's inequality depend too much on a frequency conception of probability, but that is not so. If probability claims are contingent, then no matter which semantics for probability claims we adopt, Williamson's inequality will be true in some worlds and false in others. The only way to prevent this result in the

17

face of the objections I raise is to insist on an interpretation of probability in which probabilistic claims are necessarily true if true at all. If we adopt such an interpretation, then my objections should be recast to argue that the probability involved here is simply inscrutable, for none of us are in a position to measure the proportion of worlds that have friendly or hostile environments or require truth for pragmatically effective belief. So whether probability claims are contingent or necessary, we have sufficient grounds for refusing to endorse Williamson's inequality as a sound explanation of the value of knowledge over that of true belief.

My argument has focused on Williamson's technical formulation in terms of the language of probability, as opposed to the more intuitive initial formulation in terms of rational undermining by future evidence. I don't think that resorting to the more intuitive formulation is helpful, however, for it, too, ignores the roles of pragmatic factors in belief fixation and cooperative environments for the existence of knowledge. It is possible for pragmatically useful beliefs to be highly resistant to being undermined by future evidence, and it is possible for beliefs known to be true to be highly fragile. Williamson could appeal to the qualifier of *rational* undermining and insist that pragmatically useful beliefs would be abandoned were the cognizers in question more rational, but such a response is weak. First, one need not be irrational to hold pragmatically significant beliefs in the face of contrary evidence. The most one could defend is that it would be irrational *from an epistemic point of view* to do so.

What happens if we reformulate Williamson's intuitive idea along these lines? We get something like the following: True belief is more susceptible than is knowledge to being abandoned in the face of contrary evidence for cognizers who are rational from an epistemic point of view. Why is that so? Because, according to Williamson, knowledge is incompatible with the existence of such contrary evidence, whereas true belief is not.

The question we should ask, however, is why this result is significant. We should have no doubt that there is some respect in which knowledge is immune from loss in which true belief is not. They are, after all, logically distinct. When we compare the different ways in which one of the two can survive while the other is lost, the particular immunity from loss that knowledge possesses yields no immediate and direct advantage to it over the kinds of immunity from loss possessed by true belief.

We can thus draw together the variety of points in the preceding discussion of Williamson's proposal in the following way. We have seen

18

some possible ways in which knowledge is more susceptible to loss than is true belief and other possible ways in which true belief can be more susceptible to loss than is knowledge. In the face of this variety, merely identifying one set of conditions that favor the persistence of knowledge will not explain the value of knowledge over that of true belief. For the existence of such conditions is compatible with the existence of other conditions under which true belief would survive and knowledge would not. What is needed is some reason to think that one of these considerations trumps the other, and Williamson gives no such reason. Moreover, it is exceedingly difficult to imagine what such a reason might be. That is, even if one agrees that we want an account of the value of knowledge that shows it to be more valuable than true belief, we have no reason to think that we will find such an account by looking for a reason to prefer persistence factors favoring knowledge as opposed to persistence factors favoring true belief. Williamson may be right that we do not value knowledge for instant gratification, but we can enjoy such a pleasantly pithy remark without being misled into searching among persistence conditions for an account of the importance of knowledge over that of true belief.

Given the infallibilist assumption about the nature of knowledge that dominates the history of epistemology, it is not difficult to be tempted to look in such a direction. For if knowledge is infallible in the sense of requiring the possession of evidence or information guaranteeing the truth of what one believes, no amount of further learning could threaten it. Furthermore, it could be just such an assumption that underlies Socrates' analogy about the statues of Daedelus, yielding as a conclusion that an account of the value of knowledge in terms of persistence conditions is much more attractive given this mistaken assumption about knowledge. We must not forget, however, the depth of the mistake here. Knowledge is fragile in a variety of ways, susceptible to being undermined by future events, by learning of such events, and by learning of present and past events that are misleading in their evidentiary force.

For those familiar with the Gettier literature in epistemology,[17] these last remarks will be akin to epistemological platitudes. The significance of the Gettier problem for the nature and value of knowledge will be discussed at length in future chapters, but a quick example and some

17. Edmund Gettier, "Is Justified True Belief Knowledge?" *Analysis*, 23 (1963): 121–3.

general remarks may prove helpful here. First, consider the following example:

Suppose Joe has strong evidence that his friend Fred has a silver dollar in his pocket. Fred is deceiving Joe, but Joe is unaware of this fact. Joe infers from the claim that Fred has a silver dollar in his pocket the claim that someone in this room has a silver dollar in his pocket, for the person at the podium in this room has just said, "Does someone here have a silver dollar in their pocket?" and Joe stands and says, "Yes, Fred does." So Joe believes two things: Fred has a silver dollar in his pocket, and someone here has a silver dollar in his pocket. Joe is wrong about the first claim, however, for Fred is deceiving him, but it turns out by happenstance that Joe is right about the second claim, for the speaker has a silver dollar in his pocket. So Joe's belief in the second claim is true and is held for good reasons because it is correctly inferred from another belief of Joe's that he has good reasons for holding. But it is not knowledge, since his reasons in this case bear no connection with what makes the belief true.

Notice that examples like this one require that one be a fallibilist about good reasons. If one thought that one could never have good reasons for a belief unless those reasons guaranteed the truth of one's belief, cases like this one could not arise. The difficulty with such infallibilist assumptions about good reasons is that such assumptions imply that we almost never have good reasons for anything we think, contrary to what we know to be true. Even if our reasons don't guarantee the truth of what we believe, they are nonetheless often good reasons for those beliefs. If so, however, we can't identify true belief accompanied by good reasons with knowledge.

Furthermore, once we see the possibility of knowledge even when our reasons for belief are defeasible, the fragility of knowledge becomes apparent. The very same constellation of evidence can be present in cases of knowledge and in cases where knowledge is lacking. Moreover, while the adoption of a fallibilist account of knowledge leaves open the possibility of statistical knowledge, this openness signals further the fragility of knowledge, for such knowledge is compatible with the existence of pockets of misleading information of which one is unaware. For example, a carefully controlled collection of data can yield knowledge that most members of the entire population have a certain characteristic, and it is compatible with this knowledge that there are enough members of the population lacking the characteristic that, if added to one's data, one would no longer have sufficient evidence to confirm the claim in question. It is this fragility of knowledge arising from such fallibilism that undermines the attempt to account for the value of knowledge in terms of its persistence. The conclusion we must draw, therefore, is that Williamson's efforts to find in Socrates' analogy a cross-temporal explanation of the value of knowledge are unsuccessful.

KNOWLEDGE AND ACTION

The final proposal I want to examine for defending the value of knowledge on the basis of things extrinsic to it has to do with its relationship to things that we do, that is, to human actions. Perhaps some of our actions will be inadequate or unacceptable or deficient in some other way if they are not based on knowledge. We have already seen that they cannot be judged unacceptable by their fruits, for knowledge is not required in order for our actions to turn out well. But perhaps there is something more internal to the action itself that calls for a negative judgment when the action is not based on knowledge.

One might suggest, for example, that there is something immoral or blameworthy in performing an action that is not based on knowledge. Such a suggestion faces the same difficulty encountered by the practical usefulness theory presented earlier, for if actions are based on true beliefs, then it is hard to see how the actions could be immoral in virtue of the cognitive dimension of the act. The action could still be immoral because the desires that led to it are bad desires, but replacing true beliefs with knowledge will not correct this problem. For example, if after hurting a friend's feelings one desires to make amends and believes that sending flowers with an apology will do so, it is hard to see why it would matter whether one knows that sending flowers with an apology will make amends or merely believes this correctly. In either case, sending the flowers with an apology is a good thing to do, and in the absence of some better approach to the situation, it may be the right thing to do as well.

One might still hold that in such a situation, one can be legitimately blamed for sending the flowers, even if it is the right thing to do, if one lacked good reasons for thinking that this action is the right thing to do. If one is doing the right thing only in virtue of what one learned from a fortune cookie, for example, we might still show legitimate disapproval even though we grant that the action was the right one. So we might require not only true belief about what to do, but true belief based on good reasons. Still, though, true belief based on good reasons is not knowledge.

Perhaps we might think of strengthening the cognitive requirement for blameless action so that knowledge of the beliefs the action is based on must be known to be true in order for the action to be blameless. Such a

21

requirement is too strong, however. Consider the hurt feelings case again. Suppose one has good reasons for thinking that flowers and an apology would solve the problem because another friend is playing a practical joke. That friend tells you that sending flowers is the right thing to do (perhaps he claims he's been in the same situation several times with the hurt friend, and flowers plus an apology have always been effective, in fact singularly effective, because nothing else has ever worked). He's attempting to deceive you, relying on substantial experience that the hurt friend hates flowers, but the hurt friend has just acquired a love of fresh bouquets. So you have a true belief based on testimony that is ordinarily reliable, but you do not have knowledge. Your lack of knowledge, however, does not make your action blameworthy in any way. The only blame deserved applies to your deceitful friend.

So we might be able to defend the view that actions need to be based on true beliefs plus good reasons, but we cannot defend the view that actions need to be based on knowledge. Perhaps, though, there is a special kind of action that needs such a basis even though actions in general do not. Williamson has proposed such a theory for the special action of assertion, according to which assertion must be based on knowledge if the assertion is to be free of wrongdoing.[18] This view that knowledge is the norm of assertion can be used to account for the singular importance of knowledge, because on it, knowledge is a necessary condition for legitimate assertion.

Thus, even though it cannot be defended that actions in general must be based on knowledge in order to be legitimate, the proposal here is that there is a special kind of act for which this claim is true, namely, a speech act. The speech act theory of the value of knowledge posits conditions under which acts of speech — assertions in particular — are legitimate. We can call these conditions "assertibility conditions." One way to discover such conditions is to investigate how we go about getting persons to take back an assertion. Sometimes we do so by claiming that they don't believe what they are saying. For example, a student, after failing a test, might discouragingly claim, "I never do well on multiple-choice tests." We can get the student to recant by reminding the student that the remark is the result of discouragement and not honest conviction: He really doesn't believe that he never does well; he's merely exaggerating because of discouragement. Such reminders often prompt retractions. He might say, "Yes, you're right, I shouldn't have said that."

18. Timothy Williamson, "Knowing and Asserting," *The Philosophical Review*, 105, 4 (1996): 489–523.

Retractions are also appropriate when the remark is false. If I said a month ago that the Yankees wouldn't make the playoffs, you can come to me now and require a retraction from me because what I claimed is false. So among assertibility conditions seem to be both truth and belief: An assertion is illegitimate unless it is true and is believed to be so by the assertor.

Just as in the case of action generally, we might also have reason to insist on good reasons for belief in addition to truth and belief. Fundamentalist Christians often claim that there have been more earthquakes in the twentieth century than in prior centuries. There is empirical evidence for this claim, but many make the claim unaware of the evidence. They say what they do because it fits their eschatological views, and I will assume here that this fit is insufficient in itself to warrant their assertion. If challenged by pointing out that they have no empirical evidence, they may recant. And even when they won't, their sheepishness and embarrassment often indicate that they should. So, even if they believe the claim, they shouldn't have said it without adequate evidence.

If we think of the Gettier problem as teaching the lesson that knowledge is justified true belief plus some condition aimed at handling the Gettier problem, then we may be tempted to say that retractions are in order when the Gettier condition is violated as well. In the preceding case used to show that knowledge is something more than true belief plus good reasons, we could get Joe to take back his claim that someone in the room has a silver dollar in his pocket by showing him that Fred's pockets are empty.

Given this procedural test of what we can use to get people to take back what they say, there is some plausibility to the view that knowledge is required for legitimate assertion; or, as Williamson puts it, knowledge is the norm, or rule, of assertion.[19] I want to argue, however, that this conclusion is mistaken and that the test of retraction employed earlier is a bit misleading. First, I'll engage in a bit of border skirmishing to the effect that the connections between legitimate assertion and knowledge are weaker than the preceding suggests. Afterward, I'll get to the main reason the proposal fails.

Let's begin by being precise about the proposal. First, it claims a logical relationship between the assertibility of p and knowing p: p's being assertible by S entails S's knowing p, where p's being assertible is understood to mean that it is permissible for S to assert p. This claim is false. Consider

19. Ibid., p. 519.

23

someone wishing to be a theist who takes Pascal's advice of going to Mass and hoping for the best; in line with such advice, a person may sincerely avow that God exists even though that person does not (yet) believe it. Furthermore, no one in such a condition need be moved to retract the assertion upon the complaint that the assertion is not backed by belief. All that would be required is an explanation and a defense of Pascal's advice and how the assertion fits with that advice. Again, consider someone who, moved by William James's pragmatic arguments,[20] comes to believe that God exists and asserts it, all the while knowing that there is insufficient evidence to confirm this claim. Such a person need not retract the claim when the absence of evidence is noted; all that is needed is a defense and an explanation of James's viewpoint and of how the assertion is supported by that argument. For a third case, imagine Churchland or Stich asserting, "I believe nothing that I assert," something their writings imply.[21] On the speech act proposal, no such sentence is assertible, but it is easy to see that neither would be guilty of any impropriety in asserting their position, even if it should turn out that they are philosophically mistaken in claiming that there are no beliefs. This latter case is a special instance of skeptical and Pyrrhonian assertion.[22] Skeptics are quite comfortable asserting that knowledge is not possible, and Pyrrhonian skeptics assert not only that knowledge is not possible but also that it is best not to hold any beliefs at all (though the interpretation of their belief–appearance distinction is controversial, a point to be pursued later). In each of these cases, assertion is legitimate even though the question of whether it is backed by knowledge is left open.

So it would appear that the most that can be claimed is that knowing *p* is *ordinarily* a requirement for legitimately asserting *p*. What, precisely, does such a claim mean, however? It is, of course, confused to say that one claim ordinarily entails another. Perhaps the notion of a requirement should be understood differently. Instead of thinking of requirement in terms of entailment, perhaps we should think of it as a defeasible relation, so that

---

20. In "The Will to Believe," in *The Will to Believe and Other Essays in Popular Philosophy* (New York: Habnev, 1897).
21. See Stephen Stich, *From Folk Psychology to Cognitive Science: The Case Against Belief* (Cambridge, MA: MIT Press, 1983); Paul Churchland, *Scientific Realism and the Plasticity of Mind* (Cambridge: Cambridge University Press, 1979).
22. As an aside, such possibilities of appropriate assertion show that Moore's paradox, the paradox that arises from a person's asserting that a certain proposition is true but that he or she doesn't believe it, is not always paradoxical; it is paradoxical only given certain assumptions about how standards for belief and standards for assertion are correlated.

x can require y even though $x \& z$ does not require y. If we understand the notion of requirement in this way, we might still be able to claim that the assertibility of p requires knowing p even though in the unusual cases described previously, additional factors come into play so that the assertibility of p in those circumstances does not require knowledge.

Even such retrenchment cannot save the proposal, however. Recall the way in which the proposal began. We look for ways in which we can require a person to take back an assertion, and it turns out that the conditions for knowledge are among those ways. There are, however, two quite different things a person might be doing in taking back an assertion. The person might be taking back only *what is said*, or she might be taking back *the saying of it*. So, for example, if Joe says, "I don't know why I keep trying to be friendly; nobody likes me at all," and Mary says, "Joe, you don't really believe that; you're just upset," Joe might apologize for saying what he knows is false. Such cases support the view that belief is ordinarily a requirement on assertion because the retraction involves taking back the saying itself. Moreover, when people assert things with no good reason whatsoever, we reprove such utterances, realizing that even though what is said might be true, *those individuals* have no business saying so. So once again, it is the saying itself that is at fault. But when new information is presented that undermines an assertion, only a retraction of what is said is in order. In the case of Joe and the silver dollar given earlier, pointing out that Fred's pockets are empty should lead Joe to retract his claim that someone in the room has a silver dollar in his pocket. It would be quite bizarre, however, to hear Joe apologizing for having made the claim at all. It is what was said that was mistaken, not the saying of it. Again, if I assert what is false and you show me that it is false, I'll retract my statement. But I wouldn't say that my uttering of it was out of order.

This distinction thus suggests that there is a better account of assertibility conditions than the speech act proposal developed by Williamson. Instead of conditions of knowledge being assertibility conditions, only belief and justification are among such conditions. The appeal to knowledge is superfluous, for all the explanatory work can be done by the concept of justified belief. When *the saying itself* is inappropriate, that is so in the ordinary case where standards of assertion and standards of belief converge because justified belief was not present when the assertion was made. When *what was said* must be retracted, as occurs when one learns that one has been gettiered or that one's statement is false, that is so because justification for belief is no longer present. That is all the explanation that is needed, and no appeal to concept of knowledge is involved in it.

25

There is, however, still a smidgen of a difficulty. For when you find out that you've been gettiered, there is some residual embarrassment or regret for your assertions. If Joe says that someone has a silver dollar in his pocket because he believes that Fred has one and then is shown that Fred does not have one, he might not only retract his statement, but also experience some embarrassment or regret for the assertion. Does he thereby show the inappropriateness of assertion in the absence of knowledge? No. He shows only the common human inclination against being duped, and one can be duped because of truths that undermine knowledge and because of truths that do not undermine knowledge. You'd experience the same embarrassment or regret if the defeater mentioned were a misleading one. A classic case involving misleading defeaters is the case of Tom stealing a book from the library.[23] You see Tom steal the book and have a justified true belief that he stole it. But his mother, an inveterate liar, tells the police that it was his twin brother, Tim, who stole it. The police know the story is concocted; they know she is an inveterate liar and will say anything to protect Tom. They also know Tom has no twin. But you don't know all this, and if you were told what the mother said, you'd be every bit as inclined to take back the assertion that Tom stole the book and to experience some embarrassment or regret for having confidently claimed it. But the defeater is a misleading one; without having been told it, it does not undermine your knowledge, because it is so obviously farcical. Yet, even misleading defeaters, when discovered, undermine knowledge; that is what makes them defeaters in the first place.

The lesson, then, is that your embarrassment, shame, or regret is not an indicator that knowledge is a prerequisite of appropriate assertion. Instead, it is only a sign that none of us is comfortable with the existence of information of which we are not aware that would undermine the justification of our beliefs. To have justifications immune from defeat is, of course, a valuable characteristic of a belief (provided that justification itself is). To conclude, however, that one should never say anything for which one lacks immunity from defeat is, to paraphrase William James, to show a preoccupation with not being duped.[24]

23. From Keith Lehrer and Thomas D. Paxson, Jr., "Knowledge: Undefeated Justified True Belief," *Journal of Philosophy*, 66, 8 (1969): 225–37.
24. The actual quote is: "He who says 'Better go without belief forever than believe a lie!' merely shows his own preponderant private horror of becoming a dupe." William James, *Essays in Pragmatism* (New York: Hafner, 1948), p. 100.

I suspect there are logically possible alternative explanations of the value of knowledge in terms of things external to it that I have not considered here. Still, I think the proper conclusion to draw is that there is good reason to doubt that the value of knowledge will be accounted for adequately in these terms. The theories I have considered here include the most obvious and most defended of such accounts, and though we lack any proof that no such account can be adequate, canvassing these available possibilities and seeing their faults gives us adequate reason to think that this approach to the value of knowledge will not be successful. I turn, then, to other approaches.

2

The Value of True Belief

If the value of knowledge cannot be explained adequately in terms of things external to it, such as its usefulness or its permanence or its role as a foundation for acceptable action, we will have to look at internal features in order to find the value of knowledge. Perhaps the value of knowledge will emerge as we look at its (purported) constituents, and because knowledge is ordinarily conceived to involve true belief, I begin with the value of true belief here. There are those who doubt that knowledge involves true belief, maintaining that belief itself is a quite different state from knowledge.[1] There are even those who maintain that there is no such thing as belief.[2] I do not want to become embroiled in these controversies, because these disputes will take us too far afield from the focus of this work on the value of knowledge. Given that focus, our interest can concentrate on the connection between the shared informational content that exists both when a person knows something and when that person only believes it. When a person knows something, there is informational content in the cognitive, as opposed to the affective, mental realm, informational content endorsed by the person, or to which that person is committed, or to which that person assents. This same informational content can be endorsed even if knowledge is not present, and it is the presence and endorsement of this informational content that allow a person to produce that content honestly and sincerely when queried about

1. See, for example, H. H. Price, *Perception* (London: Methuen, 1932).
2. Among defenders of this view are Stephen Stich and Paul Churchland. See Stephen Stich, *From Folk Psychology to Cognitive Science: The Case Against Belief* (Cambridge, MA: MIT Press, 1983); Paul Churchland, *Scientific Realism and the Plasticity of Mind* (Cambridge: Cambridge University Press, 1979).

that particular subject matter. When I speak of the beliefs of a person in this chapter, I mean to refer to this cognitive endorsement of information. When I claim, as I will in this work, that belief is required for knowledge, I mean to be understood as claiming only that such endorsed informational content can be present both when one knows and when one does not know.

Our question, then, concerns the value of true belief, and our strategy is to see if we can locate the value of knowledge by finding some value in its constituents. This chapter is devoted to skeptical concerns about the assumption of the discussion between Socrates and Meno that true belief is valuable because of its practical usefulness. Once we see Socrates' strategy for constructing counterexamples to Meno's claim about the value of knowledge, it is relatively easy to see how to construct similar counterexamples to the claim that true belief has practical value. One needn't believe that the way to Larissa is such-and-such, for one can find one's way to Larissa every bit as successfully if one merely *acts as if* that is the correct way to go. So there is a reason to doubt that belief has practical value. Furthermore, even if one does hold beliefs about which way to go, these beliefs needn't be true in order to be useful. All that is needed are beliefs that *make adequate sense* of the course of experience, beliefs that are *empirically adequate*.

So there are two skeptical questions to face in this chapter, the first concerning the value of belief and the second concerning the importance of truth.

THE VALUE OF BELIEF

If we follow Socrates' lead in the *Meno*, we will want to explain the value of belief in terms of its practical benefits. In particular, belief is a guide to action, and without some guide to action, our ability to satisfy our wants, desires, and purposes will disappear. Without beliefs to guide decisions about what actions to perform, we would be reduced to the position of random selection of actions, hoping that the one selected was useful. If, for example, one has a headache and desires to be rid of it, that alone provides no guidance as to what to do in order to eliminate the headache. One could arbitrarily choose one action among the infinite variety of actions available, but a better idea would be to have something to guide one's choice. That is what belief does − it guides action − and when the belief is true, it guides action successfully. So if one wants to get rid of a headache and correctly believes that taking aspirin will do so, one has a reason to take aspirin, and these features of action generate an account of the value of true belief. In summary form, the view is that belief is valuable because it is action-guiding, and true belief is valuable because the actions to which belief guides us are successful in satisfying desires and in achieving purposes when those beliefs are true.

Some, not impressed with this argument, still think that belief lacks value. The historical school most directly connected with a denial of the value of belief is the Pyrrhonian skeptical school. According to Pyrrhonians, quietude is achieved only by ridding oneself of beliefs, directing *epoche* – the suspension of belief – toward one's doxastic commitments and replacing them with the attitude of "acquiescing to the appearances." Such counsel implies that belief is not a good thing, but is rather something to be avoided, and thus Pyrrhonism might give some ground for doubting the value of belief and hence of knowledge.

There is some debate, however, about whether Pyrrhonists endorsed the idea of abandoning belief entirely or only beliefs of a certain type – those, for example, that are not among the common beliefs of everyday life, especially beliefs about philosophical and scientific matters. Jonathan Barnes calls the former view "rustic Pyrrhonism" and the latter "urbane Pyrrhonism,"[3] and he has argued that "the general tenor of [Sextus Empiricus's *Outlines of Pyrrhonism*] is, I think, indubitably rustic."[4] Miles Buryeat agrees with Barnes,[5] while Michael Frede argues to the contrary.[6]

In the present context, there are two major reasons not to find the Pyrrhonian counsel of suspension of belief troubling. First, we must note the force of the argument against rustic Pyrrhonism that such skeptics are incapable of action. This objection appeals to the action-guiding role of belief, arguing that if one lacks beliefs, one will be incapable of determining which course of action to follow in order to satisfy one's desires or achieve one's goals. Pyrrhonists attempt to answer this charge, but it

---

3. Jonathan Barnes, "The Beliefs of a Pyrrhonist," *Proceedings of the Cambridge Philological Society*, E. J. Kenny and M. M. MacKenzie, eds. (Cambridge: Cambridge University Press, 1982), pp. 2–3.

4. Ibid., p. 18.

5. Miles Burnyeat, "Can the Sceptic Live His Scepticism?" *Doubt and Dogmatism*, M. Schofield, M. F. Burnyeat, and J. Barnes, eds. (Oxford: Clarendon Press, 1980); "The Sceptic in His Place and Time," *Philosophy in History*, Richard Rorty, J. B. Schneewind, and Quentin Skinner, eds. (Cambridge: Cambridge University Press, 1984).

6. Michael Frede, "The Skeptic's Two Kinds of Assent and the Question of the Possibility of Knowledge," *Philosophy in History*, pp. 255–78; "The Skeptic's Beliefs," *Essays in Ancient Philosophy* (Minneapolis: University of Minnesota Press, 1987), pp. 179–200.

is extraordinarily difficult to find their answers acceptable. Sextus, for example, says:

Adhering, then, to appearances we live in accordance with the normal rules of life, undogmatically, seeing that we cannot remain wholly inactive. And it would seem that this regulation of life is fourfold, and that one part of it lies in the guidance of Nature, another in the constraint of the passions, another in the tradition of laws and customs, another in the instruction of the arts.[7]

Barnes has tried to make some sense out of how to live a life without belief along these lines, treating the guidance of Nature, for example, as a kind of automatic or instinctive response – activity that is hardwired in rather than relying on the software of the organism.[8] Robert J. Fogelin comments on this attempt, highlighting how difficult it is to interpret Sextus's statement in a compelling way on this point:

But, as Barnes himself sees, this automatic-response account of the Pyrrhonist's ways of acting becomes less and less plausible as we move down the list from the guidance of Nature to the tradition of laws and customs and finally to the instruction of the arts. In fact, it is already implausible when applied to passions and desires. Without possessing a complex set of beliefs, a person could not hanker after a seat on the New York Stock Exchange or want to see Lhasa before she dies.[9]

Fogelin's point appeals straightforwardly to the kind of account presented earlier concerning the value of belief. He also goes further, suggesting that some of our affective states are impossible without holding a complex set of beliefs. Whether or not we go along with the second point, however, the first is sufficient to undermine Pyrrhonism, at least in its rustic form.

Urbane Pyrrhonism is not as significant a threat to the claim that belief is valuable as is rustic Pyrrhonism. It is well known that certain beliefs are best not held – racist views, for example. The existence of disvaluable beliefs need not cast doubt on the value of belief itself, for such disvalue can be explained in terms of overriders of the basic value that belief has, much as we can do with cases in which pain is to be welcomed. Pain, we can maintain, is intrinsically disvaluable, but that does not mean it is

7. Sextus Empiricus, *Sextus Empiricus*, 4 vols., R. B. Bury, trans. Loeb Classical Library (London: William Heinemann, 1961–71), vol. 1, p. 23.
8. Barnes, "Beliefs of a Pyrrhonist," p. 27, n. 90.
9. Robert J. Fogelin, *Pyrrhonian Reflections on Knowledge and Justification* (Oxford: Oxford University Press, 1994), pp. 8–9.

always a bad thing to have, for its intrinsic disvalue can be overridden by special features of a case so that, all things considered in a given case, it is a good thing.[10] That is how we should explain the fact that in some victims of leprosy, their lack of capacity to experience pain is a bad thing. Because they cannot experience pain, they don't quickly remove themselves from damaging contact with fire, for example; whereas if they did experience pain, they would withdraw by reflex action from the fire. Such cases are compatible with the view that pain is intrinsically disvaluable. Its disvalue is overridden by the benefits that would be derived in this case by the experience of pain. Just so, some beliefs are overall bad to hold, but their badness is a result of the value of belief being overridden by special features of the content of that belief and the willingness of holders of such beliefs to act on them.

So if it is only urbane Pyrrhonism that is true, that is not incompatible with the position that maintains that belief is valuable. On the urbane view, beliefs become disvaluable when they involve subject matter beyond the reach of the common or ordinary, and one can hold that view and still maintain that belief, by its very nature, is valuable. It is just not indefeasibly valuable, and when the object of belief extends beyond the reach of the common or ordinary, we have a case in which the value of belief is defeated or overridden by other factors.

An urbane Pyrrhonist might argue that the explanation ought to go otherwise, that acquiescing to the appearances is valuable in itself, but that its value is defeated or overridden when the subject matter in question is the common or ordinary, the realm of nondogma. I think, however, that there is some preference for the former explanation over the latter. Recall that for Pyrrhonists the goal is quietude, and acquiescing to the appearances is what is required to achieve this state. For the urbane Pyrrhonist, some means for achieving this goal is required only when we move beyond the reach of the common and ordinary and enter the realm of *dogma*; otherwise, acquiescing to the appearances is simply not required. This description strongly favors the view that acquiescing to the appearances has value only within a certain domain, and its value is an instrumental one, directed toward the goal of quietude. Acquiescing to the appearances, that is, *takes on* a value when outside the domain of the common and ordinary because its value is wholly instrumental, and within the domain of the common and ordinary no such means to quietude is necessary or useful.

10.   For a contrary viewpoint, see Jonathan Dancy, *Moral Reasons* (Oxford: Blackwell, 1993).

This explanation also fits with the way in which suspension of belief is tied to skepticism for Pyrrhonists. The denigration of belief arises for Pyrrhonists only because of their skepticism; as Sextus says, "We must . . . remember that we do not employ them [the methods for achieving suspension of belief] universally about all things, but about those that are non-evident and are objects of dogmatic inquiry."[11] If we identify the nonevident with what is not known, Sextus is saying that there is no reason to pursue suspension of belief about what is, or can be, known, and such a claim strongly suggests that suspension of belief has no value within the domain of the known or evident.

I do not claim that it is impossible to construe the value of these various states in a way that denies that beliefs are valuable. The dialectic I am pursuing, however, does not require such a strong claim. We began with a plausible story of why belief is valuable, a story that emphasizes the action-guiding role of belief, and are now considering a philosophical viewpoint that threatens to undercut the plausibility of this story. The version of this philosophical viewpoint that implies the falsity of the story is rustic Pyrrhonism, but it is an implausible viewpoint in virtue of having no adequate answer to the problem of paralysis. There is a weaker version of this viewpoint, but it does not require abandoning the plausible story with which we began about why belief is valuable. So it should not lead us to abandon the view that belief is valuable because of its action-guiding character. Thus, Pyrrhonism is not a threat to the claim that belief is valuable.

We can appreciate this conclusion a bit more by considering a related view for denying the value of belief due to Bas van Fraassen in his work *The Scientific Image*.[12] Van Fraassen argues that we should take an attitude other than belief toward scientific theories because a realist attitude toward such theories is not warranted. He is, instead, a constructive empiricist, maintaining that the adequacy of a theory to experience is the distinguishing mark of a good scientific theory but is insufficient to warrant believing the theory to be true.

One option here would be to take no attitude whatsoever and merely act as if one believed the theory, and van Fraassen's view is close to this. He argues that we ought to accept the theory rather than believe it. The difference between accepting and merely acting as if is that one can do the latter without taking any positive attitude whatsoever, whereas to accept a

---

11. Sextus Empiricus, *Sextus Empiricus*, vol. 1, p. 208.
12. Bas van Fraassen, *The Scientific Image* (Oxford: Clarendon Press, 1980).

theory is to take something of a positive attitude toward it – for example, to be disposed to use it for explanatory purposes.

Van Fraassen's advice holds only with respect to scientific theories, but it is not hard to see how to extend his viewpoint to beliefs of any type. One would argue, in good Pyrrhonian fashion, that the best we can hope for regarding any theory of the world is that it is adequate to experience, but that this mark is insufficient for believing the theory to be true, and if we add to this claim that all belief is theory-laden in one way or another, we get the result that we should never hold any beliefs. This extension of van Fraassen's ideas would give us a thoroughgoing version of rustic Pyrrhonism, with an analogous counsel to the advice of the Pyrrhonists that we should acquiesce or adhere to the appearances. This analogous counsel is that we should accept our theories for purposes of explanation, prediction, and so on, but we should not believe them.

For van Fraassen, the problem with the attitude of belief, as opposed to acceptance, is its connection to the concept of truth. Belief and truth are supposed to be intimately related: To believe a claim is to take it to be true, to endorse it as being true, to believe it to be true. And it is this commitment to the truth that must be deemed problematic and unwise because there is no reason to take the claims in question to be true (as opposed to empirically adequate). To believe is to take a dogmatic attitude, that is, an attitude unwarranted by the evidence.

There are two things I wish to point out about this objection to belief. First, to believe p is not the same as to believe that p is true, even if we grant the logical equivalence of 'p' and 'p is true'. To hold otherwise is to hold that having the concept of truth is a precondition of thought, that no one can think or believe anything without having the concept of truth. Truth, however, is not a precondition of thought. It is possible to believe that it is raining outside without believing that the proposition *it is raining outside* is true, for a person might not yet have acquired the concept of truth. The best that can be defended about the relationship between believing and believing the truth is that if a person believes p, has the concept of truth, and considers whether p is true, that person cannot believe p and fail to believe that p is true.

The second point I wish to make is that any defensible connection between the mental attitude of belief and the semantic notion of truth exists for any of the ordinary cognitive attitudes: In the sense in which to believe p is to believe that p is true, we must also say that to presuppose p is to presuppose that it is true, to assume p is to assume that it is true, to be psychologically certain of p is to be certain that p is true. It is most

34

telling to note that the same applies to the language of acceptance: To accept p is to accept it as true. So, if belief is dogmatic because of the connection between believing and truth, then so should accepting be viewed as dogmatic. What this point shows is that van Fraassen's preferred mental attitude cannot be the ordinary notion of acceptance but must rather be a technical notion, similar to the ordinary notion but stripped of its connection to truth.

The pressing question, though, is, why should we think that there is any such mental attitude that a person can take toward a proposition? It is coherent, of course, to maintain a thesis only for certain purposes, such as for purposes of argument, or explanation, or self-comfort; and so it is coherent to accept a theory for theoretical purposes. Such a position replaces the two-place relation of belief or acceptance with a three-place relation, a relation between a person, a proposition, and a purpose. Even here, though, to accept a theory in this way is to accept it *as true* for these purposes. That is, the special purposes do not replace the concept of truth in the attitude taken, but govern it instead. So if it is dogmatic to believe a claim to be true, it should also be viewed as dogmatic to accept a claim as true for theoretical purposes.

So what van Fraassen needs is a notion of acceptance on which to accept a claim *as true* is unwarranted and to be avoided, whereas to accept the claim is not. I don't see any good reason to think that such a cognitive attitude is possible, for every cognitive attitude of which we are capable is tied to truth. There is no cognitive gulf between hoping that p and hoping that p is true, between fearing that p and fearing that p is true, between wishing that p and wishing that p is true, between presupposing that p and presupposing that p is true.

Perhaps this point can be made a bit more forcefully by considering the position in the theory of truth called "minimalism." According to minimalists, truth is not a substantive notion; it adds nothing of semantic content to a proposition expressed by a sentence containing it. Minimalism is a somewhat attractive theory of truth, though I do not wish to endorse it. I think, however, that it could not be attractive at all if mental attitudes of the sort van Fraassen proposes are possible. Acceptance, of the sort van Fraassen requires, must be a mental attitude completely at odds with minimalism about truth, for accepting *as true* must be a substantively different state to be in than merely accepting, in van Fraassen's technical sense of acceptance. As the preceding examples show, mental attitudes do not pose such a threat to minimalism, so any proposal of a technical type of attitude posing such a threat is at a severe disadvantage.

We should conclude that there are grave difficulties in trying to replace the action-guiding role of belief with some surrogate mental attitude, but perhaps no such surrogate is needed. Instead of suggesting a surrogate, why not simply suggest that one guide one's actions merely by *acting as if* certain claims are true? There is a bit of discomfort here, for the proposal sounds very much like the proposal that one *pretend* that certain claims are true, and pretending is a mental attitude with all the ordinary ties to truth. Perhaps not, though; perhaps one only pretends in the face of belief to the contrary. In any case, the problem could be avoided by insisting that one take no attitude toward the claim while at the same time acting as if it is true.

I don't think that such an account is ultimately coherent, for I think that acting as if a certain claim is true is parasitic on belief (or some surrogate mental attitude for belief). To see this, suppose one wishes to act as if taking aspirin will get rid of a headache. What actions will one perform? The answer is that there are no limits. In particular, it depends crucially on whether or not one believes that one has a headache. If I think I have a headache and want to get rid of it, then to act as if taking aspirin will get rid of the headache will be to take the aspirin. The point is that we get action-guiding principles out of this account only if we assume that certain beliefs are already in place.

One might claim that it is not necessary to believe that one has a headache; it is only necessary that one in fact have a headache. I think the only reason to suppose this is that it is somewhat plausible to suppose that it is always transparent to one whether or not one has a headache. One need only change the example to something nontransparent to see the point. What is it to act as if throwing a life jacket will keep one's child from drowning in the pool? Surely the answer to that question depends on whether one believes that one's child is drowning in the pool, not on the facts of the matter.

One can answer on behalf of the act-as-if theory as follows: One should both act as if one's child is drowning and as if throwing a life jacket will help (or, to use the earlier example, one should both act as if one has a headache and as if taking an aspirin will get rid of it). Even so, it is implausible to think that belief or some other endorsement of content can drop out of the picture entirely. For we need an explanation of why one should act as if these claims are true, of what makes this behavior the rational one to follow. When we have belief or some surrogate for it in the account, we have an answer to the question of the rationality of action, for the rationality of action is clearly parasitic on the rationality of the beliefs (or surrogates for such) that underlie it. If we attempt to rid our account of an element of mental endorsement of content, then we have no basis in cognition for explaining the rationality of action.

That leaves us only the possibility of explaining the rationality of action in terms of two things. The first is in terms of the nonmental features of the world, such as the truth or likelihood of truth of the propositions in question; the other is in terms of mental features other than belief. It is obvious that nonmental factors regarding the claim that one's child is drowning do not make it rational to throw a life jacket. In the absence of information about the child, the parent will be behaving irrationally (even though serendipitously). Because any plausible account of action must leave intact the possibility of rational action, one will need to appeal to mental factors other than belief in order to explain how actions can be rational even when one has no beliefs. Such denials of the value of belief appeal instead to the contents of experience, or appearances, in order to explain the rationality of action. Appearances carry informational content and thus are capable of providing information without the need for belief. On this proposal, one should throw a life jacket, and doing so is rational when it appears to one that one's child is drowning.

As we have already seen, however, an account in terms of acquiescing to the appearances does a poor job of explaining the range of human action. Most particularly, the appeal to appearances is of little help in explaining fully deliberate human action. Deliberation involves reasoning and the weighing of reasons, a process involving belief and other mental attitudes at its core. It is simply insufficient to substitute appearances for belief when accounting for the recognition of support for an action by a reason, for apparent support is merely a first stage through which the process of deliberation passes along the way to a decision to act. Acquiescing to such appearances often leads to actions based on poor judgment, because such appearances pop up when deeper reflection reveals their misleading character.

One can try to account for this need for deeper reflection in terms of contrary appearances, so that one shouldn't trust appearances when it also appears to one that the first appearance has a strong chance of being misleading. One shouldn't trust first appearances under such circumstances, but it is also true that one shouldn't trust them when one *believes* or has *reason to believe* that they may be misleading. The only hope here for the defender of acquiescing to the appearances is for there always to be appearances to take the place of beliefs and reasons to believe in this latter claim, and this hope disappoints. Beliefs are possible in the absence of appearances, and reasons to believe need not be accompanied by them either. Human psychology simply does not satisfy such requirements.

This fact can be masked by the multiple roles that the word 'appears' and its cognates play in ordinary language. One such use is for the phenomenological element of belief, so that if one believes that Frege's comprehension axiom is false, then it appears to one that it is false. It is clear, however, that this kind of appearance will be of no help in the denial of the value of belief, for there is little plausibility to the claim that one can have this kind of appearance without belief. In another use of the language of appearance, it can appear to one that the comprehension axiom is true even while one believes that it is false: It has that attractiveness to the mind that is hard to describe but that inclines us strongly to believe that it is true. This use of the language of appearance is more useful in the denial of the value of belief, because it is logically independent of belief. But it is in this sense of appearance that it is most obvious that one can believe that one's appearances are misleading without it appearing to one that they are.

In the end, then, it is hard to see how the proposal merely to act as if a claim is true will be able to avoid the importance of belief, and so I doubt that there is any good reason to question the significance of belief on these Pyrrhonian and quasi-Pyrrhonian grounds. If there are legitimate skeptical worries about the value of true belief, these worries will have to focus on the question of the importance of truth, rather than on the importance of belief, and it is to the topic of the value of truth that I now turn.

THE VALUE OF TRUTH

I begin with a weak, but quite common and understandable, attempt to deny the value of truth. This attempt is based on a sense that getting to the truth is not very likely, that finding the truth is simply too high a goal for us to attain. It is not within our cognitive reach and so is not valuable for that reason.

Such an attempt is a prime example of philosophical sour grapes. It denies the value of a thing simply because we can't have it. The basis of this viewpoint is philosophical skepticism, but it is an inferior sort of skepticism to that of the Pyrrhonians. The Pyrrhonians inferred skepticism from the danger of dogmatism and found in the suspension of belief an antidote to this danger. As such, they have not perceived danger where there is none, and their sense of a need for protection is correct. The present view, however, has no such virtues. It infers that truth cannot be important because knowledge of it (or perhaps something stronger, such as metaphysical certainty or infallibility regarding it) is beyond us. For there is no reason whatsoever to think that believing the truth is always impossible; the best that could be claimed is that there is no guarantee in any given case that we have achieved the state of believing the truth. Perhaps it follows that we should not hope for the chimera of infallibility, but nothing whatsoever follows about the value of truth itself.

There is also another reason to question the value of truth that we can dispense with quickly. Stephen Stich has argued that there is a multiplicity of predicates, any of which can mimic the intuitive notion of truth, and uses this fact to argue that there is no unique property expressed by our linguistic practice involving 'true' and its cognates.[13] It might be thought that this position threatens to undermine the view that truth is valuable, but it does not. This semantic thesis does not threaten this idea any more than it threatens any other idea about truth. For example, consider the claims that truth is distinct from belief, hope, fear, and other mental attitudes. Stich's semantic thesis does not undermine such claims on pain of self-refutation. For Stich's argument employs the word 'truth' and its cognates, and if his semantic thesis undermines anything one might say about truth, it also undermines his argument as well as the thesis itself. So whatever interest Stich's thesis might have, it is not relevant to the present question of whether truth is valuable.

There is, however, a deeper worry about the value of truth, one that bears important connections to van Fraassen's constructive empiricism. If we generalize van Fraassen's claims about scientific theories to all beliefs of any sort (perhaps on grounds that all belief is theory-laden), the complaint is that empirical adequacy seems to have precisely the same value as truth. An empirically adequate theory is one that will never be revealed to be false in virtue of some false prediction it makes about the course of experience, and so no matter what use we make of our beliefs, we will be just as well off employing empirically adequate beliefs as employing true ones.

There are other concepts in the neighborhood of empirical adequacy that have the same implication. One may choose to highlight the capacity of a theory to make sense of the course of experience, where this sense-making feature of a theory will obtain only if that theory is adequate to

---

13. Stephen Stich, *The Fragmentation of Reason: Preface to a Pragmatic Theory of Cognitive Evaluation* (Cambridge, MA: Bradford Books/MIT Press), 1990.

the course of experience as well. I mention other ways of describing the virtues a theory might possess only to focus on the implication of such descriptions to be adequate to the course of experience. In what follows, I will use the concept of empirical adequacy, but the only implication of this description that is important in the present content is this adequacy to the course of experience, and so if some other feature of theories is preferred as picking out the central virtue of a theory, that feature can be substituted in what follows as long as it, too, has the implication of adequacy to the course of experience.

Had Meno been quicker of intellect, he could have corrected Socrates' claims about the practical benefits of cognition. Socrates is right that true belief is every bit as valuable from the practical point of view as is knowledge, but Meno could have correctly pointed out that the practical benefits Socrates discusses could just as easily have been gained without true belief. All that is needed is empirically adequate belief. The result of noticing such a point would be that the question of the value of knowledge would have taken on much broader significance for Socrates than merely that of distinguishing its value from that of true belief. He would have needed to explain why knowledge has more value than empirically adequate belief as well.

An assumption of this argument is that the concepts of truth and empirical adequacy are logically distinct, but this is an assumption I will grant here. If we deny this assumption, then the view that truth is valuable faces no difficulty from this quarter. If we grant it, we cannot account for the value of true belief in terms of practical utility. Even so, there is a sense that true belief is nonetheless more valuable than empirically adequate belief, for if one were to discover that a belief is empirically adequate but false, that discovery would provide strong motivation for change. In such a case, one would experience having been duped, even though the conduct of one's affairs would not be affected at all by the mistake.

These claims suggest that the value of truth is not in its capacity to further other interests we might have, but is rather intrinsic to truth itself. Perhaps truth is remote in a certain sense, so that attaining it is too much to ask and we will have to settle for something less. Still, such remoteness casts no doubt on the value of truth, for it can still legitimately be what we want in spite of the fact that we would have to be lucky to find it. I do not mean to endorse here these skeptical remarks about truth, but merely to grant them for the sake of argument. For even if such skepticism should be embraced, finding the truth remains the ideal and is valuable in itself. We might settle for empirical adequacy because we have no route to truth other than through empirical adequacy, but what we are after, and legitimately so, is the truth. Empirical adequacy may be sufficient for our practical concerns, but it does not satisfy the intellect.

Ernest Sosa demurs concerning the claim that truth itself is valuable, however. He says:

> At the beach on a lazy summer afternoon, we might scoop up a handful of sand and carefully count the grains. This would give us an otherwise unremarked truth, something that on the view before us is at least a positive good, other things equal. This view I hardly understand. The number of grains would not interest most of us in the slightest. Absent any such antecedent interest, moreover, it is hard to see any sort of *value* in one's having that truth.[14]

Sosa doesn't think that just any truth is valuable to believe and does not understand any account of value that isn't dependent in some way on antecedent interests. But we do have an interest in the truth, both pragmatic and purely intellectual. It is the nature of interests to lack specificity: We do not have an individuated interest in the truth of the claim that our mothers love us, that the president is not a crook, that Wyoming is north of Mexico, and so on. What we have is a general interest in the truth, and that interest attaches to particular truths in the manner of instantiation in predicate logic. The default position for any truth is that our general interest in the truth applies to it, though, of course, there can be special circumstances involved so that the general interest in the truth is overridden by other factors. That seems to me to be what happens in Sosa's example concerning the grains of sand. We are finite beings, with limited time and resources for enhancing our well-being; and without some special situation in which counting the grains brings pleasure to a person, perhaps only by passing the time in a way not completely boring, our general interest in enhancing our well-being comes into conflict with our general interest in the truth. Perhaps it is even true that most of the time when our interest in enhancing our well-being conflicts with our interest in the truth, the former overrides the latter. In any case, there is no obstacle to interpreting Sosa's example in this way, and if we do, we leave intact the earlier point, that obtaining the truth is valuable in itself, apart from any contribution it makes to our well-being.

14. Ernest Sosa, "The Place of Truth in Epistemology," in *Intellectual Virtue: Perspectives from Ethics and Epistemology*, Michael DePaul and Linda Zagzebski, eds. (Oxford: Oxford University Press, forthcoming), p. 2 typescript.

We have arrived at the conclusion that true belief is valuable, but not in terms of practical utility. That theory is partially correct, however, for belief is valuable because it is action-guiding, and no substitute for belief, such as acceptance or acting as if one believes, gives an adequate basis for action. In this sense, belief itself is of practical utility. Truth, however, is not; put more carefully, we cannot account for the value of truth in terms of its practical utility. For empirical adequacy is just as successful as is truth, and hence empirically adequate belief is as useful for practical purposes as is true belief. Truth is important intrinsically, for even if our beliefs are empirically adequate, we desire, and legitimately so, to find the truth.

Should a critic press us on this point, we will find ourselves in an awkward position, for when pressed to account for the intrinsic value of anything, it is very hard to know what to say. In the present case, I claim that having the truth is preferable to that which is merely empirically adequate, and if pressed on this point, I can do little else than resort to possible cases in which one learns that one's beliefs are empirically adequate but untrue and ask whether readers share my reaction to such cases, which involves a negative affective sense of having been duped. I then consider whether there are any reasons for thinking that this response should be explained away as not revealing anything significant about the value of truth over that of empirical adequacy, and I find no reason for thinking that this reaction is misleading. Should the critic point out that none of this guarantees the conclusion I draw, I will agree – pointing out, at the same time, the irrelevance of the point. If the critic has something of more substance, such as a reason for thinking that the feeling of being duped is a misleading indicator of what is truly valuable, the discussion can proceed. In the absence of such reasons, I propose that the conclusion that truth is intrinsically valuable is the best explanation of the data before us, and I further propose that the fact that none of the reasons given have the power to compel assent to this conclusion does not in any way cast doubt on the cogency of the argument given. I grant that claims of intrinsic value are deeply troublesome claims to defend, but one cannot philosophize about normative areas of philosophy without such claims, and I see no way to defend a claim of intrinsic value other than in the manner done here. I therefore maintain that the desire for truth is a desire for something intrinsically valuable, not replaceable without loss of value by the empirically adequate.

Furthermore, this desire is legitimate even if truth is unattainable, that is, if some version of skepticism is true. Should skepticism be true, there may be a sense in which we shall have to settle for less than we want, but having to settle for less than we want in no way tends to show that finding the truth is not valuable. So in our attempt to account for the value of knowledge, we can say at least this much: If knowledge is not valuable, this failure cannot be laid at the door of true belief.

Thus Socrates' approach in the *Meno* is vindicated, for Socrates assumes the value of true belief and asks what additional value might be found in knowledge. Because we have found that true belief is valuable, a promising idea to pursue would be to find some other element that is a constituent of knowledge and is also valuable. Here we have the history of epistemology on our side, for that history repeatedly endorses the idea that there is some normative dimension to knowledge, often identified in terms of the need for adequate evidence, or certainty, or justification, or some such related notion. In more recent times, the most common ways of thinking about the difference between knowledge and true belief distinguish between internalist and externalist approaches to the one or two primary differences that theorists see between knowledge and true belief. The next two chapters will be occupied with these approaches.

3

The Value of Justification

Recent discussions of the nature of knowledge have yielded two divergent paths to follow. On the one hand are reliabilists and other externalists, and on the other hand are justificationists and internalists. Sometimes members of the former camp claim to be offering a theory of justification,[1] but for present purposes I am going to treat such claims as idle explanatory wheels of their theoretical machine. If they turn out to be right, it will make their theories no better than they would have been as theories of knowledge, and if they are wrong, their theories of knowledge might still survive the amputation of this aspect.

We shall see in this chapter that ordinary reliabilist theories of knowledge cannot explain the value of knowledge over true belief, but this point is not my ultimate target. My ultimate target is to determine whether a justificationist account of knowledge can do any better. I will argue that it can, but that the picture of justification required for success is quite unusual. The conclusion will be a slightly disturbing account of what a theory of justification must look like if it is to have a chance of accounting for the value of knowledge.

EXTERNALIST ACCOUNTS

To see the difficulty of providing a good answer to the question of the value of knowledge over true belief, consider the following theory of knowledge. On this theory, what closes the gap between true belief and knowledge is objective likelihood of truth for belief. (For purposes of this

---

1. For example, Alvin Goldman, "What Is Justified Belief?" in *Knowledge and Justification*, George Pappas, ed. (Dordrecht: Reidel, 1979), pp. 1–25.

chapter, I propose to ignore the need for a fourth condition to address Gettier-induced concerns. We will have ample opportunity to consider such a need later.)

At first glance, this theory (the theory that distinguishes knowledge from true belief in terms of objective likelihood of the belief being true) seems to provide some hope of answering the question of why knowledge is more valuable than true belief. The reason it does is that objective likelihood of truth is itself a valuable property for a belief to have. Should a theorist take this fact to be decisive for answering the *Meno* problem we are addressing, the assumption made is as follows:

Assumption 1: The *Meno* problem can be solved if there is a property *P* that (i) distinguishes knowledge from true belief and (ii) is a valuable property for a belief to have.

Assumption 1, however, is false. To see that it is false, consider some simple analogies. If we have a piece of art that is beautiful, its aesthetic value is not enhanced by having as well the property of being likely to be beautiful. For being likely to be beautiful is a valuable property because of its relationship to being beautiful itself. Once beauty is assumed to be present, the property of being likely to be beautiful ceases to contribute any more value to the item in question. Likelihood of beauty has a value parasitic on beauty itself and hence has a value that is swamped by the presence of the latter.

Take anything that you care about: happiness, money, drugs, sports cars, and so on. Then consider two lists about such things, the first list telling you where to obtain such things and the second list telling you where you are likely to obtain such things. Now compose a third list, which is the intersection of the first two lists. It tells you of ways and places that both are likely to get you what you want and actually will get you what you want. But there would be no reason to prefer the third list to the first list, given what you care about.

These analogies show that when the value of one property is parasitic on the value of another property in the way that the likelihood of *X* is parasitic on *X* itself, the value of the first is swamped by the presence of the second. So even if likelihood of truth is a valuable property for a belief to have, adding that property to a belief already assumed to be true adds no value to the resulting composite that is not already present in true belief itself. So Assumption 1 is false; one cannot solve the *Meno* problem simply by finding a valuable property that distinguishes true belief from knowledge. In addition, the valuable property would, at a minimum, have

45

to be the kind of property whose value is not swamped by the value of truth itself.

Note that this swamping problem affects not only the present theory on which knowledge is objectively likely to be true belief, but also the exceedingly minor variant of this theory called "reliabilism." Richard Swinburne has recently argued in *Providence and the Problem of Evil*[2] that the swamping problem just discussed undermines any reliabilist account of the value of knowledge over true belief, though he does not use my terminology. Swinburne argues on the negative side that reliabilism and other externalist theories of knowledge have no good explanation of the value of knowledge, whereas at least one kind of internalist theory does have a good explanation. Swinburne's argument against reliabilism is powerful and instructive. It is powerful because it is very hard to see how a reliabilist can escape the criticism. It is instructive because it shows what a good explanation of the value of knowledge must look like. Put differently, Swinburne's argument against reliabilism is not only worth looking at in itself, it also establishes a clear condition of adequacy for correctly addressing and accounting for the value of knowledge.

Swinburne divides theories of knowledge into internalist and externalist varieties and argues that the former can account for the value of knowledge but the latter cannot. An internalist holds, according to Swinburne, that the warrant that turns true belief into knowledge "arises (in major part) from something internal to the subject (i.e. something to which she has ready access)," whereas an externalist "claims that warrant arises solely from something external to the subject to which she may have no access."[3] Swinburne cites reliabilism as the most common version of the latter viewpoint, the theory according to which a belief has warrant when produced by a process that normally produces true belief.[4]

Swinburne argues that reliabilism cannot give an adequate account of the value of knowledge:

Now clearly it is a good thing that our beliefs satisfy the reliabilist requirement, for the fact that they do means that . . . they will probably be true. But, if a given belief of mine is true, I cannot see that it is any more worth having for satisfying the reliabilist requirement. So long as the belief is true, the fact that the process

---

2. Richard Swinburne, *Providence and the Problem of Evil* (Oxford: Oxford University Press, 1999), pp. 57–66.
3. Ibid., p. 57.
4. Ibid.

which produced it usually produces true beliefs does not seem to make that belief any more worth having.[5]

This argument contains an important lesson about what needs to be done in order to defend the value of knowledge. Our first approach to the problem inclines us to think as follows. "Suppose knowledge is composed of X, Y, and Z; and further suppose that all these components are valuable, that is, that the value of X is greater than its lack, and so on for Y and Z. Then knowledge is value because it is composed of valuable elements." Swinburne's argument attacks this assumption, the assumption I have labeled Assumption 1. His argument begins by endorsing the claim that reliable belief is better than unreliable belief on the grounds that the former is more likely to be true than the latter. This presupposes another value judgment, that truth in belief is important. So, letting $V(p)$ represent the value of p, Swinburne assumes

(VT) $(Value\ of\ Truth)$: V(true belief) $>$ V(false belief)
and
(VR) $(Value\ of\ Reliability)$: V(reliable belief) $>$ V(unreliable belief)

On the initial approach suggested previously, these claims are all that is needed to secure an adequate explanation of the value of knowledge, for on the proposed theory, knowledge just is reliable true belief.[6] But Swinburne balks at this conclusion, claiming that the value of reliable true belief does not exceed the value of unreliable true belief. His reason for this latter claim is that once truth is in the picture, its value so swamps the value of reliability that the value of reliability simply disappears. That is, Swinburne rejects Assumption 1.

Swinburne gives an analogy for the way in which the value of truth can swamp any value that reliability has, one concerning a beautiful piece of furniture produced by a factory that ordinarily produces defective pieces.[7] We have already seen some examples of this sort, one of which concerned things a person might value. Consider the following particular example of this: Suppose I am interested in chocolate (which I am). I check the Internet for information on where I can buy chocolate locally and find

---

5. Ibid., p. 58.
6. To assume that reliabilists hold that knowledge is to be identified with reliable true belief presumes that the Gettier problem does not affect reliabilism. I don't know why Swinburne assumes this; it is patently false. The falsity of this assumption does not affect Swinburne's argument, however, so I ignore this issue in the text.
7. Swinburne, *Providence and the Problem of Evil*, p. 58.

two lists. One gives sites within walking distance that *sell* chocolate; the other gives sites within walking distance *likely to sell* chocolate. It is fairly obvious that I'd be more impressed with the first list than with the second, leading by analogy to endorsing the claim that the value of truth exceeds that of reliability (likelihood of truth). But that is not the central point. Suppose a visitor in my office quickly generates a third list containing the intersection of the first two lists: sites that both sell and are likely to sell chocolate. I'd have no reason whatsoever to prefer the intersection list to the first list, given only my interest in chocolate. The first list tells me where to find chocolate, the second list is a bit inferior to the first, and the third list is no better than the first. So by analogy, we should endorse the claim that knowledge is no more valuable than true belief if knowledge is reliable true belief.

The central feature of this argument against a reliabilist account of the value of knowledge is, to repeat, the *swamping effect* that the value of truth has over the value of reliable belief. Once truth is in place, it has a kind of value that makes the value of reliability otiose. The general lesson of this argument is that when accounting for the value of knowledge, we must always be alert to ways in which the various values interact. This point implies that more is required to account for the value of knowledge than merely finding it to have valuable constituents. If we want to answer Plato's question about what makes knowledge more valuable than true belief, it is insufficient to cite a further property of knowledge beyond true belief *even if that property is itself valuable*. The parts may each have value, but when put together, the whole still may have no more value than if one of the parts were missing altogether.

Perhaps failing to heed this lesson explains in part why the issue of the value of knowledge has not received much attention in recent epistemology. It is common to presume that justification is a valuable property, so it would be easy to assume that if knowledge is justified true belief, then it is more valuable than mere true belief. And even if knowledge is more than justified true belief, the additional requirements look valuable, too. It is valuable not to reason through false premises; it is valuable to have a justification that is undefeated or that presupposes no falsehoods; it is valuable to be a truth tracker; it is valuable to have a warrant that would remain in relevant alternatives to the actual situation; perhaps it is valuable as well to function in accord with one's design plan.[8] These are among the

---

8. For examples of these approaches to the nature of knowledge, see, respectively, Roderick Chisholm, *Theory of Knowledge*, 2nd edition (Englewood Cliffs, NJ: Prentice-Hall, 1973);

most promising attempts to say what distinguishes knowledge from justified true belief, and we will have an opportunity to look closely at these
proposals later. For purposes of this chapter, however, we need to note
the lesson of Swinburne's argument against the value of knowledge on a
reliability theory of it. That lesson is that merely citing properties claimed
to characterize knowledge that also are valuable properties of a belief is
insufficient to yield an adequate explanation of the value of knowledge.
Without attending to the way in which the values of the constituents of
knowledge might interact, we are in no position to conclude that the
value of these properties gives us an unproblematic account of the value
of knowledge.

Let us pause for a moment and recap the discussion to this point.
We introduced the notion of objective likelihood of truth and argued
that this property is a valuable one. We then introduced the swamping
problem and argued that even though objective likelihood is a valuable
property of belief, its value succumbs to the swamping problem. That is,
in the context of true belief, the addition of this valuable property creates a composite item – belief that is both true and objectively likely to
be true – with no more value than true belief itself. We then turned to
reliabilism, a popular contemporary approach to knowledge. What distinguishes reliabilism from the theory just examined is a restriction on
the basis required for objective likelihood: The objective likelihood has
to result from being produced or sustained by a process or method that
ordinarily produces true beliefs. This restriction, as Swinburne argues,
takes us no distance beyond our original proposal in addressing the *Meno*
problem, for objective likelihood derived from the process or methods
employed is also a property that, though valuable, is still valuable in a
way parasitic on the value of truth. Thus, once it is assumed that truth
is present, this special kind of objective likelihood has no power to increase the value of the composite beyond that involved in true belief
itself.

Swinburne is not the first or the only theorist to notice this problem for reliabilism. Linda Zagzebski argues against it as well by claiming
that a beautiful piece of furniture is no more valuable aesthetically for

Keith Lehrer and Thomas D. Paxson, Jr., "Knowledge: Undefeated Justified True Belief,"
Essays on Knowledge and Justification, George Pappas and Marshall Swain, eds. (Ithaca, NY:
Cornell University Press, 1979), pp. 146–54; Robert Nozick, *Philosophical Explanations*
(Cambridge, MA: Harvard University Press, 1981); Alvin Goldman, "Discrimination and
Perceptual Knowledge," in Pappas and Swain, *Knowledge and Justification*, pp. 120–45; and
Alvin Plantinga, *Warrant and Proper Function* (Oxford: Oxford University Press, 1993).

having been produced by a factory that ordinarily produces beautiful furniture.[9]

One primary difference here between the objective likelihood theory of knowledge and various versions of reliabilism concerns the normative dimension of knowledge, and this difference may suggest a possible avenue of escape from the swamping problem. The normativity of knowledge arises because of its involvement with evaluative concepts such as justification, good reasons, or adequate evidence. Perhaps reliabilist theories can claim to be immune to the swamping problem because the value derived from reliability is just that value involved in the normativity of knowledge. So even though the truth conditions for reliable belief are just special cases of the truth conditions for objectively likely belief, perhaps the special case in question is just special enough for normativity to piggyback on.

One might argue this line as follows. Normativity is usually thought to be a supervenient property, by which we mean that the presence of nonnormative factors implies the presence of normative ones but not vice versa. So, any normativity found in knowledge must have its basis in some nonnormative factors. According to the variety of reliabilism envisaged, the basis of the normativity in knowledge is reliability. This nonnormative basis is very much like the property of objective likelihood of truth, and it would have the same value when attached to true belief as this latter property, but for the fact that it is the nonnormative basis of the normative features of knowledge. Mere objective likelihood of truth is not the basis of the normative features of knowledge and so succumbs to the swamping problem. Reliability of belief is different, however, for it is the basis of the normative features of knowledge and so does not succumb to the swamping problem.

The easiest way to see the idea here is to take reliabilism to be offering a theory of justification, though this assumption is not crucial. If we assume it, however, reliabilists can claim to have a better time with the swamping problem because their theory does not merely identify knowledge with true beliefs that are likely to be true. Instead, knowledge requires justification, and the central difference this notion introduces is that of normativity. When the right kind of objective likelihood of truth is found, a normative dimension appears that was not present heretofore. Once this normative dimension is in place, the swamping problem, it is

<hr />

9. I borrow this example from Swinburne, *Providence and the Problem of Evil*, p. 58.

claimed, can be handled, for though the value of objective likelihood of truth is swamped by the value of truth itself, the normative dimension that accompanies the right kind of objective likelihood of truth introduces a new valuational element distinct from the value of objective likelihood of truth. The normativity arising from the nonnormative base of reliability is positively valuable and thus adds an element of value not present with mere objective likelihood of truth. In this way, it might be argued that reliabilism escapes the swamping problem.

It must be admitted that this reply looks magical, something like pulling a rabbit out of a hat. If we just reach into the right hat, the rabbit of normativity pops out, rescuing our theory of knowledge, even though all the available hats appear identical. The reliabilist nonetheless insists that it is the intrinsic properties of one of the hats that makes all the difference. At least in magic, we can find out the relevant difference: Some hats have false bottoms, for example. But not here; no inquiry will reveal any property of reliable belief that makes it plain why normativity appears with it and not with objectively likely belief. So, unlike the magic to which we are accustomed, the truth of this theory would require something truly magical, different in kind from the explicable illusions used by magicians to entertain us.

I do not wish to dismiss this reply quite so quickly, however, for it is significant in several ways. First, there may be a way for reliabilists to avoid the magical appearance of the previous reply if they can explain how the property of reliability gives rise to normativity. I want to explore this issue closely in the next chapter, where I will argue that it is precisely on this point that virtue epistemology holds special promise. It is also important to note the significance of this appeal to the normative dimension for knowledge. Without an appeal to such normativity, theories that appeal, in one way or another, to likelihood of truth as a fundamental feature that distinguishes knowledge from true belief – in short, typical externalist theories of knowledge – have no resources for explaining the value of knowledge. Such theories succumb to the swamping problem, so that only by finding some value independent of the value of truth can externalism survive the Socratic inquiry of the *Meno*. The most natural place to look for such an independent value is in the arena of the normative dimensions of knowledge, so naturalistic theories that eschew any such talk of normativity will be at a deeper disadvantage in attempting to answer the question of the value of knowledge.

In this way, the appeal to normativity on behalf of reliabilism is quite significant, for in such an appeal lies the best hope for standard versions

51

of externalism to address the problem of the *Meno*. There is a further way in which this appeal to normativity is significant, one that touches theories of knowledge beyond standard versions of externalism. In the remainder of this chapter, I want to explore the consequences for an account of the third condition for knowledge if this reliabilist appeal to normativity is assumed to be a failure. I will argue that if such an appeal cannot be sustained, the standard accounts of knowledge and justification, whether internalist or externalist, must be abandoned. I will spend the rest of this chapter arguing for this point, in part to set the stage for further investigation of this reliabilist appeal to normativity in the next chapter. Our discussion will be significant in its own right as well, for it will yield an account of justification on which justification is valuable in a way that does not succumb to the swamping problem. This discussion thus will provide an account of one way in which knowledge is more valuable than true belief if justification as conceived here is a constituent of knowledge.

JUSTIFICATIONIST ACCOUNTS

If we suppose that all versions of reliabilism succumb to the swamping problem, we are assuming that no appeal to normativity by reliabilist theories can be successful, either because no normativity is involved in such theories or because the attempt to pull the rabbit of normativity out of the hat of reliability is simply too magical to satisfy. If so, theories of knowledge that explicitly employ the concept of justification would seem to have an advantage over reliability theories, because justification is a normative or evaluative property. Such theories have, already at hand, the normative dimension that the magical version of reliabilism tries to produce. The question of the nonnormative basis of this normativity may arise at some point for such theories, but here we bypass that question to focus on the significance of adding a normative property to true belief in our account of knowledge.

If justification is valuable in virtue of being a normative or evaluative property, it can be so by being either intrinsically or extrinsically valuable. Suppose we opt for the latter approach. If we do, then we will be holding that justification is valuable in virtue of its relationship to some other thing that is valuable. The natural candidate here is truth: Justification is valuable because it is a mark of truth. A mark of truth is an indicator of it, and it is natural to understand these locutions in terms of likelihood – objective likelihood – of truth: Something is a mark or indicator of truth if its presence renders the claim in question objectively likely to be true.

52

By now, the danger of shipwreck for this view should be obvious, for if justification is valuable because it renders beliefs that have it objectively likely to be true, then the value of justification will be parasitic on the value of truth. And if that is so, then the value of truth will swamp the value that justification contributes to belief, rendering justified true belief no more valuable than true belief itself.

One response to this quandary is to reach quickly for the other option – namely, that justification is an intrinsically valuable property of belief. Such a view is not without precedent, for in the third edition of his *Theory of Knowledge*, Roderick Chisholm abandoned the idea that our primary intellectual duty is to (do our best to) find the truth and avoid error in favor of the claim that our primary intellectual duty is to believe rationally and fail to believe irrationally.[10] This latter claim entails that believing rationally (or believing justifiedly) is an end in itself, not a means to some other goal that is itself intrinsically valuable. More recently, Michael DePaul has argued that inquiry has dual goals of truth and rationality, with neither being reducible to the value of the other.[11]

There are powerful objections to this view, however. Consider a baseball analogy. Various statistical categories are recorded regarding the performance of a team and its members during a game, and the reason they are kept is that they are related in some important way to winning the game. Fielding percentage is important, for example, because errors allow the other team base runners, and having base runners increases the chances of scoring, and scoring runs contributes to winning. Batting averages are kept because hits lead to base runners and to runs batted in. Suppose, however, that I propose a new statistical category that ought to be kept: what percentage of the time a batter steps on home plate on his way to first base. I claim that lower percentages are better (because right-handed batters have to cross over home plate in some way to get to first, this new statistical category favors left-handed batters, which in the view of this author is all to the good). You ask why I think that lower percentages are better; in fact, you are audacious enough to ask why I think any percentage here is of any interest at all. I claim, in response, that a lower percentage here is not valuable in an extrinsic way, as it would be if it contributed somehow to winning games. I claim, instead, that a lower percentage is intrinsically valuable, independent

---

10.   Roderick Chisholm, *Theory of Knowledge*, 3rd edition (Englewood Cliffs, NJ: Prentice-Hall, 1989), p. 1.

11.   Michael R. DePaul, *Balance and Refinement* (London: Routledge, 1993).

of any relation to any factor that contributes to winning baseball games.

I suggest you would be utterly perplexed by my proposal. The point of statistical categories for baseball is their connection to winning, for that is the goal of the game (though, I grant, the point of *playing* the game might be something other than winning – that is a different, and unrelated, matter). The claim that there is some important statistical category that is important in its own right, apart from the goal of the game (and apart from the goal of playing the game, for that matter), is preposterous. It should, and would, leave the audience incredulous.

The same, I suggest, goes for the game of belief. The goal of the game is to find the truth (we will find later that this simple claim requires some qualifications, but they do not affect the present discussion). Any claim that there are properties of belief that have value intrinsically, independent of any relationship to the truth, should be met with incredulity. Perhaps there is some kind of aesthetic or moral or political value that a belief might have that is unrelated to the truth of the belief, but the proposal here is that the property that is intrinsically valuable has the kind of value characteristic of intellectual achievements, of inquiry for its own sake. The goal of inquiry, however, is nothing other than getting to the truth and avoiding error,[12] so any property of belief that is valuable from a purely intellectual point of view had better find some connection between that property and truth. So if justification is a valuable property of belief, it simply cannot be because it has value in and of itself, independently of any relationship to the truth.

An example may help at this point. In *Epistemic Justification*, Richard Swinburne claims to defend the intrinsic value of what he terms "objective internalist justification." He does so by comparing two people who come to believe the same thing, one (a scientist) guided by the evidence and the other by dreams. Swinburne rightly points out that we find belief guided by evidence to be more valuable than belief guided by dreams and wants to hold that this fact shows the intrinsic value of justification. Yet, his explanation betrays him; he says, "We value our scientist because he shows a grasp on those a priori truths that I described in Chapter 4,

12. There is a related view on which truth is not the goal of inquiry, but rather empirical adequacy. I wish to bypass discussion of this dispute here, for it is irrelevant to the issues I'm addressing about the value of knowledge. To make it explicitly irrelevant, I could introduce the idea of a truth surrogate, a property a belief has when it is empirically adequate, and then formulate the goal of inquiry in terms of truth or truth surrogates, but the additional complexity would have no value, so I ignore it here.

and is consciously guided by them in his belief formation."[13] The a priori truths Swinburne refers to in this quote are those truths that determine to what extent a belief is justified. If so, however, it is a mistake to think of beliefs justified in this sense as having a value that is completely independent of the value of truth – you can't have such justified beliefs without grasping these a priori truths and being guided by them in belief formation. Moreover, it is in virtue of these truths that justified beliefs are objectively likely to be true, so it is hard to see how Swinburne can claim that the value of justification derived from these truths is independent of the concept of truth. In particular, it is hard to see how he can so claim when his explanation appeals to the concept of truth, namely, the a priori truths that establish the objectivity of the concept of justification under discussion.

Instead of defending the intrinsic value of justification, I think all Swinburne wants to defend is the value of having justification for false beliefs, for he explicitly states that his goal is to show that it is valuable "to have epistemically justified beliefs . . . even if they are not true."[14] In one sense, establishing such a conclusion would show that justified beliefs have a value independent of the value of truth, but not in the sense under discussion here. For justification could be valuable because of its connection to truth, and in virtue of this value, justified beliefs could be valuable even when they are false. So in spite of advertising a defense of the intrinsic value of justification, Swinburne's account of the value of justification does not succeed in avoiding an appeal to the connection between justification and truth. His explanation of the intrinsic value of justification renders it false that justification has value that is in no way dependent on the value of truth.

So we face a dilemma: Justification can't be conceived to be intrinsically valuable, having a value that depends in no way whatsoever on the value of truth, and yet if it is conceived to be extrinsically valuable, its value must derive from some connection to the truth, in which case it looks as if the swamping problem plagues not only reliabilist theories of knowledge but justificationist theories as well. In light of this dilemma, what is a self-respecting epistemologist to do?

Swinburne thinks he knows what to do. Recall that Swinburne argues first that reliabilist theories of knowledge are hopeless because of the swamping problem. He argues next that internalist theories of knowledge

13.   Richard Swinburne, *Epistemic Justification* (Oxford: Oxford University Press, 2000), p. 163.
14.   Ibid.

provide more hope. According to Swinburne, the key component of knowledge for an internalist is justification. Swinburne distinguishes between two notions of justification. The first is a very subjective notion having to do with whether a person is epistemically at fault in holding a belief. In this sense, a belief is justified by the criteria a person holds for how best to get to the truth. The objective sense requires that these criteria be correct. The correct criteria, according to Swinburne, are all a priori, related intimately to theorems derivable from the probability calculus.

Swinburne claims that the value of subjectively justified belief exceeds that of subjectively unjustified belief, and he also holds that the value of objectively justified belief is greater than that of subjectively justified belief. We can postpone consideration of the former claim, for Swinburne's primary interest is in the latter claim. Swinburne's reason for this claim is that if a belief is objectively justified, it is probably true, whereas if it is only subjectively justified, it is only probably true relative to the criteria employed. Put more simply, objective justification is superior to subjective justification because objectively justified beliefs are more likely to be true than subjectively justified ones.

These endorsements are preliminary to the main question, which concerns the value of knowledge. Had we not seen the argument against reliabilism, we might have thought that these endorsements provide sufficient ground for proclaiming knowledge valuable. For internalists typically think of knowledge as composed of truth, (objective) justification, and belief (as well as some clause for the Gettier problem). But once we have seen the earlier swamping objection to reliabilism, things are more complicated. Our suspicions should be raised especially by the fact that, for Swinburne, the value of objective justification is clarified in terms of likelihood of truth, for it is that very feature of reliability that led to the swamping problem for reliabilism.

So, suspicions suitably alerted, consider what Swinburne has to say about the value of knowledge on this internalist theory:

If we respond to our evidence in accordance with correct criteria for assessing it, it is more probable that we shall get true beliefs than if we assess it in accordance with incorrect criteria. But why should it matter if an individual true belief has been formed in accordance with incorrect criteria? I claimed earlier that it would not matter if an individual true belief was not formed by a reliable process. But there is a difference here, arising from the fact that forming beliefs in accordance with criteria is normally a process of which the subject . . . is almost always at least half-conscious. We are at least half-conscious of the criteria we use in inferring from evidence to hypothesis. . . . But then, one who operates on false criteria will have false beliefs about what is evidence for what, about the right way to assess beliefs. And false beliefs here are false beliefs about something very central to human rationality. So if true belief matters, true belief which is justified is even more valuable. . . . I conclude that knowledge in the internalist sense is a better thing to have than mere strong true belief.[15]

Swinburne initially suggests the same approach for the internalist used by the externalist: that justified true beliefs are good because they are objectively likely to be true. He quickly reminds us of the swamping effect of truth but claims that there is a difference here. The difference is that beliefs formed in accordance with criteria are "almost always at least half-conscious." Qualifiers aside, what Swinburne wants to affirm is that when we form beliefs in accordance with criteria, we have implicit beliefs about those criteria. Because true belief is better than false belief, it is better for these beliefs to be true, and if our beliefs are objectively justified, then the believed criteria will be true. So, Swinburne concludes,

(*VJTB*) (*Value of Justified True Belief*): V(objectively justified true belief) > V (objectively unjustified true belief)

The argument cannot be sustained, however. The problems derive from the qualifiers Swinburne is forced to use in describing beliefs formed in accordance with criteria. He says "almost always," we are at least "half-conscious" of the process of belief formation. If we are charitable and grant that half-consciousness implies at least dispositional beliefs or awarenesses, we are still left with the "almost always" clause, and I see no way to get it to disappear. If Swinburne leaves this clause as it is, he has not shown that objectively justified true belief is superior to objectively unjustified true belief, but rather only that it almost always is, a qualified claim insufficient to establish the unqualified value of knowledge over true belief.

Moreover, there is the assumption here that when we form beliefs, we always form them in accordance with criteria. I'm not sure what such a claim involves, but an overly reflective account of belief formation results when we combine such a claim with the assumption needed regarding the half-consciousness claim, the assumption that this claim implies the existence of (at least) dispositional beliefs or awarenesses. It may be that our belief-forming practices embody or display a set of criteria for belief formation, but it is simply false that we have beliefs, even dispositional ones, about what those criteria are. Sometimes we are reflective in belief

15.   Swinburne, *Providence and the Problem of Evil*, p. 64.

formation and thereby hold beliefs about such criteria, but sometimes we do not. So, I don't think Swinburne's defense of (*VJTB*) works; it can be successful only by strengthening the half-consciousness claim in a way that requires an overly intellectual account of the process of belief formation.

The same problem plagues Swinburne's more recent defense of the value of justification.[16] Swinburne's latest account of the concept requires a distinction between basic and nonbasic beliefs, where that distinction exists only when the subject distinguishes between beliefs caused by other beliefs and beliefs not so caused.[17] As Swinburne recognizes, such an account implies that small children do not have justified beliefs, and this result undermines any account of the value of knowledge dependent on this concept of justification. If knowledge is valuable and more valuable than true belief, it is valuable in this way both to children and to adults.

It is also worth noting in passing that even if Swinburne's preceding explanation were adequate, he would not have given an adequate account of the value of knowledge, contrary to what he claims to have done. For such a conclusion fails to honor the lesson learned in his discussion of reliabilism. If his defense of (*VJTB*) were adequate, Swinburne would have made an advance past the reliabilist theory discussed earlier. If the preceding defense were adequate, it would show that the value of justification, internalistically conceived, is not swamped by the value of truth. Yet, Swinburne knows that internalists do not identify knowledge with justified true belief. He knows that there must be a condition added to assuage Gettier. Given the lesson learned in the discussion of reliabilism, Swinburne is entitled to claim that he has an adequate account of the value of knowledge only if he can defend the claim that the value of knowledge exceeds that of justified true belief, that is, if he can defend

(*VK*) $V(K) > V(JTB)$.

It is a very interesting and important question whether *VK* is true, one that will occupy us in a later chapter. Swinburne's claim in *Providence and the Problem of Evil* to have successfully defended the value of knowledge amounts to the claim that there is no further question concerning the value of knowledge beyond that of justified true belief.[18] Such a

16. Swinburne, *Epistemic Justification*, esp. chapter 6.
17. Ibid., p. 158.
18. It is interesting to note the development in Swinburne's epistemological views, from this oversight in *Providence and the Problem of Evil* to the more sophisticated discussion at the end of *Epistemic Justification*. In the latter work, he notes the significance of the Gettier problem,

conclusion ignores the very lesson Swinburne's argument against reliabilism teaches us.

So Swinburne's account of the value of knowledge is unsatisfying in two respects. First, he fails to show that the value of objectively justified true belief exceeds that of true belief. In order to demonstrate this point, he will have to find some feature of objectively justified belief *other than likelihood of truth* that accounts for its enhanced value, and it is hard to see where to find such a feature. In any case, Swinburne's own hypothesis, that having objective justification requires having implicit beliefs about the proper criteria for justification, fails. In addition, this proposal fails to address the problems raised by the need for a fourth condition for knowledge. Such an oversight ignores the important lesson his objection to reliabilism shows, which is that demonstrating the value of knowledge requires considering the difficulty that the values of the constituents of knowledge interact in such a way that, even though the components are valuable, the enhanced value is lost through interaction.

We have seen two dead-end paths, one that depended on claiming that justification is intrinsically valuable and Swinburne's approach that highlighted the connection between justification and truth. In the face of the failure of both of these approaches, one might decide to succumb to the dilemma and abandon hope for finding an answer to the *Meno* problem. Embracing despair for a solution commits one to the view that knowledge simply is not more valuable than true belief, but this is a hard doctrine to accept. Apart from identifying knowledge with true belief, there is only one theoretical view that offers any hope for the value of knowledge when the value of justified true belief cannot be held to be greater than that of true belief. Richard Foley holds that knowledge is comprehensive enough true belief,[19] and given this view, one could hold that knowledge is better than mere true belief. It is better not because it has some special feature in each given case that makes it superior, but because one has to have *many* true beliefs in order to have knowledge. So knowledge is better than true belief in the same way that a million dollars is better than a thousand: not in virtue of having a value different in kind, but merely in terms of the quantity of the value in question.

and addresses the question of the value of knowledge separately from the question of the value of justification. We will have a chance to look at this later proposal when looking at the Gettier problem and its significance for giving an account of the value of knowledge.

19. Richard Foley, "Knowledge Is Accurate and Comprehensive Enough Belief," in *Warrant in Contemporary Epistemology: Essays in Honor of Plantinga's Theory of Knowledge*, Jonathan L. Kvanvig, ed. (Totowa, NJ: Rowman & Littlefield, 1996), pp. 87–96.

Even on Foley's view, though, there is a related problem. For if the only difference between the value of knowledge and the value of true belief is in terms of quantity – that is, if we clarify comprehensiveness of belief in terms related to the number of beliefs – then we should be able to achieve the value of knowledge by just believing enough truths, even if these truths are not related in the way required for knowledge. Such a conclusion is wrong, though. Knowledge is supposed to have a value greater than that of true belief, and it cannot be mimicked merely by adding a greater number of true beliefs (think of performing the rule of or-introduction on an unknown true belief until one has as many true beliefs as would be required by Foley's theory in order for the original belief to count as knowledge).

Whether these questions can be answered is not the only concern, for both theories mentioned earlier will be found by most epistemologists to be intolerable precisely because they ignore the normative dimension of knowedge. For such theorists, then, such theories cannot be used as an elixir to alleviate the discomfort of the *Meno* problem.

So, if our discussion contains a mistake, where is it? I think it does contain a mistake, and seeing it will help us to understand just where a theory of knowledge must go in order to answer the *Meno* problem through appeal to the normativity of knowledge.

TWO KINDS OF MEANS TO A GOAL

The mistake in the preceding section, I want to argue, is contained in the discussion of how one might conceive of justification having extrinsic value. That discussion could be presented using the language of means and ends (or goals), but there is an important ambiguity in the concept of a means to a goal that needs to be elucidated to see the mistake. First, I will explain the ambiguity. Then I will turn to the way in which the ambiguity opens a path out of the previous dilemma for justificationism.

The ambiguity in the concept of a means to a goal is easiest to see in the arena of action. The ambiguity I have in mind is that between *intentional* means and *effective* means. In the arena of action, the first concept is instanced when a person performs a certain action with the intention of realizing a certain goal. If I am chosen to take a shot from half-court at a Houston Rockets basketball game for one million dollars, I will perform certain actions as a means to the goal of making the shot. I will, for example, face the basket; I'll even shoot the ball. But I will perform no action that constitutes an *effective* means toward winning the million dollars. For, to be an effective means, the action must make it objectively likely that the goal is realized, or at least more likely than it would have been otherwise. In many cases, however, there simply are no effective means available. In this example, nothing I could do will make it likely that I make a shot from half-court, and nothing I could do will even raise the likelihood of my making such a shot. After all, I'm not as young as I used to be; maybe I'm beyond the point of even throwing the ball that far (certainly I am if not given a significant amount of time to warm up). Nonetheless, I would still try and, in trying, adopt some intentional means to the goal of making the basket.

One might object here that if my tryings are known not to raise the chances of making a basket, then I must have other reasons besides wanting to make a basket to explain why I engage in the particular actions in question.[20] Perhaps I am merely going along with the contest, trying only to fit in with ordinary expectations of what to do, but my goal simply can't be to make a basket and win a million dollars, for I know that won't happen, regardless of what I do.

This view of the relationship between what you know and what we try to do is implausible. It may be irrational in some way to try to achieve a goal that one knows one won't achieve, but it is certainly possible to be irrational in this way. Furthermore, it is not clear that it is irrational. For one may also know that there is a nonzero chance that the goal will be achieved (there is, after all, quantum theory to appeal to for some serendipitous convergence of random motions to make the ball go into the basket) and that trying in such-and-such a way is as good as any other way to try to realize that goal, even though none of the ways of trying increase the chances of the goal being realized. One might also choose to do nothing in the hope that the goal will be achieved without any trying on one's part, but if it is irrational (or, worse, impossible) to try when one knows that the goal won't be achieved, it would be equally irrational to choose to do nothing (hoping that the goal would be realized anyway).

One might also balk at the probability assessments I have made about the case. One might think, for example, that following standard procedure has to raise the likelihood at least slightly over that of the ball going into the basket as a result of behavior at the quantum level. This objection is mistaken, and I want to be explicit enough about the case to make it obvious why it is mistaken. If we want, we can change the case so that

---

20. Michael DePaul raised this objection to the example in question at the 1999 Spindel Conference at the University of Memphis.

there is a small opening created in the roof of the building and I am required to make the shot from the far corner of the parking lot, through the small opening, and into the basket. The objector will have to admit, at some point, that the shot can become so difficult that nothing I do will increase the chances of the ball going into the basket. I am pretty confident that this level of difficulty has been reached by the distance from half-court, but we can move the distance out further to satisfy the concerns of the objector.

The objector might still complain that the standard procedure I use to shoot the ball is a procedure that, in general, raises the likelihood of making a basket, even though it doesn't do so in this particular case. That point is true. If we change the reference class relative to which probability assessments are made, we can get different probabilities, some of which will conform to the view that actions taken as means to a goal must always raise the likelihood of achieving that goal and some of which will not. The important question then becomes which probabilities are the right ones for assessing this claim that all means must be effective means.

In the preceding discussion, I intended the probability claims to be single-case probabilities, not probability assessments that implicitly require some reference class. If there are such single-case probabilities, it is those probabilities that are relevant to the assessment of the claim that all means must be effective means. One fairly substantive argument on behalf of the existence of such probabilities is that well-confirmed contemporary scientific theories presuppose them. Even without such single-case probabilities, however, the case for the distinction between intentional and effective means can still be made. For the relevant reference classes in the specific example of shooting a basketball must be picked in order to make sense of the claim that the likelihood of making a basket decreases the farther away one gets from the basket. If we pick the reference class of all shots attempted throughout my life, then the probability of making a shot from half-court is the same as that of making a free throw. Imagine trying to convince the architects of the contest to let me shoot from the free throw line instead of half-court on the grounds that the likelihood of making the shot are the same! It is clear that the reference classes must be chosen to honor the obvious fact that likelihoods vary with distance, and if they are chosen in this way, then there will be some distance at which nothing that is done can make a difference to the antecedent likelihood of the ball going into the hoop.

So why follow standard procedure? Why, for example, shoot with one hand rather than the other? These questions return us to the earlier objection, that there must be some reason for preferring one method to another in order to explain what is done, and if likelihood of making a basket doesn't change, then some other goal must be involved to explain the difference.

Besides the reply made earlier to this objection, there are two other points that I want to make about it. First, we have the makings of a Buridan's ass paradox here, for if one must have a reason to prefer one course of action over another in terms of likelihood of success, one will be forced to wonder why Buridan's ass does not starve to death when faced with the choice between two equally attractive hay bales. We know, however, that such an event won't happen: Even if both bales of hay are equally attractive, the ass will not simply starve to death, unable to find some ground for choosing between them. Once the choice is made, we will have no basis for explaining the choice of one bale over the other in terms of any goal the ass is pursuing, and any theory of explanation that requires such will have to treat the failure of the ass to starve to death as inexplicable. Second, if you ask the shooter, for example, why he is shooting with his left hand rather than his right, the answer you are most likely to get is something like "Because I'm left-handed." If you ask whether the shooter thinks that shooting with one hand rather than the other will increase the chances of success, you'll get the answer "No." If you then badger the shooter about what his additional goal must be to explain the choice of shooting left-handed rather than right-handed, you'll get a reply about as informative as the one given by the ass about his choice of hay bales. My point is that the need for some additional goal can only be defended if one is willing to adopt a position generating the Buridan's ass paradox.

So the conclusion stands. There is a difference between intentional and effective means in the arena of action, a difference that is crucial in understanding many of the things that we try to achieve when we know full well how limited our abilities are. We try for the goal, knowing that we are no good at all at the task, and in so doing adopt a means for achieving that goal. But the means are not effective means, so there must be some other kind of means to a goal – namely, intentional means.

There is another way to put the same point. There is a difference between extrinsic and instrumental value. If an item has instrumental value, then there is some other thing to which it contributes. To have instrumental value, a thing must raise the likelihood of securing this other thing. Extrinsic value does not require this. To be extrinsically valuable, a thing's value must be explicable in terms of the value of some other thing.

One way to be extrinsically valuable is to be instrumentally valuable, but it is a confusion to assume that the only way to be extrinsically valuable is to be instrumentally valuable. The procedures followed in trying to make a shot from half-court are extrinsically valuable in that the explanation of their value must advert to the goal of making the shot, but these procedures are not instrumentally valuable because they do not raise the likelihood of securing the goal.

The distinction between intentional and effective means gives some hope that there might be a way to hold that justification is extrinsically valuable in virtue of its connection to truth without succumbing to the swamping problem. For, as the examples from the arena of action show, there is no implication from intentional means to the objective likelihood of achieving the goal in question, and it is the assumption that ties the language of means and ends to a conception of justification characterizable in terms of objective likelihood of truth that threatens justificationism with the same swamping problem faced by externalist accounts of a third condition for knowledge. The root of the swamping problem is that justification must be conceived to be instrumentally valuable with respect to truth (only such a conception undergirds the idea that justification implies objective likelihood of truth), and our discussion in the arena of action shows that justification can be extrinsically related to a goal without being instrumentally related to that goal.

The question remains, however, how one is to extend this discussion of means and ends in the arena of action to the doxastic realm. In particular, we must be careful not to assume that beliefs are voluntary in the way actions are.[21] We do not choose what to believe as we choose which shirt to don when dressing. This issue is crucial because the language of means and ends in the arena of action is easily construable in terms of the degree of voluntary control the agent possesses. In the case of winning a million dollars at a Rockets game, that goal cannot be achieved directly; it is not within the scope of things that I immediately and directly control. Because of this lack of control, I must adopt some means for achieving my goal, a goal over which I have at most indirect control. The first means I adopt is that of making a basket from midcourt. So that becomes my secondary goal. But note that it, too, is something over which I have at most indirect control, so I must adopt some further means in order

---

21. The most prominent critic of belief voluntarism is William P. Alston. See his *Epistemic Justification: Essays in the Theory of Knowledge* (Ithaca, NY: Cornell University Press, 1989), especially "The Deontological Conception of Epistemic Justification."

to achieve it. Notice that this process of developing means toward goals stops when I get to actions that I can control with relative ease. It is, for example, fairly easy to turn and face the basket, much more within my direct and immediate control than making a basket is. If you're a fan of basic actions in action theory, you might want to insist that I go further, perhaps all the way to tryings: In order to reach the goal of turning and facing the basket, I must *try* to do so. The impetus for positing basic actions is that they are actions that are within our immediate and direct control, whereas achieving goals such as making a basket is not. So it might appear that the concept of intentional means to a goal is thoroughly infected with issues of voluntariness, making it inapplicable to the realm of belief, where voluntariness should not be assumed.[22]

Intentional Means and Reflective Transparency

That conclusion is a bit hasty, however, even though it raises an issue of serious concern. In order to assuage this concern, we need some notion of directness and immediacy applicable to the cognitive realm and yet without any imputation of the kind of control central to the concept of voluntary action. A standard way to proceed here is Cartesian. We want to identify which beliefs to hold, and our goal is to hold a belief if and only if it is true. Of course, we don't hold beliefs thinking that they are not true, so an uncharitable reading of the Cartesian project would have each of us hold all and only those beliefs we actually hold. The Cartesian idea, however, puts more stress on reflectively identifying beliefs to hold given the goal in question. Truth is not a property that is always reflectively accessible, however, and so we must adopt some means for identifying beliefs to hold in order to achieve the indirect goal of believing a claim if and only if it is true. So we should try to have, or value, beliefs with some

22. Note that nothing I say implies anything about whether the issue of the voluntariness of belief threatens certain conceptions of justification, especially deontological conceptions of it. William Alston has argued that the nonvoluntary character of belief threatens deontological conceptions of justification (see his articles on the subject in *Epistemic Justification*), and others have argued that this objection is not telling (see, e.g., Richard Feldman, "Epistemic Obligations," in *Philosophical Perspectives 2, Epistemology*, James Tomberlin, ed. [Atascadero, CA: Ridgeview, 1988], pp. 235–56). This discussion is orthogonal to my discussion in the text, where the problem of voluntarism arises because of features of my appeal to the language of means and ends. What is important to my discussion is that I do not assume that beliefs are voluntary in the same way actions are, and it is compatible with that concern that I side with either Alston or Feldman on the issue of the implications of this point for deontologism.

other property, one that we can tell directly and immediately whether a belief has. This latter point is crucial: If the presence of the property we look for is no more reflectively transparent than is the presence of the property of truth, then we will not have adopted, in the appropriate sense, any means toward the goal of having all and only true beliefs. In order to count as an analogue of an intentional means to a goal in the arena of action, the property must be one whose presence is more transparent to reflection than is the property of truth. Justification, then, must be understood so that its presence is easily recognizable. And if one is a fan of basic actions, the appropriate analogue in the doxastic realm will be a property that is reflectively transparent. Just as whether one is trying to do X is completely up to the agent, so the detection of the presence of the property of justification will be completely within the control of the believer. All that needs to be done is to reflect on the matter, and it will be transparent whether or not the belief is justified.

This description of the constraints on a theory of justification generates the appropriate analogue in the arena of belief of a concept most at home in the arena of action, and it does so without requiring beliefs to be voluntary. Yet, it is a very strong requirement. There is nothing in Descartes's writings, for example, that implies that the presence or absence of metaphysical certainty is reflectively transparent. It is true that, for him, whether a belief is metaphysically certain is knowable a priori, but reflective transparency is a much stronger concept than that of a priori knowability. The proof of Gödel's second incompleteness theorem is a priori knowable, but it is hardly reflectively transparent. Even after seeing it and grasping its structure, one can legitimately wonder whether it succeeds.[23] A requirement of reflective transparency imposes an internalist constraint on justification, but it is hardly a constraint with which internalists are comfortable. If the constraint were simply that it can be

---

23. On this score, I recall a conversation with Carl Hempel in which he described a course he and Hans Reichenbach were taking from Hilbert. Halfway through the course Hilbert received the incompleteness results and so dropped the format of the course, which was on his formalist program, to focus on the new information. After the course was over, Hempel reported sitting with Reichenbach and asking him if he thought the proof worked. Reichenbach said, "I don't know." Note that it won't do here to say that they didn't know because they didn't understand. It may be true that if they understood the proof completely, they would see that it worked, but they certainly understood it fairly well (they are, after all, very competent and intelligent philosophers who had studied the proof carefully), and that understanding was insufficient to determine whether it worked. That it is a (successful) proof is knowable a priori if anything is, but its being a successful proof is not reflectively transparent.

known a priori whether a belief is justified, many internalists would endorse such an idea. But none of whom I am aware endorse the stronger view – not Descartes,[24] not Roderick Chisholm,[25] not Carl Ginet,[26] not Keith Lehrer,[27] not John Pollock,[28] not Richard Feldman,[29] not Richard Foley,[30] not Richard Fumerton.[31] For the view is simply much more subjective than the one any of them endorse, even more subjective than the theories that subjectivists such as Lehrer and Foley endorse.

Moreover, there are serious objections to be raised against the very idea of transparency. Some question the epistemic privilege granted by such a position to points of view acquired through reflection, withholding such an honor from viewpoints acquired through other cognitive faculties such as perception, memory, intuition, and the like.[32] Such an objection becomes easier to answer when we follow the path laid out in the *Meno*, accepting its endorsement of twin desiderata on a theory of knowledge. When we attend to the need to account not only for the nature of knowledge but also for its value, we find ourselves following a path of inquiry that leads straightforwardly to such a favoring of the products of reflection. If such a favored status is rejected, it is far from clear how any decent answer can be given to the swamping problem faced by externalists. If the alternative to such a favoring of the faculty of reflection is to deny that justified true beliefs are any more valuable from a purely theoretical point of view than are mere true beliefs, it becomes a bit more understandable why a theory of justification needs to treat the products of reflection in a way different from those of other faculties.

24. See *Meditations on First Philosophy*, Laurence J. Lafleur, trans. (New York: Bobbs-Merrill, 1951).
25. See especially *The Theory of Knowledge*, 2nd edition (Englewood Cliffs, NJ: Prentice-Hall, 1977).
26. Carl Ginet, *Knowledge, Perception, and Memory* (Dordrecht: Reidel, 1975).
27. Keith Lehrer, *Knowledge* (Oxford: Clarenden Press, 1974).
28. John L. Pollock, *Contemporary Theories of Knowledge* (Totowa, NJ: Rowman & Littlefield, 1986).
29. See, e.g., Richard Feldman and Earl Conee, "Evidentialism," *Philosophical Studies*, 48 (1985): 15–34; and "Internalism Defended," *American Philosophical Quarterly*, 38 (2001): 1–18.
30. Richard Foley, *The Theory of Epistemic Rationality* (Cambridge, MA: Harvard University Press, 1987).
31. Richard Fumerton, *Metaphysical and Epistemological Problems of Perception* (Lincoln: University of Nebraska Press, 1985); and *Metaepistemology and Skepticism* (Totowa, NJ: Rowman & Littlefield, 1995).
32. This complaint is voiced forcefully by Thomas Reid, and it is echoed regularly by externalists in arguing that one can be justified in holding a belief without knowing or being able to tell that one is so justified.

Still, the viewpoint under consideration goes far beyond merely favoring the products of reflection over those of other faculties. It requires reflection to be capable of grasping a property whose presence is transparent to reflection. Coherentists have long objected to foundationalist theories built on the idea that some properties (e.g., empirical ones) are transparent. These arguments typically proceed in terms of constructing counterexamples to foundationalist claims about transparency,[33] but Timothy Williamson recently has proposed a more general attack on the idea of transparency itself, an attack independent of any particular property that might be proposed as being transparent. Williamson terms this argument the "antiluminosity argument," and it deserves discussion here in virtue of the way in which it threatens the very idea of any property being transparent to reflection.

Williamson develops this argument with respect to the property of feeling cold. In explaining the argument, I will follow his lead and make remarks later about generalizing the argument to other properties. Using this particular property, the central premise of Williamson's antiluminosity argument is the luminosity assumption:

Luminosity: If S knows in α_i that S feels cold, then in α_{i+1} S feels cold,

where the α's form a sequence of situations that go from a situation in which S definitely feels cold to a situation in which S definitely does not feel cold. Moreover, the α's are individuated finely enough so that S cannot discriminate between adjacent α's, that is,

Indiscriminability: If S feels cold in α_i, then S feels cold in α_{i+1}.

One way to secure the indiscriminability claim is to identify the α-sequence with objective measures of temperature that are fine-grained enough that adjacent members of the sequence are indiscriminable.

In defense of the central premise, Williamson uses two claims about the nature of knowledge. First, he holds that if S knows that p, then S can reliably discriminate between situations in which p is true and situations in which p is not true. Second, he holds that if S knows that p, then S is not easily mistaken about whether p is true. At times, it appears that he thinks of these two claims as making essentially the same point, but he does not explicitly endorse that view. Because it is not obvious that these two claims are identical, I will interpret Williamson as endorsing two

---

33. For a recent quite interesting argument along these lines, see Lehrer's pain/itch example in *The Theory of Knowledge*, 2nd edition (Boulder, CO: Westview Press, 2000), p. 57.

separate theses about knowledge, each of which provides an argument for the antiluminosity claim. In particular, because adjacent members of the α-sequence are indiscriminable, it would be impossible for a person to know that one feels cold in one situation and not in the adjacent situation. For by hypothesis, one cannot discriminate between adjacent situations, and reliable discrimination is required for knowledge (or, alternatively, if the antiluminosity claim were false, one could too easily have been wrong, and knowledge is incompatible with having been easily mistaken).

The formal structure of this antiluminosity argument is precisely analogous to that of sorites arguments, and a primary objection against it is that it is faulty in just the way that sorites arguments are faulty. Williamson holds, however, that there is a crucial difference between this antiluminosity argument and standard sorites arguments. According to Williamson, when the predicates involved in a standard sorites argument are made precise, the sorites argument has a false premise, but that is not true of this antiluminosity argument.

This response to standard sorites arguments is easiest to appreciate when one adopts an epistemic view of vagueness, according to which it is our lack of knowledge that gives rise to vagueness rather than some imprecision in reality.[34] So, for example, a precise number of hairs must fall to be bald (if we assume that baldness is measured in terms of numbers rather than patterns of hair). So even if we do not know which premise of a sorites argument (to the conclusion that someone totally lacking hair is still not bald) is false, the epistemic view of vagueness guarantees that one of them is and hence that the sorites argument is unsound.

Williamson holds that the antiluminosity argument avoids this result and hence that the only way to escape the argument is to reject the luminosity premise. To see whether he is correct, let us consider several possibilities with respect to a scale of α-situations, from α_0 (where one definitely feels cold) through α_n (where one definitely does not feel cold), ordered sequentially so that S cannot discriminate between adjacent α-situations on this scale. Because both feeling cold and knowing are vague predicates, we will have to precisify both. Let us stipulate that the precise point at which one no longer feels cold is α_j.

Given this assumption, there are three assumptions we might make about where the precise cutoff for knowledge of feeling cold is: equal

---

34. Williamson defends such a view in *Vagueness* (London: Routledge, 1994).

to, greater than, or less than α_j. If the cutoff for knowledge is greater than or equal to α_j, then the central premise has a counterexample. For in both such cases, the claim that S's knowing in α_{j-1} that S feels cold, then in α_j S feels cold is false, for it has a true antecedent and a false consequent. What is required, therefore, is that the cutoff for knowledge is less than α_j, that is, α_{j-1} or less. If so, there will be no counterexample to the crucial antiluminosity premise because such a counterexample would require knowledge of feeling cold at some level without feeling cold at the adjacent level. So the antiluminosity argument contains no false premise when the predicates are precisified in this way and hence is different from standard sorites arguments.

Why should we think that the cutoff point for precisifying the knowledge predicate must occur before, or earlier than, the cutoff point for the predicate of feeling cold? We can quickly rule out the possibility that the cutoff point for knowledge is strictly after that for feeling cold, because this possibility requires denying that knowledge implies truth (you could know that one feels cold in α_j when, as we have stipulated, one does not feel cold in that situation). But that still leaves the possibility that knowledge can be precisified at exactly the same point on the scale as feeling cold is, and such precisifying leaves one of the premises of Williamson's argument false. So Williamson must have a reason for thinking that the two predicates cannot be precisified at exactly the same point. His argument here appeals to just those features of knowledge cited earlier: that to know, you must be able to make certain reliable discriminations and you cannot easily have been mistaken in your belief. The idea is that knowledge must be precisified at some distance from, and before, the precisification of feeling cold, because closeness of precisification would allow knowledge to be present when one could easily have been mistaken about whether one felt cold and when one could not reliably discriminate situations in which one feels cold from situations in which one does not feel cold. In fact, we can say more: The cutoff for knowledge must be sufficiently far away from the cutoff for feeling cold so that the difference between the feelings in the two cases is detectable to the cognizer; otherwise, we would have to allow the possibility of knowledge when one could easily have been mistaken and when one could not discriminate reliably between situations in which one feels cold and situations in which one does not feel cold.

This argument can be applied to the question of the transparency of justification. All that is needed are versions of luminosity and indiscriminability for the property of justification:

Luminosity: If S knows in α_i that S is justified in believing p, then in α_{i+1} S is justified in believing p;

Indiscriminability: If S is justified in believing p in α_i, then S is justified in believing p in α_{i+1},

where the α's form a sequence that goes from a situation in which S is definitely justified in believing p to a situation in which S is definitely not justified in believing p. Moreover, this sequence of α-situations involves members that are individuated finely enough so that S cannot discriminate between adjacent α's, as expressed in the indiscriminability claim.

As before, the argument against the transparency of justification looks like a sorites argument. In particular, the indiscriminability thesis requires that justification is vague. The α-situations, we may assume, are constructed according to quantity of evidence, where adjacent situations in the sequence differ in such minuscule amounts that one could not be justified in one such situation without being justified in the other, much as one cannot be bald with 5,000 hairs on one's head without also being bald with 5,001 hairs on one's head. The central difference between a sorites argument and the antiluminosity argument, according to Williamson, is equally true here, for when the predicates are precisified, there will be a false premise in a standard sorites argument but not in the argument against transparency. The reason for this difference, as before, concerns the features of knowledge that require reliable discrimination and not easily being wrong.

If Williamson's argument is sound, it presents an obstacle for the subjective view of justification presented earlier to address the problem of the value of justification. For on that view, what makes justification valuable is that its obtaining is reflectively accessible; in particular, it is more reflectively accessible than is truth. The nature of truth does not require any kind of accessibility to nonomniscient beings, whereas (the right kind of) justification does. So we might think of the proposal of this chapter in terms of a sequence of properties, beginning with truth, and each succeeding property as one that is slightly more accessible to reflection than the one before it. The end of this sequence is a property whose presence is transparent.

Williamson's argument, if sound, shows that there is no such endpoint to this sequence of properties. What effect would this conclusion have on the present proposal? The first point to note is that nothing in the present proposal requires that justification is a property whose presence is transparent in order for justification to be valuable. All that is required is that justification is more accessible on reflection than is truth. If we return to the arena of action and suppose that there is no such thing as a basic action, one that can be performed without the need to perform some other action, it does not follow that there are no actions that can only be accomplished by performing other actions that are more within our control. So if there is no stopping point in the arena of action and no stopping point to the sequence of properties more accessible to reflection than is truth, the lack of such stopping points will not cast doubt on the direction of our discussion aimed at explaining the value of justification.

It is nonetheless worth noting that Williamson's argument is not wholly compelling. Consider again the paradox of the heap. We construct the series of α-situations so that, pairwise, no difference with respect to the property of being a heap is detectable. (This assumption mirrors the assumption that one can't discriminate between adjacent members of the alpha series in the antiluminosity argument.)

Williamson's claim is that what distinguishes the antiluminosity argument from standard sorites arguments is that, when precisified, standard sorites arguments have a false premise, whereas the antiluminosity argument does not. So the idea is that if we draw a precise line between heapness and non-heapness, it will be false for some α_i and α_{i+1} that if an object is a heap at α_i, it is also a heap at α_{i+1}; precisification of the predicate "is a heap" guarantees that there will be some such falsehood.

There is a problem here, though. Recall that the series of α-situations was constructed to be fine-grained enough that, pairwise, no difference is detectable with respect to the property of being a heap. But detectable to whom? Suppose that O is omniscient — would the difference be detectable to O? That depends, I think, on whether and to what extent vagueness is "in the world." If we accept the epistemic view of vagueness, that there is a precise cutoff between heaps and non-heaps, but that this cutoff is not knowable by us, there is no reason to suppose that an omniscient being could not know where the cutoff is. If, however, vagueness is metaphysical rather than epistemic, then perhaps there is no pairwise distinction between heaps and non-heaps. If vagueness is metaphysical so that there is no such pairwise distinction, then any precisification of the predicate 'is a heap' will yield a falsehood in the paradox of the heap only by *violating a necessary condition for something being a heap.*

With this feature of precisification in mind, let us return to the antiluminosity argument. A defender of transparency or luminosity will want to precisify the predicate 'feels cold' and the predicate 'knows that S feels cold' at precisely the same point on the alpha scale. Williamson claims that such precisification should be rejected because it *would violate a necessary condition on knowledge*, to wit, that if you know, then you cannot easily be mistaken. And it would violate this condition precisely because the series of α-situations is constructed so that you cannot discriminate between adjacent members of the scale.

Yet, if vagueness is in the world in the strong sense that there is no pairwise distinction of feeling in the series as constructed, then it should not surprise us that necessary conditions are violated by precisification. After all, such a violation occurs in the paradox of the heap when the predicates are made precise if vagueness is strongly in the world.

Note again that if we adopt an epistemic view of vagueness, this appeal to precisification carries much more weight. On the epistemic view of vagueness, there really is a precise point at which a person becomes bald; it is just that we are in no position to know what that point is. It may not be surprising, then, that Williamson is a primary proponent of the epistemic view of vagueness.[35]

The question of the degree to which vagueness is in the world is a difficult and perplexing one, and the connection between this question and the ordinary meaning of vague terms such as 'heap', 'bald', 'feels cold', and the like is troublesome as well. To the extent that one is attracted to a theory of meaning on which it is strongly connected with appropriate use, it is hard to avoid the conclusion that the meaning of the predicate 'is a heap' requires no pairwise distinction among members of the series as constructed previously, and the same would hold for other vague predicates as well. In that case, the necessary conditions violated by precisification would be semantic in nature. Whether the violations in question are metaphysical or semantic in nature, such violations would cast doubt on the relevance of the appeal to precisification by Williamson to distinguish his antiluminosity argument from standard sorites paradoxes. For if such precisification violates metaphysically necessary conditions on being a heap or if it violates semantically necessary conditions on the predicate 'is a heap', there will be no good reason to quibble with the defender of transparency who wishes to precisify the predicate 'feels cold' at precisely the same point as the predicate 'knows that one feels cold'.

---

35. See Williamson, *Vagueness*, especially chapter 7.

I must confess here to sympathies with Williamson's views on vagueness, though I think the proper appraisal of the matter is that one needs to be forced into the epistemic view by failures of explanation as to how vagueness could be a more metaphysical matter. We end up with the epistemic view, that is, because we can't come up with an adequate nonepistemic account. To the extent that the antiluminosity argument depends on prior conclusions regarding vagueness, the argument is less than compelling, especially in the face of this kind of defense of the position on vagueness that coheres best with the response needed to distance the antiluminosity argument from sorites arguments.

I conclude, therefore, that Williamson's argument against the possibility of a transparent concept of justification is not decisive and that ascertaining its force would require a sustained detour through the issue of vagueness. It is not necessary, however, to take such a detour here, for we have already seen that the present account of the value of justification does not strictly require the transparency of justification. The fundamental aspect of this account is that justification is valuable independently of the value of true belief in virtue of being more accessible to reflection than is the property of truth. The boundary of this continuum is transparency, but the continuum does not cease to exist if the boundary is not an endpoint, just as the sequence of real numbers between 0 and 1 does not cease to exist because it has no endpoint.

Without an endpoint, one might wonder where on the posited continuum to find the property of justification, that property necessary for knowledge and valuable in virtue of its accessibility to reflection. That question is a thorny theoretical one that I will not pursue here, for it raises no threat to the position articulated. Either there is one such point on the continuum that is the correct one or there are several, any one of which could do adequate service in the theory of knowledge.

The position developed here is one way of extending the lessons learned in the arena of action to the arena of belief, and that fact leads to the question of whether there is another way to extend the lessons learned in the arena of action regarding intentional means to the cognitive realm. There may be such a way, but I am unaware of it. We have seen that any theory of knowledge that honors the importance of accounting for the value of knowledge over true belief will have to be a justificationist theory (given our assumption that no reliabilist account of the normativity of knowledge is adequate), and if the theory of justification involved is not strongly subjective, some other way of relating talk of means and ends to cognitive activity will have to be found than the one previously given.

Once we recognize the constraints imposed by the need to account for the value of knowledge over true belief, I see no path toward an account of the value of knowledge that is not strongly subjective and internalist in character. Other theories fail to identify a property more accessible to reflection than truth and thereby lack resources for solving the swamping problem.

This conclusion is provisional, for we have shelved for purposes of this chapter the question of normativity and reliabilism, reserving that discussion for the next chapter. That is, we have supposed for the purposes of argument here that the swamping problem cannot be solved by reliabilism. If that conclusion is correct, we end with a somewhat surprising conclusion: that only a subjective, internalist theory of justification has the capacity to account for the value of justification and avoid the swamping problem. This sort of justification, even in the presence of true belief, adds value to the composite in question. Hence, given this understanding of justification, we can endorse the claim that justified true belief is more valuable than true belief. That would still not solve the *Meno* problem, for knowledge is more than justified true belief. Giving a complete account of the value of knowledge will therefore require some discussion of the Gettier problem. But first, we turn in the next chapter to the relationship between reliabilism and the normativity of knowledge and justification to see if in fact reliabilism must succumb to the swamping problem.

4

Reliabilism, Normativity, and the Special Promise of Virtue Epistemology

The motivation for the present chapter arises from the swamping problem regarding the property of objective likelihood of truth. This property is one that it is better for a belief to have than to lack, but it is also a property that adds no value to true belief itself. That is, a belief that is both true and objectively likely to be true is no more valuable than a belief that is merely true. The value of objective likelihood of truth is wholly parasitic on the value of truth itself, so once truth is in the picture, objective likelihood of truth can add no further value. In the same way, Swinburne and others claim, reliabilism cites a property of belief that it is better to have than to lack, but that is also one that adds no value to true belief itself.

Reliabilists can attempt to evade this argument by citing the normativity of knowledge. Perhaps reliability is precisely that natural property on which the normativity of knowledge supervenes. If so, reliabilists can lay claim to a theory immune to the swamping problem because the value derived from reliability is just that value involved in the normativity of knowledge. The easiest way to see the idea here is to take reliabilism to be offering a theory of justification, though this assumption is not crucial. If we assume it, however, reliabilists can claim to have a better time with the swamping problem because their theory does not merely identify knowledge with true beliefs that are likely to be true. Instead, knowledge requires justification, and the central difference this notion introduces is that of normativity. When the right kind of objective likelihood of truth is found, a normative dimension appears that was not there before. And once this normative dimension is in place, the swamping problem can be handled, it can be claimed, for though the value of objective likelihood of truth is swamped by the value of truth itself, the normative dimension that accompanies the right kind of objective likelihood of truth introduces a new valuational element that is distinct from the value of objective likelihood of truth and so escapes the swamping problem.

As noted in the previous chapter, this attempt appears at first glance to be nothing but sheer sophistry. It is true that justification is a normative notion, and I will grant here that normativity supervenes on the nonnormative.[1] That is, it is not possible for two complete possible worlds to be identical in all their nonnormative features and yet diverge along normative dimensions. Furthermore, the relationship of supervenience need not be semantic so that the connection between the two is analytic, nor need it be knowable a priori whether a claimed supervenience relationship between two things is in fact correct. For example, in the moral sphere, it is somewhat plausible to think that the nonnormative features of the world involving pleasure and pain form part of the supervenience base for what is morally good and bad. Yet, G. E. Moore's open question argument shows that it is not known a priori that pleasure is good or that pain is bad.[2] Moore concluded from this fact that it isn't a necessary truth that pain is bad, but that inference is faulty, for there can be necessary truths that are neither knowable a priori nor analytically true.

So when a reliabilist suggests that reliability is the supervenience base for the normative property of justification, we cannot object to that claim by arguing that reliability and justification are not linked either analytically or a priori. Still, the appearance of sophistry remains strong. For if reliabilists can make this claim, so can those who identify justification with objective likelihood of truth.

Why should we reject such a claim by objective likelihood theorists? I suggest we should reject it on precisely the same grounds that we used to question such a move by standard reliabilism. Earlier I pointed out how magical and sophistical such an appeal to supervenience seems to be. It appears this way because the explanations offered seem so empty once one notices the connection between normative concepts and questions concerning value. Sometimes people use the terminologies of normativity and evaluation interchangeably, but even if they are not interchangeable, a positive normative concept is still one it is good or valuable to exemplify.

1. Keith Lehrer has recently attacked the claim that the normative supervenes on the nonnormative. See his *Self Trust: A Study of Reason, Knowledge and Autonomy* (Oxford: Oxford University Press, 1997).
2. G. E. Moore, *Principia Ethica* (Cambridge: Cambridge University Press, 1903).

Furthermore, this connection between normativity and value appears to be conceptual in nature. At least, such a connection is a plausible starting point in thinking about normativity and should be rejected only in the face of strong arguments for doing so. Yet, if we accept the connection, then the appeal to normativity as an answer to a value question is hardly informative. We ask, for example, why is justification valuable? The answer we get is that it is valuable because it is a positive normative concept. Such an explanation gives us no useful information whatsoever because positive normativity and being of value are conceptually linked. The explanation is akin to explaining why a certain liquid makes one sleepy by appealing to its soporific powers.

It is at this point that virtue epistemology is especially attractive. What a supervenience theorist needs to do to make the appeal to supervenience more than an empty explanation is to explain how a kind of value arises from the supervenience base that is different from the value that inheres in the base solely in virtue of its relationship to the truth. I will argue that virtue epistemology, as defended most prominently by Ernest Sosa and John Greco,[3] has such resources. Linda Zagzebski has defended a version of virtue epistemology, but her version does not hold the promise that is offered by the Sosa and Greco theories. So before turning to the more promising versions, I need to say a few things about Zagzebski's approach and why it will not be helpful in the present context.

Before turning to her view, however, a brief overview of virtue epistemology may be helpful. The core idea of the view is that progress can be made on important epistemological issues by theories that have recourse to the concept of an intellectual virtue. For example, some virtue epistemologists may wish to define the concept of justification in terms of beliefs produced or sustained by an intellectual virtue instead of attempting to understand that concept in terms of the concept of adequate evidence for belief. This development in epistemology mirrors a similar interest in ethics, where there is a renewed interest in exploring the subject matter of ethics from a standpoint that makes fundamental appeal to the concept of a moral virtue. In both ethics and epistemology, the hope is that this new approach will help resolve the fundamental problems of each discipline.

---

3. Ernest Sosa, *Knowledge in Perspective: Selected Essays in Epistemology* (Cambridge: Cambridge University Press, 1991); Linda Zagzebski, *Virtues of the Mind: An Inquiry into the Nature of Virtue and the Ethical Foundations of Knowledge* (Oxford: Oxford University Press, 1996); John Greco, *Putting Skeptics in Their Place* (Cambridge: Cambridge University Press, 2000).

78

It is this new approach and its promise of accounting for the value of knowledge that I wish to explore here. I begin by arguing that Zagzebski's prominent version of virtue epistemology will not help here, though the ideas contained in her view will be relevant later.

ZAGZEBSKI'S VIRTUE THEORY

Unlike other epistemologists, Zagzebski devotes a separate section to the issues surrounding the value of knowledge and the value of the intellectual virtues, showing a clear understanding of the significance of this question for epistemology. When she undertakes to explain the value of the virtues, she engages the issues in two parts, depending on which theory of the virtues one is considering. The first theory of the virtues is a teleological one connected with the notion of human flourishing. The value of the virtues on this theory will then be teleological as well, tied in some way to human flourishing. Because this theory of the virtues is not the one favored by Zagzebski, she does not carry out such an explanation but says that she sees no reason to doubt that it is possible.[4]

In our context, though, we cannot be satisfied with such a promissory note. The intellectual virtues are not necessary for the practical dimension of human flourishing for the same reason that knowledge is not necessary for it. So there must be a purely intellectual or theoretical dimension of human flourishing to which the virtues contribute. I have no doubt that the virtues contribute in some way to human flourishing, but this fact does little to help us understand the value of knowledge. Knowledge also contributes to human flourishing in a purely intellectual way, we may suppose, but that fact alone does not show that knowledge is more valuable than true belief or any other subset of its components. In order to address these deeper questions about the value of knowledge and the value of the virtues, we need substance over chits.

Zagzebski favors the other theory of the virtues, a motivation-based theory, so this complaint about her treatment of teleological theories is not pressing. On a motivation-based theory, according to Zagzebski, the virtues have two aspects, one motivational and the other reliabilist. When she shows that the virtues are valuable, she argues as follows:

We are now in a position to explain the goodness of intellectual virtue in a motivation-based fashion. . . . I have argued that (1) the motive for knowledge is an intrinsic good that is not dependent for its goodness upon its relations to

4. Zagzebski, *Virtues of the Mind*, pp. 201–2.

other goods, not even to the good of the possession of knowledge, and (2) the motivations component of each of the intellectual virtues is derived from this motive. . . . Since it is a reasonable maxim that (3) reliable success in achieving the aim of a good motive is itself a good thing, it follows that (4) the goodness of the reliability component of an intellectual virtue derives from the goodness of the motivational component. Therefore, (5) the goodness of both components of intellectual virtues is agent-based.[5]

So, Zagzebski begins with an argument that the motivation for knowledge is itself valuable and that the virtues are valuable in part because of their connection to this motivation. She then claims that the reliability of a character trait is presumably valuable as well because of its relationship to a good motive and hence that the virtues, constituted by a motivational aspect and a reliability aspect, are valuable.

There are two fundamental reasons why this explanation will be of no help in the present context. The first and less significant one is that there really is no reliability component of the intellectual virtues on her theory, contrary to what her official pronouncements about the theory claim. She considers objections by James Montmarquet to the idea that the virtues are truth-conducive[6] and ends up claiming that the virtues are truth-conducive in an extended sense – namely, that they are truth-conducive in virtue of being necessary for the formation of some true beliefs.[7] For example, open-mindedness may not generate mostly true beliefs (in fact, it may not generate beliefs at all), but open-mindedness may be needed to open up the possibility of discovering certain truths. Such a relationship to true belief is not truth-conduciveness, however. If it were, then belief itself would be truth-conducive, for one cannot have a true belief without having a belief. Moreover, believers are truth-conducive in this extended sense, because there has to be a believer in order for there to be a true belief, and being a believer would be a truth-conducive property even if one were such an inept believer that one never found the truth. So when Zagzebski speaks of the reliability aspect of the virtues, it is a misnomer.

The second and more important reason for finding Zagzebski's approach of little use in the present context is that the order of explanation we need goes contrary to the order of explanation she employs. We are trying to see if we can explain the value of knowledge in terms of the

---

5. Ibid., p. 209.
6. James Montmarquet, *Epistemic Virtue and Doxastic Responsibility* (Totowa, NJ: Rowman & Littlefield, 1993).
7. Zagzebski, *Virtues of the Mind*, p. 182.

value of its constituents, not the other way around, as her account goes. We will examine approaches to the question of the value of knowledge that do not attempt to explain the value of knowledge in terms of the value of its constituents, approaches that focus on features of human motivation such as the ubiquity of human curiosity and the desire to know. I will address such viewpoints in a later chapter and thus am not arguing that Zagzebski's position is of no interest. Instead, I am only arguing that her position is not relevant at the present point of this inquiry, aimed as it is at the attempt to provide an account of the value of knowledge in terms of the value of its constituents.

VIRTUE EPISTEMOLOGY AND CREDIT FOR TRUE BELIEF

Here, however, we are looking for a way of explaining the value of knowledge at least in part in terms of the value of the intellectual virtues, and we do so with the hope that there is something about an appeal to the virtues that avoids the swamping problem that undermines the explanation offered by standard reliabilism. Recently, several epistemologists have proposed such an idea, to the effect that credit accrues to the agent who has intellectually virtuous beliefs. This idea is new and quite promising in our context, for it offers hope for explicating a kind of value for belief that may not be swamped by the value of truth. Because of the newness of the idea, I will devote extended discussion to three theorists who have proposed it, exploring not only the common idea they share about how an appeal to the virtues helps explain the value of knowledge but also the distinguishing details of each view and the development within the thinking of these theorists from earlier to later work as well. In so doing, we will not exhaust the possibilities a virtue theorist might explore in attempting to find value in intellectually virtuous belief, but we can learn much about the landscape of possibilities from these three proposals. We will also find difficulties in common to the three, and my strategy here is to organize the three so that a line of development toward an adequate view that avoids the swamping problem will emerge. The theories are those of John Greco, Wayne D. Riggs, and Ernest Sosa.

All three share a common theme about the value of the virtues, for they think of this value in terms of some kind of credit due to the agent whose belief is virtue-based. For example, Sosa says:

Take a subject who believes in a large grey object nearby when he hears the cannonade in Tschaikovsky's *1812 Overture*, where by coincidence there happens

81

to be an elephant nearby from whose neck there happens to hang a radio, which happens to be tuned to a classical station, one which happens to be playing the relevant passage of that *Overture*. Relative to that highly specific set of circumstances that is of course an excellent doxastic mechanism to have. *Has it thereby earned much credit*, however, as a faculty to have, develop, exercise, retain, and admire? Of course not.[8]

I have italicized the crucial idea here, for what distinguishes excellent doxastic mechanisms from intellectual virtues, Sosa implies, is that the latter but not the former have earned credit as faculties "to have, develop, exercise, retain, and admire." In this way, the intellectual virtues share a common feature with other virtues:

The guess that by luck is true is comparable in value to the act of recklessly shooting a gun in the air, accidentally hitting and maiming a tyrant, and thereby preventing him from signing an unjust proclamation. I have brought about a good, but I hardly get any credit for it.[9]

Just as actions that result from virtues yield credit for the actor, beliefs resulting from faculties that count as virtues generate credit for the believer (or the faculty). Furthermore, these faculties that are the source of credit are involved in the notion of justification itself:

What interests us in justification is essentially the trustworthiness and reliability of the subject with regard to the field of his judgment, in situations normal for judgments in that field. That explains also why what does matter for justification is how the subject performs with regard to factors internal to him, and why it does not matter for justification if external factors are abnormal and unfavorable so that despite his impeccable performance S does not know. What we care about in justification are the epistemic endowments and conduct of the subject, his intellectual virtues.[10]

So the intellectual virtues are central to the concept of justification and generate a kind of value that Sosa refers to as "credit."

There are several different accounts compatible with these remarks, however. First, Sosa is a bit ambivalent about the locus of the credit. In the first quote, the credit seems to go to the faculty itself, whereas in the second quote the credit goes to the person. Second, it is not clear whether

---

8. Sosa, "Intellectual Virtues in Perspective," in *Knowledge in Perspective*, pp. 276–7 (italics mine).
9. Zagzebski, *Virtues of the Mind*, p. 206.
10. Sosa, "Knowledge and Intellectual Virtue," in *Knowledge in Perspective*, p. 240.

Sosa has in mind one or two different (though perhaps compatible) explanations of the value of justification. The third quote suggests that justification is important and worth caring about for essentially prudential reasons: It is important because of the need for trust in people as sources of information.[11] Sosa may wish to identify the two approaches – the approach in terms of credit due and the approach in terms of the prudential importance of justification – in some way, or he may think of them as two aspects of one theory.

John Greco's thinking about the value of knowledge has undergone development along these very lines, so we can use his ideas to bring out the strengths and weaknesses of these alternative ways of clarifying Sosa's approach. Greco's earliest thinking about the subject led him to claim the following:

Put simply, knowledge is valuable because intellectually virtuous believing is valuable, and knowledge is intellectually virtuous believing.

But why is intellectually virtuous believing valuable? The answer is as follows, and here I draw from Ernest Sosa. It is of prudential importance to the subject herself that she be a reliable judge of various truths.

Moreover, it is of prudential importance to her group that she can be relied upon in situations requiring cognitive cooperation. . . . We are a social species, dependent on each other for information sharing. It is therefore of utmost importance to us that we and our peers are reliable partners in the information-sharing business. But then this explains why knowledge is valuable. Knowledge is belief arising from intellectually virtuous character, and it is important to us as an information-sharing species that both ourselves and our peers believe out of intellectually virtuous characters. Persons who believe out of intellectually virtuous character are by definition reliable in the circumstances we normally find ourselves. They are the sort of person you can trust to deliver the truth, in the situations that you need to trust them.[12]

11. Such a position is a close cousin of the view of Edward Craig in *Knowledge and the State of Nature* (Oxford: Oxford University Press, 1990), according to which we should approach the questions of epistemology by asking about the function of the concept of knowledge, identifying that function in terms of the need to identify reliable sources of information. From this function, we can identify the value of knowledge, giving us a theory very much like that of Sosa, though not originating from any concern to develop a version of virtue epistemology.

12. John Greco, "Why Knowledge Is Valuable: Response to Jonathan Kvanvig," comments given at the Wheaton Philosophy Conference, October 14, 1995, p. 3, typescript. Edward Craig holds a similar viewpoint, according to which the concept of knowledge has a primary function of flagging approved sources of information (*Knowledge and the State of Nature*, p. 11).

Greco here maintains that knowledge is valuable because intellectually virtuous believing is valuable, and "knowledge is intellectually virtuous believing." He then claims that the value of intellectually virtuous belief is a special kind of prudential value, a value deriving from the trust that we need to place in ourselves and in others in the process of gathering information.

Neither of these points is adequate, however. First, knowledge is not identical to intellectually virtuous belief, as is shown by Goldman's fake-barn example.[13] In that example, a person is driving through a county where the residents have planted barn façades, leaving only one real barn in the area. In teaching some vocabulary to his son, he points to what looks like a barn and says, "That's a barn." As it happens, he is pointing to the one real barn in the area, so even though his belief is intellectually virtuous because it arises out of his perceptual abilities, it is not knowledge. Moreover, Greco knows that knowledge is not identical to intellectually virtuous believing; he says:

The partial account of knowledge I want to propose is this: S knows p only if S believes p, p is true, and S believes p from an intellectual virtue. Alternatively, when S knows p, S's believing p is both true and intellectually virtuous.[14]

Notice here that Greco is careful to call this account a "partial" account, formulated not in terms of necessary and sufficient conditions, but rather only necessary conditions. So even if Greco is right that intellectually virtuous belief is valuable, that will not quite explain the value of knowledge, for knowledge is more than intellectually virtuous belief. Hence, for knowledge to be valuable, it has to be more valuable than intellectually virtuous true belief, for a central challenge regarding the value of knowledge is to explain how knowledge is more valuable than some subset of its constituents.

Greco's other point, that intellectually virtuous belief has prudential value, cannot be sustained either, for the same reasons Socrates gave to Meno about the value of true belief if you want to get to Larissa. Socrates' objection applied to Greco's language is as follows:

It is true that "persons who believe out of intellectually virtuous character are by definition reliable in the circumstances we normally find ourselves" and that "they are the sort of person you can trust to deliver the truth, in the situations

13. Alvin Goldman, "Discrimination and Perceptual Knowledge," *Journal of Philosophy* 73, 20 (1976): 771–91.
14. Greco, "Why Knowledge Is Valuable," p. 2 typescript.

that you need to trust them"; but so are true believers. In fact, true believers are maximally reliable, and hence better sources of information than intellectually virtuous believers. So there is no practical advantage that intellectually virtuous believers have over true believers.

The heart of this response to Greco's early proposal regarding the value of intellectually virtuous belief is that it is easy to confuse two different issues when discussing the value of knowledge. On the one hand, there is the question of which properties of a belief are valuable; on the other hand, there is the question of which properties might add value to a true belief. If one focuses on the first question, it is easy to find attractive some pragmatic theory. An adequate theory with respect to the first question, however, is only part of the problem of the value of knowledge. As Socrates' discussion in the *Meno* highlights, there is also the second question, and pragmatic accounts fail in that context.

My suspicion is that pragmatic accounts such as Greco's early view are found attractive because we don't know who the true believers are and so must sort out who to trust without that information. There are two problems with this perspective here. A general problem is that taking such a perspective focuses our attention on the first question proposed at the expense of the second, thereby yielding answers likely to be adequate for the first question but not the second. In the context of assumed ignorance about who believes truly and who does not, we will look for ways of assessing sources of information independent of the question of truth. Even if we get a good account of how to do so, there will still be another issue left unaddressed, namely, the question of how knowledge is more valuable than its subparts, including the subpart of true belief. In order to provide a suitable answer to that question, the context will have to shift from one in which one is ignorant about which sources of information have accurate information to a context in which sources are assumed to be accurate but not always possessing knowledge. Once one's perspective on sources of information shifts in this way, pragmatic accounts begin to look much less plausible.

There may also be another problem with motivating such a pragmatic theory by appeal to a context in which one does not know which informants have the truth and which do not. Such a context would be most relevant if one began from an assumption about the remoteness and lack of direct accessibility of truth, requiring us to look for properties other than truth in order to determine what the truth is. The problem with this way of motivating a pragmatic theory is that we have as much reason to assume ignorance about the intellectual virtuousity of sources of information as we do about their alethic qualities, for it is no more obvious who the intellectually virtuous believers are than who the true believers are. If worries about the the lack of direct accessibility of truth underlie this development of a virtue theory, the remedy is to go back a chapter and relearn its lessons rather than work on a virtue theory. An assumption about the lack of direct accessibility of truth is an assumption that leads directly to the subjective internalist theory of justification outlined in the previous chapter, not to any virtue theory of that notion. This assumption leads us to look for *marks* of truth, where the property of being a mark of truth is transparently so (or at least more so than truth itself); its being such a mark is not something that one can be confused about (or at least one that is much harder to be confused about than whether the claim in question is true), and its possession by the claim whose truth we attempt to ascertain is also not something that one can be confused about (or at least one that is much harder to be confused about than whether the claim in question is true).

So Greco's early virtue theory is not very successful in developing an account of the value of knowledge. Recently, however, Greco has advanced a new approach to the question of the value of knowledge, one that is more plausible than his earlier theory, and also one that brings his theory much closer to the remarks of Sosa cited earlier.

Greco's new theory begins from the launching pad of his virtue theory of knowledge, which requires virtue-related concepts of subjective and objective justification; that is,

S knows p only if

1. S's believing p is subjectively justified in the following sense: S's believing p is the result of dispositions that S manifests when S is trying to believe the truth,
2. S's believing p is objectively justified in the following sense: The dispositions that result in S's believing p make S reliable in believing p. Alternatively, the dispositions that result in S's believing p constitute intellectual abilities, or powers, or virtues.[15]

On this theory, an intellectually virtuous belief is one that is both subjectively and objectively justified. Greco holds that these conditions are

15.   John Greco, "Knowledge as Credit for True Belief," *Intellectual Virtue: Perspectives from Ethics and Epistemology*, Michael DePaul and Linda Zagzebski, eds. (Oxford: Oxford University Press, forthcoming), pp. 19–20 typescript.

necessary only for knowledge and proposes a third necessary condition to complete the picture:

3. S believes the truth regarding p because S is reliable in believing p. Alternatively: The intellectual abilities or powers or virtues that result in S's believing the truth regarding p are an important necessary part of the total set of causal factors that give rise to S's believing the truth regarding p.[16]

Greco proposes "that adding this third condition makes the three [conditions] sufficient as well as necessary for knowledge,"[17] thereby solving the Gettier problem. He says, "[I]n cases of knowledge S's reliable character has salience in an explanation of how S comes to get things right. In Gettier cases, S's reliable character loses its salience in favor of something else."[18]

So here we have Greco's account of the nature of knowledge, but what of the question of the value of knowledge? What is new in Greco's latest theory is that he no longer tries to explain the value of intellectually virtuous belief in terms of its prudential importance. Instead, he introduces a new notion, the notion of credit due a person for holding a true belief, and gives the following partial clarification of it:

S deserves intellectual credit for believing the truth regarding p only if

a. believing the truth regarding p has intellectual value
b. believing the truth regarding p can be ascribed to S, and
c. believing the truth regarding p reveals S's cognitive character. Alternatively: S's cognitive character is an important necessary part of the total set of causal factors that give rise to S's believing the truth regarding p.[19]

Our discussions in previous chapters have defended clause (a) of this account, so we can grant that clause (a) always obtains when a person believes the truth. Clause (c) is just Greco's new necessary condition for knowledge cited earlier, so the only additional feature required beyond the new third condition for knowledge is clause (b).

Greco spends considerable time defending and clarifying clause (b), and we will turn to this task shortly, but I want first to press the question of what all of this has to do with the value of knowledge. First, we aren't told what it is to deserve credit for true belief. We are given three necessary conditions for it, but the question remains what else might be required.

16. Ibid., p. 21 typescript.
17. Ibid.
18. Ibid.
19. Ibid., pp. 14–15 typescript.

This problem could be avoided if we interpret the 'only if' in the previous account of credit as a slip by an author who really intended 'if and only if'. In the remainder of Greco's discussion, there is no hint that he thinks his list of necessary conditions is not also sufficient, so I think we lose no plausibility to the view if we take the list to be both necessary and sufficient. Moreover, it is important that we be given a complete set of conditions for the concept of deserved credit if he is going to use that concept to explain either the nature or the value of knowledge.

Even if we solve the first problem in this way, there is a more difficult problem here. The title of Greco's article is "Knowledge as Credit for True Belief," suggesting that an account of credit will give us both an adequate account of the nature of knowledge and an explanation of its value. In fact, however, Greco's account of knowledge does not require that a person receive, or deserve, credit for true belief. Knowledge requires objective and subjective justification, as Greco defines them, plus one of the necessary conditions for deserving credit for true belief. I have granted that the condition about the value of true belief always obtains, so that yields the result that two of the three conditions needed for deserved credit obtain, but that still leaves clause (b), the claim that believing the truth can be ascribed to the person in question.

We are left, then, with somewhat of an interpretive dilemma. If the ascription clause, clause (b) in the account of deserved credit, is a substantive requirement, then Greco cannot claim that knowledge is to be identified with credit for true belief. In order to yield the conclusion that knowledge is credit for true belief, Greco will have to change his account of deserved credit or treat the additional clause as redundant.

The problem with changing the account by dropping the ascription clause is that it is too central to Greco's discussion simply to be dropped. In order to appreciate this claim and see whether there is a way to salvage Greco's approach, we need to look more closely at Greco's account of deserved credit and the place of the ascription clause in it. This clause is included in the account because Greco derives the account of intellectual credit from an account of moral credit that is itself founded on Feinberg's account of moral blame.[20] The account of moral blame that Greco attributes to Feinberg requires that the action "can be ascribed

20. The account is elicited from three essays in Feinberg's *Doing and Deserving: Essays in the Theory of Responsibility* (Princeton, NJ: Princeton University Press, 1970): "Problematic Responsibility in Law and Morals," "Action and Responsibility," and "Causing Voluntary Actions."

to" the person in question.[21] Greco does not explain what is included in the idea of ascribing action to a person, but he does give a short example: "[W]e will say that Mary murdered Paul only if we think that Mary's actions figure importantly enough into the explanation of Paul's death – only if we think that Mary's actions were the cause of Paul's death."[22]

This example may help us understand what it is to ascribe an action to a person, but it does not help very much regarding belief. The example assumes that some actions have been performed (call these the "assumed actions") and licenses labeling as further actions some of the causal consequences of the assumed actions (call these the "inferred actions") based on whether the assumed actions "figure importantly enough into the explanation" of why the inferred actions occurred. In the case of Paul's murder, we attribute the inferred action of Mary murdering Paul when the assumed actions, such as Mary's shooting a gun, "figure importantly enough into the explanation of Paul's death."

If we are supposed to understand the clause involved in the notion of intellectual credit by analogy with this clause regarding moral credit, we end up saying something literally incredible: We assume that some beliefs are held (call these the "assumed beliefs") and license labeling as further beliefs some of the causal consequences of the assumed beliefs (call these the "inferred beliefs") based on whether the assumed beliefs "figure importantly enough into the explanation" of why the inferred beliefs exist. But this analogical account makes no sense. One reason it doesn't is that the account is geared in the arena of action to address the question of how to distinguish between mere events and actions (the difference between my arm going up and my raising my arm), and there is no analogous perplexity in the realm of belief between a person's relationship to a proposition being a belief or only some more general category not involving belief.

So I am not sure what the ascription clause is meant to involve, and in thinking about it, it is hard to see what it could involve beyond the simple claim that the person believes the claim in question. That is, under what conditions might we say that a person has a true belief but that the true belief cannot be ascribed to that person? The claim that there is some distinction here escapes me, and hence I see no reason whatsoever for distinguishing the two. If so, however, the ascription clause is redundant

21. Greco, "Knowledge as Credit for True Belief," p. 11 typescript.
22. Ibid.

in the account of intellectual credit because the other clauses imply that the person holds the true belief in question.

Such a conclusion has interpretive advantages, for it allows us to make sense of Greco's claim that knowledge involves credit for true belief. As we saw earlier, the ascription clause seemed to require more for credit than is required in Greco's account of knowledge, but if the ascription clause is redundant, then the account of deserved credit and the account of knowledge mesh easily, yielding the result that on Greco's view, knowledge involves credit for true belief.

The issue, however, is not merely one of interpretation of Greco's views, for if the attribution clause regarding belief is redundant, that fact makes it more difficult to hold that a person ever deserves credit for a belief. For in the arena where credit is obviously due, the arena of action, the attribution clause is essential and nonredundant. If I aim to assassinate the president, but through lack of marksmanship miss and hit another would-be assassin instead, I deserve no credit for saving the life of the president, even though my actions lead to that consequence. In the case of action, it is essential that the event in question is an action of the individual who is the potential recipient of credit, leaving us with the temptation to think that the idea of credit has something essential to do with whatever it is that distinguishes actions from events. And whatever that is, it is not something that beliefs have, on pain of having to count beliefs as actions of the person. Because they are not actions, it looks as if the disanalogy is central, leaving Greco with no good answer to the question of why beliefs are the sorts of things that can function so as to generate credit for a believer at all.

There is one idea that might be pursued here to answer this objection. One might think that what is central to the nature of action, as opposed to events, is having a certain kind of internal cause, perhaps being caused by beliefs and desires. The idea is not that all actions are of this type, but that the more basic, fundamental kinds of actions are. Other events would then count as actions, on Feinberg's theory, only when a fundamental action is an important part of the causal story behind the further event that is a causal consequence of the fundamental action. On this theory, credit is due in the primary sense for events with the right sort of internal cause, and in an extended sense when a causal result of an action has an explanation that appeals to the fundamental action in an important way. Just so, credit is due for belief in the primary sense when beliefs have the right sort of internal cause. The difference between this case and that of action is that there is no extended sense of credit in the case of belief, as there is in the case of action. Perhaps, then, the right sort of internal cause in the case of belief is being caused by an intellectual virtue.

I will argue later that something like this idea is part of a successful virtue approach to the question of the value of knowledge, but I have two reservations about it in the context of Greco's specific theory. First, Greco presents a problem for Feinberg's view that moral blame and praise are due only for actions that reveal the character of a person, noting that we often rightfully blame people for actions that are out of character.[23] If we pursue the analogy between credit for action and credit for belief, this criticism ought to lead Greco to say the same thing about belief – that is, that a person can deserve credit for a belief that is out of character. Yet, if production by the virtues is the appropriate internal cause of beliefs for which one deserves credit, one could not deserve credit for a belief that is out of character, for such a belief would not be produced by the virtues.

There is another problem as well. If causation by an intellectual virtue is the right sort of internal cause to imply credit for true belief, then a credit clause in Greco's account of knowledge would be redundant. For the requirements of subjective and objective justification already imply a role for the intellectual virtues in holding the belief, and credit due for true belief would be a by-product of satisfying these clauses. Greco holds, however, that the credit-due clause is essential and nonredundant.

So I do not see how to interpret Greco's account to give a satisfactory answer to the question of the value of knowledge. The ascription clause appears to be required to play a substantive, nonredundant role in order to allow the analogy with action to help generate an account of credit due for belief, but it is hard to get the analogy to come out right. Furthermore, if the ascription clause is nonredundant, Greco is no longer entitled to the title of his article, that knowledge is credit for true belief. We must conclude, therefore, that Greco's approach to this account of the value of knowledge in terms of credit is not entirely successful.

The idea of credit for certain kinds of true beliefs encounters some fairly severe problems in the particular context of Greco's thought, but if we abstract from that context, it may be that we can find a readier defense of this idea. Some progress in defending the idea of credit for true belief can be found in Wayne D. Riggs's treatment of the problem of the value of knowledge.[24]

23. Ibid., p. 10 typescript.
24. Wayne Riggs, "Reliability and the Value of Knowledge," *Philosophy and Phenomenological Research* 64, 1, pp. 79–96.

Some of what Riggs claims looks like an attempt to rescue standard reliabilism from the swamping problem. He begins by distinguishing between the value that accrues to a *true belief* in virtue of having been produced by a reliable process – which he admits is none, on the basis of the swamping problem – and the value that accrues to the *true believer* in virtue of being the person whose true belief was produced by a reliable process. The value differences that exist are to be explained by appeal to the concept of accidentality, claiming that "what makes a reliably produced true belief more valuable than its accidentally true counterpart is precisely this lack of accidentality."[25] He holds that the relevant sort of non-accidentality should be clarified by analogy with skillful actions. When an Olympic athlete wins a gold medal in virtue of her abilities, more value is found in her total situation than in the situation of someone who merely finds a gold medal on the beach. Moreover, the greater value obtains even if the one who finds a gold medal on the beach is equally gifted athletically.[26] Riggs claims that this difference, the difference between having a medal as a result of a display of skill and having a medal as the result of something else, "is precisely the kind of accidentality that reliabilism is addressed to."[27]

These claims might be taken as a response to the swamping problem. Riggs might be suggesting that reliabilists have found something of value, but if we look only at the value that accrues to a belief on the basis of having been produced by a reliable process, we will be disappointed (at least, we will be disappointed if we have already assumed that the belief is true). Instead of looking at the value accruing to the belief, we should look at the value accruing to the person, and if we look there, we will find value even when we assume that the belief in question is true.

There are a couple of problems with this interpretation of Riggs's remarks. First, it makes for a weak argument. I have tried to find value by focusing on the person instead of on the belief, but I don't find it. At least, I don't find it without importing information gleaned by analogy from his example of skillful action and credit due for such accomplishments. This point leads to a second problem with this interpretation, for the interpretation finds no role at all for Riggs's appeal to the Olympic athlete.

I think there is a better interpretation of Riggs's ideas, one that distinguishes between two versions of reliabilism. The kind of accidentality

25. Ibid., p. 89.
26. Ibid., pp. 90–1.
27. Ibid., p. 91.

ruled out by skillful action is incompatible with some versions of reliabilism and not with others. In particular, virtue versions of reliabilism aim to rule out this kind of accidentality, but versions of reliabilism that focus more on methods or processes of belief formation are not aimed in the same direction. For example, Robert Nozick's intuitive truth-tracking theory is aimed at avoiding such accidentality,[28] for truth trackers arrive at the truth in much the same nonaccidental fashion as skillful athletes succeed in competition. Nozick modifies this intuitive theory in the face of counterexamples so that it aims at ruling out a different kind of accidentality. He considers a case of perceptual knowledge that such-and-such a building is a theater, which is knowledge, according to his theory, only if the person would not believe it is a theater if it was one. He imagines the following possibility: If it weren't a theater, it would be a secret testing facility for the government, which would put in place barriers to detection. Perhaps, for example, a gas could be emitted in the vicinity of the building to make anyone investigating the nature of the building too sick to find out that it was not a theater. In response to this counterexample, Nozick claims that the focus should be on the method of belief formation, not on the person holding the belief, so that the relevant counterfactual should put the focus on the methods of belief formation instead of on the truth-tracking character of the person holding the belief.[29]

In another example, Goldman's reliabilism puts the focus on processes and methods rather than on the skills or abilities of a person. Yet, processes and methods can be fleeting and ephemeral in their use, and beliefs produced by a passing fancy for the use of one such process or method over another does not rule out the kind of accidentality ruled out by successful action by skilled athletes.

In spite of some of Riggs's comments, I don't think a failure to rescue reliabilism in all its forms from the swamping problem is on his agenda. Instead, I think he hopes to find some version of the view on which the elimination of a particular kind of accidentality results in value for the agent, a kind of value left untouched by the swamping objection to standard reliabilism. What he wants to argue for is that there is a kind of accidentality that is eliminated when the belief is "*sufficiently causally determined* by the abilities, powers, skills, etc. of the person herself."[30]

28. Robert Nozick, *Philosophical Explanations* (Cambridge, MA: Harvard University Press, 1981).
29. Ibid., p. 179.
30. Riggs, "Reliability and the Value of Knowledge," p. 94.

Riggs need not defend reliabilism, on this interpretation, unless that view is a version of virtue epistemology, the version that requires that the ground of reliability is found in the abilities, skills, and powers – in a word, the intellectual virtues – of the person in question.

I must note, however, that the way Riggs reaches this conclusion is subject to some of the same difficulties as Greco's. For Riggs claims that "[t]he degree of accidentality of some event E is inversely proportional to the degree of causal efficacy the person in question has in bringing about E,"[31] language a defender of the theory of agent causation would love,[32] and he uses the term "human agency" in reference to his topic.[33] Such language, and the accompanying analogies from the arena of action that prod theory development, suggest something different from the conclusion Riggs draws. Such language suggests that credit due has something to do with performing actions that constitute earning the prize in question. So, the Olympic athlete deserves credit for her gold medal because she earned it, whereas the person who finds one on the beach has not earned it, even if the finder has all the same athletic abilities as the Olympic winner. To earn a prize in this sense involves essential reference to human agency: to actions performed by a person and perhaps to the athletic abilities displayed in the actions. Yet, if credit is due in virtue of this essential role for human agency, then the concept is simply not at home in the realm of belief. For at least in many cases, belief is not the product of human agency in this way.

I think Riggs could try to avoid this problem by analogy, employing the dialectic between libertarians and soft determinists regarding human freedom. If human freedom is really of the libertarian sort, then credit is due an agent only when libertarian freedom is displayed in that person's actions. Soft determinists, because they deny the existence of libertarian freedom, look for other grounds on which to attribute credit and claim to find it when the actions in question are caused in the right way. There are two central claims here. First, the event in question must be an action in order for the agent to deserve credit for it; second, the source of the action must be certain types of internal states of the agent.

31. Ibid., p. 93.
32. A defense of the idea of agent causation can be found in Roderick Chisholm, "Human Freedom and the Self," in *Reason at Work*, Steven M. Cahn, Patricia Kitcher, George Sher, and Peter Markie, eds. (New York: Harcourt Brace, 1990), pp. 536–46.
33. Riggs, "Reliability and the Value of Knowledge," p. 18 typescript.

Riggs can claim that their account of credit in the realm of belief will fail if a libertarian account of credit due in the realm of action is the only acceptable one. He can argue, however, that the soft determinist position is not incoherent, that credit can be due for action even when the action is causally determined by other events. What matters is the nature of causal determination, which minimally must be internal to the agent. If that is so, then it should be possible for a person to earn credit for a belief as well when the belief is produced or sustained by the right sorts of causes. Presumably, the right sorts will be analogous to those posited by the soft determinist in cases of action – ones that are internal to the believer.

This suggestion was presented earlier in connection with Greco's theory. There is a difference here, however, for the major difficulty in the context of Greco's theory is the need to explain the significance in his account of the ascription clause for credit due and the role of the concept of credit in his complete theory of knowledge. It would be enough for Riggs if beliefs involving a display of intellectual character generate credit for the believer, even if there might be other ways to generate such credit. So perhaps the appeal to the right sort of internal causation can be more useful to Riggs than it was to Greco.

The difficulties arising for a virtue account of credit due for true belief that arise through dependence on the analogy with action are addressed most explicitly in Sosa's recent development of this proposal. Sosa begins by distinguishing a special kind of extrinsic value, what he calls "praxical value," the value possessed by the event of an agent's bringing about something valuable. Such value can obtain with respect to a person's true beliefs either by the actions of a guardian angel or by one's own actions. In either case, the world contains the same amount of intrinsic and praxical value. So the key, for Sosa, is to explain the value of knowledge over true belief in terms of praxical value deriving from one's own agency. Sosa thus concludes:

So the grasping of the truth central to truth-connected reliabilist epistemology is not just the truth that may be visited upon our beliefs by happenstance or external agency. We desire rather truth gained through our own performance, and this seems a reflectively defensible desire for a good preferable not just extrinsically but intrinsically. What we prefer is the deed of true believing, where not only the believing but also its truth is attributable to the agent as his or her own doing.[34]

34. Sosa, "The Place of Truth in Epistemology," in DePaul and Zagzebski, *Intellectual Virtue*, forthcoming, p. 20 typescript.

This idea of there being a "deed" of true believing, of the truth of one's believing being "attributable to the agent as his or her own doing," raises precisely the problem we have been discussing. Beliefs are not actions and thus are not creditable or attributable to the agent in the way actions are.

Here Sosa's discussion makes significant advances over the previous discussion, for he devotes considerable attention to this question of agency regarding belief. Sosa begins with the analogy to action, citing the enhanced value in archery of hitting the bulls-eye by a display of skill versus hitting it by luck. He then asks whether this result in the case of action can be used to explain the value of knowledge over true belief in terms of praxical value.[35] After asking that question, he immediately turns to a discussion of agency, beginning with the claim that "In a very weak sense even a puppet 'does' something under the control of the puppeteer, and even to stumble across a stage unintentionally is to 'do' something."[36]

Sosa holds that agency, even in this weak sense, is tied to evaluation. He says, "An artifact like our temperature control system that 'does' things, that 'works,' might be evaluated variously, along with its performances."[37] So, whether there is agency of a distinctively human kind or not, there is agency in enough of a sense to undergird the evaluation of the agent and its performance. Weak agency is all that is needed to undergird attributing credit to the agent.

Sosa does not address the obvious objection to this account, that his felt need to put words like 'does' in quotation marks signals an awareness that the use of such language is not literally true. When we speak of what a thermostat accomplishes, why not think of such language as metaphoric? That is, we pretend that the thermostat is an agent in order to describe its behavior, but if we wished to speak literally, we would drop such language altogether. Such a phenomenon is common when characterizing evolutionary processes involving biological organisms. We characterize the mating behavior of certain birds in fully intentional language – for example, speaking of a male's intentions to impress females or of a female's attempts to entice interest in males. In some cases, it may be that such behavior involves the type of intentionality characteristic of agency, but it is highly doubtful that this claim is true in all cases. Much of evolutionary pressure happens at a subintentional level, in spite of our predilection to adopt that type of language to characterize such pressure. Nothing much

35. Ibid., pp. 9–10 typescript.
36. Ibid., p. 10 typescript.
37. Ibid., p. 12 typescript.

is damaged by this practice, though, for most recognize that such language could be replaced with more accurate characterizations of evolutionary pressure if the intentional descriptions should mislead.

Shouldn't we say the same about our statements regarding the actions of a puppet or the behavior of a thermostat? I see no reason to take such language as anything more than metaphorical expression in service of efficient communication, expression that could be replaced with more accurate descriptions that would not involve agency if the metaphors mislead. Such strictly accurate descriptions may not be as efficient as a form of communication, however, so the easiest path is to resort to such nonliteral language.

It may be that there is some way to handle this objection, but I don't think an answer to it is required in order to maintain the heart of Sosa's position. His approach involves two steps. The first step is his account of the language of agency where it strictly does not belong. It is this step that the objection challenges. There is still the second step, however, the step that ties the first step to the language of evaluation. A thermostat that controls the temperature as it was designed to do is evaluated positively; one that malfunctions is evaluated negatively. What is important to notice about this second step is that it need not assume the strict accuracy of the language of agency applied to the thermostat. Sosa can allow the critic his or her choice of a strictly accurate characterization of the operation of the thermostat. All Sosa needs is the link between an accurate characterization and the language of evaluation, and that link is not threatened at all by a rejection of the literal significance of the language of agency applied to the thermometer.

Thus, it is not sufficient to undermine a virtue approach to credit for true belief by insisting that beliefs are not voluntary and do not count as actions or accomplishments of the agent. Instead, a much stronger claim is needed, a claim to the effect that the language of evaluation is appropriate only when undergirded by the language of agency. This claim, however, has little to recommend it. We are not the least inclined to abandon the idea that some thermostats are better than others when it is pointed out to us that thermostats are not agents capable of voluntary actions.

As Aristotle reminds us, a good knife and a good person are both evaluated positively, but in different senses of 'good'. So it may be that when the language of agency undergirds evaluation, we have a different sense of the evaluative terms than we do with other kinds of evaluation. That point, however, does not threaten the substance of the virtue position here. All that is needed is that credit is due to a believer for true beliefs that result from the employment of the intellectual virtues. A virtue theorist can let the chips fall where they may as to whether this evaluation is the same as or different from the credit due a skilled archer for hitting the target.

Even if we grant that the language of evaluation can be appropriate without an appeal to agency, there still must be something in the thing itself to explain when positive evaluations apply to that thing and when they do not. In the case of Sosa's virtue account of credit due for true belief, the difference needed must involve an appeal to the intellectual virtues of the believer. Sosa argues for this claim by analogy, comparing a rank beginner in tennis serving an ace with that of a skilled profession:

An agent might be nearly incompetent and yet perform most effectively on a particular occasion. This evaluates the performance in the light of its wonderful outcome. Someone with a barely competent tennis serve may blast an ace past his opponent at 130 mph. This is a most effective serve given its outcome. . . . But from another point of view it may not have been so positively evaluable after all. If the player is a rank beginner, for example, one most unlikely to reproduce that performance or anything close to it, then one may reasonably withhold one's encomium. . . . Performances that are creditable must be attributable to the agent's skills and virtues, and thus attributable to the agent himself.[38]

Sosa's position is that successful results deserve a certain kind of positive appraisal, but the distinctive kind that generates credit for the agent must involve a display of skill or virtue.

Such a view of credit due an agent is not true in cases of action, as we saw earlier that Greco has recognized in his discussion of credit due for actions that are out of character. I recall an article in *Sports Illustrated* by an author who had played golf only once in his life. He shot a 71 and found it very easy, so boringly easy that he never played again. He deserves credit for having shot a 71, but not because he is a skilled player.

One might think he was a skilled player, that if he had played again, he would have shown how skilled he was. I don't think so. I'd be even more amazed if he continued to shoot that well had he continued. He nonetheless deserves credit for his spectacular round. After all, it is not as if the wind blew his shots into the hole or a squirrel dropped a nut just right to make the ball end up in the hole. His round was lucky in

38. Ibid., pp. 12–13 typescript.

certain respects, but all of our achievements are lucky in some respect or other, so the mere presence of luck does not imply that no credit is due. One might even grant that more credit would be due if his round were a display of skill developed over a lifetime, but that does not undermine the point in question.

It is important, however, not to be confused about the force of this difficulty for virtue theories. The point we are currently investigating is the idea that value is found in displays of intellectual virtue, and nothing in the preceding example suggests that this point is mistaken. When virtue theorists turn to the task of defending a virtue theory of knowledge, they will have to address the threat to their view posed by credit due for out-of-character actions and examples such as the preceding golf example. Our procedural policy here, however, asks us to grant a theory of knowledge its assumptions about the nature of knowledge to see if something of value can be found in knowledge beyond that of true belief. Even if we find a positive answer to that question, the theory will still face the formidable task of defending its account of the nature of knowledge. Though, as we have already noted, there is considerable dependence between the questions of the nature and value of knowledge, our task here calls for us to table questions about the nature of knowledge to the extent possible in order to focus on questions concerning the value of knowledge. So even though the preceding example poses a threat to virtue epistemology as a whole, it does so at a point tabled for purposes of our present discussion of the value of knowledge, the point at which a virtue theorist wishes to connect credit for true belief due to the operation of the intellectual virtues with the concept of knowledge. What is important in our context, however, is that if we grant to virtue epistemologists their account of the nature of knowledge, we have found a value for knowledge within their theoretical perspective that is not swamped by the value of true belief and is distinct from the value of subjective justification discussed in the previous chapter. Such a discovery is important in its own right, even if virtue epistemologists face questions about the nature of knowledge raised by our discussion.

A FURTHER BENEFIT OF VIRTUE EPISTEMOLOGY?

To this point, then, we can identify as valuable not only true belief but also subjectively justified true belief and intellectually virtuous true belief. It would be a great benefit to a theory of knowledge if one could give a unified treatment of these apparently unrelated properties, and

John Greco has proposed just such a theory.[39] Let us look to see if such unity can be achieved.

Greco desires a theory of knowledge with five features: (1) It needs to imply that not all evidential relations are inferential, and in particular (2) why sensory evidence can be noninferential. (3) It must also be a foundational theory of knowledge. Finally, (4) it must reveal how inferences that are only contingently reliable can yield knowledge and (5) how knowers can be sensitive to the reliability of their inferences (p. 164).

Greco believes that simple reliabilism, the view that identifies knowledge with beliefs produced by reliable methods or processes, explains adequately the first four claims. He holds, however, that agent reliabilism, his particular version of virtue epistemology, is needed in order to account for the last.

On the first point, I think Greco misleadingly endorses simple reliabilism as an explanation of (1)–(4) because it implies all of them. It is a foundational theory of knowledge, at least in its formal structure (some beliefs are known apart from being based on other beliefs), and this foundational knowledge can be sensory knowledge that is noninferential. It also implies that knowledge can arise from contingently reliable processes or methods.

We might be willing to grant that no problems arise with the reliabilist explanation of (1)–(3), but we shouldn't grant the adequacy of the explanation of (4). For simple reliabilism does not provide a theoretical explanation of (4) unless knowledge is present in a number of cases where we know it isn't. An explanation is not adequate simply because it implies a number of things that it ought to imply. If that were true, we could theoretically explain everything by citing a contradiction. An adequate theoretical explanation must not only imply things that are true, but also fail to imply things that are false. So simple reliabilism is an adequate explanation of (4) only if knowledge is present in BonJour's clairvoyance case (where Norman, who is unknowingly clairvoyant and possesses overwhelming evidence against the existence of such, still believes a claim on the basis of clairvoyance and is correct because he is clairvoyant),[40] in Plantinga's serendipitous lesion case (where a brain lesion causes the very

39. Greco, *Putting Skeptics in Their Place.*
40. Laurence BonJour, *The Structure of Empirical Knowledge* (Cambridge, MA: Harvard University Press, 1985), pp. 41–5. The case involves Norman, who is unknowingly clairvoyant, forming clairvoyant beliefs but having strong evidence that clairvoyance is unreliable. His beliefs are thus reliable, but he does not know them to be true.

belief that one has such a lesion, in spite of having no evidence of it),[41] and in a number of other cases that constitute counterexamples to simple reliabilism.

This problem will be innocuous enough if Greco's way of supplementing simple reliabilism so as to yield agent reliabilism eliminates these counterexamples. Perhaps this is the way Greco conceives the relationship between simple and agent reliabilism; at the very least, this way of conceiving the relationship would explain the perplexing dialectic in Greco's discussion. Greco's official account of the relationship between (1)–(5) and simple and agent reliabilism is as follows: Simple reliabilism explains (1)–(4), and agent reliabilism adds something to simple reliabilism to enable an explanation of (5) as well. Yet, Greco introduces agent reliabilism by considering the problem of "strange and fleeting" processes, processes such as Plantinga's serendipitous lesion that happens to cause a true belief that such a lesion is present or BonJour's clairvoyant who forms (true) beliefs based on clairvoyance even though he knows better. When Greco finally turns to (5), the explanatory work is done by a distinction between subjective and objective justification, which I will comment on later. Yet, if simple reliabilism adequately accounted for (1)–(4), why doesn't Greco simply jump to the agent reliabilist's explanation of (5) in terms of the distinction between subjective and objective justification?

The answer may be that Greco knows that simple reliabilism's explanation of (4) is inadequate and that the first thing agent reliabilism must do is to offer a better explanation of (4), one lacking the untoward implications of simple reliabilism regarding strange and fleeting processes such as those involved in the Plantinga and BonJour cases. If my suspicions are correct that it is this awareness that explains Greco's dialectic, then Greco sees that two tasks, and not just one, are demanded of agent reliabilism: to correct the explanation of (4) given by simple reliabilism and to explain (5).

According to Greco, agent reliabilism claims that "A belief p has positive epistemic status for a person S just in case S's believing p results from stable and reliable dispositions that make up S's cognitive character."[42] The account involves two ideas not present in simple reliabilism. First, the disposition that results in belief must be part of S's cognitive character.

---

41. Alvin Plantinga, *Warrant: The Current Debate* (Oxford: Oxford University Press, 1993), p. 199. The case involves a brain lesion, among whose effects is the very belief that the person in question has a brain lesion. This process of belief formation is reliable but not knowledge-producing.
42. Greco, *Putting Skeptics in Their Place*, p. 177.

Second, in addition to being a reliable disposition, the disposition must be "stable."

What is it for a disposition to be stable? Greco introduces agent reliabilism to solve the problem for simple reliabilism raised by strange and fleeting processes, one of which is Plantinga's serendipitous lesion example. Stability of a disposition does not seem incompatible with strangeness (and Plantinga's lesion case is certainly strange), but it is to be contrasted with fleetingness. Yet, the problem of strange and fleeting processes is not centrally a problem about what period of time the process is operative. Plantinga's lesion might have been present from birth; BonJour's clairvoyant might have formed clairvoyant beliefs most of his or her life. Making the dispositions in question more permanent in the cognitive lives of the persons in question does nothing to relieve the force of the counterexamples. So adding stability doesn't seem to help.

Moreover, stability doesn't seem to be required. Suppose God is in a playful mood when creating Adam, and suppose a disposition for belief is stable only if it lasts for n units of time. God's playfulness leads him to consider the array of sets of dispositions toward belief and to change the set Adam has over the course of his life. How often does he do this? For some m, such that $0 < m < n$, God changes the set every n-m units of time. He begins by giving Adam all the ordinary dispositions toward belief that we all have. So Adam looks at a ripe pear on a tree and believes *That is yellow*. Adam has perceptual knowledge of the color of the pear, but Greco's account implies that Adam doesn't have such knowledge, because God is being too playful with his creation. There may be possibilities of playfulness that are incompatible with knowledge, but the sort in question here isn't one of them (though it may be that once the changes to character begin, knowledge will not result when the new character is displayed; that is, my counterexample may work only for the initial created character of Adam, but nothing in the example requires more). Those familiar with the inevitable degradation of our cognitive equipment, whether graceful or otherwise, will see any appeal to stability of dispositions toward belief as a red herring. For some humans the degradation occurs over decades, for others much more quickly. The facts about present knowledge, however, don't seem connected at all with how long we will maintain the integrity of our cognitive mechanisms.

The second difference between Greco's agent reliabilism and simple reliabilism appealed to the person's cognitive character, but this condition is of no help here. For Adam's cognitive character is constituted by the set of dispositions during the time he has those dispositions. The only problem is that Adam doesn't have those dispositions long enough for Greco's theory to allow him perceptual knowledge of a very simple sort.

It is interesting to note in this regard that Greco introduces examples of strange and fleeting processes of belief formation to motivate his appeal to stability, but he never uses that concept to explain why knowledge isn't present in the examples of BonJour and Plantinga. I think that fact is telling, because lack of stability is not what is missing in those cases. What is wrong is, rather, a matter of lack of coherence between the understanding a person has of the reliability of various ways of forming and holding beliefs and how the beliefs are formed in these cases. What is wrong, in the language of Sosa, for example, is that there is no reflective knowledge in such cases.[43]

Greco's explanation of (5) touches on this very point, so we might hope that his explanation of (5) will simultaneously solve the problem simple reliabilism has in explaining (4). Greco's explanation of (5) centers on his distinction between subjective and objective justification. According to Greco, objective justification amounts to a belief being the result of dispositions that make a person reliable regarding that belief in the conditions in question, and subjective justification involves a belief being "the result of dispositions that S manifests when S is thinking conscientiously" (p. 218). The hope is that this combination of positions will block the difficulties that confront other versions of reliabilism.

To see if the attempt is successful, we need to look more carefully at Greco's remarks about the dispositions involved in conscientious thinking. First, Greco identifies conscientious thinking with the "default mode" of being motivated to get to the truth (p. 191). The contrast is thus between thinking honestly and being motivated by nonalethic factors such as greed, prestige, comfort, and the like.

Second, Greco does not identify subjective justification with such proper epistemic motivation; in fact, his definition does not even require proper motivation. For his definition only requires the activity of the dispositions that are present when one is properly motivated, and those dispositions might be active both when one is properly motivated and when one is not. I think this may be too weak a connection between subjective justification and proper epistemic motivation. For example, if the same disposition can accompany both well-motivated and ill-motivated belief,

---

43. Sosa's concept of reflective knowledge is found in *Knowledge in Perspective*, especially "Knowledge and Intellectual Virtue."

it will be possible to display that disposition ill-motivatedly while rationally believing that an ill-motivated display on this occasion is highly unlikely to get one to the truth. Such a situation strikes me as paradigmatic for lack of subjective justification rather than one in which subjective justification is present, as Greco's theory may allow.

Moreover, Greco's appeal to subjective justification does not explain away the standard counterexamples to simple reliabilism. In BonJour's clairvoyant case, Greco needs to charge the clairvoyant with not manifesting the dispositions that he manifests when trying for the truth. I don't see why the clairvoyant has to be guilty of this charge. The clairvoyant knows better than to trust clairvoyance, but that doesn't imply that he is manifesting dispositions different from the ones manifested for him when aiming for truth. The clairvoyant's failure is that he doesn't take into account possessed defeating information, but one can fail to do this, and even fail to be disposed to do this, and nonetheless manifest the dispositions one normally does when proceeding honestly.

Most of us do not behave this way cognitively, but that is a contingent fact about us. As we improve cognitively, we learn to monitor for defeating information and we learn to withhold belief when we learn of the presence of defeating information. Even so, in the process of so improving, we often think honestly and display the dispositions that we ordinarily display when honestly trying for the truth without monitoring for defeating information and without withholding belief in the presence of known defeaters. Greco's response to the clairvoyance case requires that the only explanation for retaining a belief in the presence of known defeaters is that we are being moved by dispositions other than those operative when thinking honestly, but there are other options. Habits are often overly general, displaying themselves even where not especially useful or desirable. Transparently honest people sometimes hurt others' feelings by unthinkingly displaying such honesty, and belief formation can exemplify this same feature. The motivations present when one is honestly trying for the truth might be unthinkingly displayed when attention to the presence of known defeaters would have prevented the display of these motivations.

This point is not merely a trifling failure of detail, but rather a particular instantiation of a more general weakness of reliabilism. On the face of it, justification is a function of the information or evidence we possess, but reliabilism wishes to talk in terms of belief-forming mechanisms and so must try to mimic evidential relations with these mechanisms (say, by individuating mechanisms or character traits in such a way that the reliability of these mechanisms coincides with the intuitive idea of information or evidence possessed). I have argued on other occasions that the prospects for successful mimicry are hopeless,[44] and my point here is that the preceding difficulty is simply another example of the difficulty. The concept of defeating information is, intuitively, one concerning the epistemic relationships between semantic contents, and the hope of any version of reliabilism is to mimic these relationships by appeal to the right kinds of mechanisms or character traits. Greco's attempt on this point is not entirely successful, I think, for there are no grounds for thinking that in order to display dispositions involved in trying for the truth, one must be disposed always to avoid belief when defeating information is present. So there is no reason to think that the clairvoyant case is explained away by an appeal to such dispositions.

Let me hasten to add that I think Greco's approach to these counterexamples to simple reliabilism is on the right track. In these cases, the persons involved have beliefs that are subjectively unjustified, preventing their beliefs from being known to be true. The problem is that Greco's account of subjective justification doesn't sustain this reponse. A more general point is that it is highly unlikely that any disposition-based proposal can yield an adequate response to the counterexamples to simple reliabilism. Dispositions, by their very nature, can be overly general and hence will be able to be displayed while failing to take into account the presence of defeating information. Not even an appeal to the disposition to take into account such information can help, for one needn't have that disposition in order to have subjectively justified beliefs. Sensitivity to such information is learned behavior, behavior that can be learned by forming subjectively justified beliefs that turn out to be false.

If I'm right in concluding that no disposition-based account of subjective justification can be adequate, Greco will have to abandon one of the most attractive features of his account. Greco's hope is to use features of character to elucidate the concept of subjective justification, thereby unifying his account of objective and subjective justification in terms of an appeal to cognitive character. If I am correct, however, he'll have to sacrifice theoretical unity in order to find an adequate account of subjective justification.

44. See, e.g., "The Basic Notion of Justification," Christopher Menzel, co-author, *Philosophical Studies,* 59 (1990): pp. 235–61; of *The Intellectual Virtues and the Life of the Mind: On the Place of the Virtues in Contemporary Epistemology* (Totowa, NJ: Rowman & Littlefield, 1992), chapter 5; "Zagzebski on Justification," *Philosophy and Phenomenological Research,* 60 (2000), pp. 191–6; and "Propositionalism and the Perspectival Character of Justification," *American Philosophical Quarterly,* 40, 1 (2003): 3–18.

So I think there is little hope for a unified theory of the two elements we have identified as valuable epistemic properties of belief. Subjective justification is valuable, and so is intellectual virtuousity, but the appearance that these are separate and distinct epistemic properties is probably accurate.

CONCLUSION

The basic idea of a virtue approach to the question of the value of knowledge over that of its subparts is that there is a special value for beliefs that arise out of intellectual virtue. When true belief is a product of the virtues, the claim is that there is epistemic credit due to the agent in question and hence that virtuous true belief is more valuable than true belief. The best defense of this idea is found in the analogy with the notion of weak agency and the kind of evaluation appropriate to such, as Sosa does. On such a view, credit requires only the proper kind of internal cause of action in order for responsibility to accrue, and the virtue epistemologist may make the same claim for belief. That is, the virtue epistemologist may claim that the right kind of internal cause for belief results in credit due.

This approach does not single out the virtues as the unique internal cause that generates credit due, for other explanations may be possible. If they are, then the approach to the nature of knowledge adopted by virtue epistemologists may not be successful. This question about the adequacy of virtue epistemology as an account of the nature of knowledge is a question for another time and place, and if we grant their account of the nature of knowledge in order to focus on the question of the value of knowledge (as we do here), virtue epistemology has an important contribution to make to the discussion of the value of knowledge, for we have seen how credit is due for virtuous belief and how the value of such credit is not swamped by the value of true belief itself. Thus, we have found another sort of value related to knowledge, a value understood in terms of credit due for true belief when such belief involves a display of the intellectual virtues.

Combining this result with that of the previous chapter, we now have two sources of value beyond true belief, the value of subjective justification and the value of virtuous belief. Neither value is swamped by the value of true belief, so both kinds of value can be cited as part of the explanation of the value of knowledge.

We close this chapter, though, on a negative note, for neither sort of value is sufficient to explain the value of knowledge. Knowledge is not subjectively justified true belief because the latter can obtain without the former, and knowledge is also more than virtuous true belief. The former is, I think, the more obvious, for a person can have a subjectively justified true belief in the chanciest of fashions. Nearly any Gettier case is easily adapted to the notion of subjective justification, showing that knowledge is more than subjectively justified true belief. It is equally true, however, that knowledge is more than intellectually virtuous true belief. Goldman's fake barn case discussed earlier is a well-known example that reveals a difference between knowledge and such virtuous belief, for impressive perceptual abilities count as intellectual virtues and could be displayed in the fake barn case. The reason the display of such virtues falls short of knowledge is that perception can be an impressive ability and still be unable to distinguish real barns from well-designed fake ones, and so a true belief could result that still was only accidentally true.

As we saw earlier, to explain the value of knowledge in a way that satisfies the constraints of the *Meno* requires showing that knowledge is more valuable than any proper subset of its constituents. So even though intellectually virtuous true belief and subjectively justified true belief are valuable, an adequate explanation of the value of knowledge requires showing that knowledge is more valuable than either of these combinations. Addressing that issue requires attention to the Gettier problem, to which we turn in the next chapter.

5

The Gettier Problem and the Value of Knowledge

The topic for this chapter arises out of two sources. In the previous two chapters, we discovered two properties of belief that are valuable beyond that of truth, the properties of subjective justification and intellectual virtuousity. Both of these properties are valuable by themselves, so that it is epistemically better for a belief to be subjectively justified than not and it is better for a belief to be virtuous than not. Moreover, these properties have a value not swamped by the presence of truth, so that it is better to have a subjectively justified true belief than one that is true but unjustified in this sense, and it is better to have a virtuous true belief than to have a true belief that is not virtuous. In the former case, what makes the property of subjective justification valuable in a way not swamped by the value of truth is that this property is a transparent mark of truth. So it has value because of its connection to truth, but its value is not swamped by the presence of truth, as are other properties such as reliability that also have value because of their connection to truth. Intellectually virtuous belief is valuable because when a belief has this property, the believer is due credit for having a true belief. If we understand the virtues in terms of truth-conduciveness,[1] then this property is valuable in part because of its connection to truth, but not in such a way that its total value is swamped by the value of truth.

Hence, the first source of motivation for the present chapter is the discovery of important epistemic properties other than truth. The other motivation is the Gettier problem, for neither of these properties is

---

1. For an argument against this construal of the virtues, see Jonathan L. Kvanvig, *The Intellectual Virtues and the Life of the Mind: On the Place of the Virtues in Contemporary Epistemology* (Totowa, NJ: Rowman & Littlefield, 1992), chapter 6.

sufficient, either individually or jointly, in the presence of true belief for knowledge. Thus, we must face the further Socratic query of what makes knowledge more valuable than true belief plus either or both of these properties.

I begin with a brief summary of the Gettier problem and some of the more important counterexamples in the literature. I then outline the basic approaches to the Gettier problem before turning to the question of whether any of these approaches offer the hope of explaining what makes knowledge better than subjectively justified true belief, virtuous true belief, and true belief that is both subjectively justified and virtuous.

THE GETTIER PROBLEM

The heart of the Gettier problem arises whenever the requirements other than truth for knowledge do not guarantee the presence of truth itself. I will call such a position "fallibilism." The position Gettier attacked is the position that knowledge is justified true belief, where justification can obtain even though it provides no guarantee of truth. In our case, the problem arises because neither subjective justification nor intellectual virtuosity is a guarantee of truth.

Gettier provided two counterexamples against the theory of knowledge he rejects.[2] The first example involved ten coins in the pocket of someone in the room, and the second involved a friend, Smith, being in Boston. In both cases, sufficient evidence to justify a belief is presented where the belief in question is false (either *Jones, who is in this room, has ten coins in his pocket* or *Smith is in Boston*). In each case, the person presented with the evidence reasons deductively from the false claim that is justified to a further claim (either *someone in this room has ten coins in his or her pocket* or *Smith is in Boston or Brown is in Barcelona*), where this further claim just happens to be true (either because somebody else in the room has ten coins in his or her pocket or because Brown just happens to be in Barcelona). Because the inference is a self-conscious and competent wielding of logical devices, any justification present for the premise ought to be transferred to the conclusion. If so, however, the conclusion is a justified true belief. The way in which it is true bears little resemblance to the path of discovery followed by the person in this

2. Edmund L. Gettier, "Is Justified True Belief Knowledge?" *Analysis,* 23 (1963): 121–3.

case, so it counts as a justified true belief where the truth of the belief is merely accidental, not related in an appropriate way to the justification that is present. Because it is accidental in this way, it does not count as knowledge, and hence knowledge cannot be identified with justified true belief.

These counterexamples attack a theory that is not in play at this point in our study, but it is not hard to adapt them to attack the theories that are in play. Consider first the claim that knowledge is subjectively justified true belief. Because subjective justification involves transparent marks of truth, and whether a mark of truth is transparent or not is such a subjective matter, there is nothing to prevent us from imagining the Gettier cases to involve an individual for whom all the justification presented and the inferences involved are transparent marks of truth. They may not be such marks for most people, but it is not impossible that they be such; and if they are, Gettier's examples adapted to such an individual count straightforwardly against the idea that knowledge is subjectively justified true belief.

Moreover, the same strategy shows that knowledge is not virtuous true belief. The individual in the Gettier cases could easily be a competent logician and an excellent handler of empirical evidence, thereby making his original belief and the inferences drawn displays of intellectual virtue. Even so, knowledge would not be present, so knowledge is more than intellectually virtuous true belief.

A final extension of the Gettier cases shows that knowledge is not intellectually virtuous and subjectively justified true belief. Simply let one individual have both the characteristics of the previous two paragraphs: She is both subjectively justified and intellectually virtuous in believing the concluding propositions of the Gettier cases. Still, she lacks knowledge, so knowledge is more than true belief plus the valuable properties elicited from our discussions in Chapters 3 and 4.

GETTIER-LIKE CASES

Here are four important test cases from the literature that any account of knowledge must address:

The Nogot–Havit Case: Nogot does not own a Ferrari, but he has provided Smith with overwhelming evidence that he, Nogot, owns a Ferrari. Smith comes to Nogot's office, where he talks with Nogot and the janitor, Havit. Because

Smith believes that Nogot owns a Ferrari and believes that Nogot is in the office, Smith infers that someone in the office owns a Ferrari. This belief is true because the janitor owns a Ferrari. Further, the belief is justified because it is knowingly inferred from other justified beliefs, the beliefs that Nogot owns a Ferrari and that Nogot is in the office. Yet, Smith does not know that someone in the office owns a Ferrari, even though he has a justified true belief that this is so.[3]

The Fake Barn Case: Henry is driving in the countryside with his son, teaching him the kinds of objects found in it. "That's a cow," says Henry; "that's a tractor," "that's a silo," "that's a barn," and so on. Henry has no doubt about the identity of these objects, and his vision is fully adequate and functional. In particular, Henry is aware of no grounds that would cast doubt on the last claim about a barn. Each of the identified objects has features characteristic of its type, Henry is reasonably careful in his identification, and there is little traffic to distract him. Unknown to Henry, the county he travels in is full of fake barns. These fakes look from the road exactly like barns, but are without back walls or interiors, quite incapable of being used as barns. The object Henry sees, however, is the lone real barn in the area, so Henry is correct in identifying it as a barn. Yet, if he had been looking at a fake, he would have mistaken it for a barn. So Henry does not know that it is a barn, even though he has a justified true belief that it is a barn.[4]

The Tim–Tom Case: Joe, the library detective, sees his good friend Tom take a book from the library and leave without checking it out. On the basis of perception and personal acquaintance, Joe justifiably believes that Tom stole a book. Joe informs the police officer of what he saw, but after talking to Joe the officer speaks to Tom's mother, who claims that Tom is out of town and that it may have been Tom's identical twin brother, Tim, who stole the book. Unknown to the officer, Joe, or anyone else, Tom's mother is lying. Tom stole the book, he was not out of town, and Tom does not have a twin brother. In spite of the fact that Joe has a justified true belief that Tom stole the book, the testimony of Tom's mother undermines his knowledge.[5]

The Assassination Case: A political leader is assassinated, but his associates, fearing a coup, decide to pretend that the bullet hit someone else. The false report appears on national television, stating that a secret service person has been killed in a failed assassination attempt. Before the announcement is made, however, a

3. Keith Lehrer, "Knowledge, Truth and Evidence," *Analysis*, 25, 5 (1965): 168–75.
4. Alvin Goldman, "Discrimination and Perceptual Knowledge," *Journal of Philosophy*, 73, 20 (1976): 771–91.
5. Keith Lehrer and Thomas Paxson, Jr., "Knowledge: Undefeated Justified True Belief," *Journal of Philosophy*, 66, 8 (1969): 225–37.

reporter files the correct story, which is reported in his newspaper. Jill buys a copy and reads the correct report, a report in a credible news source by a reliable reporter. Everyone else has seen both the newspaper article and the television report, and they are in a state of confusion. Because of the existence of evidence she does not possess that is possessed by everyone else, Jill does not know even though her belief is justified and true. How could she know because her belief is so dependent on her lack of generally available information?[6]

Some adaptation of these cases is required in order to make them threaten the account of the value of knowledge that we have achieved to this point. On that account, knowledge is valuable because it involves true belief, which is valuable, and involves one or both of the properties of intellectual virtuosity or subjective justification. The adaptations are not difficult, however; we need only include the relevant properties in each of the cases. Doing so creates no inconsistency in the cases and no greater inclination to think that knowledge is present once these properties are included.

The result of such cases is something we noticed earlier in our discussion of Swinburne's account of the value of knowledge. Swinburne defended the value of knowledge through an internalist conception of justification. His account of the value of that kind of justification is inadequate, as we saw, but we also noticed something equally important. Even if his account of the value of justification had been adequate, the preceding examples show that knowledge is not justified true belief and hence that the value of knowledge cannot be identified with the value of justified true belief. An adequate account of the value of knowledge must explain why it is more valuable than any subset of its constituents. If we assume that there is some property like justification that distinguishes knowledge from true belief, then an adequate explanation of the value of knowledge could be achieved by giving an adequate account of the value of justification. Because knowledge is more than justified true belief, such an explanation is only one part of a complete explanation. In addition, what is needed is an explanation of why knowledge is more valuable than justified true belief.

In the previous two chapters, we identified two properties slightly different from Swinburne's concept of internal justification that are valuable, but the lesson learned in discussing Swinburne's theory applies here as well. In order to understand fully the value of knowledge, we need an explanation of why knowledge is more valuable than subjectively justified

6.   Gilbert Harman, *Thought* (Princeton, NJ: Princeton University Press, 1973), pp. 120–72.

true belief, more valuable than virtuous true belief, and more valuable than subjectively justified, virtuous true belief.

Our success in finding valuable properties related to knowledge in the previous two chapters gives us hope that the same result may be forthcoming here, but I will argue that there is a general difficulty in attempting to explain the value of knowledge over the value of its components here that is new. I want to explain the general difficulty and then canvass particular attempts to provide a fourth condition for knowledge to show how these attempts fail to provide resources for addressing the general difficulty. The conclusion at which I aim is that the prospects are dim for an explanation of the value of knowledge arising out of the search for a solution to the Gettier problem.

I begin with the general problem. The heart of the Gettier problem involves some degree of slippage between what makes a belief true and what makes a belief justified (or intellectually virtuous), leaving the person in question with a justified belief that is only *accidentally* true. When epistemologists attempt to describe the general features of the problem they address, the concept of accidentality plays a central role along with other concepts such as "fortuitousness," "luck," and the like. This terminology leads to the guiding idea that knowledge is justified belief whose truth is no accident or the truth of which is neither lucky nor fortuitous.

These characterizations are on target, but they can be misunderstood. For they might be taken as a suggestion that we can arrive at an adequate account of knowledge by finding ways to rule out accidentality or luck or fortuitousness in having a true belief. It is instructive that epistemologists attempting to solve the Gettier problem have not made such attempts, for it is a mistake to think of the appeal to accidentality as supplying some theory that needs only minor tinkering in order to solve the Gettier problem. A more accurate picture of what epistemologists are doing when they cite accidentality as somehow central to the Gettier problem is that they are identifying some genus under which they believe they will find a species that provides a solution to the problem they seek to solve.

The idea that the appeal to accidentality is a theory only in need of refinement has not been pursued by epistemologists, and I think there is a very simple and compelling reason why it shouldn't be pursued. This idea ignores the role a suitable, cooperative environment plays in the acquisition and possession of knowledge. We have found that an intellectually virtuous character is valuable on the basis of credit due to the believer for the accomplishment of true belief, and if we combine this approach with the idea of eliminating luck from true belief, we will begin to think of knowledge in terms of true belief achieved through the display of intellectual character excellent enough that no accidentality in the possession of true belief is present. Such an approach is hopeless, however, for explanations of true belief never appeal solely to the quality of our intellectual endowments. The environment itself must also be suitable for the operation of those powers. If we had infallible powers, things would be different; we would be in control of our epistemic destinies, and we could explain the difference between the value of knowledge and the value of true belief solely in terms of the value of our maximally excellent cognitive powers. But we do not have such powers, and hence the cooperation or suitability of the environment is required for a grasp of the truth to constitute knowledge.

Once we see that it is never solely in virtue of our cognitive powers that we find the truth, we must grant that a bit of fortuitousness is always present when we find the truth: Knowledge is always obtained at least in part by grace rather than totally by works.[7] So if it is fortuitousness that we hope to eliminate, we are hoping for something that cannot be had short of possessing infallible powers of discernment. I grant that such powers are surely desirable and valuable, but any attempt to account for the value of knowledge that appeals to the value of infallible powers of discernment will surely fail. For knowledge simply has little to do with infallibility.

These points do not by themselves give us a reason to think that the Gettier problem presents an insuperable obstacle to solving the *Meno* problem, for even if we cannot eliminate fortuity completely, there may still be kinds of fortuity that it is valuable to eliminate. Another point must be recognized as well, however. Given that knowledge is always obtained at least partially by grace, there will be elements of fortuity that we should not want to eliminate if knowledge is valuable. We cannot endorse the idea that any time any kind of fortuity is identified, it will be valuable to eliminate, for if we eliminate all fortuity, only infallible beings will have knowledge. Consider, for example, the fortuity of having been conceived,

---

7. I borrow this apt phrase from Robert J. Fogelin, *Pyrrhonian Reflections on Knowledge and Justification* (Oxford: Oxford University Press, 1994).

of having been born alive, of still being alive. There is also the fortuity each of us experiences of having many more beliefs about a particular locale rather than other locales (because of where we are physically located in space-time). Moreover, fortunate accidents bless us constantly, from the failure to acquire diseases that degrade our cognitive equipment to the failure of our enemies to carry out the work of the evil demon by breaking connections between what is rational to believe from our own perspective and what is true or likely to be true.

We might say, then, that the best approach to the Gettier problem would be one that identifies a kind of fortuity that, as it were, wears its disvalue on its sleeve. That is, it would be most useful for solving the *Meno* problem if the kind of accidentality eliminated by the fourth condition for knowledge were one that is intuitively disvaluable. Such a proposal would mimic the proposal that justification is required for knowledge in addition to true belief. Justification is, by its normative or evaluative nature, a valuable property. It takes no transcendental deduction or complex theoretical framework to establish this point. As such, the property of justification appears, prima facie at least, to be well suited for use in an explanation of the value of knowledge over that of true belief.

We have seen that the explanation of the value of justified true belief over that of mere true belief requires complexities not accounted for by this prima facie perspective. Yet the point remains that it is the intuitive value of justification that undergirds the search for an adequate and useful solution to the difficulties encountered. If it were not obvious from the outset that justification is a valuable property, the problems encountered would have provided sufficient reason in themselves to look elsewhere to account for the value of knowledge.

The same points should drive discussion of the Gettier problem and the prospects for solving the particular version of the *Meno* problem that arises only after noticing that knowledge cannot be identified with justified true belief. If we can identify some property that is intuitively valuable to eliminate, then there is hope for a solution to the problem of the value of knowledge. If, however, the best we can do is to offer a proposal that is so gerrymandered and ad hoc that we cannot identify this solution with any recognizably disvaluable kind of luck, accidentality, or fortuitousness, except to say that it is just that kind eliminated by whatever closes the gap between justified true belief and knowledge, we face a serious problem. For if such a characterization is all that could be provided, we would have no reason whatsoever for thinking that a solution could be found to the problem of the *Meno* on the basis of the value of knowledge's constituents.

This point is a straightforward implication of the twin desiderata on a theory of knowledge I have been stressing. On the assumption we have been making in the past several chapters (that the value of knowledge is in some way a function of the value of its parts), the need to account for both the nature and value of knowledge requires that we identify a fourth condition that not only yields a counterexample-free account of knowledge but also provides some basis for explaining the value of knowledge over the value of its constituents. The point I have been arguing is that this dual requirement can only be met when the identified fourth condition is something more than a gerrymandered, ad hoc way of avoiding counterexamples to one's account of knowledge. The identified fourth condition must identify some species of accidentality or luck, where such an identification provides a basis for defending the value of eliminating such luck.

The labyrinthine complexity of solutions to the Gettier problem is well known, and it is common to characterize the search as one where the complexity involved is ad hoc and gerrymandered in excess. Williamson, for example, argues that the very complexity of analyses of knowledge is incompatible with the value knowledge possesses:

Even if some sufficiently complex analysis never succumbed to counterexamples, that would not entail the identity of the analyzing concept with the concept *knows*. Indeed, the equation of the concepts might well lead to more puzzlement rather than less. For knowing matters; the difference between knowing and not knowing is very important to us. Even unsophisticated curiosity is a desire to *know*. This importance would be hard to understand if the concept *knows* were the more or less ad hoc sprawl that analyses have had to become; why should we care so much about *that*?[8]

I do not wish to endorse all that Williamson says here, but only to point out the inverse proportionality he sees between the complexity and ad hoc character of an account of knowledge and the usefulness of such an account in an explanation of the value of knowledge. His remarks present a nice summary of the point I am arguing. We might put the point in terms of being pulled in two different ways when addressing the Gettier problem. On the one hand, the variety of cases in which one can fail to know and yet have a justified true belief inclines one toward more complex, ad hoc, and gerrymandered proposals. On the other hand, the felt need

8. Timothy Williamson, *Knowledge and Its Limits* (Oxford: Oxford University Press, 2000), pp. 30–1.

to address the question of the value of knowledge over its subparts leads one toward simpler proposals in which the value of the condition is intuitively obvious. The twin desiderata on a theory of knowledge, the desiderata of accounting for both the nature and value of knowledge, threaten in this way to become the Scylla and Charybdis that sink the project entirely. I want to argue that this threat is real in the following sense: The Gettier problem shows that no component-based account of the value of knowledge will be successful. This conclusion leaves open the possibility that the value of knowledge can be accounted for in other ways, but it closes the door on the idea that we can account for the value of knowledge in terms of the value of its subparts.

APPROACHES TO THE GETTIER PROBLEM

I will canvass some of the more popular attempts to solve the Gettier problem to see how they fare with regard to this tension between the desiderata of the nature and value of knowledge. As might be expected, most such theories founder by focusing on the complexities needed to account for the nature of knowledge, thereby undermining any ability to explain knowledge's value. I want to begin, however, with a theory having the opposite problem, a simplistic version of the relevant alternatives approach.[9] I will argue that this version begins with a property that is intuitively valuable but has no hope of success in accounting for the nature of knowledge because it refuses to define the concept of "relevance."

On a relevant alternatives approach, the difference between knowledge and justified true beliefs is determined by whether one would be immune to error in alternatives to the actual situation. For example, in Goldman's fake barn example, an alternative to the actual situation is one where one is referring to a fake barn rather than a real barn when saying, "That's a barn."

This theory handles the fake barn case quite well, but it also risks implying global skepticism if we consider the alternative situation to the actual one in which Descartes's evil demon is operative. In order to avoid this skeptical consequence, this approach introduces the qualifier "relevant" and holds that the evil demon scenario is not a relevant alternative to the actual situation. The pressing issue for this approach is to specify

9. For an early version of the view, see Alvin Goldman, "Knowledge and Perceptual Discrimination," *Journal of Philosophy*, 73 (1976): 771–91.

what makes a situation relevant, and here relevant alternatives theorists have had little of help to say. The most simplistic version of the view would simply rely on our intuitive understanding of the concept of relevance, claiming that no more precise theoretical specification is needed.

Such a theory is well suited to addressing the issue of the value of knowledge. Immunity from error is itself a good thing, and it would be hard to argue that one should prefer such immunity in *irrelevant* alternatives to immunity in *relevant* alternatives. Whether this value could withstand the scrutiny needed to provide a complete answer to the question of the value of knowledge remains to be seen, but the theory provides some hope of such. It provides such hope by identifying a property with obvious evaluative dimensions and in this way follows the strategy of addressing the question of the value of knowledge by identifying evaluative features of knowledge not present in mere true belief.

Those schooled in the esoterica of the literature on the Gettier problem will be impatient with this defense of such a simplistic version of the relevant alternatives theory. For without some clarification of the concept of relevance, this approach is a nonstarter for addressing the problem of the nature of knowledge. It is important to recognize explicitly the significance of the intuitive concept of relevance, however. For the evaluative nature of this concept is precisely what one would wish for if one were focusing primarily on the question of the value of knowledge. It is unfortunate that the simplistic version of this approach has no similar hope of adequately addressing the question of the nature of knowledge. As such, it provides a good example of how a myopic focus on one of the two desiderata on a theory of knowledge leaves one with a theory holding little promise for success.

I do not wish to be misunderstood here as claiming that all versions of the relevant alternatives approach are of precisely the same sort as this simplistic version, for there are ways in which relevant alternatives theorists have gone beyond a simple appeal to the concept of relevance. One of the more interesting attempts is to appeal to contextualism here, claiming that what is relevant varies by context. This answer can be successful in addressing the question of the value of knowledge only if what is valuable covaries with this concept of relevance, and we will have a chance to examine this position in detail in a later chapter.

A relevant alternatives theorist might resort to a circular account of knowledge, claiming that a relevant alternative is one in which the failure to arrive at the truth is a failure that undermines knowledge. Such an approach is an obvious nonstarter, but it is interesting to compare this strategy with others that we will see later. This approach offers a substantive start on the problem of the value of knowledge and founders by offering an obviously circular nonstarter on the issue of the nature of knowledge. Other approaches to the Gettier problem end up doing the opposite, I will argue. These approaches offer a substantive start on the question of the nature of knowledge, but can offer only a circular nonstarter on the issue of the value of knowledge. They identify a condition on knowledge that can only be seen as valuable by assuming that the value of knowledge must be dependent on the value of its constituents. Such, we will see, is the lot of theories that focus myopically on the question of the nature of knowledge.

We will need to put this point on hold for the time being, however, for some ground clearing is necessary before we can take a look at the most promising approaches to the Gettier problem, approaches that share with the relevant alternatives theory this feature of offering false hopes. The ground clearing is necessary because of the interplay between the twin desiderata on a theory of knowledge, of accounting for both the nature and value of knowledge. Many of the approaches to the Gettier problem suffer from such deep defects in the attempt to account for the nature of knowledge that it is pointless to ask what use they have in addressing the problem of the value of knowledge. The goal of this ground clearing will be to isolate those approaches that have some prospect of success in providing an account of knowledge that is, at a minimum, free from counterexample in order to assess whether such approaches can be of any use in accounting for the value of knowledge. I'll begin with some general classificatory remarks about the kinds of approaches available for addressing the Gettier problem.

Some of the earliest attempts to explain the difference between knowledge and justified true belief emphasize the role that falsehoods play in yielding cases of justified true belief that are not cases of knowledge. Some claim, for example, that one cannot have reasoned through any false steps in arriving at the belief in question or that one's reasoning cannot involve these false steps essentially.[10] This approach emphasizes actual beliefs in the reasoning process, whereas other theorists employ the notion of "falsehoods" without requiring actual beliefs. Roderick Chisholm, for example, has suggested that knowledge requires evidence that confirms no

---

10. See, for example, Harman, *Thought*, chapter 9.

falsehood,[11] and Ernest Sosa claims that knowledge cannot epistemically presuppose any falsehoods.[12]

Defeasibility theorists provide a different approach. According to them, knowledge requires that justification be undefeated, where a defeater is a claim that, if believed, would undermine whatever justification is present. For defeasibility theorists, this necessary condition for being a defeater is not itself sufficient, and one difficult task for such a theory is to determine which subclass among those claims that satisfy this necessary condition is defeaters. One prominent suggestion is that a defeater is also a proposition that the individual in question is justified in believing to be false.[13]

Other approaches emphasize concepts such as "causality," "reliability," or "conclusive reasons," where the last idea is clarified in terms of counterfactuals. In the first group is Mark Steiner, who claims that knowledge of p requires that the sentence that expresses p be used in a causal explanation of the person's belief that p is true.[14] Reliability theories must appeal to reliability in a way different from reliability theories of justification, on pain of having to identify knowledge with justified true belief and thereby affirm the presence of knowledge in the cases presented earlier. One example of a different, and stronger, appeal to reliability to distance knowledge from justified true belief is offered by Adam Morton, who holds that knowledge has to be produced or sustained by a process that produces or sustains no false beliefs, and that is such that there is an explanation in terms of the laws of nature and the facts of the case, of why on this occasion a true belief results.[15]

Conclusive reasons approaches are clarified in terms of counterfactuals. Fred Dretske's original conclusive reasons account required that if the proposition were false, one would not believe it, and if one did not believe the proposition, it would not be true.[16] L. S. Carrier suggests the following: a person S knows that p only if (a) the reasons for S's believing p are such that in S's circumstances, if it were not the case that p then S

11. Roderick Chisholm, *Theory of Knowledge*, 2nd edition (Englewood Cliffs, NJ: Prentice-Hall, 1977), chapter 6.

12. Ernest Sosa, "Epistemic Presupposition," *Justification and Knowledge: New Studies in Epistemology*, George Pappas, ed. (Dordrecht: Reidel, 1979), pp. 79–92.

13. See, for example, Lehrer and Paxson, "Knowledge."

14. Mark Steiner, "Platonism and the Causal Theory of Knowledge," *Journal of Philosophy*, 70 (1973): 60.

15. Adam Morton, *A Guide Through the Theory of Knowledge* (Encino and Belmont, CA: Dickenson, 1977), p. 58.

16. Fred I. Dretske, "Conclusive Reasons," *Australasian Journal of Philosophy*, 49 (1971): 1–22.

would not believe p, and (b) the reasons for S's believing p are such that, in S's circumstances, if S were not of the belief that p, it would not be the case that p.[17] In his comprehensive summary of the search for a fourth condition for knowledge, Robert Shope defines the conclusive reasons approach as one involving either Carrier's condition (a) or one of the following:

(a′) There is some subset H of existing circumstances that are logically [and causally] independent of the truth of p, such that unless p were the case, S would not believe p; or (a″) . . . unless p were the case, S would not have the reasons S does for believing p.[18]

Such conclusive reasons theories are close cousins, at least, of the relevant alternatives theory. If we adopt something like the standard semantics for counterfactuals, then a conclusive reasons approach requires that we be immune from error in certain close counterfactual situations. It is easy to use this language to explain the relevant alternatives theory. What it requires is the same immunity from error in situations that are relevantly close to the actual situation.

Each of these approaches begins from an intuitively attractive starting point, responding as they do to certain subsets of counterexamples that have arisen in response to Gettier's original counterexamples. My goal is to show how the promise each approach provides disappears as refinements to the approach are introduced. In some cases, the promise of the approach founders on unanswerable difficulties regarding the nature of knowledge, and I want to move past these approaches first in order to focus on those approaches that appear to have some possibility of correctly explaining the nature of knowledge.

Consider first the approaches that focus on the role falsehoods play, approaches that claim that the absence of knowledge is a result of reasoning that contains falsehoods, or evidence that contains or presupposes or confirms falsehoods. Such approaches suggest that knowledge might be important because it insulates us from error, beyond the object of belief itself, and such extended insulation from error is certainly a valuable property to have. For if truth itself is valuable, then more truth will be valuable as well.

17. L. S. Carrier, "An Analysis of Empirical Knowledge," *Southern Journal of Philosophy*, 9 (1971): 6.
18. Robert K. Shope, *The Analysis of Knowing: A Decade of Research* (Princeton, NJ: Princeton University Press, 1983), p. 122.

The problem, however, is that knowledge doesn't require such insulation from error. The first of these approaches to be abandoned is the view that knowledge requires reasoning through no false steps. Such a claim is of no help with examples such as the fake barn case, in which no reasoning takes place at all. So the only approaches with any promise at all are those that emphasize bodies of evidence that contain, presuppose, or confirm falsehoods. These approaches, though they have a bit more promise, cannot withstand scrutiny either. First, among the lessons of the preface and fallibility paradoxes are that we nearly always have evidence in support of some false propositions. The lottery paradox begins by imagining a fair lottery with a thousand tickets in it. Each ticket is so unlikely to win that we are justified in believing that it will lose. So we can infer that no ticket will win. Yet we know that some ticket will win. In the preface paradox, authors are (sometimes) justified in believing everything in their books. Some preface their book by claiming that, given human frailty, they are sure that errors remain, errors for which they take complete responsibility. But then it appears that they justifiably believe both that everything in the book is true and that something in it is false.

There are a number of attempts to solve these paradoxes, but no such attempt can deny the possibility of knowing that some ticket will unexpectedly win the lottery and knowing that undetected errors remain in our best work on a topic. If such knowledge is possible, however, the evidential base for such knowledge will support some falsehoods. To know that errors remain undetected in a work requires knowing something of our fallible natures and knowing the contents of the work. And such knowledge must also involve seeing each of the claims in the book as true, for that is what it is for the errors to remain undetected. Similar remarks apply to the lottery case: To know that some unknown ticket will win requires knowing something about the nature of the lottery, but it also involves strong evidence for each ticket that it will lose, for that is what is involved in the case of the lottery in knowing that some ticket will unexpectedly win the lottery. So knowing that some ticket will unexpectedly win requires epistemic support for some falsehoods, and knowing that undetected errors remain in a work also requires epistemic support for falsehoods. So even though these types of insulation from error look like nice properties to have, they are not properties implied by knowledge.

There is another lesson that the preface paradox teaches, for a natural extension of that paradox raises the fallibility paradox. Let the book in question be a compilation of all of our beliefs. The preface statement then becomes an assertion of our own fallibility, that among our beliefs are undetected falsehoods. For those of us aware of our own fallibility, we have knowledge that presupposes some falsehoods. So once again, the paradoxes teach that knowledge does not require some blanket insulation from error that would be exceedingly nice to possess.

Second, the possibility of statistical knowledge undermines such an approach as well. A statistical sample can deviate in statistically significant ways from what it confirms about a population and still be used to gather knowledge about that population. For example, a sample might give us knowledge that most swans are white even though the actual percentage of white swans is significantly different from what our sample confirms. In such a case, the statistical sample grounds some knowledge but also confirms some falsehoods. Suppose our sample has 80 percent white swans, and, being somewhat sophisticated statistically, we know that the range for two standard deviations is 76 to 84 percent, that is, there is a 95 percent chance that the actual population is in that range, given the randomness of our sample. I use this information to conclude that most swans are white and acquire knowledge on this basis. The sample confirms other claims – for example, that the actual population is between 78 and 82 percent white, because the likelihood of this claim is fairly high given my sample (not 95 percent, but, say, 90 percent). Suppose, then, that the population is actually 83 percent white. Then I know that most swans are white on the basis of evidence that confirms a falsehood for me.

If the actual population were quite skewed from my sample (suppose it is only 60 percent white), then we would need to grant, I think, that the sample can't give inductive knowledge. Furthermore, in the preceding case, I assume that if a probability for a claim is known to be .9, that's enough for confirmation. One might choose to set the threshold for justification higher, but the same conclusion can still be employed that knowledge can be present when one's evidence confirms some falsehoods.

The lesson is that approaches that emphasize the role that falsehoods play in Gettier problems will have to be restricted in order to avoid such difficulties for this approach. Once defenders of this approach back away from the claim that knowledge issues a blanket protection against falsehoods related in some special way to one's body of evidence, they will need to appeal to some feature of this set of falsehoods *different from their falsity* to explain why immunization from these particular falsehoods is valuable. No such approach of this type has attempted such an explanation, and I know of no promising approach along these lines (in part because every approach along these lines is subject to counterexample[19]).

A second approach to the Gettier problem emphasizes concepts such as causality, reliability, or conclusive reasons characterized in terms of counterfactual claims. We have already seen reasons for thinking that reliability approaches succumb to the swamping problem, so approaches that employ such concepts will be unsuccessful here as well in explaining the value of knowledge. Moreover, standard causal theories of knowledge simply are not general enough to be adequate to all the kinds of knowledge that we have, including mathematical knowledge and moral knowledge. Steiner's approach cited earlier, which tries to salvage the generality of the causal approach, requires that sentences play a causal role in belief formation in order for knowledge to be present (in particular, he requires that the sentence that expresses p be used in a causal explanation of why the belief that p is true), but that approach simply cannot work. Some animals and prelinguistic children have knowledge, but sentences play no causal role in the explanation of the truth of their beliefs.

Perhaps what Steiner intends is not that the sentence plays a causal role, but rather that we, the explainers, must use that sentence in providing an explanation. Still, such a theory implies the existence of explainers, possibly distinct from those who hold the beliefs in question. Some worlds contain both explainers and believers, and some do not; so this attempt to salvage full generality for the causal approach cannot work either. Nor will it work to make the appeal to explainers conditional – that if a successful explanation were carried out, it would appeal to a sentence that expresses p. Just think of the attempt to explain the possibility of God knowing that he has created a world in which no linguistic items exist. The only worlds in which an explanation could be carried would be worlds in which the claim in question would be false, and hence the explanation would be unsuccessful.

Among this group, we are left, then, only with the conclusive reasons approach, which emphasizes what would happen, epistemically, in close counterfactual situations. This approach in terms of counterfactuals and the defeasibility approach provide the most promising approaches to the Gettier problem. The defeasibility theory is formulated in terms of what happens to justification when additional evidence is taken into account, for a defeater is a claim that, in conjunction with the evidence that justifies

19. See ibid., for a catalog of such attempts and counterexamples to each.

the belief, fails to justify that belief. In the remainder of this chapter, I want to focus on these more promising approaches to the Gettier problem. I want to argue that neither approach has much hope of accounting for both the nature and value of knowledge.

COUNTERFACTUAL AND DEFEASIBILITY APPROACHES TO THE GETTIER PROBLEM

Consider first how the defeasibility approach fails regarding the value of knowledge. At first glance, this approach offers much promise regarding the question of the value of knowledge, for it is a valuable to have an epistemic standing that is not defeated by any additional information. The difficulty is that this explanation of what is valuable is too strong, for knowledge doesn't require immunity from defeat by just *any* additional information, for one of the lessons of the literature is that not all defeaters undermine knowledge.[20]

How is this possible? That is, how can there be additional information that defeats justification but doesn't undermine knowledge? Consider a minor variant on the earlier Tim–Tom case. In that case, what defeats Joe's justification for believing that Tom stole the book is the testimony of Tom's mother. In particular, it is her claim that Tom was out of town and that Tom has a twin brother, Tim, that defeats Joe's justification. But now imagine the testimony also including an admission of lying. That is, suppose that Tom's mother, just after claiming that Tom was out of town and that he has a twin brother, says, "Oh, my gosh, what am I saying? I'm tired of trying to protect him. I recant this poor excuse of an alibi for Tom." Then the testimony of Tom's mother does not undermine Joe's knowledge, even though it contains a defeater of the justification that Joe has.

So even if we value undefeated justification, that gives us no reason to value knowledge over justified true belief, for knowledge does not eliminate defeaters. Part of what makes the concept of defeat significant is what it implies about further learning. If your justification is undefeated, then you could pursue further investigation in an unlimited fashion and never encounter information that justifies changing your mind. You would have the assurance that further investigation would continue to confirm exactly what you currently believe, giving one clear license

---

20. To my knowledge, Peter Klein first saw this. His own theory of the distinction is presented in *Certainty* (Minneapolis: University of Minnesota Press, 1981).

to stop the investigation if one chooses. Such assurance is lost, however, once we note that not all defeaters undermine knowledge.

The language used to describe the two kinds of defeaters I have been discussing is noteworthy and instructive. In cases where a defeater is present that does not undermine knowledge, the defeater is said to be a "misleading" one. Knowledge can then be understood in terms of justified true belief that is subject to no nonmisleading, or "genuine," defeaters. This language signals, I believe, an implicit recognition of the need to address the question of the value of knowledge, for these terms are clearly value-laden.

The difficulty for the defeasibility approach is precisely the one we encountered with the relevant alternatives approach earlier. The concept of relevance, too, serves to indicate the need to address the question of the value of knowledge, but fails to give an adequate account of the nature of knowledge unless it is explained in terms other than to say that an alternative is relevant if what happens in it can undermine knowledge. In the same way, if one's explanation of the distinction between a genuine and a misleading defeater were that the first undermines knowledge and the second doesn't, we would again have no successful addressing of the question of the nature of knowledge. In both cases, resources for explaining the value of knowledge are retained at the cost of circularity in the account of the nature of knowledge.

So if the defeasibility theory is an advance over the relevant alternatives theory, it can only be so by offering some more substantive account of the distinction between misleading and genuine defeaters. To their credit, defeasibility theorists have devoted considerable attention to this issue. The problem, I will argue, is that their attempts do not track any distinction in value, as the language of genuine and misleading suggests.

For example, one might try to redeem the defeasibility approach by claiming that when you are subject only to defeaters that do not undermine knowledge, you could learn everything epistemically relevant to your belief and still be justified in believing what you currently believe. This reply is at the heart of defeasibility approaches that appeal to the power of overriders to explain why some defeaters are misleading and others are not. When a defeater is misleading, there is a further piece of information that, together with one's original justification and the misleading defeater, still provides justification for one's belief. Moreover, this hierarchy of defeat and overriding is not limited to two levels but can go indefinitely high, so that one's understanding of knowledge is in terms of justifications for which any defeaters are ultimately overridden.

To see why this approach does not go very far in addressing the question of the value of knowledge, compare this hierarchy of defeaters and overriders with cases in which one's justification is simply defeated. In this latter case, it is still true that one's belief is correct and that one would still be justified in believing what one believes were one to learn everything epistemically relevant to what one believes. It is for this reason that one can define omniscience in terms of being justified in believing p if and only if p is true.[21] So we have two cases, one of knowledge and one not, but in both cases, there is information that, if learned, would undermine our justification. Furthermore, there is additional information beyond this defeating information that, if learned, would restore our justification. In the one case, these additional pieces of information are so related that knowledge is present. In the other case, they are not. Yet, nothing in the account gives any reason to suggest that additional pieces of information so related that knowledge is present constitute something of special value, over and above additional pieces of information so related that knowledge is not present. Hence, the defeasibility approach based on the hierarchy of defeaters and overriders is unhelpful in explaining the value of knowledge in terms of the value of its constituents.

Peter Klein has a slightly different proposal, one relying on the distinction he formulates in terms of "effective" and "initiating" defeaters. An effective defeater is one that breaks the chain of confirmation for one's belief. An initiating defeater is one that renders plausible some effective defeater, and such a defeater is misleading when the chain between it and the effective defeater depends essentially on misinformation independent of the evidence a person has. As Klein puts it, "The defeating effect of the initiating defeater is essentially parasitic upon misinformation which does not depend upon any false proposition in E_s [the set of evidence for the person in question]."[22]

There are concerns about this account that arise from the point of view of both the nature of knowledge and the value of knowledge. First, it is critical for the success of Klein's account that misleading defeaters, by themselves, do not undermine chains of confirmation. For example, in the Tim–Tom case, the testimony of the mother is supposed to be misleading evidence when it is part of a pattern of protective behavior of which the police are fully aware and regarding which there is a long

---

21. See Jonathan L. Kvanvig, *The Possibility of an All-Knowing God* (London: Macmillan, 1986), for a full defense of this account of omniscience.
22. Klein, *Certainty*, p. 148.

history. For Klein's account to succeed, the claim that the mother so testifies to the police cannot itself be an effective defeater. If this account is to succeed, that information cannot, by itself, undermine the confirming power of perceptual evidence and background acquaintance with the person who stole the book. The difficulty, from the point of view of the nature of knowledge, is that this restriction is not obviously satisfied. It is true that the testimony of the mother confirms other propositions that also defeat the confirming power of one's evidence regarding who stole the book, propositions such as *Tom has a twin brother whom I cannot distinguish from Tom, and this twin was at the library yesterday*. Klein's position requires, however, that only such propositions as the latter undermine the confirming power of one's evidence. I think that view is implausible. The contrary testimony of people deemed to be in a position of greater authority on a particular subject is, by itself, sufficient to undermine the confirming power of one's evidence. A sufficient explanation for abandoning a complex claim about probability is that my friend, Daren, an expert on probability theory, says the claim is false. That is all the reason I need for abandoning the claim, and it is a reason for abandoning the claim because in normal circumstances it is sufficient, in itself, to undermine the confirming power of whatever evidence I had for the claim.

My claim here may suggest a strongly nonholistic conception of confirmation, but it does not require it. Whether one thinks of the confirmation relation as a two-place relation between propositions or as a three-place relation between two claims and some background information, the point still holds. Expert testimony, by itself, is enough to undermine confirmation (given normal kinds of background information).

This objection to Klein's proposal is a concern over its adequacy as an account of the nature of knowledge. Concerns over its adequacy to help account for the value of knowledge are equally pressing. There are several ways, on his account, that defeaters can be present and yet not undermine knowledge. Consider again Klein's characterization of misleading defeaters quoted earlier:

The defeating effect of the initiating defeater is essentially parasitic upon misinformation which does not depend upon any false proposition in E_s.

In attempting to account for the value of knowledge, we need to consider some contrasting kinds of defeaters. One kind is a "one-step-removed" defeater: information that renders plausible some other information that undermines one's evidence. We can contrast such a defeater with a "direct" defeater, a bit of information that simply undermines the confirming

128

power of one's evidence. If we use Klein's account to explain the value of knowledge over that of justified true belief, we might try to maintain that it is better to be subject to a one-step-removed defeater than to a direct defeater (because, on his account, one-step-removed defeaters are less likely to undermine knowledge than are direct defeaters). Such a proposal is akin to saying that second cousins are better than first cousins. From some perspectives, that may be true: Second cousins are perhaps less likely to ruin one's reputation by association. From other perspectives, it is simply not obvious. My selfish genes, it is said, find more at stake in the welfare of first cousins than second cousins, for example. Similar points can be made regarding Klein's distinction in types of unpossessed information.

There is, of course, a circular way to get the desired explanation of the value of knowledge: We could identify one kind of unpossessed information as more valuable because of its association with knowledge and then cite that value as the basis for explaining the value of knowledge over that of its subparts. If we are careful to avoid such obvious circularity, however, no account will be forthcoming, for there is no reason to think that immunity from direct defeaters is preferable to immunity from defeaters once removed.

One might try to explain the value difference here in terms of the possibility of confirming falsehoods, that a once-removed defeater may confirm falsehoods and a direct defeater won't, but that proposal will not work. Almost any (contingent) falsehood can confirm a falsehood, as we saw earlier in this chapter. The only relevant difference here is whether the confirmation of falsehoods is the kind that allows or prevents the certification of a knowledge claim, but we can't use that information to infer that one kind is better than the other without endorsing a blatantly circular account of the value of knowledge.

There is one more feature of Klein's proposal that bears noting. The proposal that "The defeating effect of the initiating defeater is essentially parasitic upon misinformation which does not depend upon any false proposition in Es" distinguishes between misinformation that depends on false claims in one's body of evidence and misinformation that does not depend on false claims in that evidence. The first kind is "false-evidence-dependent," the second not. When a defeater is parasitic on false-evidence-dependent misinformation, it cannot undermine knowledge; when a defeater is not parasitic on misinformation that is false-evidence-dependent, it can.

It is hard to see this distinction as anything more than gerrymandering needed to prevent counterexamples to one's account of the nature of knowledge, and it is easy to side with Williamson in remarking, "Why should we care about *that*?" The distinction between these kinds of defeaters tracks no intuitive difference in value, leaving us with an account of the nature of knowledge incapable of helping to explain the value of knowledge. As noted before, there is a circular account available, one that presumes on the value of knowledge to explain the significance of the proposed distinction, but we have rehearsed the error of this way enough already.

Klein's proposal is instructive regarding the pattern to be found among defeasibility theorists and more generally among the more sophisticated approaches to the Gettier problem. The initial formulation shows signs of sensitivity to the need for giving an explanation of the value of knowledge, for the initial formulation normally cites a property of belief that would be valuable to have. After the initial formulation, however, emendations are introduced with no apparent eye at all to the issue of the value of knowledge. The procedure appears to presuppose that the issue of the value of knowledge has already been solved by giving an initial formulation sensitive to that issue, so that emendations can be made to the initial formulation that ignore the question of the value of knowledge. Of course, no one reasons explicitly in this way, but the pattern of refinement for the initial approaches has all the flaws of theorizing based on this reasoning.

A more likely explanation concerns the myopia that sets in when one is trying to solve an exceedingly difficult problem, and Klein's language is instructive in this regard. Just prior to offering his characterization of which defeaters fail to undermine knowledge, Klein says, "But *there is a common feature* in all of the cases in which the initiating defeater is misleading."[23] This language betrays a focus solely on the issue of the nature of knowledge, for the point of looking for a common feature among a group of cases is to find a criterion for dividing them that is immune from counterexample. It is no wonder, once such myopia takes over, that the result is a condition on knowledge with nothing to commend it for the task of explaining the value of knowledge.

It may be thought that such myopia is present from the start when dealing with the Gettier problem, but I remain unconvinced. The point is not all that important, but it is instructive to notice that the usual approaches to the Gettier problem are presented in value-laden terminology: relevant

23. Ibid; italics mine, added to highlight the instructive phrase.

130

alternatives, undefeated justification, conclusive reasons, and so on. Even if the theorizing pays no explicit attention to the question of the value of knowledge, this language shows the significance of the question and some (perhaps only implicit) interest in addressing it. The difficulty raised by the Gettier problem soon comes to dominate, and proposals become qualified with no eye whatsoever to the problem of the value of knowledge.

Once one becomes sensitized to the problem of the value of knowledge and its particular incarnation regarding the Gettier problem, it is easy to spot flaws in other versions of the defeasibility theory. For example, consider that version proffered by John Pollock and Richard Swinburne, aimed at accounting for the assassination case presented earlier, in which information generally available undermines any claim to knowledge. Swinburne says:

I concur with Pollock that the difference lies in what 'we are socially expected to be aware of'. 'We are expected to know what is announced on television' ... (I have replaced Pollock's phrase 'expected to know', question-begging in this context, by 'expected to believe'.)[24]

Swinburne notes that we cannot give a noncircular account of knowledge if we use the phrase "expected to know" and so prefers to formulate the position in terms of what we are expected to be aware of or to believe.

One problem with this approach is that it does not generalize well to other cases involving the difference between misleading and genuine defeaters, such as the difference between the two Tim–Tom cases discussed earlier. In one of these cases we have only the mother's testimony, and in the other we have her testimony plus an admission that she is lying and wishes to retract her testimony. Whatever the explanation of the difference between these cases, it has nothing to do with what we are socially expected to be aware of or to believe.

Furthermore, once we are sensitive to the need to account for the value of knowledge, we will question the usefulness of this approach, even if we had thought the approach was counterexample-free. We will wonder why it is important or valuable to possess information we are expected to be aware of, questioning how our contemporaries could be so unfailingly right about which information is important to possess and which isn't.

24. Richard Swinburne, *Epistemic Justification* (Oxford: Oxford University Press, 2001), pp. 191–2. The reference to Pollock's view is from *Contemporary Theories of Knowledge* (Totowa, NJ: Rowman & Littlefield, 1986), p. 192.

Immediately after noting his agreement with Pollock, Swinburne expresses some worries about the approach:

But, of course, such expectations vary with the society, and give rise to large border areas with respect to which experts may well differ about what is socially expected or about which they agree that expectations are diverse. There may well be societies in which everyone consults a suspect's mother before reaching judgments about guilt. And how 'nationwide' would the television coverage need to be, in order to undermine Jill's claim to knowledge?[25]

Swinburne uses these considerations about the variability of expectations to introduce a discussion of contextualism, which may rescue this approach. These considerations suggest the need for a strong form of relativism about the concept of undefeated justification, a form of relativism whose weaknesses are not mitigated by an appeal to contextualism. One of the most difficult problems for any version of relativism regarding evaluative concepts is how infallibility could plausibly be vested in the attitudes of peoples or groups. If relativism is offered as an account of what is morally good and bad, the question is how a society could be incapable of error about such matters. If relativism is offered as an account of when certain defeaters undermine knowledge and when they do not, a similar question is pressing. Once we have focused on the question of the value of knowledge and are looking for an account of the fourth condition for knowledge that helps explain why knowledge is more valuable than mere justified true belief, we will want an answer to the question of how people's expectations could infallibly track this difference in value. There is simply no reason whatsoever to think that expectations can't be off-base about what is valuable in this respect, just as there is no reason to think that groups of people can't be mistaken about what is morally right and wrong.

The appeal to contextualism at this point is a nonstarter. I will discuss the contribution contextualism might make to the question of the value of knowledge in later chapters, but the point to note here is that if contextualism gives us nothing beyond the relativizing of questions of value to the attitudes of one's peers or any other group, it will be no help in addressing the problem of the value of knowledge. As we will see, contextualism comes in much more plausible forms, leaving room for contextualists to incur no obligation to solve this knotty problem for relativism. Contextualists are free to agree that from the perspective

25. Ibid., p. 197.

of the question of the value of knowledge, an account of the difference between misleading and genuine defeaters in terms of expectations of peers tracks no important difference between kinds of unpossessed information.

So, to turn away from specific kinds of defeasibility theories to the general approach that such theories take, we encounter once again a bald and unqualified approach that suggests a possible explanation of the value of knowledge over subsets of its constituents. Yet, the bald and unqualified approach yields an inadequate account of the nature of knowledge, so qualifications are necessary. The urged qualifications eliminate the attractiveness of the approach for explaining the value of knowledge, however, even if they raise the prospects for such an approach to succeed as a counterexample-free explanation of the nature of knowledge. The sad reality is that the hopes for satisfying the dual requirements on a theory of knowledge once again seem reciprocally related: As hope for satisfying one requirement rises, hope for satisfying the other diminishes, leaving us with an epistemology inadequate for explaining either the nature of knowledge or its value.

The last remaining approach is the conclusive reasons approach or, more generally, approaches that attempt to elucidate the nature of knowledge in terms of certain counterfactuals relating the claim believed with the holding of the belief. Labeling the approach as a conclusive reasons approach is a little misleading, because versions of this approach do not appeal to the concept of a reason at all but instead use counterfactuals containing only the concepts of belief and the truth and falsity of such, counterfactuals such as *If the claim in question were false, one would not believe it* and *In similar situations in which one believes the claim, it is true.*

To see why the language of reasons is out of place in this approach, note that which possible situations are closest to the actual situation is often an objective feature outside our understanding or grasp of a situation, and thus outside of, independent of, the reasons we possess. Consider a case where one has strong evidence for a claim, where one has checked and rechecked some simple arithmetical sums on a sheet of paper, confirming that all the work on that sheet is correct. In some such cases, the counterfactuals in question will be true, and in other cases with precisely the same quality of reasons, the counterfactuals will be false. For the reasons themselves do not *make* the counterfactuals true or false. A more natural suggestion is that the counterfactuals are true or false, depending on the nature of the persons involved. That nature might be the kind of nature that would result in the acquisition of the reasons in question, so reasons do play a role, perhaps, in some way, but it is not the quality of reasons but rather the quality or character or nature of the person having the reasons that carries explanatory weight. That is, the reference to quality of reason is not nearly as important as, say, the reference to the person's ability to track the truth of what is believed.[26] The counterfactuals in question express the power or ability of a person with respect to the truth, because the person is such that the claim in question would not be believed if it were false, nor would one fail to believe the truth in close counterfactual circumstances, slightly different from the actual circumstances, in which the claim is true. With Ernest Sosa, we can call these two conditions "sensitivity" and "safety."[27] A belief is sensitive when it is abandoned in conditions where its content is false, and a belief is safe when it is held only when it is true.

Unfortunately, this approach is not as successful as one would like. First, note that the truth of the counterfactuals in question is of little interest. A benevolent demon might devote himself to making the appropriate counterfactuals true so that some person's beliefs are technically safe and sensitive; another, malevolent demon might make those same counterfactuals false regardless of the quality of my evidence or the content of one's intellectual character. Hence, the truth or falsity of these counterfactuals alone is of no special interest to us, so if their truth is what makes the difference between justifed true belief and knowledge, then knowledge is of no special importance either.

There is a reply here, that it is not the truth of the counterfactuals that interests us, but the *explanation* of their truth. We want the counterfactuals to be true in virtue of capacities or abilities we have in finding the truth, so even though the mere truth of the counterfactuals may not be important or valuable, their truth in virtue of our powers is. If the counterfactuals are true because of the activity of some demon, they don't interest us much; but if they are true in virtue of our cognitive powers, they interest us, and properly so.

The question we must ask, however, is what all this has to do with knowledge. It is not hard to see that knowledge is not found simply by adding this condition to those already determined to be valuable. First, there are counterexamples to the claim that sensitivity is a requirement

---

26. Robert Nozick, *Philosophical Explanations* (Cambridge, MA: Harvard University Press, 1981).
27. Ernest Sosa, "Plantinga on Epistemic Internalism," *Warrant in Contemporary Epistemology*, Jonathan L. Kvanvig, ed., (Totowa, NJ: Rowman & Littlefield, 1996), pp. 73–86.

for knowledge. Consider, for example, Goldman's dog example.[28] I look at a dachsund and know that it is a dog. If the animal confronting me weren't a dog, it would be a wolf (by whatever details of nature one wishes to include to make this particular claim true). I am not very good at distinguishing wolves from dogs, we might suppose, so if I were not currently confronted with a dog, I would still believe that what I was confronted with is a dog. Still, my failure to be able to distinguish wolves from dogs should have no bearing on the present case, for I am not at all confused about whether a dachsund is a dog.

For another example, consider a case of knowledge by induction. June drops a trash bag down a garbage chute at her apartment building. A short time later, the bag is in the basement garbage room. June knows about the structure of the garbage chute and has often gone to the basement to retrieve something from her garbage that she hadn't meant to throw away. On the basis of past experience and relevant background knowledge, June knows on this occasion that her garbage is in the basement. But her belief is not sensitive. In the extremely unlikely event that her trash bag does not end up in the basement, it would be because it became snagged on the wall of the chute, and if it did, June would still believe that her garbage is in the basement. Nonetheless, June now knows, on inductive grounds, that her garbage is in the basement.[29]

Sosa's safety clause, which requires that June would believe that her garbage is in the basement only if her garbage would be in the basement, fares no better with this case. First, note that we cannot read this safety clause in accord with the standard semantics for counterfactuals where any subjunctive is true when it has a true antecedent and a true consequent. Doing so would result in judging every true belief to be safe. And if every true belief is safe, then it is obvious that knowledge is not true belief that is both justified and safe – Gettier's own examples would undermine the view.

What Sosa has in mind regarding the truth conditions of this safety requirement is what goes on in close possible worlds. In particular, we are to consider close worlds in which the antecedent is true and see if the consequent is true in those worlds as well. For Sosa's account to succeed, he will have to maintain that no worlds are close enough to affect the assessment of the safety condition if such worlds contain an extremely unlikely event (such as the garbage not making it to the bottom of the

28. Goldman, "Discrimination and Perceptual Knowledge," p. 779.
29. Ernest Sosa, "Skepticism and Contextualism," *Philosophical Issues*, 10 (2000): 1–18.

chute). Put slightly differently, the truth of the safety condition is not affected by counterfactual situations in which extremely unlikely events occur. For if close worlds can contain unlikely events, then one close world would be one where June believes her garbage is in the basement when in fact it is hung up somewhere in the chute.

Such a requirement, the requirement that close worlds cannot contain extremely unlikely events, forces unacceptable conclusions in lottery situations. It forces one to hold that one can know that one's ticket will lose. The belief that one's ticket will lose can be justified if the lottery is large enough, but we should balk at the idea that such a belief can count as knowledge. If someone says that he knows his ticket will lose, he should be reprimanded: He is justified in being very confident that it will lose, but he does not know that it will lose.

Such a belief is nonetheless safe on the interpretation of safety required to render the safety requirement immune from the garbage chute example. On that interpretation, close worlds cannot contain extremely unlikely events. If so, however, then the belief that one's lottery ticket will lose is safe. It is true that a person would believe that his or her ticket lost only if it did in fact lose, if the interpretation of this conditional excludes worlds in which extremely unlikely possibilities, such as one's ticket winning the lottery, are excluded.

One might suggest, as does Greco, that we interpret safety a bit more weakly, so that a belief is safe when usually it would be held only if it is true.[30] Such a weakening makes the account even more susceptible to counterexamples, however. Consider a 1,000-ticket lottery and construct increasingly large disjunctions claiming that certain tickets win as follows: One of tickets 1–500 will win, one of 1–501 will win, one of 1–502 will win, and so on. At some point in this sequence, before reaching the claim that one of 1–1,000 will win, we will reach the threshold at which safety, on this interpretation, will have been reached, implying that it is possible to know that such a claim is true. We must reject such a claim, however, for we can construct an incompatible set of propositions of the same likelihood, all having the same claim to knowledge. Suppose the threshold is achieved at the 75 percent level, so that the belief that one of tickets 1–750 will win is a safe belief. Then so is the belief that one of tickets 2–751 will win, and so is the belief that one of tickets 3–752 will

30. John Greco, "Knowledge as Credit for True Belief," *Intellectual Virtue: Perspectives from Ethics and Epistemology*, Michael DePaul and Linda Zabzebski, eds. (Oxford: Oxford University Press, forthcoming), p. 4 typescript.

win. If we take the set of all combinations of 75 percent of the tickets and consider beliefs that each member of this set will win, we get an inconsistent set of beliefs that are nonetheless all safe by this weakened account of safety. Not all members of this set can be true, and yet every member of the set is in precisely the same epistemic condition on the interpretation of safety under consideration. The proper conclusion to draw is that this epistemic condition is insufficient for knowledge.

Timothy Williamson also has argued against a sensitivity requirement,[31] endorsing instead something like a safety requirement, claiming that when one knows, one cannot easily be mistaken – the very language used by Sosa to introduce the concept of safety. He gives a counterexample to sensitivity that contains language that provides the basis for learning a more general lesson. He says:

> I tend slightly to underestimate the distances I see. When I see a distance of twenty-one metres I judge it to be less than twenty metres, although when I see a distance of twenty-three metres I do not judge it to be less than twenty metres. This may mean that when I see a distance of nineteen metres and correctly judge it to be less than twenty metres, I do not know it to be less than twenty metres. It surely does not mean that when I see a distance of one metre and correctly judge it to be less than twenty metres, I do not know it to be less than twenty metres. . . . Suppose that a mark on the side of a ship is one metre above the waterline. . . . I judge by sight whether the mark is less than twenty metres above the waterline. Let p be the proposition that the mark is less than twenty metres above the waterline. If p had been false, I might still believe p. I believe p insensitively. Surely I can still know p, because I believe p on quite different evidence from that on which I would have believed it had it been false.[32]

This example is important for both sensitivity and safety theories, for Williamson's example is easily adapted to form a counterexample to safety as well as sensitivity. Williamson would still have knowledge in the case he describes even if his estimates of distance were much more unreliable. Suppose, for instance, that he judged anything over five meters to be no less than twenty meters. He can still know that the mark that is in fact one meter above the waterline is less than twenty meters above the waterline. His belief is not sensitive, but neither is it safe: In most cases where he judges the mark to be less than twenty meters above the waterline, he is wrong.

---

31. Timothy Williamson, *Knowledge and Its Limits* (Oxford: Oxford University Press, 2000), chapter 7.
32. Ibid., pp. 159–60.

Williamson's discussion contains an explanation of why such examples pose problems: The evidence would be different from the evidence on which the actual belief is based. So if any of the approaches that employ counterfactuals is going to succeed at identifying the nature of knowledge, the antecedent of such counterfactuals will have to include a clause requiring sameness of evidence. Failure to do so will leave such theories open to Williamson-like counterexamples.

Other refinements are possible as well. Nozick, for example, wants to restrict the antecedent of the sensitivity requirement so that the same method is employed.[33] As before, however, refinement occurs at the expense of attention to the question of the value of knowledge. The question we must always ask is whether the refinement proposed makes a difference in the realm of value. For example, suppose that a justified true belief is not safe or sensitive when these conditions are defined with no restriction on the method employed. Suppose further that a justified true belief is both safe and sensitive when these conditions are defined with a restriction on the method employed (or, if one prefers, with a restriction to ensure sameness of evidence). Terms like 'safe' and 'sensitive' are value-laden terms and seem like the kinds of properties it would be good for a belief to have. These terms, however, are merely placeholders for certain counterfactual conditionals, one set being restricted by the method employed and the other set not. As far as I can see, the only way to arrive at the conclusion that it is more valuable to satisfy one such set of counterfactuals is by first identifying that set as the one connected with knowledge and assuming that knowledge is valuable. If so, however, we have precisely the same difficulty here as I highlighted with the relevant alternatives approach. We have, that is, no resources for explaining the value of knowledge in terms of the value of its constituents, because the identified constituent has no claim to value except in virtue of some supposed connection with knowledge, which is assumed to be valuable.

So we arrive at the same point with the more promising approaches to the Gettier problem that we began with concerning the relevant alternatives approach. In each case, such approaches offer something of value that might be used to explain the value of knowledge, but each such approach faces immediate difficulty concerning the nature of knowledge. Counterexamples to the initial formulation of the approach force alterations in the approach, and the alterations are guided exclusively by concern

33. Nozick, *Philosophical Explanations*, pp. 179ff.

138

over the nature of knowledge, resulting in emendations of the original suggestion that appear entirely ad hoc from the point of view focusing on the question of the value of knowledge. That is, if we devote attention not only to the adequacy of such approaches in terms of the nature of knowledge but also to the adequacy of such approaches in terms of the value of knowledge, no such emendations have much to recommend them. As the prospects rise for providing a counterexample-free account of the nature of knowledge, the prospects sink for providing an account of knowledge in terms of the value of its constituents.

CONCLUSION

Two conclusions are warranted by our discussion. Extant approaches to the Gettier problem offer no basis for explaining the value of knowledge over and above the value of true belief, subjective justification, and the display of virtuous intellects. The failure of these approaches gives a strong inductive argument for thinking that success is unlikely.

Sometimes such inductive evidence is compatible with optimism about ultimate success, as may be the case regarding scientific theories. Even though we have a scientific track record of failed theories, that record may also contain signs of progress so that the inductive argument for thinking that present and future theories will all be false fails. Here, though, the evidence points otherwise, leaving little ground for optimism here. When we look carefully at the variety of failed attempts to satisfy the twin desiderata concerning the nature and value of knowledge, we do not find signs of progress. We find, instead, a repeated pattern in which progress with respect to one desideratum is balanced by greater weakness with respect to the other. The heart of the Gettier problem concerns the presence of a certain kind of accidentality or luck, and our discussion provides a long and sustained basis for thinking that any value found in eliminating this kind of luck can only be found by assuming first the value of knowledge.

We have, therefore, a strong argument against the approach to the question of the value of knowledge pursued in the past four chapters: the approach that attempts to explain the value of knowledge in terms of the value of its constituents. The difficulties encountered in attempting to explain the value of knowledge through the value of its constituents show that we need a different approach. If knowledge is valuable, it is so on the basis of factors other than the value of its constituents. I turn to such alternative attempts in the next two chapters.

6

Knowledge as Irreducibly Valuable

It will be helpful to take a moment to reflect on where we are in our study of the value of knowledge. We began with the assumption that knowledge is valuable, arguing that this assumption is one of two central desiderata on any adequate theory of knowledge. First, an adequate theory of knowledge must give a correct account of the nature of knowledge. Second, an adequate theory of knowledge must account for the value of knowledge.

After defending the Socratic view that the value of knowledge is not to be found in relation to the practical realm or to other things external to knowledge, we pursued the idea that we should seek its value among its constituents. Traveling this path has led to some useful results, including accounts of the value of true belief, subjective justification, and displays of intellectual virtue. We have had to conclude, however, that this path fails to lead us to our destination, for the Gettier problem raises issues that give us reason for pessimism. In particular, we have seen grounds for thinking that a clause aimed at solving the Gettier problem will not cite some further constituent of knowledge that is valuable that explains how knowledge is more valuable than subsets of its constituents.

This conclusion has been anticipated by Timothy Williamson in a passage quoted in the previous chapter, and his reaction to it is instructive at this point in our inquiry. He says:

Even if some sufficiently complex analysis never succumbed to counterexamples, that would not entail the identity of the analysing concept with the concept *knows*. Indeed, the equation of the concepts might well lead to more puzzlement rather than less. For knowing matters; the difference between knowing and not knowing is very important to us. Even unsophisticated curiosity is the desire to *know.* This importance would be hard to understand if the concept *knows* were the more or less ad hoc sprawl that analyses have had to become; why should we care so much about *that*?[1]

Williamson anticipates the results of our study to this point, noting that the value of knowledge is not redeemable by the history of proposals regarding the Gettier problem. Williamson is so committed to the value of knowledge that he concludes that knowledge simply cannot be identified with any proposed analysis of it, but that conclusion is unwarranted. First, as I will argue later in this chapter, dictionary definitions can be misleading, and such is the case regarding curiosity. A more careful assessment of its nature will sever the link between curiosity and knowledge enough that the phenomenon cannot be used to demonstrate the value of knowledge. Moreover, Williamson's discussion confuses two quite different issues. In his argument against extant analyses of knowledge, he appeals to the claim that the difference between knowing and not knowing is important to us. I agree that this difference is important, but an explanation of the difference in value between knowing and not knowing is not necessarily an explanation of how knowledge is more valuable than its subparts. An account of the importance of the difference between knowing and not knowing could proceed as follows: Our chances of success in practical matters are higher, conditional on our knowing rather than not knowing. Such an explanation generates no explanation of how the value of knowledge exceeds that of its subparts. It is important to notice here that only the second issue, the issue of the value of knowledge in relation to that of its subparts, can give rise to Williamson's skepticism about proposed analyses of knowledge, for if knowledge is important, but not more valuable than its subparts, we would have no reason to object to ad hoc accounts of knowledge. So, instead of the importance of knowing versus not knowing, Williamson needs to appeal to a positive answer to the guiding issue of this study. He needs to claim that the value of knowledge must exceed that of its subparts, and here I think a more circumspect attitude is appropriate, at least by this point in our study. I am not counseling a rejection of this claim, but rather a more provisional acceptance of it than Williamson needs for his argument. The more we search for the value of knowledge and fail to uncover it, the more evidence we should acknowledge against the claim that knowledge is valuable. In fact, Williamson

---

1. Timothy Williamson, *Knowledge and Its Limits* (Oxford: Oxford University Press, 2000), p. 31.

uses precisely such a form of argument against the idea that knowledge is analyzable,[2] the form of argument that the more we fail in our attempts to analyze knowledge, the stronger our evidence that it is not analyzable. So it would be awkward for him to insist on the presupposition of the preceding passage, to wit, that we are so certain that knowledge is more valuable than its subparts that knowledge simply cannot be identified with anything like the various proposed analyses of it. Williamson should grant the same form of argument here, that the more detailed and penetrating our failed searches for the value of knowledge are, the more evidence we acquire that knowledge is not valuable.

Still, the search for a special value of knowledge is not complete if we only look for that value in terms of the values of its subparts, and Williamson's pessimistic conclusion about analyses of knowledge follows only on the opposite assumption. If we suppose that knowledge has special value explicable in terms other than the value of its parts, the ad hoc character of recent analyses of knowledge would not lose any credibility in the face of claims about the special value of knowledge.

So Williamson's preceding argument is too quick in a number of ways. It misidentifies the relevant question concerning the special value of knowledge, and it takes this special value as more of a given than is warranted. Most important for this chapter, it fails to consider the possibility that knowledge has a special value that cannot be accounted for in terms of the value of its constituents. Even if the value of knowledge cannot be accounted for in terms of the value of its constituents, there are other avenues to explore in search of the special value of knowledge. Contrary to Williamson's assumption, there is no decisive reason to suppose that the value of knowledge must be explicable in terms of the value of its constituents. That point remains true regardless of whether we view knowledge as simple, as analyzable, or as composite in some nonanalytic way. In this chapter and the next, we will explore these other avenues.

These other avenues attempt to find the value of knowledge more directly than by taking a route through its constituents or through pragmatic dimensions of its meaning and use. On these views, the value of knowledge is a direct and immediate property of it, a property it has in a more direct way than it would if the value of knowledge were a compilation of the value of its parts. The value is one of the whole itself, on these viewpoints, not a composite value generated by the value of its parts. As

2. Ibid., chapter 2.

a result, these approaches can stomach the failure of the previous chapter with equilibrium, for defenders of such views do not expect to find the value of knowledge by considering the value of its parts.

There are two quite different ways of attempting to defend the intrinsic value of knowledge, ways that I will term "descriptive" and "evaluative." The standard conception of knowledge places it within the realm of facts, part of the descriptive aspects of the world. It may make a difference to the world evaluatively as well, but not in any way that denies that what is known and what is not will form a part of the total set of facts, of a total correct description of the world. In recent years, however, approaches to knowledge have arisen that deny that there is any unique descriptive aspect of the world that is to be identified with knowledge. On this viewpoint, knowledge is an evaluative concept in which the valuational element distinctive of knowledge attaches to descriptive features of the world that are not to be identified with knowledge. Hartry Field is the first to have suggested such a viewpoint, but versions of it have been endorsed recently by Mark Heller and John Greco (though these latter will need to be convinced by later discussion that they in fact side with Field on this issue).[3] Evaluativism will be the subject of the next chapter, so the goal of the present chapter will be to address the issue of the intrinsic value of knowledge, making the standard assumption that, where it exists, knowledge is a factual feature of the world.

CURIOSITY AND THE INTRINSIC VALUE OF KNOWLEDGE

Consider, to begin, why someone might wish to claim that knowledge is intrinsically valuable. Upon seeing the difficulty of accounting for the value of knowledge in terms of its constituents, one might be convinced that no such account of the value of knowledge is forthcoming, but remain unmoved in one's view that knowledge is more valuable than its subparts. After all, the desire to know is ubiquitous; it is identified in the dictionary with human curiosity, a feature that pervades our species (and presumably any intelligent species with much survival value). After

---

3. Hartry Field, "The A Prioricity of Logic," *Proceedings of the Aristotelian Society*, 96 (1996): 359–79; "Epistemological Nonfactualism and the A Prioricity of Logic," *Philosophical Studies*, 92 (1998): 1–24; Mark Heller, "The Proper Role for Contextualism in an Anti-Luck Epistemology," *Philosophical Perspectives, 13, Epistemology*, James Tomberlin, ed. (Cambridge, MA: Blackwell, 1999), pp. 115–29; John Greco, "Knowledge as Credit for True Belief," *Intellectual Virtue: Perspectives from Ethics and Epistemology*, Mark DePaul and Linda Zabzebski, eds. (Oxford: Oxford University Press, forthcoming).

noticing this aspect of human nature, the rhetorical question "How *could* knowledge fail to be valuable?" is pressing. For human curiosity seems to require that knowledge is an object of our desires, and there is no reason whatsoever for thinking that there is anything illegitimate in this desire (even if certain expressions of curiosity are objectionable). So if knowledge isn't uniquely valuable in virtue of its contribution to other valuable things such as health and happiness, and if it isn't uniquely valuable in virtue of the value of its constituents, that gives no reason to think that knowledge isn't of unique value. If we can't find an explanation for the value of knowledge in terms of its relationship to other things, we should hold that it is intrinsically valuable rather than entertain the idea that it does not have the value we suppose it to have.

Before looking more closely at the nature of curiosity, I want to sound a cautionary note by way of reminder. It is easy at this point to lose track of the guiding question of our inquiry, which is whether knowledge is more valuable than its subparts. When we look at human inquiry and the nature of curiosity, it would be shocking to hear it argued that these features have no implications for the question of the value of knowledge. Nothing I will say here undermines the view that knowledge is important. Our question, however, is not whether there is some way to demonstrate that knowledge is valuable or intrinsically valuable. Rather, we inquire what kind of value knowledge has, in particular whether it has a value that exceeds that of its subparts.

With this reminder before us, let us look carefully at the phenomenon of curiosity and its connection to knowledge. First, we need to go beyond the quick definition of curiosity given earlier, for the dictionary definition that identifies curiosity with the desire to know isn't quite right. The dictionary picks desire as the internal motivational state involved in curiosity, but desire need not be the driving factor. There are other motivational states, such as one's interests or needs or instincts or drives, which need not be representational and which might underlie curiosity. Desire, I take it, is a representational mental state, so it need not be involved in curiosity.

Second, curiosity often drives inquiry even when one already knows something. For example, one can know by testimony that one's neighbor is a cross-dresser and still, out of curiosity, attempt to see for oneself. The result of looking will carry much more information than merely that one's neighbor is a cross-dresser, but the desire to see for oneself can be simply the desire to experience the cross-dressing itself and not a desire for the extra information that may be conveyed with that experience.

Neither of these points presents a serious difficulty for the defender of the special intrinsic value of knowledge based on the pervasiveness of curiosity. The first point leaves intact the idea that knowledge is the object of curiosity, and the second point can be accommodated as well. The desire to see for oneself is a desire for firsthand knowledge and is thus still a pursuit of knowledge, even if only a special kind. Knowledge can have special intrinsic value even if some kinds of it are more interesting to us than others.

There is, however, a third point about curiosity that is more pertinent, for there is an alternative account of curiosity, one that specifies the goal of the activity in terms of attempting to discover what is the case, in terms of attempting to find out (perhaps in the firsthand way) what is the actual character of the world. In short, the goal of curiosity is to find the truth. Such a search for truth will proceed via one's subjective standards for ascertaining truth, and thus when the motivational state is satisfied in the search for truth, one will have subjective justification for the claim that one has found the truth (or that such-and-such is the case).

This picture of curiosity is intimately tied to a question raised first in Chapter 1 of this book concerning the goal of inquiry. As we saw there, Sartwell claims that the goal of inquiry is knowledge, whereas the standard epistemologist's formulation of the epistemic goal is in terms of getting to the truth and avoiding error.

Here I side with standard epistemology, with some qualifications, for we need to describe the goal of inquiry so that it is applicable across the entire range of cognitive beings. My concern here is with attributing complex intentional states to small children and nonhuman animals that lack the conceptual resources to be accurately characterized by those states and yet display curiosity and engage in inquiry. Given this concern, the concept of truth has advantages over those of knowledge, for knowledge is a more complex concept than truth: A cognitive being can have the concept of truth without that of knowledge, but not vice versa, because truth is a conceptual component of knowledge. Still, the concept of truth is not itself innate, leaving open the possibility that curiosity can be displayed and that one can engage in inquiry absent even the concept of truth. Even so, such inquiry or curiosity is teleological, directed at some goal. The aim of such inquiry, from within the intentional states of the cognizer, is not to find the claims that are true, for such a characterization requires possession of the concept of truth by the cognizer. From the perspective of the cognizer with respect to a particular proposition p, the goal in question is to ascertain whether p or *not-p*,[4] not to ascertain whether or not p is true.

Once we see the teleological nature of inquiry and curiosity from the inside in this way, the most accurate way to describe it from the outside is in terms of some motivation for finding the truth, for the concept of truth allows us to generalize across all the particular instances of attempting to ascertain whether p or *not-p*, which is the accurate portrayal from the inside of the nature of inquiry and curiosity. It is in this way that the goal of inquiry and the nature of curiosity are to be identified with finding the truth and avoiding error.[5]

We have been approaching the issue of the goal of inquiry from the inside, from within the intentional realm of the individual inquirer. Goals can also be described from the outside, independently of how they are conceived or represented by the individual in question. This distinction leads to the question of what characterization of the goal of inquiry is appropriate from an external third-person perspective, for even if a first-person perspective does not favor the view that the goal of inquiry is knowledge, it may be that a third-person perspective is more favorable to that view.

From such a third-person perspective, we can assess the goals of an inquirer in two ways. We can look at the conditions under which the appetite for information is sated and characterize the goal in terms of that which typically sates the appetite for information. If we approach the question in this way, it is difficult to see how the concept of knowledge is going to play a role in explanation. A more plausible account than one that appeals to knowledge, on this approach, would be one that appeals to the concept of perceived truth. On this account, the phenomenon of curiosity and the goal of inquiry are characterized in terms of finding that which is perceived to be true regarding the subject matter in question, not in terms of coming to know the truth about that subject matter. For the sating of the appetite in question occurs when a perception or conviction of truth arises, and such conviction sometimes will constitute knowledge and sometimes it will not.

---

4. I note here that this formulation begs the question regarding bivalence and the related principle of the excluded middle, but because I am a fan of bivalence and the excluded middle, I will leave it as an exercise to those less enamored to reformulate the points so as not to beg that question.
5. I leave open the question of whether the goal of inquiry is all truths or only the important ones (or some other subclass). Interesting and important as that question is, it is not at issue here.

One way to think about this approach is to ask oneself what conceptual resources a mature science would need to describe inquiry and curiosity in as nearly a lawlike way as the phenomena permit. Is there any reason to suppose that such a mature science would appeal to the concept of knowledge? I think not. All that is needed is concepts such as "information," "belief," "strength," and "degree of conviction," perhaps some associated idea of reasons for such, and truth. One may try to argue that the concept of "knowledge" would still be present – for example, one might suggest that the concept of information possessed by a cognizer would be synonymous with what a cognizer knows – but that path would be difficult to follow. I see no reason to think that a mature science of human inquiry needs to be sensitive to Gettier issues in order to give adequate explanations of the human phenomenon of curiosity and the related search for truth.

I see parallels between this issue and the issue investigated in Chapter 1 concerning the nature of legitimate assertion. There I argued against the idea that knowledge is a norm of assertion, defending the view that justified belief is all that is needed. Here I think something similar is true about the resources needed to explain human inquiry from a third-person perspective. A mature scientific account of human inquiry and curiosity, just like a mature philology of legitimate assertion, needs less in the way of epistemology than some would like.

Another way to assess the goal of inquirers from a third-person perspective is to consider what their behavior would be if they were given full information about their situation. For example, if we consider the situation of an inquirer whose appetite for information has been sated by some found answer, but who does not know that answer to be correct, we could ask what such an inquirer would do if he or she was informed that the answer was not known to be correct. It is plausible to assume that inquiry would resume under such conditions, and this fact may be thought to lend credence to the view that knowledge is the goal of inquiry.

There are two points of weakness to note about this argument. The first is that we would get the same result if the person in question had not found the truth and were informed of such. So this argument for a connection between curiosity and knowledge is no better than a similar argument connecting curiosity with discovered truth. This weakness leads to a second, for if we are to compare these two proposals, we should inform our inquirers fully of their precise condition. Upon having their appetite for information sated, they are in one of three conditions: (i) they have not found the truth but think they have; (ii) they have found the truth but not in such a way that they have knowledge; and (iii) they have found the truth and know the information in question to be true. I submit that the only one of these three situations in which inquiry would resume would be condition (i). To inform someone that she had found the truth but had fallen short of knowledge would be met, I submit, with relative indifference. If one engages in curiosity-driven inquiry about who the present king of France is, and inquiry ceases when one becomes convinced that there is no present king of France, inquiry will not resume if one is told that it is true that there isn't a present king of France but that one's inquiry was not sufficient to give one knowledge that there is no present king of France. There would be no point in further effort unless one were motivated by something more than mere curiosity.

One might think that the testimony will result in one's coming to know that one's belief is true even if one didn't know beforehand. If so, the inquirer is no longer in the position of having found the truth but not knowing it to be true, and so the lack of further investigation is no argument against the view that curiosity is a desire to know.[6] It is true that testimony often generates knowledge, but it is also possible that a testifier is someone with sufficient credibility to give one grounds for doubt that one has knowledge, but not with sufficient credibility to generate knowledge of that to which he or she testifies. Cases of this sort occur, for example, when the testimony is that of experts with a mixed track record. Their track record might be good enough to provide grounds for doubting that we are right when they disagree with us, but spotty enough that their word is insufficient for knowledge. When such a testifier says that one has found the truth but lacks knowledge, such testimony does not impart knowledge, but neither would it be, in ordinary cases, a cause for further investigation (when the motivation is merely that of curiosity). "Yeah, yeah, who cares?" and "Whatever" come to mind when imagining how the curious might respond to such testimony.

The conclusion to draw, then, is that whether we look at curiosity from a first-person perspective or from a third-person perspective, there is no adequate justification for taking knowledge to be its object. In each case, a better explanation is available in terms of truth itself, either found truth, discovered truth, or a perception or conviction of truth.

As a final nail in the coffin of the idea that curiosity is intentionally directed at knowledge, let me explain the attraction of characterizing

---

6. This objection was brought to my attention by Wayne Riggs.

curiosity in this fashion. If we attend to the pragmatics of the concept of knowledge, one of the dominant features of it is a sense of closure to inquiry implied by its attribution. It makes no sense to say, "I know that it is raining, but I believe further inquiry is warranted." It is this pragmatic feature of closure or finality that makes attractive the knowledge-based conception of curiosity or inquiry. For such closure and finality is precisely what we seek when we are curious and when we engage in inquiry. Because the concept of knowledge is a primary concept for communicating such closure, it is natural to employ the concept of knowledge to characterize the nature of curiosity or the goal of inquiry, even though it is not strictly accurate.

How is this element of finality or closure achieved on the account of curiosity that characterizes it in terms of finding the truth? The answer is in terms of some level of subjective justification that achieves such finality or closure for each cognitive being. In seeking the truth, an individual acquires subjective justification for a claim, and when that level of subjective justification reaches a suitably high level, closure is experienced. We do not need to claim that the individual has a theoretical viewpoint about how high the level must be for closure or finality, for the level may itself be part of the hardware of the mechanism rather than a feature of its software.

So the reason the knowledge-based picture is attractive is that it is pragmatically suited to conveying this element of finality. Expressing this idea of closure in terms of the variable degrees of subjective justification needed for each person is quite complicated, so we resort to a simpler procedure. We express the closure sought through inquiry driven by curiosity by taking advantage of the pragmatic dimension of closure involved in the concept of knowledge. For this reason, it is natural to characterize curiosity as the desire to know, even though this definition is not strictly accurate.

There is one other point worth making about the proposal regarding the importance of curiosity and its connection to the question of the value of knowledge. We should ask what results we could expect had this approach succeeded. If curiosity is important and is conceptually linked with the concept of knowledge, we might be able to argue from these facts for the importance or value of knowledge. So if the worry under consideration was whether knowledge is important or valuable, the appeal to curiosity would be interesting and relevant. The problem is that the question to which this account would be an answer is one that we answered early in Chapter 1, where we noted the practical advantages that knowledge provides. We also noted, however, that there is more to giving an account of the value of knowledge than would be achieved by showing that it is valuable. The problem raised by Socrates in the *Meno* goes much deeper than that, raising the possibility that knowledge is valuable but not in a way that is superior to that of true belief or other of its subparts. So in appealing to the phenomenon of curiosity in defense of the value of knowledge, the defender of the value of knowledge is tilting at windmills. The point of our investigation, after the preliminary sections of Chapter 1, concerns deeper problems regarding the special value of knowledge raised in the *Meno*, not the issue of whether knowledge has any value at all. As the preceding arguments show, it is not clear that the phenomenon of curiosity could be used to establish even this preliminary point, but even if it could, it would not answer the deeper questions of the relative value of knowledge compared with that of its subparts.

THE DESIRE TO KNOW

So the ubiquity of curiosity and the nature of inquiry give no grounds for ending our investigation of the value of knowledge, even if we accept the importance of curiosity and the value of inquiry. Still, there is the pervasive element in common discourse in which people assert their desire to know, and we need to take account of such sincere assertion if we are to give a complete hearing to the idea that knowledge has a value that is intrinsic to it and not derivable from the value of its parts on the basis of the claim that the desire for it is so pervasive.

Regarding such claims, the first point to note is that it is very easy to confuse knowledge with related concepts that we have already found to be valuable. For example, it is valuable to have found the truth, and the subjective justification available for concluding that one has found the truth also provides justification for concluding that one has knowledge. In such a case, one could easily report the goal of the completed inquiry in terms of knowledge rather than in terms of having found the truth, if only because of the efficiency of the term 'knowledge' over the phrase 'found the truth'. In addition, by placing emphasis on platitudes such as "When you know, you can't be wrong," some will swear to a desire for knowledge because they value immunity from error. They want, that is, to find a resting point for inquiry that is absolutely certain and unrevisable. That desire, however, is a desire for something stronger than knowledge, not for knowledge itself.

Still, not all who claim the desire to know are confused. Consider, for example, the claims of Richard Feldman:

> I want to know things. If being sure is something like being justified, then that's not quite what I want either. I don't want to be a victim in a Gettier case. Consider an analogy, if at the end of my life I learned that my friends actually didn't much like me but instead were on a life long mission to act as if they did, I'd be disappointed. I'd feel as if I've been duped, even though my so-called friends actually did do all the seemingly friendly things I thought they did. I can imagine Jon asking why I'd care. Well, I don't know, but I would. In the knowledge case, my discovery would be that I've been right by accident. And that's not what I want. I want to know. This remains true even if I can't say why I want it, even if I can't say why knowledge is "better" than other states, and even if I can't understand what sort of value is supposed to be at issue when I'm asked why knowledge is better than true belief or accidentally true justified belief. So, I remain interested in having and theorizing about knowledge.[7]

Feldman combines these autobiographical remarks with some rather startling claims about the nature of value that might undergird some of the claims made earlier, and I want first to move past these claims about value to focus on the more important issues. Feldman says:

> The words "interesting" and "important" express relations. What's interesting to me may not be interesting to you. What's important in one setting or relevant to one set of questions or concerns may not be important to others. If one does not find certain questions interesting, or one concludes that their answers are not important for answering other questions one is pursuing, that's fine. But the unrelativized claims ought to be avoided. I am interested in knowing things and in finding out what knowledge is. It's important to me.[8]

If these claims about value were true, it would be easy to show the special value of knowledge. One would only need to find a person to whom knowledge is important, more important than whether he or she has any of knowledge's subparts. When we look at the first quote from Feldman, it is clear that there is such a person: Feldman himself.

The problem is that this account of value is inadequate, for it reduces some of the most important questions in life to trivialities. I ask, is it more valuable to devote oneself to the study of epistemology or to the study of medicine? and Feldman's answer is, that depends only on which

7. Richard Feldman, "Comments: Kvanvig on Externalism and Epistemology Worth Doing," *Southern Journal of Philosophy,* 38 (Suppl.), 2000: 49.
8. Ibid., p. 48.

is more important to me on which I value more. Feldman attributes too much infallibility to me and to himself. I can be wrong about what is valuable, just as anyone else can. It is possible to value something that is worthless, that is in fact not valuable. It is possible for something to be important to me that is utterly trivial, and it is possible for things to matter to me that ought not and need not matter to me. Feldman is simply wrong that value concepts always express relations, though that is one grammatically correct syntactic form in which terms of value occur. This paragraph contains multiple examples of another form, however, and it is a form in which terms expressing value concepts are one-place predicates. Furthermore, these linguistic facts mirror an important philosophical point: that Feldman's subjective view about value is implausible. Some things are more important than others, whether anyone recognizes it or not.

So let us put aside this subjectivism and consider what we should conclude from Feldman's sincere and unconfused avowal that he desires to know. Of course, it doesn't follow from this fact that knowledge is valuable, and some of Feldman's remarks suggest that he'll continue to value knowledge even if it isn't really valuable after all. He says he'll still want knowledge even if he "can't say why knowledge is 'better' than other states," even if he "can't understand what sort of value is supposed to be at issue." Such remarks can be taken in two ways: either "can't say" means something about the lack of a good theory, or it may mean that what is said is false. Consider the first option. Feldman may mean that he simply lacks a good theory of the value of knowledge and knows of no good direction to pursue in trying to find one. He may mean, even more strongly, that there simply isn't any good explanation of the value of knowledge, and so he "can't say" much about the value of knowledge. If that is what he means, then the more investigation we undertake that leaves the value of knowledge unexplained, the greater the inclination Feldman ought to develop to doubt that knowledge is valuable. It doesn't follow from the fact that there is no good explanation for p that p is false, but it provides evidence for that claim.

Consider cases where the inability to provide an explanation is compatible with our continued endorsement of the truth of a claim. In such cases, there is a meta-explanation available to account for this compatibility. For example, consider indeterminacies at the quantum level. Our usual pattern of searching for hidden variables is blocked in this case because of the strong evidence against hidden variable theories. So we continue to endorse the idea that such unexplained events occur precisely because we have a meta-explanation available to account for why such events occur without any adequate explanation of their occurrence.

If we pursue this analogy in the epistemological domain, we are entitled to assert the inexplicable value of knowledge only if we have a meta-explanation of why an explanation of the value of knowledge is impossible. I cannot rule out the possibility of such a meta-explanation, but no such explanation has been offered and it is very hard to see what one would look like. In the absence of progress on this front, the continued failure to find an adequate explanation of the value of knowledge counts against there being any such value. So if Feldman means that he simply hasn't found a correct account of the value of knowledge, continued failure in the search ought, at some point, to change his mind.

Consider, then, the second option. In this case, Feldman would be saying that he "can't say why knowledge is better than other states" because there is no good explanation of why knowledge is better than other states, in which case there is no truth of that sort to be found (absent some meta-explanation as to why there should be unexplained truth here). On this reading, Feldman is insisting that he'll still value knowledge even if it is not, in fact, valuable. That may be true as a piece of autobiography, but it is hard to find anything of philosophical substance in it. His preferences would amount to little more than a confession of what his hobbies are, admitting that what he cares about isn't really significant after all.

So the first thing to say about those who insist that they have a desire to know is that this desire is like many others that we have, desires that can be informed by investigation that they are misplaced. In this regard, Feldman's language is particularly instructive, for he does not claim that we have reached explanatory bedrock when it comes to the value of knowledge, as we would expect of one who thinks that knowledge is intrinsically valuable. Instead, he says that he doesn't want to have been right "by accident." I agree; I don't want to have been right by accident, but as we have already seen, we cannot identify knowledge with being nonaccidentally correct. Knowledge is always at least partially obtained by grace and never completely by works, and when we try to identify the kind of nonaccidentality that is characteristic of knowledge, we identify properties of belief that have no credible power for accounting for the value of knowledge.

Contrast this situation with that of true belief. We originally attempted an explanation of the value of true belief in pragmatic terms, but such an explanation succumbed to the equal pragmatic value of empirically adequate beliefs. Still, there is the intrinsic disvalue of being wrong, something

153

to which we are strongly averse. We do not want to be duped either by people or by nature.

Many will have noticed that the very property whose value is under discussion is appealed to in the explanation of its value. If we thought that we were making explanatory progress here, we should be accused of explanatory circularity. But there is a better explanation, one that appeals to the intrinsic value of true belief. When we find something of intrinsic value and attempt to explain its value, we are forced to resort to explanations that are apparently circular. For example, many take pain to be disvaluable. When questioned concerning its disvalue, it is hard to cite any explanation of its disvalue other than the fact that pain hurts. This is no explanation, however. Instead, what it indicates is an inability to explain the disvalue of pain in any other terms, indicating an account of the disvalue of pain on which pain is disvalued intrinsically. The same should be said about true belief. When we attempt to explain its disvalue, we do so in hopelessly circular fashion. Such hopeless circularity indicates in this case that we cannot explain the value of true belief in any terms other than itself. The value of true belief is a value that it has intrinsically.

Notice that Feldman talks in precisely these terms when it comes to true belief. He says, "if at the end of my life I learned that my friends actually didn't much like me but instead were on a life long mission to act as if they did, I'd be disappointed. I'd feel as if I've been duped, even though my so-called friends actually did do all the seemingly friendly things I thought they did. I can imagine Jon asking why I'd care. Well, I don't know, but I would." Feldman has a hard time explaining why true belief is valuable to him, even if it has no practical consequences, and is forced into just such an apparently circular explanation: He'd feel duped. An uncharitable interpretation of such remarks would simply note the circularity, but a more accurate understanding of what is occurring would attribute to Feldman a sense that the value of true belief is intrinsic to it, inexplicable in any terms other than itself.

The contrast between true belief and knowledge here is telling. When Feldman addresses the question of value, he does not engage in any such apparently circular explanation. Instead, he points to an explanation, albeit one that we have already seen to be inadequate: He doesn't want to be right only by accident. Such a reply suggests strongly that for Feldman the value of knowledge is not intrinsic but depends on the value of the constituents of knowledge. Furthermore, the difference Feldman expresses between true belief and knowledge is, I think, the common one. When trying to explain the value of true belief, we resort to circular explanations until we see that what we are after is an appeal to intrinsic value. In the case of knowledge, we do not resort to such circular explanations, but instead attempt to explain knowledge in other terms. That is, our natural inclination is not to think that knowledge is intrinsically valuable. We pull that idea out of the hat only in desperation at our inability to find any other adequate account.

I think, for these reasons, that it is not a plausible maneuver at this point to appeal to the intrinsic value of knowledge to address the problem of the value of knowledge. One other factor suggests the same. Even if we suppose that knowledge has intrinsic value, we have already granted that true belief does. The appeal to the intrinsic value of knowledge is a good answer if the question is whether knowledge has any value at all. As we have seen before in this chapter and elsewhere, however, that question is only the first part of the problem of the value of knowledge raised in the *Meno*. The problem bequeathed to us by Plato also requires an explanation of why knowledge is more valuable than true belief, and even if knowledge is intrinsically valuable, that fact by itself provides no explanation whatsoever of why its value exceeds that of true belief. If anything, the natural explanation goes in the opposite direction: If x is both intrinsically valuable and a component of y, then y's intrinsic value is explicable in terms of the intrinsic value of x. So not only does it appear to be a mistake to claim that knowledge is intrinsically valuable (except in virtue of the intrinsic value it has because true belief is one of its constituents). No such value can be derived on the basis of the pervasiveness of curiosity or the desire to know. Even more important, however, is the fact that such a conclusion could not answer the entire problem of the value of knowledge anyway.

CONCLUSION

Two points capture the force of the arguments in this chapter. First, even if knowledge is intrinsically valuable, this fact does not explain the value of knowledge over true belief. Second, it is implausible to explain the value of knowledge by appeal to some intrinsic value it possesses, for such an appeal belies our practice of trying to explain the value of knowledge in other terms — in particular, in terms of its constituents. We saw in the previous chapter that such an explanation fails, so it is perhaps understandable why that project would be abandoned in favor of an appeal to intrinsic value. This latter appeal, however, is an appeal of last resort, not commended to us by our ordinary attempts to explain the value of knowledge.

Perhaps, though, we are misconceiving of knowledge so radically that we are missing something completely obvious. We are assuming that knowledge is a descriptive feature of the world, as has the entire history of philosophy on the subject. If that assumption is mistaken, perhaps we have been laboring unnecessarily. In the next chapter, I look more closely at the nature of value and valuation and see what can be made of the idea that our attitudes about knowledge give direct, immediate grounds for thinking that knowledge is valuable.

7

Epistemic Attitudinalism: Semantic and Pragmatic Approaches

The conclusion to which our investigation seems to be pointing is that ordinary thinking about knowledge is mistaken, that knowledge does not have the kind of value it is ordinarily thought to have. In particular, we seem to be heading for the conclusion that knowledge does not have a value that exceeds that of subsets of its constituents. Knowledge cannot be identified with intellectually virtuous, subjectively justified true belief, and it appears that its value does not exceed the value of this combination of ingredients.

Perhaps, though, we are missing what is right under our noses. Language is a perplexing combination of semantic and other features, and to this point, we have largely ignored features other than semantic ones. Moreover, within our exploration of the semantic features of the concept of knowledge, we have been assuming a descriptivist standpoint about knowledge. We have been assuming, that is, that the concept of knowledge applies to objective, factual features of the world. It is, perhaps, this combination of assumptions that leads us toward a pessimistic conclusion such as that there is no good answer to the problem of the *Meno*.

A different proposal is that the value of knowledge is found in certain attitudinal features involved in the concept or use of the concept of knowledge. One approach along these lines would involve making claims about knowledge that emotivists in ethics make about moral concepts.[1] We might call this the "boo/hiss" theory of knowledge. On it, to ascribe knowledge is just to cheer for a particular mental state, and to deny knowledge is to boo that mental state. This particular theory is not especially

---

1. See, e.g., C. L. Stevenson, *Ethics and Language* (New Haven, CT: Yale University Press, 1945).

promising, but perhaps there are other, more promising approaches along these lines. The core idea to be explored here is whether the value of knowledge is a function of certain evaluative attitudes expressed when employing that concept, rather than a function of certain properties that are the constituents of knowledge. In recent years, several approaches to knowledge have been aired that connect the concept of knowledge to such attitudes either in virtue of semantic features of the concept of knowledge or in virtue of pragmatic features of our use of that concept.

SEMANTIC AND PRAGMATIC VERSIONS OF EPISTEMIC ATTITUDINALISM

I will refer to the theories just described as versions of epistemic attitudinalism. In this section, I will describe three different theories of this sort so that we may gain some general understanding of and critical perspective on them. I begin first with Hartry Field's version.

Field's Evaluativism

Hartry Field holds that ascriptions of knowledge and justification are evaluative rather than factual.[2] He says:

[W]e should have a non-factualist attitude toward justification . . . ; it is a matter of policy rather than fact, . . . and the question is only whether it is a good policy. It makes no sense to ask whether logic *really is* justifiable a priori; the only issue is whether it is advantageous to employ an evidential system that licenses adhering to a logic whatever the empirical evidence may be.[3]

Some clarification of terminology is needed here. Field means by an "evidential system" a system of rules governing what to believe in which circumstances.[4] He holds that such a system can be ascribed to each person by idealizing away from "performance error"[5] and that an attribution of justification to a belief can be factual if it is nothing more than a description of whether such a belief is sanctioned by the evidential system of that

---

2. Hartry Field, "The A Prioricity of Logic," *Proceedings of the Aristotelian Society*, 96 (1996): 359–79; "Epistemological Nonfactualism and the A Prioricity of Logic, "*Philosophical Studies*, 92 (1998): 1–24.
3. Field, "The A Prioricity of Logic," p. 377.
4. Ibid., p. 362.
5. Ibid., pp. 362–3.

person,[6] the system a person actually uses in forming and retaining that belief.[7] Field doubts, however, that usual ascriptions of justification are subjective in this way, and when they are not, ascriptions of justification also evaluate the evidential system in question, positively or negatively evaluating the standards that permit the belief in question.[8] Hence, standard determinations of whether a particular belief is justified (or a priori justified, as in Field's example in the previous quotation) is one of "policy" rather than "fact," where the mark of good policy is whether it is "advantageous" – as he puts it elsewhere, "whether or not it is a good thing to have an evidential system that licenses" the belief in question.[9]

One of the first questions that comes to mind here concerns clarification of the nature of the advantage in question. In particular, we need to be told *in what respects* a good policy in epistemology is good or advantageous. Field makes it clear that he holds a *teleological* conception of justification, identifying justification in terms of suitable means for achieving epistemic goals; he says, "what is involved in deciding to employ a certain sort of evidential system is seeing how well such a policy would accord with one's epistemic goals."[10]

So far, Field's conception of justification is fairly mundane, for nearly every epistemologist holds that justification is teleological. There is one surprise in Field's language, for in stating his teleological conception, he speaks of "what is involved in deciding to employ" a certain sort of evidential system. Such a remark is a bit too suggestive of the idea that we choose which practices of belief formation to adopt, as are his remarks about attributions of justification constituting policy recommendations. Epistemologists who resort to this language, language much more at home in the arena of action than belief, can usually be paraphrased so as to avoid the unwanted implications that we can choose how to go about forming and holding beliefs, however, and I will assume that the same can be done

---

6. Ibid., p. 363.
7. Ibid. Sometimes Field talks as if the evidential system were imputed to a believer, with no implication that it is a functioning item in the formation and sustenance of belief. Yet, when he clarifies the nature of evaluativism, he is forced to speak of evaluating the system that is, in fact, in use in the formation and sustenance of belief. So I think the former reticence suggests only that when we attribute a system to a person, we are theorizing, and in theorizing, we are subject to all the usual problems of underdetermination of theory by evidence. Even so, there is a fact of the matter about which evidential system a person employs.
8. Field, "Epistemological Nonfactualism," p. 6.
9. Field, "The A Prioricity of Logic," p. 364.
10. Ibid., p. 377.

here for Field's language. If it can, then Field so far appears only to endorse a teleological conception of justification, a conception mundane enough to leave us wondering how such a creative conclusion as nonfactualism could follow from such a conception.

Field's answer appeals to the multiplicity of epistemic goals. His earliest formulation of this point is as follows:

> Questions about whether something is a good thing typically have no simple yes–or–no answers, in part because they typically involve an interplay of a great many considerations. In the case of cognitive practices (as for moral practices), we tend to positively evaluate practices similar to ours; we also tend to positively evaluate practices that we can see lead to various sorts of practical benefits.[11]

Field says that whether something is good in a particular respect usually is a function of a great many things. In the case of practices of belief formation, two things he says are relevant are whether the practice is similar to our own and whether it leads to practical benefits. Yet, such claims hardly provide the basis for such a novel position as epistemological nonfactualism for two reasons. First, the teleological character of justification is not directed toward either of the considerations mentioned: We don't call a belief (epistemically) justified because it is part of a practice similar to our own or because it is a belief that leads to practical benefits. It may be true that most of the beliefs we judge to be justified have these additional properties, but it is not these properties that explain our attributions of justification. We do not, that is, look for beliefs similar to our own or beliefs that lead to practical benefits when trying to determine whether those beliefs are epistemically justified (justified in the way required for knowledge, let us say). Instead, the teleological character of justification is revealed by the standard account of the epistemic goal in terms of finding the truth and avoiding error. We judge the epistemic status of a belief by its relationship to this goal and by whether the proper standards have been met by the belief in question in the attempt to achieve this goal. Second, the notion that some sort of nonfactualism follows in either epistemology or ethics because there are no simple yes–or–no answers to questions about whether something is good is a complete non sequitur. If the answers were easy, they would be part of the lore of common sense, not part of the most disputable areas of theoretical philosophy. Moreover, if the lack of a simple yes–or–no answer implied nonfactualism, not only would most of philosophy have to be classified as nonfactual, so would

11. Ibid., p. 364.

160

most of science. For one simple example, consider the scientific question of the nature of light: Is it a wave or is it a particle? Because there is no simple yes-or-no answer to this question, Field's initial reason for counting knowledge ascriptions as nonfactual would lead to counting statements about the nature of light as nonfactual as well.

Field replaces this first approach by a more sophisticated attempt to undergird nonfactualism by appeal in later articles to the teleological character of justification. Field abandons the preceding arguments in favor of ones that cite the dual goals of reliability and power, noting the trade-offs between each: A method can be highly reliable if it is extremely cautious, but for a method to be powerful, it cannot display such caution.[12] He also notes the different ways of emphasizing each of these desiderata: There is reliability or power in the long run, in the short run, and in runs of different lengths.[13] When there is conflict between different proposals for the best methods to adopt, Field says:

> In that case it is hard to see how the issue of which method to prefer could be over a matter of fact. Advocates of the different methods would still disagree, but on attitude or policy, rather than over any facts.[14]

Besides this point about the teleological character of justification and the inevitable disagreements about how to weight the competing factors of power and reliability, Field believes there is another reason to adopt his nonfactualist position. He holds that there are also "varying degrees" to which a method can succeed in satisfying a goal, and "how high a degree of meeting the goal is *good enough* is itself a matter of evaluation."[15] He maintains that we cannot reasonably expect our methods to be the best possible for achieving our goals, but that leaves open the possibility that an adequate method at one time may be superseded by a more adequate method at another time.[16] In such a case, Field holds that the factualist seems forced to count the use of our present methods as unjustified, whereas Field holds that a more interesting evaluation would regard the less good methods as more relevant because the better methods are not yet available.[17]

To get a clear picture of Field's position, we need some clarification. In particular, we need to be a bit more careful in the use of the concept

12. Field, "Epistemological Nonfactualism," p. 8.
13. Ibid.
14. Ibid.
15. Ibid., p. 9.
16. Ibid.
17. Ibid., pp. 9–10.

of a goal in formulating Field's points. Note that the multiplicity of goals for Field's first point involves the concepts of reliability and power. On the standard teleological conception of justification, however, these concepts are not themselves goals of cognitive activity, but are related to the epistemic goal of finding the truth and avoiding error as means are to ends. To speak of them as epistemic goals is to speak in a way that can easily mislead.[18] When we turn to the second point, which defends the appropriateness of satisficing rather than maximizing means to ends, a more standard account of epistemic goals can be assumed. Furthermore, if there is a way to put Field's position in terms of the standard account of the epistemic goal, we should put it that way in order to minimize interpretive difficulties.

I think we can explain Field's position in this way. As just noted, Field's second point is that there are many incompatible evidential systems that provide satisfactory means to the goal of getting to the truth and avoiding error. Field's first point will have to be recast somewhat, but perhaps the following is an acceptable reconstruction. Various trade-offs are involved in any evidential system between reliability and power, between minimizing false belief (here reliability is more important) and maximizing true belief (here power is more important), and it is hard to see how there is any fact of the matter as to which balance between these two aspects of the standard epistemic goal is correct. Instead, there is only a nonfactual evaluation that an equal balance is best, or that erring on the side of caution is best, or that placing one's emphasis on the range of true belief is best.

One might still question the power of this argument for evaluativism, but my intention at this point is not to criticize but to explain the position to see its relevance to the question of the value of knowledge. In this view, when we say that a person is justified or has knowledge, we are not engaging in description but are instead evaluating. Thus, to say that a person has knowledge is automatically and directly to evaluate the situation in question positively. In the picture that dominated discussion in earlier chapters, the concept of knowledge is a concept whose value, if there be such, is a function of the value of the constituents of this concept.

---

18. The epistemologist best known for appealing to the concepts of reliability and power (as well as to speed, which Field does not mention) is Alvin Goldman. See especially *Epistemology and Cognition* (Cambridge, MA: Harvard University Press, 1986). It is interesting to note that Goldman is crystal clear on the point in the text: Truth is the goal, and reliable, powerful, and fast processes or methods are the means, with the theoretical task being to determine the proper balance between these virtues of processes or methods.

Epistemic attitudinalism takes a different approach, claiming that the value of knowledge arises from the attitudes expressed in the use of the concept. Knowledge is valuable in this view because the concept itself includes a positive evaluative component. For something to count as knowledge requires our taking a favorable attitude, a pro-attitude, toward it. So when we are asked why knowledge is more valuable than true belief, the answer is that true belief need not be accompanied by this pro-attitude, but knowledge must be.

Those enamored of subjective approaches to value questions will find in this pro-attitude the end of the story, but those more attracted to objective theories of value will have a residual worry. The worry is that we can take pro-attitudes toward things that have no (objective) value whatsoever. Field's position, relying on the distinction between factual and nonfactual components of language, denies the propriety of such assumptions of the objectivity of value. For Field's attitudinalism, there is no question of the value of knowledge beyond the pro-attitude that is part of it.[19]

Field's version of attitudinalism depends on justification being a component of knowledge in order to address the problem of the value of knowledge. The next version does not.

Heller's Contextualism

Mark Heller defends what he terms "antiluck" epistemology.[20] He claims that the fundamental intuition in this view is that knowledge requires "there to be a kind of necessary connection between . . . belief and . . . truth."[21] He claims that there is a family of theories of knowledge, including reliabilism, a relevant alternatives approach, and a counterfactual theory, that equivalently satisfy this antiluck approach. Heller makes the strong claim that the three approaches are equivalent,[22] but he does not need that strong a claim. All he needs is the claim that there are versions of each such approach that are equivalent.

---

19. At the Rutgers Epistemology Conference in 2000, Field indicated an affinity with the kind of relativism developed by Alan Gibbard in *Wise Choices, Apt Feelings* (Cambridge, MA: Harvard University Press, 1992). Such a view could be used to undergird the rejection of the objectivity of normative claims that is part of Field's position.
20. Mark Heller, "The Proper Role for Contextualism in an Anti-Luck Epistemology," *Philosophical Perspectives, 13, Epistemology*, James Tomberlin, ed. (Cambridge, MA: Blackwell, 1999), pp. 115–29.
21. Ibid., p. 115.
22. Ibid., p. 116.

So, before finding a role for context, Heller first presents a theory of knowledge, the official version of which is:

S's true belief that p is knowledge iff S does not believe p in any of the selected not-p worlds.[23]

Heller's theory is also contextualist, however, and the contextualism arises in the selection of not-p worlds. Heller says, "If the same set [of worlds] were selected for every knowledge claim in every context our work would be done. But the same set is not selected in every context, and that is where contextualism comes in."[24]

It is easiest to see the contextualism using the relevant alternatives approach to knowledge. On this approach, knowledge requires being right in alternatives to the present situation when those alternatives are "relevant." If we understand alternatives in terms of possible worlds, then some possible worlds are relevant to knowledge and some are not. Contextualism is affirmed if the set of relevant worlds varied according to context, and Heller claims it does.

The relevance of this version of contextualism for our question concerning the value of knowledge arises out of the mechanism that drives contextual shifts in standards for knowledge in Heller's view. To get clear on the mechanism in question, we need a bit of terminology. If we suppose that we have an ordering of worlds around the actual world (perhaps in terms of closeness or overall similarity), then a *standard* for knowledge is delineated by drawing a line between worlds that count and worlds that don't for assessing whether knowledge is present in a given case. A person *satisfies* such a standard if she fails to believe *p* in any of the not-*p* worlds that count according to that standard. Finally, a person's *total epistemic condition* is simply a summary of which standards for knowledge that person satisfies and which standards that person does not satisfy.[25]

Heller then uses this terminology to distinguish between the nonvaluational parts of epistemology and the valuational component:

A report of someone's total epistemic condition is wholly non-valuative – to describe S's epistemic condition is not to assign a value to that condition in any way. In contrast, to say of someone that she has knowledge is to pass such a value judgement. . . . By attributing knowledge we are saying that someone who

23. Ibid.
24. Ibid.
25. Ibid., p. 118.

is in that epistemic condition has the epistemic property we care about in that context. That is why two evaluators can agree about S's epistemic condition and still disagree about whether she has knowledge; the two evaluators simply care about different properties.[26]

Thus, the mechanism that drives contextual shifts is a valuational mechanism. What we care about causes us to focus on different standards in different contexts and to withhold or endorse the attribution of knowledge based on such care.

Some qualifications are needed regarding this preliminary account of this theory. The first qualification Heller proposes himself. He recognizes that his description of which property we care about is a bit too specific. He says:

All of this talk of which property an evaluator cares about is a bit too simplistic. We never care about any one specific property – we never care exactly in which situations S would believe p. . . . What we really care about is that S have any one of a set of properties, any one of which would serve our purposes.[27]

What Heller has in mind here is a kind of vagueness about which standards are satisfied in a given case. He holds that we don't care about satisfying any one specific standard but rather about a vague range of standards.

I think the theory needs even more imprecision than Heller admits here. Most people, myself included, have never had a possible world as part of the object of their concerns, at least not if possible worlds are maximal and complete. We wish the world were a bit different, we hope that things turn out a certain way, and these connative states are often directed at nonactual possibilities. It is a far reach, however, from finding such possibilities among the objects of our concern and finding possible worlds themselves in our concerns.

It would be rash to abandon Heller's theory for this reason, for the theory could be modified to remove the language of possible worlds from the proposal. Because it is the appeal to standards a person cares about that drives Heller's contextualism, the change to the theory will need to take place regarding the concept of a standard. Instead of treating a standard for knowledge as a line between some ordering on possible worlds, some looser account will be needed. Perhaps we could understand a standard for knowledge simply in terms of some notion of the risk of

26. Ibid.
27. Ibid., p. 119.

165

error, and then claim that knowledge ascriptions depend on what kind of risk sensitivity we care about in a particular situation. In any case, the language of possible worlds here should not be viewed as an indispensable part of the theory, but rather as an item of convenience that can be jettisoned.

Moreover, Heller is much too restrictive about the kinds of epistemic concerns we might have. Consider the sentence quoted previously that "[b]y attributing knowledge we are saying that someone who is in that epistemic condition has the epistemic property we care about in that context." Well, maybe that person has *one* of the epistemic properties we care about in that context, but it is hard to see why there has to be a unique such property.

At times, Heller seems to think that there can't be more than one such property. He says, "But 'knowledge' is the word we use for epistemic praise; we have no other to take its place."[28] The latter part of this quote may be true, that there is no other term we have for the particular kind of epistemic praise we ascribe when we ascribe knowledge. But it is simply false that we have no other terms for epistemic praise. Some observations are astute, some claims are insightful, some remarks are perceptive, some people have understanding and wisdom, some thoughts are discerning, some criticisms are penetrating, some theories are ingenious or clever or creative, some opinions are judicious, others are probing. And I have not even mentioned the standard epistemological stable of justification, rationality, and support by good evidence. So it is patently false that we have only one term for epistemic praise, for praise of the sort that is appropriate when we evaluate things from the perspective of the goal of getting to the truth and avoiding error.

Heller does mention one such term, recognizing that it provides a counterexample to the claim he makes that 'knowledge' is the word we use for epistemic praise. He says:

We seem also to have a word for saying that S's epistemic condition is good enough even when she has a false belief, namely "justification", but this word seems tied to an evidentialist concept, and knowledge is not always evidential.[29]

The fact that Heller addresses the concept of justification in the context of claiming that we have only one term of epistemic praise shows, I think, that he sees counterexamples to his claim. If he sees such counterexamples,

28. Ibid.
29. Ibid.

however, he sees only through a glass darkly, for his response is not to the point. He claims that justification may not be a component of knowledge, but that does not address the point that an ascription of justification may well be a way of ascribing epistemic praise.

What is clear is that there is a rather large array of terms of epistemic appraisal, one of which is 'knowledge'. The only way to defend the view that ascribing knowledge is our only way of expressing epistemic praise would be to draw a clear distinction between terms of epistemic praise and terms of epistemic appraisal. I doubt that this can be done, for to epistemically appraise a belief positively is to praise it in a certain way.

So Heller should claim no more than that there is some property we care about in a given situation that is uniquely associated with our ascription of knowledge in that situation. It is the property associated with meeting the range of standards that we express when we ascribe knowledge to a person in that situation. Such an emendation of the theory does not alter anything central to it, as far as I can tell, and still leaves the attitudinalism that is central to it intact.

Both Field's theory and Heller's theory put the attitudinal element in knowledge ascriptions into the content of the ascription itself. That is, their versions of attitudinalism are *semantic* in character. Not all versions of attitudinalism need be semantic, however, and it will be helpful to our understanding of this position to see a nonsemantic version of the view as well.

Greco's Credit Theory of Knowledge

Earlier, we saw John Greco's theory of the virtues in which credit accrues to an agent when the belief in question is a display of the virtues. Greco thinks that the concept of credit is central to the concept of knowledge as well. As we shall see, the best interpretation of Greco's theory makes the evaluative dimension of ascribing credit a pragmatic, rather than a semantic, feature of knowledge.

We saw earlier that Greco takes the following two conditions to be necessary for knowledge:

1. S's believing p is *subjectively* justified in the following sense: S's believing p is the result of dispositions that S manifests when S is trying to believe the truth, and
2. S's believing p is *objectively* justified in the following sense: The dispositions that result in S's believing p make S reliable in believing p. Alternatively, the dispositions

that result in S's believing p constitute intellectual abilities, or powers, or virtues.[30]

Greco proposes to add a third condition to these two to complete his account of knowledge:

I now want to add a third condition on knowledge, understanding knowledge attributions to imply attributions of intellectual credit. . . . I propose that adding this third condition makes the three sufficient as well as necessary for knowledge.

3. S believes the truth regarding p *because* S is reliable in believing p. Alternatively: The intellectual abilities (i.e. powers or virtues) that result in S's believing the truth regarding p are an important necessary part of the total set of causal factors that give rise to S's believing the truth regarding p.[31]

This third condition is related intimately to Greco's account of intellectual credit, which we have already seen but which bears repeating for the sake of familiarity:

S deserves intellectual credit for believing the truth regarding p only if

a. believing the truth regarding p has intellectual value,
b. believing the truth regarding p can be ascribed to S, and
c. believing the truth regarding p reveals S's cognitive character. Alternatively: S's cognitive character is an important necessary part of the total set of causal factors that give rise to S's believing the truth regarding p.[32]

As we saw in Chapter 4, there are important concerns about the notion of intellectual credit on this account stemming from clause (b), for it is not clear that (b) can be endorsed without involving in the realm of belief the concept of agency appropriate only in the realm of action. Because we discussed that issue fairly thoroughly in that chapter, we will bypass it here, assuming that this clause is satisfied for every case of belief. If we do so, granting as well that true belief has intellectual value, then Greco's account of deserving intellectual credit reduces to clause (c) of this account of intellectual credit and is just Greco's third condition for knowledge. So, Greco claims, knowledge is belief that is both subjectively and objectively justified and is such that the person in question deserves intellectual credit for believing the truth.

30. Greco, "Knowledge as Credit for True Belief," *Intellectual Virtue: Perspectives from Ethics and Epistemology*, Michael DePaul and Linda Zabzebski, eds. (Oxford: Oxford University Press, forthcoming), pp. 19–20 typescript.
31. Ibid., pp. 20–1 typescript.
32. Ibid., pp. 14–15 typescript.

Greco says that he wants attributions of knowledge to imply attributions of credit. If we understand 'implies' in its semantic sense, this theory implies only that a person *deserves* credit when such a person has knowledge, for it is the concept of deserved credit that Greco defines earlier. His account does not imply semantically any attribution of credit, and hence Greco's theory is not a semantic version of attitudinalism.

One could try to alter the theory to make it yield a semantic implication here. One way would be to take clauses (a), (b), and (c) as elucidating what it is to *receive* intellectual credit for a true belief instead of elucidating what it is to *deserve* such credit. Presenting the theory in this way distances it from Feinberg's account, the account on which Greco models his theory of intellectual credit, for one might deserve moral credit for an action but not receive any. The idea of credit received implies a relationship to other persons, just as do the related concepts of approval and honor, praise and blame. To receive honor, approval, praise, or credit for an accomplishment signals recognition. To deserve honor, approval, praise, or credit does not signal a relation, for one can deserve honor even if there is no one available to do the honoring. So there are significant disadvantages to altering the theory in this way to secure its evaluative dimension.

There is another reason not to alter the theory in this or any other way to secure a semantic connection between attributions of knowledge and the concept of credit for belief. The reason is that I don't think such a view is what Greco intends to defend. When he uses the concept of implication, I don't think he has in mind semantic implication, so let us present a way of understanding his claims that yields a nonsemantic connection between ascriptions of knowledge and credit for true belief.

Let us begin by supposing that Greco's central claims, formulated previously and in his work in terms of necessary and sufficient conditions, are semantic in nature. Thus, we will suppose that there is a semantic connection between the concept of knowledge and the three conditions Greco cites, and we will assume that the semantic interpretation of the phrase 'deserves intellectual credit for true belief' is given by clauses (a), (b), and (c) (with the additional understanding that (a) and (b) can be treated as superfluous). So when knowledge is attributed to a person, part of the meaning of what is being claimed is that the person deserves intellectual credit for his true belief. The connection between attributions of knowledge and credit for true belief would then be part of the pragmatic dimension of language in the following way. When we say that a person deserves credit for something, part of what we are doing by making such an assertion is, in ordinary circumstances, attributing credit to that person for that thing. So the implication between attributions of knowledge and attributions of credit, on this reading of Greco's theory, is a pragmatic implication, yielding a nonsemantic version of epistemic attitudinalism.

This way of understanding Greco's theory has an additional exegetical advantage. Greco claims from the outset that the connection between knowledge and credit is one of "illocutionary force."[33] He claims that there are two different questions one might try to answer in giving a theory of knowledge:

> The first is the "What is knowledge?" question. . . . The second is the "What are we doing?" question. This questions asks what illocutionary act is being performed when we say that someone knows. . . . I think the key to solving our two problems for fallibilism is in the "What are we doing?" question.
>
> So what are we doing when we attribute knowledge to someone? . . . [O]ne of the central functions of knowledge attributions is to give credit for true belief.[34]

Greco does not explain how his official theory gives the results he intends, but if we interpret the theory in the way described, we get the desired connections. We get, that is, a *semantic* connection between knowledge and deserved credit for true belief, and we get a *pragmatic* connection between attributing deserved credit and ascribing credit for true belief, thereby giving us Greco's desired result that the connection between knowledge and credit is one of illocutionary force. The result is a version of attitudinalism that is pragmatic rather than semantic in character, one providing an interesting contrast to the versions of semantic attitudinalism seen earlier.

EPISTEMIC ATTITUDINALISM AND THE VALUE OF KNOWLEDGE

Each of these three theories treats the concept of knowledge as implying evaluation. On Field's and Heller's views, the implication is semantic; on Greco's view, it is pragmatic. To say that their theories are attitudinal is to say that in ascribing knowledge to someone, a positive attitude is expressed or implied. Furthermore, because of this implication, attitudinalism presents a significantly different approach to addressing the question of the value of knowledge. Such a view need not explain the value of knowledge in terms of some descriptive conditions that are themselves valuable or in terms of some intrinsic value that knowledge possesses. Its

33. Ibid., p. 1 typescript.
34. Ibid., pp. 6–7 typescript.

value derives from our pro-attitudes toward it, which are expressed either semantically or pragmatically in our ascriptions of knowledge.

This characterization of attitudinalism makes it seem very much like a theory that attempts to defend the value of knowledge on the basis of the pervasive desire for it. In both cases, for example, the value of knowledge depends on attitudes of persons. There are, however, two fundamental weaknesses of the desire-based approach not shared by attitudinalism.

First, it is not strictly accurate to say that there is a pervasive desire for knowledge, for the conceptually fundamental concept here is truth, and curiosity of the fully intentional variety is plausibly taken to be displayed both by small children and by nonhuman animals lacking the concept of knowledge. They may also lack the concept of truth, but we saw earlier that the appropriate way to express, in terms of a generalization, what they are seeking uses the concept of truth rather than that of knowledge. Furthermore, we have found an explanation of why we should express the nature of curiosity in terms of a desire to know even though it is not strictly accurate. At the heart of this desire, or motivation, is an interest in finality and closure, and a pragmatic feature of attributions of knowledge is just the sort of finality and closure in question. One can say of other people, "They believe the truth, but they need to investigate further," but one cannot say in as coherent a way, "They know the answer, but further inquiry is needed." Attributions of knowledge have this pragmatic dimension of closure of inquiry, whereas attributions of having found the truth need not. Yet, note that in the first-person case, no such difference is to be found. It is just as incoherent to say "I have found the truth but I need to investigate further" as it is to say "I know the answer but I need to investigate further." The difference between first- and third-person attributions suggests the following: Human curiosity is a motivation to find the truth with finality and closure, and we ordinarily express the content of such a motivation using the concept of knowledge. So we say that human curiosity is a desire, or motivation, for knowledge, pragmatically communicating the idea we are after, even though, semantically, what we say is not true.

The second point is that this approach to the question of the value of knowledge is merely a pointer toward the value of knowledge rather than a full defense of it. The mere fact that we desire something does not show, by itself, that what is desired is good. A full defense would need to go beyond the appeal to the desire in order to find something in the object of desire to account for its goodness.

In both of these respects, epistemic attitudinalism has advantages over the theory based on curiosity. If semantic attitudinalism is true, it makes little sense to ask any further for an account of the value of knowledge, for it is a presupposition of the role of that concept in our language that it is valuable. The only possibility for its lacking value, if attitudinalism is correct, would be for our pro-attitudes to differ radically from the objective value that things have. Some attitudinalists think that all value is based in the attitudes we take toward things, thereby rejecting this possibility, but even for those who admit that what is valuable can differ from what we value, attitudinalism has a response here. If we were to find out that our pro-attitudes differ radically from the objective value that things have, such a discovery would have an effect on our ascriptions of knowledge. If attitudinalism is correct and we learned that certain of our ascriptions of knowledge involved epistemic conditions that are not valuable, we should take back such ascriptions. For the pro-attitude involved in attributing knowledge would be out of place, and hence the attribution should be withdrawn.

The pragmatic version of epistemic attitudinalism regarding the connection to the value of knowledge fits this picture as well. Consider promising as a pragmatic implication, or illocutionary accompaniment, of saying "I promise." It makes little sense to ask what explains the connection between uttering the sentence and having made that promise; that connection is part of the function of the concept of promising, and no further explanation is necessary. One might inquire as to why any language would contain such performative utterances in the first place, but an answer to that question will not yield any further explanation of why saying "I promise" pragmatically implies the act of promising. Just so, according to the pragmatic version of epistemic attitudinalism, saying "He knows that" pragmatically implies an ascription of credit for true belief. On this view, part of the function of the concept of knowledge is to ascribe credit, just as part of the function of the concept of promising is to make promises. Thus, according to this view, knowledge is what it is at least in part because an ascription of it involves the assigning of credit for true belief, and so it is equally accurate to say on the pragmatic version of attitudinalism that knowledge expresses a pro-attitude by its very nature, and its value is presupposed by such.

One may complain here that we are seeking an *explanation* of the value of knowledge and not just a *defense* of it, and there is some legitimacy to this complaint against attitudinalism. It may be that the most satisfying versions of attitudinalism are ones that take attitudinal approaches to all questions of value, arguing that value is always and everywhere a product of the mental attitudes taken toward descriptive aspects of the world. Even without this additional commitment, though, attitudinalism is useful at this point in our study. For we have seen enough failed attempts to explain the value of knowledge that we should have begun by this point to question whether knowledge really has special value. So even if attitudinalism can only give us a defense of the value of knowledge, that accomplishment would be significant here even if we were left with no explanation of its value.

Such a defense of the value of knowledge is only as adequate as the position on which the defense is based. So, we must ask, is epistemic attitudinalism correct? In the next section, I argue that this question should be given a negative answer.

THE FAILURE OF EPISTEMIC ATTITUDINALISM

The problem for these approaches to the question of the value of knowledge is not the quality of their explanations, but rather the acceptability of their starting point. For knowledge simply is not evaluative in the ways demanded by these positions. Let us begin with semantic versions of the theory.

Field's position is, I will argue, the least helpful version of attitudinalism in our context. First, there is a theory-specific problem for Field concerning the charge of hasty generalization. He concludes that there is no correct balance between the conflicting goals of finding the truth and avoiding error simply because it is not obvious how to resolve disputes over the correct weighting. Yet, if he were to adopt as a general principle that any use of language is nonfactual when it is difficult to see how to resolve disputes, then he would have to claim that his own theory is not true (because nonfactual). Worse yet, he would have to claim that hardly anything in philosophy involves descriptive uses of language. For it is part of the common experience in philosophy that disputes are not easily resolved, and it is rarely easy to see how to resolve them.

There are also more general problems for Field's theory. First, there is a historical point against it. Suppose we return to the glory days of Logical Positivism and Logical Empiricism. Philosophers of these persuasions had a fondness for science and for descriptive or factual language, such a fondness that all else was pronounced semantically meaningless. The sad thing for such philosophers is that far too many concepts turned out to be empty on their accounts of the distinction between descriptive and nondescriptive, factual and nonfactual, language. But no one accused them of going overboard in their enthusiasm by ruling against the meaningfulness of ascriptions of knowledge. No one, that is, even hinted that our knowledge of the world might be in jeopardy because of the austerity of the Positivist/Empiricist program. Why not? The answer, I think, points to the implausibility of Field's theory. If this version of attitudinalism had any plausibility, we should have expected epistemologists to voice objections to Logical Positivism, even as ethicists, metaphysicians, and philosophers of religion did. No such objections were voiced, and no such implications were drawn by the Positivists themselves. These facts give some reason for thinking that Field's ideas are simply on the wrong track.

The second, general problem is more telling. For Field, the evaluative element of knowledge derives completely from the evaluative character of justification, and Field's attitudinalism arises from his dissatisfaction with ordinary descriptive characterizations of justification. He objects to them, claiming that they treat justification as a kind of liquid that squirts from premises to conclusions of arguments.[35] Here Field shows his sympathy with Alan Gibbard's account of norms, which Field admits to being the source of his expressivism.[36] Gibbard's account is supposed to apply equally to moral and epistemic norms, and he argues that, given an account of natural Darwinian representation, there is no need to posit normative facts to explain what we are doing when we express normative judgments. Instead, our behavior can be explained solely in terms of the evolutionary value of coordination between minds regarding which norms to accept and which not to accept.

The originality of Gibbard's view is the extension of expressivism outside the domain of morality and action and into the realm of epistemology, and it is this difference from ordinary versions of expressivism that Field relies on. There is a problem for such an extension, however, one arising from the fact that a defense of expressivism in any realm appeals to *arguments* and the adequacy of various proposed *explanations*, and these arguments and explanations rely on *epistemic norms*, the very items attitudinalized by Gibbard's thesis. For example, if I infer that evolutionary theory is better than some alternative because it posits fewer theoretical entities, I rely on the norm that in the search for truth the principle of Occam's Razor should be followed. For another example, if I deduce some conclusion by the canons of first-order theory, I rely on the norm that these canons are appropriate in extending our knowledge. And if I reason in accord with Bayes' theorem on some probabilistic matter, I rely

---

35. Field, "The A Prioricity of Logic," p. 377.
36. Gibbard, *Wise Choices, Apt Feelings.*

on the principle that this theorem is a suitable guide in determining what to believe.

The problem created by the attitudinalizing of these norms is that if the norms are not true, the arguments and explanations fail to provide sufficient epistemic grounds for endorsing their conclusion. Gibbard remains unmoved, however:

> My explanations were of course guided by norms – epistemic norms. Why, say, did no basic tendency toward perfection figure in the explanations [of the beliefs of physicists regarding electrons] I gave? No such thing should be posited, I assumed, when observed patterns can be explained just as well without it. This is a normative judgment, and it and others like it guided me . . . The norms that guide explanation, though, are not themselves parts of the explanation. I did not suggest that we developed our normative capacities because basic tendencies to perfection should not be posited gratuitously. Epistemic norms tell us what constitutes a good explanation, but that does not make them part of that explanation.[37]

Of course, Gibbard is right that the norms that guide reasoning are not themselves part of that very reasoning. Norms are not *constituents* of explanations, but that is not the appropriate level of concern here. Explanations have *presuppositions* as well as constituents, and the adequacy of Gibbard's explanation depends on the truth of Occam's Razor in the way distinctive of such.

What is a presupposition? I offer no general theory of them, but we can say this much: The class of presuppositions is a subset of the class of implications of a statement or set of statements. One quite clear example is the following: The validity of *modus ponens* presupposes the truth of the corresponding conditional to *modus ponens*. In the preceding quote, Gibbard admits that he *assumed* the truth of Occam's Razor. I think Gibbard is recognizing that Occam's Razor is a presupposition of the cogency of his arguments. That is, the quality of his arguments depends crucially on Occam's Razor in just the way that the validity of *modus ponens* depends on the alethic status of its corresponding conditional. In the language I am employing, his arguments presuppose the truth of Occam's Razor.

Gibbard might claim that the corresponding conditional to *modus ponens* is not a norm of reasoning (because it has no normative concept in it), whereas Occam's Razor is normative (it refers to what one *should not* posit), and thereby try to distinguish the two cases in such a way that

---

37. Ibid., p. 122.

Occam's Razor is not a presupposition of his arguments. That difference, however, is superficial. Gibbard admits that he has been *assuming* some version of Occam's Razor, and it is pointless to try to maintain that one has been assuming *p* without assuming *p is true*. In the present context, what is assumed, just like what is presupposed, must be true. The crucial difference is that assumptions need not bear any straightforward logical relationship to the explicit contents of discussion, whereas presuppositions do. But in either case, it is the truth of the assumption or presupposition that is at stake. In particular, if Occam's Razor is false, Gibbard had better look around for a better defense of his attitudinalist views, for the present argument supports his position only if its presuppositions are true, including Occam's Razor.

One can get distracted here by the metaphysically tendentious language of facts, but that is not the issue at all. The question is not whether Occam's Razor is a fact, but rather whether it is a presupposition of certain explanations. Its being such requires that it be semantically evaluable, and whatever else it demands in terms of the existence of facts and the like depends on results in the theory of truth. The simple point is that arguments and explanations presuppose the truth of epistemic norms, and if the norms themselves are given nonalethic status, then the explanations and arguments are simply defective in virtue of the fact that their presuppositions are not true. Good arguments presuppose logical and epistemic norms, and the concept of presupposition itself involves the concept of semantic evaluation.

We should also note that there is a more straightforward reason for rejecting Field's attitudinalism in the present context concerning the value of knowledge in addition to the previous more general difficulty. If the attitudinal component of knowledge derives solely from the attitudinal character of justification, then knowledge will have no special value derived from this attitudinal component beyond the value possessed by justified true belief. Because knowledge is more than justified belief, Field's attitudinalism cannot provide a defense or explanation of the value of knowledge over that of subsets of its constituents. So if semantic attitudinalism offers any hope regarding the question of the value of knowledge, it will have to be a version in which the attitudinal nature of knowledge does not derive solely from that of justification.

Recognizing this point makes Heller's version of semantic attitudinalism much more attractive than Field's version, for Heller does not presume that knowledge and justification are related semantically. I think, however, that semantic attitudinalism must be rejected, for every version of semantic

176

attitudinalism faces a problem that I will term the "Spock problem." Against Heller's theory stands the possibility of Spock-like individuals, both as evaluators and as possessors of knowledge. Such Spock-like creatures could employ our concept of knowledge in describing the epistemic situation of various individuals, but they would do so without caring at all about anything. Psychologists say that severe depression can leave people with very few concerns in life, sometimes with none at all. Nothing is important to them anymore; they really don't care at all about anything. Nonetheless, such individuals do not cease to distinguish between what they know and what they don't know. What they have lost is any interest in the difference.

Most of us have experienced the loss of concern that comes with depression, and it would be surprising indeed if we retained a concern for matters epistemic when we have lost much more personal concerns. In introspecting on my own case, I notice no hesitancy to distinguish between knowledge and the lack of it even when I am most depressed, and I expect that experience is fairly common. If so, however, any attitudinalism resting on the cares and concerns of the evaluator will be undermined by the details of how actual depression works.

To crystallize these concerns into a particular example, consider a purely cognitive being with no cares or concerns whatsoever; call him "Spock." Can Spock have knowledge, on Heller's view? At first glance, the answer seems to be "yes," for we can correctly ascribe knowledge to Spock in virtue of the fact that he satisfies the standards that matter to us regarding his situation.

This explanation of Spock's knowledge depends essentially on the existence of a distinct evaluator and would be unavailable if only Spock-like creatures exist. If only Spock-like creatures exist, it appears that Spock could not correctly be said to have knowledge. That result is incorrect, however. As Trekkies all know, individuals like Spock can be very smart and can know quite a bit more than ordinary humans know. Moreover, Spock would not cease to have that knowledge if only he and his kind existed.

At one point, Heller addresses the question of the role an evaluator plays in his theory, a question at the heart of the Spock problem. He says:

One word of warning. My emphasis on the evaluator and her concerns should not lead to the false conclusion that S cannot have knowledge unless S is being evaluated. The property that we are now referring to with the term "knowledge" could be had by S even if no one were evaluating whether S has it and even if no one had ever given any thought to that property. What is true is that which property we care about is dependent on who we are and what situations we are in. The point is that . . . we epistemologists should replace the single question "Does S have knowledge?" with the pair of questions "What epistemic condition is S in?" and "Which epistemic conditions do we care about?" The second of these questions is a question about us, the evaluators, not about S. But that does nothing to lessen the significance of the first question, a question to which the evaluator is irrelevant.[38]

Heller claims that a person can be in precisely the epistemic condition she is in, can satisfy precisely the epistemic standards she does, without being evaluated, and concludes from that claim that a person can have knowledge without being evaluated (note the second sentence, "My emphasis on the evaluator and her concerns should not lead to the false conclusion that S cannot have knowledge unless S is being evaluated"). There are two different problems to which such remarks may be addressed. One might worry that Heller's theory allows the presence of knowledge only when an evaluation is occurring. The worry here is that knowledge comes and goes, depending on whether the true belief in question is under evaluation: If it is currently being evaluated, it is knowledge; if it is currently not being evaluated, it is not knowledge. Heller's answer here is effective, for his theory doesn't require actual, present-tense evaluation to be occurring in order for knowledge to be present.

This issue of whether an evaluation is currently occurring is not the Spock problem, however, and the preceding passage may be taken to address that problem only by offering a counterfactual approach to the issue. Instead of requiring that Spock or some inhabitant of Spock's world have epistemic concerns, Heller may wish us to consider what *our* evaluation of Spock's condition would be if we were inhabitants of Spock's world.

There are two problems with this view, the first technical and the second more general. The technical problem involves vagaries common to all counterfactual theories in philosophy, for it is very hard to get the two sides of a counterfactual theory to covary in truth value of necessity. In the particular case at hand, what our evaluation of Spock's condition would be if we inhabited that world is simply unclear. Maybe we would be much more Spock-like, too, because of the tendency of humans to adopt attitudes of those around them. Heller might reply that the antecedent of the counterfactual should involve our presence in Spock's world with all the cares and concerns we currently have. That won't work when

---

38. Heller, "Contextualism," p. 121.

178

the evaluator is too depressed to care about matters epistemic. Moreover, even if the evaluator actually has such concerns, there is still no reason to assume that the truth value of the counterfactual will covary with whether Spock has knowledge, for there are too many possible ways in which one could have the precise cares and concerns one currently has and still hold that Spock lacks knowledge. Perhaps if one were in a world of Spock-like creatures, one would express one's cares and concerns by attributing insight to Spock but not knowledge; perhaps the shock of being so different from everyone else would simply confuse one, so that no judgments could be made. Counterfactual theories generally succumb to worries of this sort, and there is little reason to think that a counterfactual theory here will be more successful than it is in other areas of philosophy.[39]

There is also a more general worry about the contextual element of this theory. On this theory, whether a person knows is determined contextually by what he cares about in a given context. If contextualism is true, it is not likely that this version of it is the correct one. A central question for any version of contextualism is to give an adequate account of the mechanism by which the standards for knowledge are raised and lowered, and this version attributes such raising and lowering merely to what epistemic standards we care about in a given context. Such an account attributes too much infallibility to the evaluators in the same way that relativism attributes too much moral infallibility to cultures. If contextualism is true, what the standards for knowledge are in a given context is something that perplexes us, and we don't resolve the perplexity by introspecting to discover what we care about. The order of explanation is quite different. We often come to care about certain standards by carefully considering what the standards for knowledge are.

I want to emphasize that these problems are not unique to Heller's theory. Any version of semantic attitudinalism will be plagued by the Spock problem, and it is simply false that the meaning of 'knowledge' must change in order for people who lack the ordinary cares and concerns we have to ascribe knowledge to themselves and others.

We are left, then, with Greco's theory and, more generally, with pragmatic versions of attitudinalism. The explanation of the value of knowledge on his approach depends on credit being correctly assigned in virtue of some ascription of knowledge. When credit is correctly assigned, it

---

39. For a discussion of the general failure of counterfactual theories in philosophy and an application of this point to counterfactual accounts of dispositions, see my "Lewis on Finkish Dispositions," *Philosophy and Phenomenological Research*, 59 (1999): 703–10.

is deserved and hence a valuable state has obtained. Is this valuable state present even when knowledge remains unascribed or when no one cares? On Greco's theory, the answer is yes, for the valuable state is just the condition of deserving credit for true belief, and that condition is semantically implied by Greco's theory of knowledge.

One question for Greco's theory is whether there is such a semantic connection between knowledge and deserved credit. According to Greco, the concept of deserved credit for true belief solves the Gettier problem. Consider, however, the following version of the Tim–Tom case discussed in Chapter 5.

The Tim–Tom Case: Joe, the library detective, sees his good friend Tom take a book from the library and leave without checking it out. On the basis of perception and personal acquaintance Joe justifiably believes that Tom stole a book. Joe informs the police officer of what he saw, but after talking to Joe the officer speaks to Tom's mother, who claims that Tom is out of town and that it may have been Tom's twin brother, Tim, who stole the book. Unknown to the officer, Joe, or anyone else, Tom's mother is lying. Tom stole the book, he was not out of town, and Tom does not have a twin brother. In spite of the fact that Joe has a justified true belief that Tom stole the book, the testimony of Tom's mother undermines his knowledge.[40]

For Greco's theory to be successful, Joe must not deserve credit for his true belief in this case. It is very hard to see why he doesn't deserve such credit, however. He was alert, attentive, cautious in his assessment, and accurate in his diagnosis. He doesn't have knowledge, that is true, but he nonetheless deserves credit for his true belief.

Greco, I expect, would not be convinced, and perhaps some readers will not be either. So let us assume that Greco is right, that Joe does not deserve credit for his true belief. Now consider the following supplement to the Tim–Tom case. All the details occur as in the first version, but in this case the police have heard this story dozens of times before. They know that Tom has no twin brother, because they investigated it when Tom was accused of stealing in the past. They also have a long history of Tom's mother telling them lies to try to protect Tom. So the pattern is clear to them: Tom's mother is just trying to protect Tom again, but not very smartly. She is using a ruse that they already know to be false.

40. Keith Lehrer and Thomas Paxson, Jr., "Knowledge: Undefeated Justified True Belief," *Journal of Philosophy*, 66, 8 (1969): 225–37.

In such a case, Joe's knowledge is not undermined, for though the testimony of Tom's mother is a defeater of his evidence that Tom stole the book, it is a misleading defeater because it is such an obvious ruse. (Joe, remember, has no knowledge of the events at the precinct; if he did, we'd have to take account of whether he knows that the story is a ruse.) Because the defeater is misleading, it does not undermine the claim that Joe knows Tom stole the book. The explanation is that only genuine defeaters can undermine knowledge, and this defeater is not a genuine one.[41]

Greco must maintain, therefore, that credit for true belief is due in the second case but not in the first. I can see relevant differences between the two cases that can be used to explain why knowledge is present in the second case but not in the first, but those differences have no connection to credit deserved as far as I can see. Rather, the differences have to do with genuine versus misleading defeaters. If I simply consider the two situations that Joe is in, I think he deserves credit for true belief in both cases; but if one wishes to be skeptical about that, it still seems to me that Joe deserves credit for true belief in both cases or in neither. The differences between the two cases suggest no difference in that regard at all.

One might say that the explanation for Joe's being right in the first case involves luck and that credit is not deserved for products of luck. Such a response is inadequate. To repeat from a prior chapter, to say that Gettier examples involve accidentally or lucky true belief is to identify a genus under which some solution to the Gettier problem falls, but it is a mistake to think that knowledge rules out all luck. All we are entitled to assume is that a solution to the Gettier problem will rule out some luck and some accidentality, leaving luck and accidentality itself compatible with knowledge. Hence, there is no reason to think that luck or accidentality is incompatible with knowledge and plenty of reason to think otherwise – knowledge is nearly always obtained by grace and not by works. So luck and accidentality cannot be incompatible with deserved credit for true belief if Greco's theory is correct.

One might try to maintain that the luck involved in the first case is incompatible with deserved credit because it is luck incompatible with the presence of knowledge, but this response fails to grasp the force of a counterexample. It is like a utilitarian responding to a counterexample to

41. Compare Peter Klein, *Certainty* (Minneapolis: University of Minnesota Press, 1981).

the theory of moral permissibility, involving framing an innocent person in order to achieve higher overall utility, as follows: "If my theory is right, that is no counterexample." The claim is correct, but philosophically unimpressive, because it ignores the force of the counterexample. Just so with this imagined response by Greco. Greco could claim that if his theory is correct, then credit is deserved for true belief in the second case but not in the first. But that response ignores the force of the counterexample. I ask that the cases be read not with an eye to the question of whether knowledge is present in each case, but with attention to the question of whether Joe deserves credit for true belief in each case. If that is what we focus on, an honest and impartial evaluation of the cases will reveal no discernible difference in the two cases. So either Joe deserves credit for true belief in both cases, as I believe he does, or in neither. Either way, Greco's theory will not work.

The only way to get a different answer, I submit, is to read the cases with an eye to the question of whether knowledge is present and then infer an answer to the question of credit deserved from the assumption that knowledge implies deserved credit or is valuable in some other way over and above the value of its constituents. That procedure is defective. On the first option, it assumes the truth of Greco's theory. On the second option, it undermines the attempt to appeal to deserved credit to help explain the value of knowledge over that of its constituents, for it assumes that point in order to avoid a counterexample to the theory. So either way, we must judge the attempt to explain the special value of knowledge in terms of credit due to be a failure.

These problematic details of Greco's theory point to a more general problem for pragmatic versions of attitudinalism. There are a number of concepts involving cognitive achievement of various sorts that, when ascribed, ordinarily attribute something positive to the recipient. Beliefs and believers can show acumen, perspicacity, discernment, insight, genius, sagacity, wisdom, brilliance, depth, and intelligence, to name a few. In each such case, the ascription of that characteristic involves, at least ordinarily, a pro-attitude on the part of the speaker toward the belief or believer in question. In order for the pragmatic version of epistemic attitudinalism to be successful in providing an account of the value of knowledge, whatever positive element is pragmatically present when knowledge is ascribed would have to be uniquely present to ascriptions of knowledge not involved in other related cognitive achievements, especially those achievements already judged to be valuable, such as true belief, subjectively justified belief, and beliefs that are reliable in virtue of being the products of the intellectual virtues. If the pragmatic element were not distinctive in this way, no appeal to it could help explain the value of knowledge over that of its subpart.

It is implausible to think that there is a unique pro-attitude displayed for each different term of epistemic appraisal, however. What distinguishes each of the preceding terms is not some fine-grained difference in pro-attitude, but rather the semantic content of each term. There is no reason to posit some pragmatic difference in pro-attitude or in the kind of positive value accredited to the agent, as opposed to explaining these differences in semantic terms. If there is no such good reason, then the pragmatic force of different terms of epistemic appraisal will not be able to individuate any value of knowledge from the value of its subcomponents.

We can put this point slightly differently as well. For pragmatic attitudinalism to succeed, we would have to find a reason to individuate terms of epistemic appraisal on the pragmatic side rather than just on the semantic side, and though there may be some significant differences on the pragmatic side, there is insufficient reason to think that these differences are ubiquitous enough and value-related enough to sustain the pragmatic attitudinalist approach to the question of the value of knowledge. For example, there is a difference between saying that a belief is insightful and saying that it is discerning, but the difference is not explained by any difference of value credited to the agent in virtue of the pragmatic dimension of saying that one belief is insightful and another is discerning. The difference here is fundamentally one of difference in meaning between the two adjectives. Whatever of value that is pragmatically accredited is more plausibly taken to be a coarsely individuated value present across many different kinds of epistemic appraisal.

So none of the particular versions of epistemic attitudinalism are successful accounts of the value of knowledge. Perhaps, though, there is hope that some other version of the view, admittedly not yet developed, might provide an adequate attitudinalist approach to the question of the value of knowledge. Hope springs eternal, but it is worth noting that the arguments given earlier do not depend for their force on specific idiosyncracies of the theories examined. Instead, they rely only on very general features of semantic and pragmatic attitudinalism. I have no general argument that decisively confirms that there is no such possibility, but arguments such as the previous ones give strong grounds for abandoning these views.

We should conclude, then, that there are strong grounds for doubting that any version of epistemic attitudinalism will be successful in explaining the value of knowledge. Semantic versions of such made dunces out of too many philosophical luminaries in the early twentieth century for not knowing the meaning of the term 'knowledge', and cannot account for the possibility that people can know things without caring at all whether they have knowledge. Pragmatic versions lack these weaknesses, but they must try in vain to individuate pro-attitudes and value credited in a very fine-grained manner.

We are left, then, with no decent answer to the question of the value of knowledge, and we have pursued at considerable length the ways that might be suggested for answering this question, which first arises in the *Meno*. Such a conclusion is deeply unsatisfying. Stopping with the claim that we are simply wrong provides no insight, and no appeal to general human fallibility will pacify. If we are to maintain the position that there is no good answer to the problem of the *Meno*, we must do more. The next chapter is devoted to that task; there I will identify something of value in the general area of knowledge. I will show how to account for its value and how its value gives us most of what we wanted when we wished for an explanation of the value of knowledge.

8

Knowledge and Understanding

We have been unable to unearth some unique value for knowledge, contrary to the ordinary conception of things. This result leaves us with somewhat of a dilemma, for it would be hard to defend the position that the common viewpoint is wholly without merit. Not that we are anywhere close to claiming such about the common view of knowledge, for our findings that true belief, subjective justification, and displays of intellectual virtue are valuable puts us already within the general locale of knowledge, even if knowledge itself is not uniquely valuable. Furthermore, nothing argued here suggests that knowledge is not valuable. What has been argued is rather a more specialized point: that the problem suggested by Socrates in the *Meno* concerning whether knowledge has more value than its subcomponents is a problem requiring a negative answer. Knowledge is valuable, to be sure, but its value is exhausted by the value of a subset of its constituents.

This result may be in part a product of a bit of myopia on the part of contemporary epistemologists, given the debates among philosophers of the ancient period about the best translation of the Greek term that is commonly translated 'knowledge'. For some argue that the term ought to be translated as 'understanding'.[1] Given this fact, it may be a mistake to identify the problem of the *Meno* with any question about the value of knowledge. It may be that the problem of the *Meno* could just as well have been put as a question about the value of understanding, and our failure to find a unique value for knowledge is a mere sidebar to the more successful pursuit of a unique value for understanding.

---

1. See Robert Fogelin, *Pyrrhonian Reflections on Knowledge and Justifications* (Oxford: Oxford University Press, 1994), for discussion of this debate on how to translate ἐπιστέμε.

Such a result would have much to commend it. First, there is a way of looking at the relationship between knowledge and understanding so that understanding appears to be even more valuable than knowledge. Many in our information age wonder where all of our understanding has gone, replaced by knowledge of the sort celebrated on *Who Wants to Be a Millionaire?* and *Jeopardy* and in games such as *Trivial Pursuit*. A head full of trivia and detail is an amazing thing, but nothing to be compared with the reach and sweep of a person of understanding, so if knowledge is a good thing, understanding is even better. Attending to the relationship between knowledge and understanding can give us hope in our pursuit of special and unique value for epistemic achievements, even though we have had to give up such hope regarding the cognitive achievement of knowledge. If we could account for the value and centrality of understanding in our cognitive lives, we could blunt the force of our negative conclusions concerning the value of knowledge. For one need not apologize for replacing a lifelong pursuit of knowledge with a lifelong pursuit of understanding.

Such a conclusion might also contribute to a quite radical change in the discipline of epistemology. Radical changes have already occurred in recent years in the discipline in response to a new attitude toward skepticism. The history of epistemology is primarily a story of conversations with the skeptic. Skepticism provides the impetus for the origin of the discipline and has dominated the efforts of epistemologists throughout the history of epistemology, either in defense of skepticism or by way of rebuttal. The result of this dominance is that the discipline of epistemology has focused on the concept of knowledge and whatever constituents it has, such as truth and justification.

As a result of ordinary-language philosophy and the commonsense philosophy traceable to Thomas Reid,[2] but defended with greater historical significance for contemporary epistemology by G. E. Moore,[3] skepticism has come to play a less central role in epistemology over the past half century or so. Instead of providing legitimate concern that we might not know very much or anything at all, skepticism came to be viewed as a clearly false position in need only of a proper explanation of its falsity. The standard assumption came to be, it would seem, that everyone with

2. Thomas Reid, *Inquiry and Essays*, Keith Lehrer and Ronald E. Beanblossom, eds. (Indianapolis: Hackett, 1975).
3. G. E. Moore, *Philosophical Papers* (London: Allen and Unwin, 1959). See especially "Proof of an External World," "Refutation of Idealism," and "A Defense of Common Sense."

good sense *knows* that skepticism is false; the only interesting question is *why* it is false.

The result of these movements has been a freedom of exploration in epistemology, unencumbered by any need to address constantly the arguments of the skeptics. The result has been a flourishing of investigation into topics such as the nature of justification, the role of testimony in warranted belief, and the social dimension of knowledge, as well as the Gettier-inspired plethora of attempts to characterize the nature of knowledge. New approaches to epistemological questions have been developed, too, including social epistemology, feminist epistemology, and virtue epistemology.

In spite of this loosening of the shackles fastened on epistemology by skepticism, there is a deeper way in which skepticism still dominates. For even in the new era of freedom, the concept of knowledge provides the focal point of epistemological inquiry. This point is well instanced by virtue epistemology. Instead of a broad focus on cognitive achievements and excellences in general, virtue epistemologists have usually tried to make a place for the virtues in epistemology by defining knowledge or justification in terms of the virtues. I think that such a focus betrays remnants of skeptical shackles that have plagued the history of epistemology. For in the absence of such, epistemology would seem to have a large stake in inquiry regarding successful or valuable aspects of cognition, such as wisdom and understanding, regardless of the value such aspects have in addressing the skeptical challenge regarding knowledge.

It is worthwhile to contrast this aspect of virtue epistemology with G. E. M. Anscombe's early call for a return to the concept of virtue in ethics.[4] Anscombe not only proposes a kind of virtue ethics to replace standard utilitarian and deontological approaches, but also denigrates moral theories that focus on concepts such as right and wrong, good and bad. An analogue of such an approach in epistemology would be one that favored talking about the intellectual virtues and no longer focusing on the standard epistemologists' fare of knowledge and justification. Yet, no virtue epistemologist has entertained such a possibility. The shackles of skepticism remain intact, forcing inquiry into our cognitive successes and achievements to focus on questions of knowledge and justification.

Let me caution that I am not denigrating skepticism. I happen to think that skepticism is false, but I also think that it is a substantive

---

4. G. E. M. Anscombe, "Modern Moral Philosophy," *Philosophy,* 33 (1958): 1–19.

philosophical thesis requiring serious argumentation: Moorian presentations of two hands are not sufficient in themselves to settle the issue. What I lament is a lack of diversity in epistemology, and one of my goals here is to present a theoretical foundation for greater diversity of interests in epistemology. In particular, understanding deserves much more attention than it has received. First, there is at least as much intuitive support for the idea that understanding has value beyond that of its subparts as there is for the idea that knowledge has such value. As we shall see, using conclusions from previous chapters, we have resources to explain this value. Second, understanding is a cognitive achievement distinct from knowledge. Though the nature of understanding is not often addressed, it is nonetheless commonly assumed that knowledge and understanding bear a direct and intimate connection, for the common assumption is that understanding of the theoretical sort is a species of knowledge. The assumption is, I believe, that the kind of understanding at issue when regarding our cognitive successes and achievements is some type of deep and comprehensive knowledge concerning a particular subject, topic, or issue.

I will begin my discussion of understanding by questioning this latter assumption, but I want to make one point before doing so. I want to point out how the plan I will follow in discussing understanding follows the lessons we have learned from Socrates in the *Meno*. Socrates' discussion, as I have argued, gives us two desiderata to guide our theorizing about cognitive achievements, one concerning the nature of such achievements and the other concerning their value. I will not present a complete theory of understanding here, but I will present enough of a theory regarding the nature of understanding so that we will be able to give an explanation of its value. The conclusion I will draw is that the problem of the *Meno* can be solved when it is conceived as a problem regarding understanding rather than knowledge. In order to get to that conclusion, I begin with the issue of the relationship between knowledge and understanding.

UNDERSTANDING, KNOWLEDGE, AND LOGICAL FORM

We can begin by asking about the logical form of attributions of understanding. Let us first distinguish between noun, adjective, and verb clauses involving this concept. In its noun form, we have examples such as

"My understanding was that you would be finished by now."
"My understanding of Heidegger is sketchy at best."

In its adjectival form, we have examples such as

"He is in an understanding frame of mind."

In its verb form, we have examples such as

"He understands quantum theory."
"She understands that Gore might have been president."
"They understand why Germany invaded Poland."
"We understand where you are coming from."
"You understand what it takes to be a marine."
"I understand how to make dynamite."
"Everyone understands when it is time to eat."

In passing, we should also note that there are grammatical forms in which 'understanding' appears to be a one-place predicate. I saw a billboard recently that proclaimed "God understands," and we often say "I understand" in conversation. In each case, however, such statements are elliptical, with something assumed that is not said, and when the ellipses are removed, we will have instances of the forms just presented.

Among these various uses are some that are of special interest for theoretical purposes and thus of special interest to epistemology broadly conceived in terms of the study of cognitive, as opposed to practical, successes and achievements. Among the different grammatical forms in which the concept of knowledge occurs, epistemologists focus on knowledge that something is the case, ignoring for epistemological purposes knowing how and other grammatical forms that are not as central for theoretical purposes.

For such purposes, it is not wise to ignore all grammatical forms other than understanding that something is the case, however. For, given purely theoretical purposes, claims such as *He understands quantum theory* are certainly relevant. My suggestion, therefore, is that we focus on understanding in two central uses: when understanding is claimed for some object, such as some subject matter, and when it involves understanding that something is the case.

If we consider the other uses, we can see that a number of them can be explicated in terms of these two central uses. For example, understanding why, when, where, and what are explicable in terms of understanding that something is the case. In each such case there is some truth that explains the special kind of understanding in question, and the person's relationship to that truth can be explicated in terms of understanding that something is the case. For example, understanding why something is the case requires

189

understanding that a certain explanation is correct, and understanding what happened requires understanding that such-and-such happened. So quite a bit of the diversity noted previously can be explained in terms of the uses on which I will focus.

What gets left out, most significantly, is understanding how. That is as it should be, for such understanding is relevant more to practical purposes than to theoretical ones, just as knowing how is more relevant to the former than to the latter.

An initial supposition about understanding and its relationship to knowledge is that both imply truth, that both are factives. To say that a person understands that p therefore requires that p is true. There is a minor difficulty with this idea, however, for there are hedging uses of the concept of understanding. Suppose I've been told that you are angry with me, and I decide to try to remedy the situation by speaking with you about it. Not wholly convinced of the truth of the claim, I might say, "I understand that you are angry with me." In such a case I am hedging a bit on the truth of the claim that you are angry with me, so what I say can be true even though you are not, in fact, angry with me. Such a hedging use bears important connections to the noun form of 'understanding', where saying that your understanding of something is such-and-such need not imply truth. In the example, if you reply that you are not, in fact, angry with me, I might respond by saying that my understanding must have been mistaken.

There are uses of the concept of knowledge that are nonfactive as well. We sometimes talk about the present state of scientific knowledge, but such language does not imply that present theories are true. In addition, we sometimes say, "I just *knew* I was going to fail," as an expression of surprise at having succeeded. And undergraduates are increasingly given to claiming that it used to be known that the earth is flat, even though we now know that it isn't.

Our interest in the nature of knowledge or understanding requires some sorting, then, among common uses of the term. In both cases, I think the best explanation is to take the nonfactive uses to involve either misspeaking or the expression of propositions that do not involve the concepts of knowledge or understanding central to epistemological inquiry, related as it is to theoretical concerns. When undergraduates say, "It used to be known that the earth is flat," they may be misspeaking. If such expression becomes common enough, they will cease to be misspeaking, but in the process they will have ceased to express a proposition involving the concept of knowledge. Instead, the word 'knows' will have come to

190

express a different concept. Again, when a person claims in surprise, "I just *knew* I was going to fail," the intended proposition is one about how psychologically certain that person was about being headed for failure.

Just so in the cases of nonfactive uses of 'understanding' and its cognates. In the nonfactive uses, the idea communicated is that the person believes, and perhaps has good evidence for believing, that something is the case. For example, when a person says, "My understanding is that you weren't home till after midnight," the intended proposition is one about the beliefs, perhaps justified beliefs, of the speaker. In such uses, the speaker intends to cushion the force of a bald accusation, an assertion that seems too strong to be appropriate.

I want to focus here, however, on the factive uses of 'understanding' and its cognates, for these uses are more relevant to the theoretical project of epistemology. Among such uses are two primary ones: propositional understanding and objectual understanding. The propositional sort occurs when we attribute understanding in the form of a propositional operator, as in understanding that something is the case, and the objectual sort occurs when understanding grammatically is followed by an object, as in understanding the presidency, or the president, or politics, or the English language. Objectual understanding is, of course, not straightforwardly factive, for only propositions can be true or false. Still, the uses I wish to focus on are ones in which facticity is in the background. For example, to understand politics is to have beliefs about it, and for this objectual understanding to be the kind of interest here requires that these beliefs are true.

Understanding, in these forms, is importantly related to knowledge, enough so that it is plausible to think that understanding is a species of knowledge. In the senses relevant to our inquiry, both attitudes are factive, and in some contexts, the terms seem virtually synonymous. For example, it is hard to draw a distinction between saying that one knows or understands the American political process. The synonymy view is false when applied across all contexts, however, for it is possible to have knowledge without having understanding. One can know Bill Clinton, for example, without understanding him, and we can contrast knowledge of a number of facts about a subject matter with understanding of it. To be a species of knowledge, however, the two-way entailment required of synonymy need not obtain. All that is needed is that understanding implies knowledge, and that view has much to recommend it. If one understands a body of information, this would seem to require knowledge of that information; and if one understands that the 2000 presidential election

.

was at stake in Florida, it is hard to see how such understanding could obtain without knowing that the election was at stake in Florida.

So, the proposal with which we begin is as follows. When propositional understanding is attributed, knowledge of the proposition in question is implied, and when objectual understanding obtains, knowledge is implied as well. In some cases, the implication may go in the other direction as well, but the view in question is committed only to a one-way entailment.

If understanding is a species of knowledge, and not identical with it, what does understanding add that knowledge can lack? The central feature of understanding, it seems to me, is in the neighborhood of what internalist coherence theories say about justification. Understanding requires the grasping of explanatory and other coherence-making relationships in a large and comprehensive body of information. One can know many unrelated pieces of information, but understanding is achieved only when informational items are pieced together by the subject in question.

One might even propose a more radical thesis, to the effect that a change occurs metaphysically when understanding is achieved. Whereas knowledge can have as its object individual propositions, understanding may not. It may be that when understanding is achieved, the object of understanding is an "informational chunk" rather than a number of single propositions. In such a view, propositional understanding is not the primary form of understanding, but results via abstraction from this primary form.[5] Perhaps something similar occurs in ordinary perceptual experience. Though one might know a number of propositions, even together with other propositions concerning the explanatory and other coherence-making relationships between the information in question, this propositional knowledge would not constitute understanding, in this view, until a change in the object of such cognitive achievement occurs.

I will not press the metaphysical point here, however, for it is not central to the issues I want to raise about the connection between knowledge and understanding. So, for present purposes, I want to focus on this crucial difference between knowledge and understanding: that understanding requires, and knowledge does not, an internal grasping or appreciation of how the various elements in a body of information are related to each

5. Nicholas Asher has defended such an idea with respect to propositional attitudes such as belief within the context of Discourse Representation Theory, but here I restrict the view to understanding. See his "Belief in Discourse Representation Theory," *Journal of Philosophical Logic*, 5 (1986): 127–89, and "A Typology for Attitude Verbs and Their Anaphoric Properties," *Linguistics and Philosophy*, 10 (1987): 127–97.

other in terms of explanatory, logical, probabilistic, and other kinds of relations that coherentists have thought constitutive of justification.

One can see something of this character played out in Plato's philosophy if Kenneth Sayre's account of it is close to correct. Plato raises the question in the *Theaetetus* concerning the nature of knowledge, ending vaguely with the suggestion that what distinguishes knowledge from true belief is expressed by the concept of a λόγος. On Sayre's account, this suggestion is developed in the *Sophist* in terms of the method of collection and division,[6] a simplified account of which is to identify the object in question in terms of genus and species, beginning with the most general kind to which it belongs, identifying it via kind and differentia until the object itself is completely identified. Such an account of the nature of knowledge is, however, far too psychological. One can know that Fido is a dog without engaging in any such psychological process relating to kinds and differentia.

If we remember the debate about whether to translate $\epsilon\pi\iota\sigma\tau\acute{\epsilon}\mu\epsilon$ as 'knowledge' or 'understanding', however, we can make much more sense out of this proposal. For if we are talking more of the nature of understanding than of knowledge, the objection that the account is too psychological loses its force. For understanding requires, in its very nature, the grasping of explanatory connections between items of information, and if the proper form of explanation is as Plato saw it in the method of collection and division, then the theory presented looks like a good start toward a theory of understanding. It is a good start because it focuses on the question of whether the person has seen the right kinds of relationships among the various items of information grasped.

Moreover, if we turn more epistemological attention to the nature of understanding rather than focusing exclusively on the nature of knowledge, we may find a more natural home for coherentism, for coherentism may offer more promise in the exploration of understanding than as a theory of some component of knowledge, that is, justification. A central problem for coherentism regarding justification is the possibility of justified inconsistent beliefs. Such a possibility is one of the lessons of the Preface and Lottery Paradoxes discussed earlier and the related paradox concerning human fallibility: If you know that you are fallible, then you will be justifiably confident that some of your beliefs are false, which together with your other beliefs entails a contradiction.

6. Kenneth Sayre, *Plato's Analytical Method* (Chicago: University of Chicago Press, 1969).

Some have proclaimed these paradoxes the death song of coherentism,[7] but that is premature. Recently, William Lycan has suggested the idea of compartmentalizing beliefs and requiring coherence in the compartments.[8] In the paradoxes, the preface belief and the fallibility belief would be in separate compartments from the rest of one's beliefs, so inconsistency of this sort doesn't undermine coherentism. It does diminish global coherence and hence justification, according to Lycan, but it doesn't eliminate it entirely. Only inconsistency within a compartment could do that.

Such a strategy faces problems, however. If failure of global coherence diminishes justification, then we might be able to increase the overall coherence of our belief system by coming to believe that we are infallible. Lycan might reply that the benefit of consistency brought by this belief may be countered by failure of fit with other beliefs, such as the belief that we have had false beliefs in the past or that it is generally a part of the human condition to make cognitive errors. This failure of fit between these beliefs and the belief that we are infallible might result in a lower level of overall coherence of the system than the inconsistency that the infallibility belief removed. Still, we could remedy this failure of fit incoherence by abandoning those beliefs or adopting some further explanation of why things are different now than in the past and why what is generally true about human beings doesn't apply to us (after all, we all do this in one way or another anyway). But surely we would not be more justified in our beliefs about ordinary phenomena such as the weather, politics, science, and the like if we made all these adjustments. We would have eliminated inconsistency and incoherence but failed to produce any positive effect on the quality of justification.

In addition, it is hard to characterize the concept of a compartment to yield the proper results in all these paradoxes. In the Preface and Infallibility Paradoxes, compartmentalization can be done in terms of object-level beliefs and meta-level beliefs, between beliefs that are not about (other) beliefs and beliefs that are about beliefs. On this way of compartmentalizing, the belief that it is raining is an object-level belief, because its content is not about any belief, whereas the belief that I believe that it is raining

---

7. See, e.g., Richard Foley, "Justified Inconsistent Beliefs," *American Philosophical Quarterly*, 16 (1979): 247–57.
8. See, e.g., Lycan's "Plantinga and Coherentisms," *Warrant in Contemporary Epistemology: Essays in Honor of Plantinga's Theory of Knowledge*, Jonathan L. Kvanvig, ed. (Totowa, NJ: Rowman & Littlefield, 1996), p. 10.

is a meta-level belief because its content is about a belief. We might also compartmentalize here by level, leaving this last example as a first-level meta-belief, whereas my further opinion that I believe that I believe that it is raining would be a second-level meta-belief.

This way of compartmentalizing may work for the Preface and Infallibility Paradoxes, for it sorts the sources of inconsistency into separate compartments. In the case of the Preface Paradox, the statements that comprise the body of the book would be object-level statements, whereas the preface statement that some claims in the book are false would be a meta-statement. In the Infallibility Paradox, the belief that I am fallible would be a meta-belief as well. The case of the Lottery Paradox is different, however. In this case, the inconsistency arises in virtue of a number of particular beliefs to the effect that each ticket will lose and a general belief that some ticket will win, all of which are object-level beliefs. To compartmentalize in a way needed to handle the Lottery Paradox, one will have to keep these general and particular beliefs in different compartments.

Yet, sometimes the inconsistency between one's general beliefs and one's particular beliefs is decisive, implying lack of justification, as when you are convinced that telling this particular lie in these circumstances is morally acceptable when you also believe that lying is always wrong in such circumstances. In such a case, each of these beliefs is a defeater of any justification the other possesses. The most natural way to account for such is to keep the beliefs in the same compartment, but a coherentist can't always do that and use the idea of compartmentalization to escape the Lottery Paradox.

The issue of how to compartmentalize takes on a different flavor when coherentism is employed in a theory of understanding. Theoretical understanding has as its standard object a body of information, but ordinarily not a single proposition. So when we say that a person understands Special Relativity Theory, there is no single proposition of which we ascribe understanding. Rather, there is a larger body of information, composed perhaps of propositions, regarding which we ascribe understanding. This point suggests that standard ascriptions of understanding come compartmentalized already, and the worry of having to draw artificial boundary lines to avoid the difficulties that plague a coherence theory of justification may not be as pressing. So the first lesson to learn is that broadening our vision of topics suitable for epistemological investigation may allow us to find useful niches for theories that may have turned out to be inadequate concerning the standard epistemological fare of knowledge and justification.

Using coherentist ideas to help explicate the nature of understanding elucidates another difference between knowledge and understanding. Whereas it is awkward to speak of degrees of knowledge or of some knowledge being better or worse than other knowledge,[9] understanding comes in these forms. Some people have a better understanding of a subject matter than others, and others have a greater degree of understanding.

One might attempt to explain away this relativity in the same way we explain away talk of degrees of truth, for we also say that some people's views are closer to the truth than others'. Such a move is not necessary regarding understanding, however, for the two cases are significantly different. The common form of understanding in terms of some large body of information has no analogue when it comes to truth, for the concept of truth has primary application to propositional contents. If we attend to this difference, then we have two bases on which to explain the relative nature of understanding. First, justification itself comes in degrees, so two bodies of information regarding the same subject matter might differ in the degree of coherence they display. Second, the two bodies of information might differ in terms of the amount of information contained regarding the subject matter. In both of these ways, understanding can be a matter of degree, and in that way understanding is different from knowledge and from truth.

UNDERSTANDING IS NOT A SPECIES OF KNOWLEDGE

The preceding ideas about understanding also set the stage for arguing that understanding is not a species of knowledge. First, note that knowledge, too, can be ascribed relative to a body of information: A person can be said to know Special Relativity Theory just as much as she can be said to understand it. We have noted that knowledge is typically not a relative concept, as is understanding, and we might try to use that fact here to show that understanding is not a species of knowledge. Such a conclusion would be hasty, however. For when we speak of objectual knowledge, it is not unusual to resort to the language of relativity in describing it. We can coherently say, "He knows Descartes's philosophy much better than I do," so there is no basis here to distinguish between understanding and knowledge.

9. For an alternative view that defends what I term "awkward," see Stephen Cade Hetherington, *Better and Worse Knowledge* (Oxford: Oxford University Press, 2001).

There is an interesting difference between understanding and knowledge of a subject matter, however. I think we are more inclined to try to explain knowledge of a subject matter in terms of knowledge of the truths involved in that subject than we are to explain understanding in terms of such individual propositions. At the very least, the objectual type of knowledge ascription is obviously related to more standard knowledge ascriptions that relate a person and a proposition. Perhaps we can fully explain knowing a body of information in terms of knowing truths,[10] but at the very least, we should endorse the claim that knowing a body of information involves knowing a number of the truths that make up that body of information. So, if understanding is a species of knowledge, then understanding a body of information will also involved knowing a number of the truths that make up that body of information. We thus have a condition of adequacy on the claim that understanding is a species of knowledge, a condition of adequacy I will argue is false.

Note that the crucial features just discussed concerning understanding draw attention to things other than what is central to knowledge. What is distinctive about understanding has to do with the way in which an individual combines pieces of information into a unified body. This point is not meant to imply that truth is not important for understanding, for we have noted already the factive character of both knowledge and understanding. But once we move past its facticity, the grasping of relations between items of information is central to the nature of understanding. By contrast, when we move past the facticity of knowledge, the central features involve nonaccidental connections between mind and world. So our first glances at the two phenomena suggest the possibility that the logical connection proclaimed by the standard view, the view that understanding is a species of knowledge, is incorrect.

Moreover, consideration of particular cases of understanding suggests the same. Consider, say, someone's historical understanding of the Comanche dominance of the southern plains of North America from the late seventeenth until the late nineteenth centuries. Suppose that if you asked this person any question about this matter, she would answer correctly. Assume further that the person is answering from stored information; she is not guessing or making up answers, but is honestly averring

10. The issue here is the well-known one of whether *de re* belief can be explained in terms of *de dicto* belief, about which much has been written. My formulation of the connection between objectual knowledge and propositional knowledge in the text is crafted to avoid this debate, ancillary as it is to the relationship between knowledge and understanding.

what she confidently believes the truth to be. Such an ability is surely constitutive of understanding, and the experience of query and answer, if sustained for a long enough period of time, would generate convincing evidence that the person in question understood the phenomenon of Comanche dominance of the southern plains. But does she have knowledge? Ordinarily, yes; but it is not required. For, on the usual theories of knowledge, all those answers could be given from information possessed and still fail to be known to be true, because the answers might only be accidentally true. For example, most history books might have been mistaken, with only the correct ones being the sources of the understanding in question and with no basis in the subject for preferring the sources consulted over those ignored. Such a case fits the model of a standard type of case found in the Gettier literature (in particular, the fake barn case), where such accidentally true beliefs are not justified in the way needed for the beliefs to count as knowledge.

Such possibilities may lead one to wonder about the wisdom of ascribing understanding on the basis of the correct answers given to the questions asked. Correctly answering the questions doesn't *entail* the presence of understanding, after all. At most, it only constitutes very good evidence of it, evidence that might be defeated. We might find out, for example, that the person is guessing and being lucky every time. As noted previously, however, I stipulate that the case is one where the person is not guessing, that she is revealing honestly the convictions she has, the data she has, and the grasped explanatory connections involved in the large body of information possessed. Moreover, the capacity for answering is counterfactual supporting, as I have described it: Ask anything about the phenomenon, and one would get a correct answer from information possessed.

Given these parameters, reservations about ascribing understanding should be put aside even in the cases where knowledge ascriptions should be withheld. For understanding does not advert to the etiological aspects that can be crucial for knowledge. What is distinctive about understanding, once we have satisfied the truth requirement, is internal to cognition. It is the internal seeing or appreciating of explanatory and other coherence-inducing relationships in a body of information that is crucial for understanding. When we think about knowledge, however, our focus turns elsewhere immediately if we have learned our lessons from the Gettier literature: We think about the possibility of fortuitousness, of accidentality, of being right but only by chance. We focus, that is, on what kinds of further external connections there are between mind and world, beyond the fit required for the belief to be true.

The basic idea here is that although knowledge is incompatible with a certain kind of epistemic luck, understanding is not. Upon learning of the disturbed etiology of beliefs about the Comanches, as in the case imagined here, we might say that a person has true beliefs or even justified true beliefs, but no knowledge, if we have heeded our lessons from Gettier. We would not, at least we should not, say that because of these factors, she is lucky to have the knowledge that she has, for knowledge rules out this kind of luck. But we needn't say the same about the claim of understanding. If the etiology were as imagined, one would be lucky to have any understanding at all of the Comanche dominance of the southern plains. So such understanding would count as understanding not undermined by the kind of luck in question.

These remarks must contain a caveat about the lessons of the Gettier literature, which I include because some epistemologists think that knowledge can be understood in terms of true belief alone. We have already seen Sartwell's defense of such a view in a previous chapter and have chronicled some of its weaknesses, so I will devote no further attention to it here. There is, however, a more interesting version of the same thesis in a recent paper by Richard Foley.[11] Foley asks us to imagine an individual who answers correctly any question we might ask about any subject matter. The individual is not guessing; he is asserting his true convictions. Foley concludes that in such a case we should all grant that such an individual knows a lot more than you or I. Furthermore, Foley claims that this conclusion should be granted even if the individual in question has all of his true beliefs sheerly by chance. Perhaps he is a Swampman, formed in the marsh as a result of a random strike of lightning, arising cognitively formed with all the true beliefs in question.

Foley takes his example to show that all the standard responses to the Gettier problem are misconceived, for they all imply that Swampman has no knowledge. For those tempted by Foley's theory, my argument against understanding being a species of knowledge will be suspect. But I think there is a more palatable response than abandoning the Gettier tradition entirely, as Foley's theory requires. My response to Foley is to grant that there is something epistemically extraordinary about Swampman but to deny that such extraordinariness needs to be explained in terms of

11. See Crispin Sartwell, "Knowledge Is True Belief," *American Philosophical Quarterly*, 28, 2 (1991): 157–65; Richard Foley, "Knowledge Is Accurate and Comprehensive Enough True Belief," in *Warrant in Contemporary Epistemology*, pp. 87–96.

knowledge.[12] To make such a rejection palatable, we need to explain what is epistemically extraordinary about Swampman, and if we distinguish rightly between knowledge and understanding, I think we can find such an explanation. Because understanding is by its very nature highly internal, constituted by seeing and grasping information and its significance, the fact that Swampman has an extraordinary range of true beliefs and can answer all the questions we might put to him shows that the understanding he possesses vastly exceeds our own. He is cognitively superior to us in this very important way, even though he may know quite a bit less than we do.

THE VALUE OF UNDERSTANDING

Given this sketch of understanding, can we do better in accounting for its value than we were able to do for the value of knowledge? Here we need to return to the notion of subjective justification, the value of which was defended earlier. Subjective justification obtains when persons form or hold beliefs on the basis of their own subjective standards for what is true or false. They follow the marks of truth defined by their own subjective perspective on the world. As we have seen, this sort of justification is valuable because it is constituted by adopting intentional means to the goal of truth. On this view, justification is extrinsically valuable in virtue of its relationship to truth, though it is not instrumentally valuable on the basis of its relationship to truth.

Given this notion, we are in a position to explain the value of understanding, conceived of in terms of a body of information together with the grasping of explanatory connections concerning that body of information. Such a description involves those features distinctive of coherence theories of justification without the liabilities that accrue to coherentism when it is applied to the entire system of beliefs. It is, in short, compartmentalized holistic coherence that is distinctive of understanding, and to the extent that coherentism is plausible as a theory of justification, it is even more plausible here because of the compartmentalization that

---

12. It is also worth noting that at the 2002 Rutgers Epistemology Conference, Foley presented his new view of knowledge but in discussion recanted. When pressed by the audience, Foley added another requirement to his theory: that a person must be in a position to know, must not be isolated from the world in a way that prevents the possibility of knowledge. Of course, Foley would not employ such language in a full explication of his theory, because it would then be circular, but it is instructive to note that he now recognizes that an account of knowledge solely in terms of a comprehensive grasp of truth is inadequate.

is assumed. In particular, inconsistency within a body of information is inconsistent with understanding that body of information.

One might worry here about theories that are themselves inconsistent: Can't one understand naive set theory, for example, even though it is inconsistent? There is a difference between understanding the claims of the theory and the understanding involved in taking the claims of the theory to be true. One can understand naive set theory in the sense of grasping the axioms and (some of) the theorems that follow from these axioms without endorsing any of the claims as being true. So in this sense, one can understand inconsistent theories, because one can have such understanding without having any inconsistent beliefs.

What is ruled out by the factive character of the kind of understanding of interest in theoretical contexts is any understanding that depends on the existence of inconsistent beliefs. We might honorifically ascribe understanding to people who unwittingly find themselves having such beliefs, much as we honorifically talk about the present state of scientific knowledge (even though we know that some of what falls under that rubric is false). Nor do I wish to claim that there is no legitimate use of the term 'understanding' that is not factive, for I have already noted uses such as the hedging uses of the term that are nonfactive. I am inclined to treat such cases in terms of pragmatic rather than semantic features of language, much as I would want to explain the cognitive significance of talk of the present state of scientific knowledge in terms of nonsemantic, pragmatic features of the concept of knowledge. From that perspective, cognitive achievements, however laudatory, do not constitute real knowledge or real understanding without the presence of truth.

There is still something of a problem here, though, for it is hard to resist the view that understanding may be correctly ascribed even in the presence of some false beliefs concerning a subject matter. For example, suppose the false beliefs concern matters that are peripheral rather than central to the subject matter in question. We might want to talk of slight imperfections in understanding or of slightly defective understanding, but that is different from saying that there is no understanding present at all because of the falsehoods involved.

The view I am defending needs to be altered slightly to accommodate this idea, but it need not be abandoned entirely. When the falsehoods are peripheral, we can ascribe understanding based on the rest of the information grasped that is true and contains no falsehoods. In such a case, the false beliefs are not part of the understanding the person has, even though they concern the very material regarding which the person has understanding. So in this way, the factive character of understanding can be preserved without having to say that a person with false beliefs about a subject matter can have no understanding of it.

For understanding, there is a need for truth and for explanatory and other coherence relations to obtain between the various beliefs involved in the achievement of understanding. Yet, the mere existence of such connections is not enough, for there is a psychological requirement concerning the coherence relations involved in understanding, to the effect that the person in question must grasp them. The way in which all the information fits together must be part of what the person is aware of. We thus get the following explanation of the value of understanding. The distinctive element involved in it, beyond truth, is best understood in terms of grasped coherence relations. Such coherence relations in this context contribute to justification. Such justification is subjective, because the person in question must grasp the marks of truth within that body of information in order to grasp correctly the explanatory relationships within that body of information. Such justification is not merely subjective, however, for the awarenesses in question must be correct in order for the factive element of understanding to obtain. Moreover, to have mastered such explanatory relationships is valuable not only because it involves the finding of new truths but also because finding such relationships organizes and systematizes our thinking on a subject matter in a way beyond the mere addition of more true beliefs or even justified true beliefs. Such organization is pragmatically useful because it allows us to reason from one bit of information to other related information that is useful as a basis for action, where unorganized thinking provides no such basis for inference. Moreover, such organized elements of thought provide intrinsically satisfying closure to the process of inquiry, yielding a sense or feeling of completeness to our grasp of a particular subject matter. In sum, understanding is valuable because it is constituted by subjectively justified true belief across an appropriately individuated body of information that is systematized and organized in the process of achieving understanding, and subjectively justified true belief that is systematized in this way is valuable.

CONCLUSION

There is another way in which an epistemological project that focuses more on understanding than on knowledge has axiological advantages. If we recall William James's assessment of our cognitive fears in terms of the

202

fear of being duped and the fear of missing something important,[13] it is not difficult to see how understanding is superior to knowledge in addressing these fears. Because both concepts are factive in character, both are equally adequate for addressing our fear of being duped, but the same cannot be said for the fear of missing something important. Whereas knowledge can be piecemeal, understanding requires more completeness. Thus, it is not possible for one to miss something important about which one has perfect understanding. Moreover, the concept of relative understanding tracks what is important in a body of information, so that failure to grasp significant items within that body of information renders a person lacking in understanding. It is only when information is less important within that body of information that one can be credited with understanding in spite of such a failure of perfect understanding.

This discussion about understanding is a sketch rather than a complete theory of the nature of understanding. Yet, brief as it is, it forms the basis for a positive answer to the issues in the *Meno* directed at the concept of understanding. Our discussion shows enough about understanding to give us confidence that a complete theory of it can successfully address both desiderata on a good epistemological theory. We can be confident, that is, that a complete theory of the nature of understanding will also give us resources for accounting for its unique value, and having this feature is another way in which understanding is superior to knowledge.

13. William James, "The Will to Believe," in *The Will to Believe and Other Essays* (New York: Longmans, Green, 1897).

9

Conclusion

I want first to point out an important misconstrual of what I have been arguing. For a quick but misleading summary of my thesis might be that knowledge is not valuable, whereas understanding is.

Such a summary is grossly misleading, for the position I have defended maintains a high value for knowledge. First, knowledge involves true belief, and true belief is valuable in virtue of the action-guiding character of belief and in virtue of the intrinsic value of finding the truth. Second, knowledge is valuable because of its relationship to subjective justification. I have not claimed, and do not claim here, that subjective justification is necessary for knowledge, but it is nonetheless true that one of the paths to knowledge is through the land of subjective justification. So, much knowledge is subjectively justified, even if not all of it is. Third, we have found also that displays of cognitive excellence or intellectual virtue are valuable as well. Once again, I have defended no position on the relationship between such displays and knowledge, but the same point is true here that is true of subjective justification. That is, even if displays of cognitive excellence are not necessary for knowledge, it is nonetheless true that much of our knowledge is explained in terms of such displays.

There are also other items that are related to knowledge that are valuable as well and lead to the conclusion that knowledge is of immense value. Reliably produced belief is valuable, and so is objectively justified belief. Each of these is instrumentally valuable because of its connection to truth, and the latter may also be valuable in another way if we agree with Swinburne that the path to objectively justified belief goes through subjective justification.[1] These properties, as well as those previously mentioned, are related to knowledge in something other than a purely coincidental way.

The proper conclusion to draw from these points is that knowledge is a vessel loaded heavily with value, not the misleading previous conclusion that knowledge is not valuable. There is, however, a reason for the preceding summary, for there is a problem concerning the value of knowledge that, I have argued, cannot be solved. That problem is first introduced in Socrates' discussion with Meno. Socrates' version of the problem was to try to explain what makes knowledge more valuable than true belief. Translated into the language of contemporary epistemology, the generic problem is to explain how the value of knowledge exceeds that of its subparts. The conclusion we have come to is that this problem is insoluble, and thus that knowledge does not have a value exceeding that of its subparts.

The same is not true of understanding on the account of understanding defended in the previous chapter. Understanding, in that view, is a construction out of true belief and subjective justification of a coherentist variety. Because both truth and subjective justification are valuable independently of each other and because neither value is swamped by the value of the other, we have the basis for an explanation of why understanding is more valuable than its subparts. To this basis, we add the value created by additional justified true beliefs regarding the general explanatory relationships (including logical and probabilistic relationships) that coherentists proclaim to be the defining features of justification. To have mastered such explanatory relationships is valuable because it gets us to the truth, but also because finding such relationships organizes and systematizes our thinking on a subject matter in a way beyond the mere addition of more true beliefs or even justified true beliefs.

Does this conclusion suggest that understanding is somehow easier to achieve than knowledge, because knowledge requires being ungettiered and understanding does not? That, too, would be a misrepresentation. It is true that in this respect understanding is easier to achieve than knowledge, but it should also be remembered that understanding only comes in big chunks of information, whereas knowledge can be acquired piecemeal. In this respect, understanding is much more difficult to achieve than knowledge.

1. Richard Swinburne, *Epistemic Justification* (Oxford: Oxford University Press, 2001).

Is understanding thereby more valuable than knowledge? I have not argued that this is so, but there is a good case to be made for it. It is interesting to note some of Sosa's comments about his distinction between animal knowledge and reflective knowledge, where the former can be obtained through the use of truth-conducive mechanisms, whereas the latter requires something more – coherentist justification. According to Sosa, one has reflective knowledge only when "one's judgement or belief manifests not only such direct response to the fact known but also understanding of its place in a wider whole."[2] Sosa makes it clear that such reflective knowledge is superior in value to mere animal knowledge.

What is important in our context is the way in which Sosa's description of reflective knowledge seems very much like the theory of understanding presented here, for Sosa describes reflective knowledge in terms of manifesting the understanding of a fact's place in a wider whole. I do not claim that Sosa identifies reflective knowledge with understanding, but given the theory of understanding presented here and the superiority of reflective knowledge to animal knowledge, it is not difficult to see the nature of the argument that understanding is superior to knowledge. Sosa's remarks do not require such an interpretation, for he can maintain that understanding is superior to knowledge only when it counts as reflective knowledge and not as mere understanding. Yet, the weaker position, that even understanding that fails to constitute knowledge is more valuable than knowledge itself, has its attractions. It comports well with our ordinary conception that understanding is a milestone to be achieved by long and sustained efforts at knowledge acquisition. By making such efforts, we move toward a goal that is more valuable than the possessions we might acquire on the way. And perhaps we can be graced by something more valuable than knowledge even when we find ourselves in the kinds of hostile environments that prevent the acquisition of knowledge in the pursuit of understanding.

2. Ernest Sosa, *Knowledge in Perspective: Selected Essays in Epistemology* (Cambridge: Cambridge University Press, 1991), p. 240.

References

Alston, William P. *Epistemic Justification: Essays in the Theory of Knowledge.* Ithaca, NY: Cornell University Press, 1989.

Anscombe, G. E. M. "Modern Moral Philosophy." *Philosophy,* 33 (1958): 1–19.

Asher, Nicholas. "Belief in Discourse Representation Theory." *Journal of Philosophical Logic,* 5 (1986): 127–89.

"A Typology for Attitude Verbs and Their Anaphoric Properties." *Linguistics and Philosophy,* 10 (1987): 129–97.

Barnes, Jonathan. "The Beliefs of a Pyrrhonist." *Proceedings of the Cambridge Philological Society,* E. J. Kenny and M. M. MacKenzie, eds. Cambridge: Cambridge University Press, 1982.

BonJour, Laurence. *The Structure of Empirical Knowledge.* Cambridge, MA: Harvard University Press, 1985.

Burnyeat, Miles. "Can the Sceptic Live His Scepticism?" *Doubt and Dogmatism,* M. Schofield, M. F. Burnyeat, and J. Barnes, eds. Oxford: Clarenden Press, 1980, pp. 20–53

"The Sceptic in His Place and Time." *Philosophy in History,* Richard Rorty, J. B. Schneewind, and Quentin Skinner, eds. Cambridge: Cambridge University Press, 1984, pp. 225–54.

Carrier, L. S. "An Analysis of Empirical Knowledge." *Southern Journal of Philosophy,* 9 (1971): 3–11.

Chisholm, Roderick. *Theory of Knowledge,* 2nd edition. Englewood Cliffs, NJ: Prentice-Hall, 1977.

Theory of Knowledge, 3rd edition. Englewood Cliffs, NJ: Prentice-Hall, 1989.

"Human Freedom and the Self." *Reason at Work,* Steven M. Cahn, Patricia Kitcher, George Sher, and Peter Markie, eds. New York: Harcourt Brace, 1990.

Churchland, Paul. *Scientific Realism and the Plasticity of Mind.* Cambridge: Cambridge University Press, 1979.

Craig, Edward. *Knowledge and the State of Nature.* Oxford: Oxford University Press, 1990.

Dancy, Jonathan. *Moral Reasons.* Oxford: Blackwell, 1993.

DePaul, Michael. *Balance and Refinement.* London: Routledge, 1993.

Descartes, René. *Meditations on First Philosophy*, Laurence J. Lafleur, trans. New York: Bobbs-Merrill, 1951.

Dretske, Fred. "Conclusive Reasons." *Australasian Journal of Philosophy*, 49 (1971): 1–22.

Empiricus, Sextus. *Sextus Empiricus*, R. B. Bury, trans. Loeb Classical Library. London: William Heinemann, 1961–71, vol. 1.

Feinberg, Joel. *Doing and Deserving: Essays in the Theory of Responsibility*. Princeton, NJ: Princeton University Press, 1970.

Feldman, Richard. "Epistemic Obligations." *Philosophical Perspectives 2, Epistemology*, James Tomberlin, ed. Atascadero, CA: Ridgeview, 1988, pp. 235–56.

"Comments: Kvanvig on Externalism and Epistemology Worth Doing." *Southern Journal of Philosophy*, 38 (2000): 43–50.

Feldman, Richard and Conee, Earl. "Evidentialism." *Philosophical Studies*, 48 (1985): 15–34.

"Internalism Defended." *American Philosophical Quarterly*, 38 (2001): 1–18.

Field, Hartry. "The A Prioricity of Logic." *Proceedings of the Aristotelian Society*, 96 (1996): 359–79.

"Epistemological Nonfactualism and the A Prioricity of Logic." *Philosophical Studies*, 92 (1998): 1–24.

Fogelin, Robert. *Pyrrhonian Reflections on Knowledge and Justification*. Oxford: Oxford University Press, 1994.

Foley, Richard. "Justified Inconsistent Beliefs." *American Philosophical Quarterly*, 16 (1979): 247–57.

The Theory of Epistemic Rationality. Cambridge, MA: Harvard University Press, 1987.

"Knowledge Is Accurate and Comprehensive Enough Belief." *Warrant in Contemporary Epistemology: Essays in Honor of Plantinga's Theory of Knowledge*, Jonathan L. Kvanvig, ed. Totowa, NJ: Rowman & Littlefield, 1996, pp. 87–96.

Frede, Michael. "The Skeptic's Two Kinds of Assent and the Question of the Possibility of Knowledge." *Philosophy in History*, Richard Rorty, J. B. Schneewind, and Quentin Skinner, eds. Cambridge: Cambridge University Press, 1984, pp. 255–78.

"The Skeptic's Beliefs." *Essays in Ancient Philosophy*. Minneapolis: University of Minnesota Press, 1987, pp. 179–200.

Fumerton, Richard. *Metaphysical and Epistemological Problems of Perception*. Lincoln: University of Nebraska Press, 1985.

Metaepistemology and Skepticism. Totowa, NJ: Rowman & Littlefield, 1995.

Gettier, Edmund. "Is Justified True Belief Knowledge?" *Analysis*, 23 (1963): 121–3.

Gibbard, Alan. *Wise Choices, Apt Feelings*. Cambridge, MA: Harvard University Press, 1992.

Ginet, Carl. *Knowledge, Perception, and Memory*. Dordrecht: Reidel, 1975.

Goldman, Alvin. "Discrimination and Perceptual Knowledge." *Journal of Philosophy*, 73, 20 (1976): 771–91.

"Discrimination and Perceptual Knowledge." *Essays on Knowledge and Justification*, George Pappas and Marshal Swain, eds. Ithaca, NY: Cornell University Press, 1979, pp. 120–45.

"What Is Justified Belief?" *Knowledge and Justification*, George Pappas, ed. Dordrecht: Reidel, 1979, pp. 1–25.

Epistemology and Cognition. Cambridge, MA: Harvard University Press, 1986.

"Knowledge and Perceptual Discrimination." *Journal of Philosophy*, 73 (1996): 771–91.

Greco, John. *Putting Skeptics in Their Place*. Cambridge: Cambridge University Press, 2000.

"Knowledge as Credit for True Belief." *Intellectual Virtue: Perspectives from Ethics and Epistemology*, Michael DePaul and Linda Zagzebski, eds. Oxford: Oxford University Press, forthcoming.

Harman, Gilbert. *Thought*. Princeton, NJ: Princeton University Press, 1973.

Heller, Mark. "The Proper Role for Contextualism in an Anti-Luck Epistemology." *Philosophical Perspectives, 13, Epistemology*, James Tomberlin, ed. Cambridge, MA: Blackwell, 1999, pp. 115–29.

Hetherington, Stephen Cade. *Better and Worse Knowledge*. Oxford: Oxford University Press, 2001.

James, William. "The Will to Believe." *The Will to Believe and Other Essays in Popular Philosophy*. New York: Hafner, 1897.

Essays in Pragmatism. New York: Harner, 1948.

Klein, Peter. *Certainty*. Minneapolis: University of Minnesota Press, 1981.

Kvanvig, Jonathan L. *The Possibility of an All-Knowing God*. London: Macmillan, 1986.

The Intellectual Virtues and the Life of the Mind: On the Place of the Virtues in Contemporary Epistemology. Totowa, NJ: Rowman & Littlefield, 1992.

"Lewis on Finkish Dispositions." *Philosophy and Phenomenological Research*, 59 (1999): 703–10.

"Zagzebski on Justification." *Philosophy and Phenomenological Research*, 60 (2000): 191–6.

"Propositionalism and the Perspectival Character of Justification," *American Philosophical Quarterly*, 40, 1 (2003): 3–18.

Kvanvig, Jonathan L. and Menzel, Christopher. "The Basic Notion of Justification." *Philosophical Studies*, 59 (1990): 235–61.

Lehrer, Keith. "Knowledge, Truth and Evidence." *Analysis*, 25, 5 (1965): 168–75.

Knowledge. Oxford: Clarenden Press, 1974.

Self Trust: A Study of Reason, Knowledge and Autonomy. Oxford: Oxford University Press, 1997.

The Theory of Knowledge, 2nd edition. Boulder, CO: Westview Press, 2000.

Lehrer, Keith and Paxson, Thomas, J. R. "Knowledge: Undefeated Justified True Belief." *Journal of Philosophy*, 66 (1969): 225–37.

Lewis, David. "Elusive Knowledge," *Australasian Journal of Philosophy*, 74, 4 (1996): 549–67.

Lycan, William. "Plantinga and Coherentisms." *Warrant in Contemporary Epistemology: Essays in Honor of Plantinga's Theory of Knowledge*, Jonathan L. Kvanvig, ed. Totowa, NJ: Rowman & Littlefield, 1996, pp. 3–24.

Montmarquet, James. *Epistemic Virtue and Doxastic Responsibiliity*. Totowa, NJ: Rowman & Littlefield, 1993.

Moore, G. E. *Principia Ethica*. Cambridge: Cambridge University Press, 1903.

Philosophical Papers. London: Allen and Unwin, 1959.

Morton, Adam. *A Guide Through the Theory of Knowledge*. Enrico and Belmont, CA: Dickenson, 1977.

Nozick, Robert. *Philosophical Explanations*. Cambridge, MA: Harvard University Press, 1981.

Plantinga, Alvin. *Warrant: The Current Debate*. Oxford: Oxford University Press, 1993.

Warrant and Proper Function. Oxford: Oxford University Press, 1993.

Plato, *Meno*. *The Collected Dialogues of Plato*, Edith Hamilton and Huntington Cairns, eds.; W. K. C, Guthrie, trans. Princeton, NJ: Princeton University Press, 1963.

Pollock, John. *Contemporary Theories of Knowledge*. Totowa, NJ: Rowman & Littlefield, 1986.

Price, H. H. *Perception*. London: Methuen, 1932.

Reid, Thomas. *Inquiry and Essays*, Keith Lehrer and Ronald E. Beanblossom, eds. Indianapolis: Hackett, 1975.

Riggs, Wayne. "Reliability and the Value of Knowledge." *Philosophy and Phenomenological Research*, forthcoming.

Sartwell, Crispin. "Knowledge Is True Belief." *American Philosophical Quarterly*, 28, 2 (1991): 157–65.

"Why Knowledge Is Merely True Belief." *Journal of Philosophy*, 89, 4 (1992): 167–80.

Sayre, Kenneth. *Plato's Analytical Method*. Chicago: University of Chicago Press, 1969.

Sextus Empiricus. *Sextus Empiricus*, 4 vols., R. B. Bury, trans. Loeb Classical Library. London: William Heinemann, 1961–71.

Shope, Robert K. *The Analysis of Knowing: A Decade of Research*. Princeton, NJ: Princeton University Press, 1983.

Sosa, Ernest. "Epistemic Presupposition." *Justification and Knowledge*, George Pappas, ed. Dordrecht: Reidel, 1979, pp. 79–92.

Knowledge in Perspective: Selected Essays in Epistemology. Cambridge: Cambridge University Press, 1991.

"Plantinga on Epistemic Internalism." *Warrant in Contemporary Epistemology: Essays in Honor of Plantinga's Theory of Knowledge*, Jonathan L. Kvanvig, ed. Totowa, NJ: Rowman & Littlefield, 1996, pp. 73–86.

"Skepticism and Contextualism." *Philosophical Issues*, 10 (2000): 1–18.

"The Place of Truth in Epistemology." *Intellectual Virtue: Perspectives from Ethics and Epistemology*, Michael DePaul and Linda Zagzebski, eds. Oxford: Oxford University Press, forthcoming.

Steiner, Mark. "Platonism and the Causal Theory of Knowledge." *Journal of Philosophy*, 73, 3 (1973): 57–66.

Stevenson, C. L. *Ethics and Language*. New Haven, CT: Yale University Press, 1945.

Stich, Stephen. *From Folk Psychology to Cognitive Science: The Case Against Belief*. Cambridge, MA: MIT Press, 1983.

The Fragmentation of Reason: Preface to a Pragmatic Theory of Cognitive Evaluation. Cambridge, MA: Bradford Books/MIT Press, 1990.

Swinburne, Richard. *Providence and the Problem of Evil*. Oxford: Oxford University Press, 1999.

Epistemic Justification. Oxford: Oxford University Press, 2000.

Van Fraassen, Bas. *The Scientific Image*. Oxford: Clarenden Press, 1980.

Williamson, Timothy. *Vagueness*. London: Routledge, 1994.

"Knowing and Asserting." *Philosophical Review*, 105, 4 (1996): 489–523.

Knowledge and Its Limits. Oxford: Oxford University Press, 2000.

Zagzebski, Linda. *Virtues of the Mind: An Inquiry into the Nature of Virtue and the Ethical Foundations of Knowledge*. Oxford: Oxford University Press, 1996.

Index

acceptance, 34, 35, 42, 141
accidentality, 92–4, 113–16, 139, 153, 181, 198
agency, 94–8, 106, 168
agent causation, 94
Allen, Colin, xvi
Alston, William, 64, 210
analysis, 19, 109, 111, 116, 121, 140, 141, 207–10
Anscombe, G. E. M., 187, 207
antiluminosity, 68, 69, 71
Aristotle, 97
Asher, Nicholas, 192, 207
assertibility, 22, 23, 25
assertible, 23, 24
attitudinalism, xv, 157, 158, 163, 167, 169–74, 176, 177, 179, 182–4
    pragmatic, 183
    semantic, 170, 171, 176, 179

Barnes, Jonathan, 30, 31, 207
belief
    true, x, xii–xvi, 4, 6–16, 18–23, 26, 28–30, 38, 40, 42–50, 52, 53, 56–60, 74–6, 79–81, 84–92, 95–9, 101, 106–16, 118–20, 125, 126, 129, 132, 134–6, 138–40, 143, 150, 151, 153–5, 157, 162–4, 168–70, 172, 176, 178, 180–2, 185, 193, 199, 202, 204, 205, 208–10
    value of, xiv, 29–33, 37, 38
    virtuous, 81, 84–7, 106–8
Burnyeat, M. F., 30, 207

Carrier, L. S., 120, 121, 207
Chisholm, Roderick, 48, 53, 67, 94, 119, 120, 207
Churchland, Paul, 24, 28, 207
clairvoyance, 100, 101, 104
closure, 149, 171, 202
coherentism, 193–5, 200
coherence theorists, 195, 196, 205
conclusive reasons, 120, 121, 124, 131, 133, 208
Conee, Earl, 67, 208
contextualism, xv, 118, 132, 135, 143, 163–5, 179, 209
counterfactuals, 93, 121, 124, 125, 134, 136, 138, 163, 178, 179, 198
Craig, Edward, 83, 207
credit for true belief, xv, 81, 86–91, 97, 99, 136, 143, 168–70, 172, 180–2, 209
curiosity, 81, 116, 140, 141, 143–50, 155, 171

Dancy, Jonathan, 32, 208
defeasibility theory, 120, 124–7, 130, 131, 133
    effective defeaters, 127, 128
    initiating defeaters, 127–30
    misleading defeaters, 126, 181
Descartes, Rene, 67, 207
desiderata, 6, 11, 67, 116–19, 139, 140, 161, 188, 203. *See also* knowledge, theory of, twin desiderata on
desire to know, 81, 116, 143, 144, 148–51, 153, 155, 171
Dretske, Fred, 120, 134, 208

213

3810000

Made in the USA
Lexington, KY
25 November 2009